The Complete ITALIAN COOKBOOK

The Complete
ITALIAN COOKBOOK

Carlo Bernasconi and Christian Teubner

WHITECAP BOOKS

This edition published in Canada in 1999 by Whitecap Books
Vancouver Toronto New York

Published in Germany as *Italienisch Kochen* in 1999 by Teubner Edition.
© Teubner Edition 1999

All rights reserved.
Without limiting the rights under copyright reserved above, no part of this publication may be reproduced, stored in or introduced into a retrieval system, or transmitted in any form or by any means (electronic, mechanical, photocopying, recording or otherwise), without the prior written of the copyright owner and the publisher.

Translation: Debra Nicol for Translate-A-Book
Editorial management: Barbara Horn
Design and production management: Richard Johnson
Photography: Christian Teubner, Odette Teubner, Ulla Mayer-Raichle, Andreas Nimptsch
Layout: Christian Teubner, René Fuchs, Annegret Rösler, Gabriele Wahl
Reproduction: PHG-Lithos GmbH, Germany
Printed in Germany by Dr. Cantz'sche Druckerei GmbH
10 9 8 7 6 5 4 3 2 1

Library of Congress Catalogue Card Number: 99-073370
ISBN: 1-55110-980-8

Contents

Italian cuisine 6
A short journey through history and the regions of Italy to discover the full range of Italian cuisine, including a quick trip to the bar for wine, liqueur, and coffee.

Antipasti Appetizers 24
The delicious little morsels at the beginning of a meal, for which Italy is famous, are easily made from salami, prosciutto, preserved or pickled vegetables, and bread with best-quality olive oil.

Insalate Salads 58
The finest vinegar, crunchy lettuce leaves, spicy herbs, and fresh vegetables are the essentials, but delicious creations can be made with seafood, or even bread.

Zuppe Soups 84
As a first course or a meal, Italian soups are substantial. Legumes are used to add substance; tomatoes, zucchini, or arugula to make a lighter soup.

Pasta Pasta 110
The food associated the world over with Italian cooking, pasta and gnocchi are presented here with their indispensable accompaniment, cheese, from fresh mozzarella to extra-hard Parmesan.

Riso Rice 196
To stir or not to stir? Wetter or drier? However they are prepared, Italy's risottos taste superb, made with seafood, vegetables, saffron, or even dandelions.

Verdure Vegetables 232
Boiling, frying, braising, grilling, and baking — there is hardly a method of preparation that isn't used in Italy for fresh vegetables and aromatic mushrooms, with highly appetizing results in every case, of course.

Pesci Fish 278
Long coastlines, and clear lakes and brooks mean that fish, shellfish, and crustaceans abound in Italy, and the exciting recipes for them are the highlights of the *secondo piatto*, or main course.

Carni Meat 322
The best cuts of pork, beef, veal, and lamb are flash-fried and juicy here, braised to tenderness in a delicious sauce there; a delight every time.

Cacciagione & Pollame Game & Poultry 352
Hunting is common in Italy, and there is a corresponding wealth of fine recipes for game; but domesticated rabbits, ducks, and hens are also prepared in a great variety of ways.

Dolci Desserts 382
Even a selection of fragrant, fully ripe fruit would make an extremely tempting Italian dessert, but sweet creations such as *panna cotta* and *zuppa inglese* are enough to make the sweet-toothed go weak at the knees.

Pane & Pizze Bread & Pizza 412
Rustic loaves, lavishly topped flatbreads, and stuffed breads with unusual fillings: Italy's bakeries boast plenty of exciting products to discover, in addition to the world-famous pizza.

Indice Index 440

Italian Cuisine
An Introduction by Carlo Bernasconi

Among the different styles of cooking in the Mediterranean region, that of Italy has, over the centuries, become one of the most popular. Italian food can be found all over the world, on supermarket shelves and in restaurants, as well as in the home. Compared to other national foods that can claim international standing, such as those of China, India, France, and Mexico, it can fairly be pointed out that outside their country of origin pizza and pasta are eaten daily by billions of people all over the globe from New York to Moscow, from South Africa to Finland.

Why this has been the case for such a long time, and will remain so, can be attributed to a common characteristic of these successful Italian dishes: They are simple to prepare and easy to digest. Only very few ingredients, and very few pots and pans, are needed to prepare a delicious plate of pasta. This shows how quickly you can bring the magic of the country and its cuisine to the table.

Restaurants on their own cannot make a national cuisine popular; you need good product availability, and the feeling that very little effort is required to produce a tasty dish and that nothing can go wrong. Both apply to Italian cooking. With a few exceptions, the essential ingredients of Italian cooking can be bought fresh anywhere, as tomatoes, garlic, onions, and other vegetables, particularly eggplant and zucchini, are to be found in markets throughout the Western world. Wheat flour, rice, and corn are also important staple foods; and chicken and pork are among the most commonly available meats. Even if you cannot drink a Barolo from Piedmont with a *brasato* made with Argentinian beef in the south of Chile, this does not make the dish less tasty.

Where women rule

The family is the center of social life in Italy to a greater extent than in any other country in the world. On warm summer nights the family members, from the *bisnonna* (great-grandmother) to the youngest *bambini*, get together to eat. They may serve the food on the terrace of the house or sit in the garden of the farm under a pergola covered in vines in front of a heavily laden table. And in colder months they all gather around the table in the dining room or the kitchen.

In the domestic kitchen women rule. From an early age, girls are taught by their mother how to handle the many ingredients and prepare the dishes for the family. They know that food is an essential part of social gatherings, and so they will devote a lot of energy and time to produce a *spaghettata*, with sauces that delight even the youngest family members.

It has always been like this. It will always remain like this. Even if the modern Italian woman now has a job and leaves the bringing up of children to the *nonna* (grandmother), she will still spend more time preparing food than many other women of the Western world. You will very rarely find men in the family's kitchen — their realm is the wine cellar. Over the centuries Italian society has maintained this classic separation of roles between men and women. The women's place is in the home, particularly in front of the stove and looking after the children. There is a tradition of mother and daughter cooking together, where in the intimacy of the kitchen secrets can be disclosed that are not meant for the ears of others. Meanwhile the men go out to work and to the soccer field. Alternatively, out of economic necessity, the men frequently emigrate and support their family from abroad. This stereotype still holds true for large parts of Italy, especially in the south of the country.

People who have visited an Italian market — and there is one in every town and village — will hardly ever have met a man doing the daily shopping, unless he was a chef. It is the women who dominate the markets, thoroughly examining for freshness the vegetables, fish, and meat they need for their evening

Temple ruins at Agrigento The remains of this Greek settlement founded in the seventh century B.C. are a popular backdrop for wedding photographs.

meal. Men might accompany the women, but only to help carry the shopping or so they can disappear into an adjacent bar for an apéritif and a few *chiceti*, little delicacies that go well with a glass of white wine.

Romans, Crusaders, and Moors

Where did Italy's cuisine as we know it originate? There is every reason to believe that Italian food culture goes back to ancient Roman times. In the Roman capital fruit from all over the Empire, which reached from the Middle East to North Africa,

Lunch *al fresco* The way people eat in rural Sicily. Different dishes are served and there are even leftovers for the dog and hens.

graced the well-supplied tables of the senators. What Romans were eating then is described in the often quoted cookbook *De re coquinaria* (also known as *De culinariae rei discplina*), written by Apicius and available in modern reprints. Even Pellagrino Artusi mentions this book in 1891 as the source of all Italian cookbooks.

After the fall of the Roman Empire, the Moors

revitalized Italian cuisine. They came to Sicily as early as the ninth century, and their culture had its heyday in the twelfth and thirteenth centuries. The Crusades to the Holy Land also played a role. The crusaders brought back spices, fruit, and other foods that were unknown to the Romans. It is this mixture of influences from Arab culture, the Crusades, and trade carried out from ports in Apulia that characterizes Italy's cuisine.

Early written sources

Claudio Benporat mentions in his *Storia della gastronomia italiana* (History of Italian Gastronomy) that the first cookbook was written in the fourteenth century by an anonymous Tuscan who listed 183 recipes in the order in which they were served. He begins with vegetable soups, ravioli, and crespelle (egg rolls), then meat cooked in its own juices, followed by seasoned, roast, and stuffed cuts of meat; he finishes with pies filled with meat or fish. One of the recipes listed by contemperaneous authors that has remained unchanged since the fourteenth century is *maccaroni siciliani*.

It was recommended in the past that macaroni be made during August — the hottest month of the year — so that the pasta could dry quickly. It was then boiled in water, stock, or almond milk (during Lent) for two hours. After that it was seasoned with "grated cheese of good quality," fresh butter, and herbs.

In the sixteenth century Italy was the undisputed artistic, literary, and secular center of Europe. Many Italian still believe that the development of French cooking took a decisive turn for the better in the sixteenth century as a result of Caterina de Medici's marriage to Henry II of France. It was, of course, the petite 14-year-old Caterina who introduced forks and porcelain plates to the tables of France, but there are no contemporary sources that mention Florentine chefs as part of her entourage who could have influenced French cooking. Indeed, Benporat notes that Italians who wrote accounts of their travels in France at that time mention with great admiration Bordeaux wine and the fact that it was drunk out of glasses, suggesting that gastronomic culture was well developed.

Be that as it may, a great age of Italian cooking ended with the sixteenth century. The new vegetables and fruits that explorers such as Columbus, Cortés, and Pizzaro brought back from the New World were for a long time not accepted in Italian cooking; even the tomato, which today is such an integral part of Italy's cuisine that no recipe for an appetizer or main

The Rialto market in Venice is famous for its large selection of fruit, vegetables, and especially fish. Tarpaulins protect the wonderful displays from the rain and from too much sunshine.

course can do without it, was always eaten raw by Italians until the end of the nineteenth century.

Pellegrino Artusi, a revolutionary in the kitchen

The change came in 1891 when Pellegrino Artusi's *La scienza in cucina e l'arte di mangiar bene* (The Science of Cooking and the Art of Eating Well) was published, a work that the author thought would not attract much attention. On the contrary, Pellegrino Artusi revolutionized Italian home cooking with his book and gave Italians a new attitude to eating. In particular he told Italians how to gain the maximum of pleasure by combining certain dishes at a certain time with a certain wine. While pleading for moderate wine consumption at meals, Artusi did not go as far as adopting recommendations by doctors to add water to the wine, which is still customary today, especially at lunchtime. Artusi's overall contribution to the development of Italian gastronomy cannot be overestimated.

A journey through the regions of Italy

Anyone who reduces Italian cooking to pasta and pizza, possibly admitting at most *scaloppine al limone* or risotto, is doing the many regions of the country a great injustice. Italy has such an exceptional wealth of regional specialties that its cuisine is easily the most varied in the Mediterranean area. Italians in the skiing resort of Cortina d'Ampezzo in the Veneto eat different dishes from those enjoyed by the peasants on the island of Pantelleria, which is nearer Tunisia than Sicily. But both belong to Italy. What divides these cuisines is not only distance but also the climate.

Along the Alpine range

The Alto Adige and the Alpine parts of Italy, northern Piedmont and the Aosta Valley, and, of course, the Valtellina have long, cold winters. Inevitably this is reflected in the food that is served there. All over the Alpine region substantial, filling, high-calorie dishes, such as cheese fonduta from the Aosta Valley, dumplings stuffed with bacon from the Alto Adige, and sauerkraut, an ancient well-proven recipe for conserving white cabbage, can be found on the menu throughout the Alpine region. In the Valtellina *pizzocheri*, short noodles made of buckwheat flour and water, are also served.

This young Italian cook proudly presents the stuffed sardines which the kitchen staff have prepared.

In the trattoria La Buca in Zibello a woman is in charge. She personally supervises every step in the preparation of the sumptuous *culatello* (salted pork) and makes all the decisions in the kitchen of her restaurant. In this picture she fries the prosciutto for a pasta sauce.

Crisp apples from the Alto Adige, red-skinned and picked when just ripe, are only one example of the large supply of fruit and vegetables that Italy's regions have to offer.

Pigs are butchered in November and December, which provides the mountain farmers in the Alto Adige and the Valtellina with a supply of dried meat throughout the year. Unsurpassed are the air-dried ham and the bresaola from the Valtellina, a beef specialty that is cut very thinly. As soon as spring starts the Alpine region returns to a mild climate, which is much appreciated by tourists and which makes it possible to grow vines in the southern part of the province of Alto Adige, on the border with Trentino and Valtellina.

The latitude of this region is responsible for several characteristics that are reflected in its cuisine. Only hardy cereals resistant to the cold are grown here, which means no wheat. However, the lack of the typical "pasta culture" in these northern regions of Italy is no disadvantage, as dairy products, especially cheese, compensate for it.

The Veneto

If you travel along the Adige as far as Verona, you are in the center of the Veneto, which for centuries supplied the inhabitants of Venice with vegetables, fruit, rice, and corn. This region, which borders on the Trentino to the north and on Friuli (Friuli Venezia) to the east, comprises a mountainous part stretching as far as the Austrian border and a large low-lying plain forming the border with the region of Emilia-Romagna to the south. From the culinary point of view the Veneto is one of the most highly developed regions of Italy, not least because it was influenced by the Venetian aristocracy, so that delicacies from the mountains are combined with those from the sea. The richness of the country is immense: Huge fields of vegetables alternate with vineyards, and grapes that produce full white wines grow on the slopes. The culinary specialty is the risotto; especially appreciated in winter, it has many variations, being made with fish, meat, or vegetables.

The Radicchio di Treviso has also become a highly regarded delicacy all over the world, which no one can prepare in as many different ways as Armando Zanotto. His cookbook lists more than 600 possibilities for serving this delicious winter salad. In spring asparagus from Bassano dominates the menus of the restaurants, usually served with butter and Parmesan cheese. Polenta is also very popular in the region around Verona and Vicenza, but here it is made from durum wheat rather than corn, and is baked and served to accompany *baccalà alla visentina*, a special Venetian version of salt cod that is very popular everywhere in Italy.

Pumpkins are cooked in many different ways in Italy. The versatile giants among the vegetables are sometimes roasted, sometimes marinated, and sometimes stirred into in a risotto. Candied, they are an ingredient in the Tuscan *panforte*.

Carinthia, Bohemia, and Venice — mixed influences in Friuli

Friuli is one of the regions of Italy where the political upheavals of past centuries have left their traces in the cuisine. Until 1866 Friuli was under Austrian rule, and today is divided into the hilly Collio and the Grave del Friuli, a plain that borders the Austrian province of Carinthia in the north. For this reason Friuli cuisine embraces various ways of making strudel and dumplings, as well as sophisticated seafood recipes and risottos that originated in the Republic of Venice. There are even undeniable traces of Slav and Bohemian influence, as Trieste was the only access to the sea in the days of the Austro-Hungarian Empire.

In the hills dishes with corn dominate, polenta being served with game, with ragout, or with herbs. From the heart of the region near the capital, Udine, comes the famous prosciutto from San Daniele, which owes its quality on the one hand to the excellent pork, and on the other to the fact that the mountain winds from the Carnic Alps blow over the gentle hills of the Collio and meet the moist air from the sea. Friuli is also a region full of wild herbs, which grow especially well in the hilly parts and are used in its cuisine. Ruccola grows nearly everywhere, and in the hills caraway is added when baking bread that is to be eaten with beer. There are also many ways of preparing mushrooms in Friuli, the classic recipe being fried mushrooms with polenta, the ubiquitous regional dish.

Bundles of wonderful asparagus — both green and white — are for sale on this stall, together with artichokes, fennel, tomatoes, and peas. You need excellent ingredients to produce a good meal, and these have just been harvested and are of top quality.

Lombardy, a region made for rice-growing

Lombardy's center is the busy industrial, trading, and banking metropolis of Milan, surrounded by the fertile Po basin, which supplies everything the families in the city need — even wine! For the rest of the world, it is two products that have made Lombardy famous: one is the blue cheese reputedly invented in Gorgonzola and named after it, and the other is rice from Mortara, a small town half an hour southeast of Milan. The experts are still arguing whether rice was introduced into the Padania (as the Po basin is called in Italian) by the Spanish or whether it found its way via India and the Arabs in Sicily to the north of Italy. Initially, farmers in the Po basin tried to grow both long-grain and short-grain. The short-grain varieties, such as Carnaroli, Arborio, and Baldo, adapted to the climate in the basin more quickly and produced an excellent yield.

Rice plays an important part in recipes for first course dishes. In the main course meat dominates, usually veal or beef, and occasionally trout from the nearby lakes (Lecco and Como) is used. Osso buco is one of the best-known dishes from Milan, which the conservative Milanese foodies prefer to eat with a white wine sauce, as they consider tomatoes and anchovies a sacrilege. This dish underlines one of the characteristics of Lombard cuisine: More time is spent in roasting meat here than anywhere else in Italy. This region is also well known for the use of pork in its excellent sausages, such as zampone (stuffed pig's trotter), cotechino, luganega, and mortadella.

Alba truffles for the gourmet

Whenever the region of Piedmont is mentioned, every gourmet immediately thinks of the white truffles from Alba that improve many a dish in winter, especially egg pasta or a simple risotto. This delicacy has its

Truffles: With few but really choice ingredients, you can conjure up real delicacies. Italians prove the truth of this principle with this expensive variety of mushroom. The truffles are simply grated over a plateful of pasta or over a risotto, which is enough to produce an incomparable meal.

Dusk in Venice Just the time for a glass of white wine or an apéritif in the Piazza San Marco.

price, fixed by supply and demand; it can reach astronomical heights in the fall, depending on the weather, which can cause a shortage. Another dish that delights many a visitor to Piedmont is the *bagna caôda*, which is traditionally served when the new wine is safely in the barrels and the wine growers meet to celebrate with a meal after the hard work of spring and summer is done. *Bagna caôda* is a sauce made with garlic, anchovies, and olive oil that is reduced until it turns into a brownish paste. The anchovies that dominate this dish made by the Piedmont wine producers come from the Ligurian coast; historically, they were traded for butter, cheese, and wheat. The *bagna caôda* is left to simmer on the stove until it is ready to be served; then an egg is added to it. *Bagna caôda* is eaten with plenty of bread and raw vegetables; leek is a must with it, so is celery, and even chile peppers. With it, the Piemontese drink their young Barbera wine. No other dish should really follow this, except perhaps a cup of strong beef bouillon.

A land kissed by the sun

One of the most versatile areas of Italy from a culinary point of view is without doubt the Ligurian coast, which stretches from La Spezia as far as Ventimiglia, and has a wealth of fish dishes. In Liguria, especially in the eastern part from La Spezia to Genoa, people have no reservations about cooking fish and vegetables together. For instance, they like to bake *brazino* (sea bass) in the oven between layers of potatoes. Two important ingredients in many recipes are anchovies and artichokes. The former are plentiful in the sea and the latter grow along the Ligurian coast from Genoa to Ventimiglia. Nearly every town and village has its own way of preparing them.

Olive oil plays an important part, especially in Liguria Ponente, west of Genoa, because there, in the Valle Argentina, north of Imperia, oil has been pressed for centuries from the aromatic Taggiasca olive. Cookbooks from the region contain very few meat recipes; where they do, the recipes feature lamb, chicken, or rabbit.

Rich pastures and a bountiful coast

The cuisine of Emilia-Romagna is without question one of the richest and most diverse in Italy. This is the home of pasta dishes, the aromatic *aceto balsamico tradizionale* (traditional balsamic vinegar), left to mature for 12 to 25 years in barrels of different sizes, and the *prosciutto di Parma*, the widely famed air-dried ham. This is also the home of Parmigiano Reggiano,

Great views and good food and drink can be combined here in the Gulf of Gaeta, north of Naples, either with a picnic or a delicious meal on the terrace of a restaurant.

the hard Parmesan cheese that has to accompany almost every pasta dish. Only when the dish contains crustaceans or fish is it omitted, which is often the case along the Adriatic coast. Emilia-Romagna offers a large variety of pasta dishes — this is where a kind of imaginary "pasta border" can almost be drawn across Italy.

Pasta is made here with wheat flour and eggs, while farther south, even in Tuscany, durum wheat with water is often preferred. The climate of Emilia-Romagna, with its hard winters, calls for nourishing and filling dishes, and this is reflected in the many potato dishes.

Tuscany, a synonym for Italy

The Apennine Mountains, which divide Emilia-Romagna from Tuscany, are the reason why one finds a rather substantial cuisine among the vine-clad hills of one of Italy's most beautiful landscapes.

The contradiction that seems to exist between highly acclaimed wines like Chianti and Montepulciano on the one hand and a rather solid cuisine with many bean dishes on the other has its historic reasons. Despite their highly sophisticated wines, the people remain a farming community, and beans play a more important role than pasta or rice.

The nourishing *costoletta alla fiorentina*, a veal cutlet usually weighing between 14 ounces and 1¼ pounds, leaves one with the impression that this regional cuisine is pretty substantial. True, but the strong Sangiovese grape demands correspondingly substantial food. A Tuscan meal can start with crostini, slices of toasted bread spread with chicken liver pâté or calf brains and Parmesan cheese, and continue with potato gnocchi. This may be followed by game or, more usually, another substantial meat dish with vegetables.

The meal may be rounded off with a *panforte di Siena*, a dessert baked with candied fruit, nuts, and honey. On the other hand the meal may consist of just a *panzanella*, a bread salad to which tomatoes and onions are added, a very tasty dish when only the best olive oil has been used.

Umbria, the land of forests and hills

Umbria, the region that borders on Tuscany, is famous for the use of olives in many of the local dishes. In fact, excellent olive oil is made here, and is often used simply as a flavoring, especially for boiled vegetables. Sausages and pasta are also on the menu,

At Tamburini's, the well-known delicatessen store in Bologna you can buy anything the heart desires, from excellent ham and delicious salami to tasty parmesan.

because here again cooking is influenced by work in the vineyards. Food has to be nourishing and the larder has to be filled with ham, sausages, and preserved vegetables, particularly eggplant and zucchini, for the colder winter months. The one thing Umbrian cooking cannot do without is the garbanzo bean — the Moorish influence becomes obvious here — served either as a kind of houmus or with meat dishes.

Rome — not a culinary capital?

There are quite a few connoisseurs of Italian gastronomy who maintain that a rich selection and variety of dishes can be found only in the north; the further one travels south, the less imaginative, plainer, and more monotonous the dishes become. None of this is to be detected in the Italian capital. In her bestseller *The Regions of Italy and Their Cuisine*, Alice Vollenweider, the doyenne of Italian lifestyle and literary commentators, enthuses about the wealth of products available in the markets in Rome, of which there are as many as columns in a Roman temple or church. Dishes with lamb, rigatoni with a tasty ragout, bean soup with pasta, and ragout of salted cod are all on the menu. Roman cuisine seems to be able to absorb anything, and pasta dishes show a southern influence — they are often sprinkled with grated sheep's-milk cheese.

Down south and on to the islands

Campania, Calabria, Apulia, Basilicata — the southern regions of Italy so long neglected by the government — impress everyone with their simple dishes of beans and vegetables (*cima di rapa*), and with pasta in many forms, of which strozzapreti and orecchiette are the most popular. Lamb plays an important culinary role here. In a restaurant I was served lamb's liver with the intestines of young lamb wrapped around them and then pan-fried. The intestines prevent the liver from drying out in the hot skillet. *Pizza napoletana* and *spaghetti al pomodoro* are the most popular dishes from Naples, making a virtue out of necessity, as even the poorest people can afford to buy tomatoes, basil, and flour or semolina. The thick fava beans, rather than the usual, smaller cannelini beans, are an indispensable ingredient in southern Italian cooking; eaten with fresh sheep's-milk cheese they become a delicacy.

Pesci azzurri, so called because of their silvery blue scales, include the different varieties of mackerel being weighed here.

Picturesque, brightly colored fishing boats in a Ligurian harbor Day after day fishermen land their catch here. The different kinds of Mediterranean fish and seafood are always sold fresh, either straight from the boat, weighed with simple hand-held scales, or at the local fish market.

Eggplant and tomatoes liven up the table served *au gratin* as *melanzane alla parmigiana*, a wonderful summer dish made with mozzarella *di bufala*, buffalo-milk mozzarella cheese, which cannot be compared to the commercial type made from cow's milk and used in so many other dishes. *Insalata caprese* is another southern specialty made with ripe tomatoes, buffalo-milk mozzarella, and basil.

Artichokes are also an essential part of the menu in the south; they flourish here, as this plant needs very little care. They play a particularly important role in the cuisine of Sicily, the largest and most southern Italian island. In a recipe from Catania artichokes are stuffed with a mixture of anchovies and fresh bread crumbs, and, as ever in Sicily, *peperocini*, chile peppers. Immacolata Fertitta, a chef who re-creates recipes from her native Sicily in Zurich, fries sliced eggplant in oil and serves it with sprinkled with croûtons and topped with a light tomato sauce. *Spaghetti al tonno* is a standard Sicilian dish. The tuna fish is first quickly seared in oil, then cut into small pieces and cooked in a tomato sauce for ten minutes before being mixed with the spaghetti. A simple salad made with freshly sliced oranges, onion rings, and olives, and seasoned with mint and olive oil, is a very popular appetizer in Sicily that is also gaining popularity in more northern regions.

Sicilian cuisine is usually simple, but this does not apply to the many desserts originating there. Sicily is famous for its *dolci*, or sweets, which leave nothing to be desired. Most are made with honey and almonds, both of which are produced locally.

The basis of Sardinian cuisine is bread and wine, but that alone would not be sufficiently nourishing. Typical appetizers are salami and ham from boars that roam the island in large numbers. *Is malloreddus*, one of the most popular Sardinian first courses, is gnocchi made from durum wheat and saffron served in a tomato sauce with pieces of salami and sheep's-milk cheese. *Sa cassola*, a fish soup served all along the coast of Italy, varies from area to area. Main courses are often based on pork or lamb, and suckling lamb and pig roasted on the spit are especially popular. Of course game is part of the Sardinian menu, especially

16 ITALIAN CUISINE

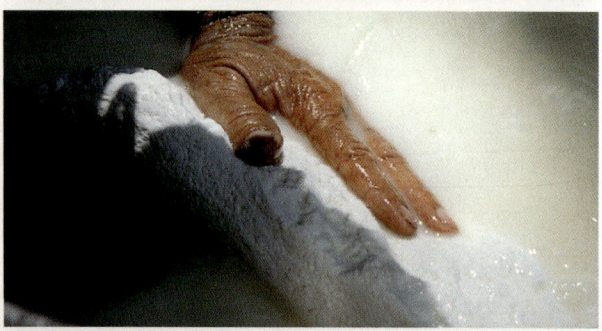

Artigianale Here pecorino *fiore sardo* cheese is made entirely by hand. First the Sardinian farmer heats sheep's milk in a large cauldron until it thickens. The broken-up whey is then pressed together by hand and placed in baskets to drain. When dry, it is pressed into special wooden molds. This gives the cheese its characteristic shape, with a pretty pattern on top.

hare, which is sometimes prepared with dried tomatoes. As in Sicily, desserts are exceptional. *Torrone* is a particular favorite on both islands, and is easy to make. Four and a half pounds of almonds are skinned by dropping them into hot water, after which they are lightly roasted in the oven. In the meantime 2¼ pounds of honey are mixed with 4 egg whites and cooked in a saucepan over a low heat for 15 minutes. Then the almonds are added and the mixture is poured onto a baking sheet lined with paper and left to cool.

Artigianale and Arcigola Slow Food

Franco Boeri's white Fiat Panda climbs slowly up the winding road into the Valle Argentina. Badalucco, a village on the Ligurian coast behind Imperia, appears smaller and smaller the further up the road Signore Boeri drives. He continues driving as the road turns into a track with deep potholes, until he eventually encounters two farmers who are striking the branches of an olive tree with long poles made of chestnut wood. The Taggiasca olives fall into the nets spread out beneath the trees, from which they are carefully collected and put into large metal buckets. The trees in the hills around Badalucco are 300 to 500 years old, and are planted on terraces that were built up by hand. "Putting up the pyramids of Giza was nothing in comparison to building these terraces," said one of the farmers.

Signore Boeri is a typical late-twentieth-century farmer. Born after the war, he worked in the family business until he took over the olive oil mill from his father. Then he began restructuring the business according to the principles of the Arcigola Slow Food movement, which was founded in 1986 and champions the environmentally friendly production of food. Signore Boeri organizes the sale of his olive oil himself rather than giving it to a consortium to market. The entire process of oil extraction is strictly based on tradition. The olives are weighed and put into huge containers, where they are crushed by two blocks of granite weighing nearly 900 pounds. After that the pulp, or oilcake, is spread on coconut mats, one layer on top of another. Liquid begins to drip out immediately; later, the oil is separated from the water with a centrifuge. Only the granite millstones and the olive press are powered by electricity.

Businesses like Signore Boeri's are essential for the future of Italian gastronomy because they limit themselves to refining their craft and hence contribute more to genuine Italian cuisine than all the industrial food firms put together. According to Carlo Petrini, the president of Arcigola Slow Food, "Everybody is entitled to high-quality foods, and the appreciation of this quality is a general tendency among buyers, even if some people — such as sociologists, marketing experts, and other opinion-formers — would have us believe that the younger generation knows only fast food and that families are conditioned to buying tasteless, unimaginative supermarket food." Arcigola Slow Food organizes an annual *salone del gusto* ("taste show") in Turin, where small entrepreneurs can introduce their products. the show attracted 126,853 visitors in 1998; very encouraging for Signore Petrini.

Educating the palate is really one of the most important tasks for champions of good Italian cuisine. As long as there are "eccentrics" (in the positive sense of the word) such as Gioachino Palestro, who processes goose meat in the same way as Jewish people did 500 years ago, the future of Italian cooking is secure. Palestro's *ecumenico* salami is among the finest delicacies Italy has to offer, and one tends to agree with him when he says "a person has to be mad to spend that much time producing a salami." Based in Mortara, Signore Palestro makes his salami using only the breasts of geese. He cuts them into fan shapes, covers them with goose fat, and seasons them with salt and pepper. He leaves them to rest for a day, then rolls up the meat like a roulade, slices it, and stuffs it into the goose necks. After that the salami is sewn up by hand and hung in a coldstore for three months.

Signore Palestro is a good example of the thousands of people, real artisans, running small businesses that produce individual high-quality products, and who act as ambassadors of good taste, people who know the difference between what is genuine and what only seems so. Tantalizing aromas lead you to a wealth of enticing products in his shop, including wine, Gorgonzola cheese, mostarda, and, of course, his own sausage. Signore Palestro is happy to share his enthusiasm for handmade country produce with any customer who wants to buy these fine foods. It becomes obvious when talking to him that there is a whole network of artisanal producers, and one comes away with the firm conviction that the gastronomic

Franco Boeri is one of the few people in the Valle Argentina who mills olive oil just as his forefathers did.

Some of the grapes that are used to make Italy's top-rated red wines can be seen in this picture. The grapes ripen in regions with extremely varied climates, from the Alpine valleys of the southern Tyrol to the sun-drenched plains of the south.

culture of Italy, in a process of constant development, is in safe hands.

A feast for the palate and the eye: *le sagre*

Gastronomic tradition is deeply rooted in the people and manifests itself in the so-called *sagre* held annually in nearly every village and small town in Italy. *Sagre* are partly religious feasts, usually celebrating a saint, and partly culinary events. There are dozens, if not hundreds, of these fairs. On April 25 in the villages in the hills around Treppo Grande in Friuli, for example, people celebrate not only the Feast of St. Mark with a church service, but also the first freshly cut asparagus. The fame of the *sagra dello stoccafisso* in Badalucco has spread far beyond the narrow valley; it takes place every September and is a competition to see who can prepare the best salted cod, with cooks turning up from as far away as Norway, the home of the *baccalà*. Many of these festivals have lost their original purpose and have become events in their own right that attract an international public. A good example is the *palio* in Siena, which was originally a feast for the many *contrade* (quarters) of this Tuscan city to which a sporting dimension was added with a chariot race in the main square. *Sagre* now serve a very particular purpose in bringing together the population of a village or an area and enabling the food producers and farmers to show the fruits of their labor and to sell them. At the same time a church service calls for blessings from above. This applies most of all to the *sagre* that are part of a village's spring events, at which prayers are said for a rich harvest. *Sagre* are also held in the fall to give thanks for a bountiful year, usually taking place in September, when the harvest has been brought in, or in October, when the wine has been pressed.

Vines as far as the eye can see

Nowhere else is the high standard of craftsmanship more obvious than in Italy's viniculture, which has undergone a series of sweeping changes over the last thirty years. The aim has been better quality and less mass production. Admittedly, the proponents of viniculture development in Italy, by restricting the grape yields in favor of stronger, more complex wines, are no longer able to satisfy the demand.

For Daniele Cernilli, one of the top Italian wine journalists, Italian wine has the highest potential for development, especially that from the southern regions, where it is still largely stored in barrels and sold in demijohns according to ancient tradition. Of the 264 billion gallons of wine from Sicily, only just over 10½ million gallons were bottled. The regions from which we can expect excellent wines in the coming years are Campania, Umbria, and Le Marche, all southern regions where full reds are made and which have since antiquity been among the classic wine producing areas of Italy.

Diversity: 2,000 different grape varieties

Growing grapes for eating and for making wine has a very long tradition in Italy. There was intensive cultivation of vines since the time of the Roman Empire, especially in the area round Rome, in Latium, and in Campania, where the Roman elite had their country houses. It was also the Romans who spread viticulture along the European trade routes within the Empire.

We cannot list here all 2,000 grape varieties that are grown in the 750 miles between the northernmost point of Italy in the Alto Adige and the southernmost island of Pantelleria, which is closer to Africa than to Italy. Piedmont and Tuscany are still the most famous and innovative wine-producing regions. While in Tuscany great mercantile houses established in the fourteenth and fifteenth centuries became rich by setting up as bankers and devoting themselves to wine

In Luciano Baffo's *enoteca* in Venice you can buy excellent *vini da tavola* straight from the cask to drink with lunch or dinner, get expert advice, and, of course, sample the wine before you buy.

production (Antinori, Frescobaldi), Piedmont remained an area of small vineyards with such famous growers as Angelo Gaja, whose wines are so hard to come by they virtually have to be taken by force from the cellars.

Top quality vintages from the Alto Adige to Sicily

Compared to other Mediterranean countries, including France, Italy is the wine country *par excellence*. Grapes are grown all over the country, and in each region there are outstanding vintners at work who produce wines with the top quality grading *Denominazione di Origine Controllata* (DOC) or *Indicazione Geografica Tipica* (IGT), which are comparable to the great vintages of the world.

The scale of wine production varies considerably in the regions, from the Aosta Valley, with an area of only 2,288 acres under cultivation, to Sicily, by far the largest grape-growing area of Italy, with over 400,000 acres devoted to the vine. The many institutes and agricultural colleges are the guardians of the knowledge gathered over centuries. They combine it with the latest technology and pass it on to those working in the field, thus ensuring the continued production of excellent vintages in the future.

Astonishing but true: a Pinot Nero is made from

grapes grown on the slopes of the Aosta Valley at over 4,000 feet. From the lower Aosta Valley comes a Muscat de Chambave, a sweet gold- to amber-colored wine, made from grapes grown at a height of up to 2,300 feet. As the cultivated area is small, it is only natural that the wine is mostly drunk locally and hardly exported. Sicily produces table wines — *vini da tavola* — even in the hottest areas in the interior of the island, which are sold directly from the cask.

The situation is completely different in Piedmont, where the tolerant Nebbiolo grape dominates; its name is derived from *nebbia*, the Italian for "fog." Barbera, Dolcetto, and Arneis grapes are grown in the area around Alba, Barolo, Neive, and Barbaresco, and are used to make wines of the same names. Neive and Barbaresco are home to such famous wine producers as Angelo Gaja, Bruno Rocca, Bruno Giacosa, and Fratelli Giacosa. Their wines can be found in nearly all the top restaurants worldwide and are priced accordingly. This is justified, as the wines are made only with grapes grown on their own estates, and great care is taken during harvesting to pick only the best.

Among the underrated wines of Italy are those from the region of Oltrepò Pavese near the town of Voghera. This wine-growing region bordering on Piedmont and Emilia-Romagna has up-and-coming growers whose best products are sold in Lombardy's capital, Milan. Unusual for Italy, for Lombardy, and for wine-production in general is the Valtellina, where Nebbiolo grapes are grown almost exclusively, with the vines clinging to the rocky mountain sides sheltered by the great massif of the Piz Bernina. There a very drinkable everyday wine is produced, which is especially popular in Germany, Austria, and Switzerland, and a *sforzato*, made from a dried grapes with a high alcohol content.

In the region known as Tre Venezie, which includes Trentino-Alto Adige, Friuli-Venezia Giulia, and the Veneto, wine-production is at its most efficient, but at a high price. The Merlots from the Veneto are still considered inferior, and wine producers are finding it difficult to build up the region's reputation. Around Conegliano excellent white wines are produced from the Prosecco grape; on the one hand, a sparkling wine that became exceptionally popular in the 1990s, and, on the other hand, a *vino tranquillo*, that is, a wine that has not been fermented in vats, and is ideal for drinking with a light lunch, especially in the middle of summer. The Soave is extremely well known, a mellow, strong white wine. There is even a dessert version available, made from grapes left to dry on the vines; it is admittedly difficult to find but is easily a match for the best dessert wines in the world.

North of the Veneto, along the river Adige and around the Lago di Caldaro is the ancient grape-growing area of the southern Tyrol, where the wine producers have changed direction radically from mass production to quality wines, and produce some excellent examples, such as a dark Lagreiner and a red Malvasier, and dessert wines such as the Rose and Gold Muscatel. The Gewürztraminer from the little village of Tramin, which gave the grape its name, often gets very high marks from experts. Further to the south in the Trentino quite a heavy red wine is produced, the Teroldego Rotaliano, which is ideal for drinking with game.

Friuli, home of high-quality white wines

Divided into a plain, the Grave del Friuli, and a hilly area, the Collio, Friuli has developed into one of Italy's outstanding wine-producing areas, with producers such as Mario Schiopetto, Giovanni Dri, and Silvio Jermann leading the way in establishing the reputation of this region. The Jermann Sauvignon Blanc is one of the best wines that can be bought in Italy. Schiopetto, with his red Rivarossa, a blend of Cabernet Sauvignon, Pinot Nero, and Merlot, has developed a wine that measures up to a Bordeaux after it has been laid down for the right period.

If the wine-growing areas of Emilia-Romagna and Tuscany are taken together, the dominance of the Sangiovese grape can be clearly seen. The Romagnoli insist that this grape variety comes from Monte Giove near Sant' Arcangelo di Romagna, but whether this is true or not, it is wine lovers who are the winner, as they will find that the earthy wines of the Emilia give perfectly respectable results, although no match for the Chiantis from Tuscany. This is to be expected, as the gentle Tuscan hills are better suited than the plains to grape-growing, as the vines growing on hillsides absorb only as much water as they need for their growth, and the soils there are chalky and stony. Outside Italy, Chianti is still regarded as the archetypal Italian wine; the unusual bulbous shape of the bottle in its raffia basket may have a lot to do with this.

Brunello di Montalcino and the Vino Nobile di Montepulciano have long since taken the place of Chianti, and a Brunello from Tenuta il Poggione impresses even the most spoiled of wine buffs, who will prefer it to a premier *grand cru* from Bordeaux.

The red and white wines of Sicily were traditionally heavy and high in alcohol content. For some time Sicilian wine producers have also been developing lighter, fresher wines, which experts think show great promise.

However, the top-ranking world wine is now the Sassicaia from Antinori, grown as a pure Cabernet, whose best vintages reach astronomical prices.

It would be presumptuous and unjust to say that no wine produced south of Tuscany can compete with the vintages of the northern regions. This is not the case. The Orvieto white wine from Umbria is very impressive; as bottled by Antinori with the Castello della Sala label, it is promised a great future by wine experts. Even a producer such as Bigi can come up with a decent white wine.

You have to go further to the south, to Apulia, Campania, to the Basilicata, and to Calabria to find the red wines, such as the Salice Salentino, that have gained a very good reputation as table wines.

Lacrimae Christi, which is a full-bodied red wine, comes from Campania, from the slopes around Naples, though it is being overtaken in quality by the Taurasi, a powerful, extra-rich red made from the Aglianico grape; the 1968 Riserva from Mastroberardino is considered legendary. This wine often has 14 per cent alcohol, and is matured in

The Italian bar, a unique institution From morning till evening it is an important meeting place, where people stop to have a quick drink.

Slovenian oak casks. The Aglianico del Vulture, made in the Basilicata from the same kind of grape and cultivated around the Monte Vulture, is comparable to the Taurasi. It grows on a lava layer which is up to 1½ inches deep, and is an excellent wine to accompany meat and game. Among the best producers are Fratelli D'Angelo in Rionero in Vulture.

Great changes are taking place in Sicily, where most of the grapes grown on the 500,000 acres of vineyards are exported as eating grapes. Now the region is making great strides in wine production too. Duca Enrico produces a full-bodied red that can be counted among the top-quality wines of Italy. A Cerasuolo di Vittoria is made that is reminiscent of a rosé in color but is stronger and more lively. To a large extent, Sicilian wine means Marsala, and its quality and image have been improved in particular by Marco de Bartoli on his Veccio Samperi vineyard. Compared with sherry and port, Marsala still lags behind in reputation. Nevertheless , we recommend ending a good Italian meal with a Vergine or Soleras, the bouquet of which is reminiscent of vanilla, citrus fruit, caramel, and wood. The Passito di Pantelleria is also excellent after a meal, because on the sun-drenched island off Tunis the Zibibbo grapes gets so much natural sugar that they do not need to dry in the sun for long before they can be turned into a tempting dessert wine.

Viniculture in Sardinia must not be underestimated either. This is where the Grenache grape is turned into a strong Cannonau, either as a dry white or a sweet red wine. Rather smooth and more suitable with a Sardinian meal is the Monica di Sardegna, but it is unclear where the grape came from. As a sweet wine it is known as Monica di Cagliari, after the capital of the island. What is different about these wines is that they do not need to mature for long in the casks; after one year they have as much warmth and strength as older red wines.

Grappa and liqueurs

Grappa is an important by-product of wine-making in Italy, and in many countries became one of the most popular drinks of the 1990s. In Italy, however, grappa (which is added in drops to a cup of espresso to make a *corretto grappa*) is more traditional than trendy. The brandy made from the residue of grapes left after pressing is produced mainly in the large distilleries of the Veneto, which turn out a semi-finished product for larger firms (Grappa Julia, Nardini), or in small distilleries in Friuli that specialize in producing pure grappas and charge extremely high prices for it. The brandy remains a mere by-product even after maturing in wooden barrels (oak, quince, or cherry) — unless, that is, clever distillers boil it with grapes, sometimes even adding the permitted amount of caramel.

A list of Italian drinks would not be complete without mentioning the many apéritifs. Martini is the most prominent, followed by Campari and Aperol, which are herb-, white wine- or rhubarb-based and made according to old secret recipes. Thanks to good promotion, they have found their way into bars all over the world. If you find yourself in the right Italian region, you may have a *bianco sporco*, a "dirty white wine" before the meal. This aptly named cocktail is a small measure of Campari or Aperol topped up with dry white wine. If you have had a heavy lunch or dinner and decide to forgo the customary grappa, you can chose between a variety of herb-based liqueurs, which vary from one region to another, such as Nocino (made from grappa, nuts,

A glass of wine can be enjoyed in the morning too. Especially if one can also discuss the latest sports news or other such important topics.

and herbs), China Martini, and Averna (which is usually drunk with ice); when in dire need, a Fernet Branca is the only solution.

Il vero caffé italiano

This chapter on Italian food and drink would not be complete without a mention of the famous espresso. The coffee is drunk in small cups, which must be neither too thick nor too thin in order to assimilate the excess heat of the liquid as it issues from the jet at a temperature of 176°F. As a rule, roasted Arabica beans are used for an espresso. The aroma and body make this drink special, because the high pressure forces the boiling water through the finely ground coffee and furthers the extraction of soluble substances that largely determine the taste.

As can be seen from the photographs opposite, the epitome of Italian coffee culture is still represented by the unchanged Caffé Florian in the Procuratie Nuove in Saint Mark's Square in Venice. It was opened on December 29, 1720 by Floriano Francesconi, and became famous for its illustrious clientele. Even when fleeing from Venice, Casanova is supposed to have drunk an invigorating "Turkish drink" there before he finally quit the Serenissima for good. But the *vero espresso italiano*, which has conquered the world, was unknown to that era. Espresso machines as we know them today were invented only after the Second World War.

The bar, a stage for everyday life

A bar in Italy is not a dark hole where a great variety of cocktails are mixed, although a good *barista* is just as capable of mixing a Negroni as of producing a steaming *ristretto*, an extra-strong coffee. He can also produce *tramezzini*, slices of toast with the crusts cut off, sandwiched with all sorts of delicacies, and cut into dainty triangles. The bar is the main meeting place for Italians. In the morning they meet for a coffee, then for an apéritif before lunch, for a *corretto grappa* in the afternoon before going back to the office, while in the evening the espresso bar is taken over by the young. Throughout the day it has served the purpose of refreshing people *espresso*, quickly, and providing a place for them to see each other and be seen. The bar is the stage where the Italians act out their little dramas and at the same time enjoy excellent catering. It is nothing other than a condensed version of the Italian lifestyle — before and after a meal, the highlight of each day.

Antipasti
APPETIZERS

The little morsels served as hors d'oeuvres to stimulate the appetite and palate are one of the most delicious achievements of Italian cuisine. Fine cold cuts of prosciutto and salami have their place in a classic selection of antipasti, as do marinated vegetables. But whether the antipasto consists of *sott'oli*, *sott'aceti*, or just bread, the one constant is cold-pressed extra virgin olive oil, whose taste differs so greatly according to region and variety, thus lending a unique touch to each of the various delicacies.

Olives & capers: both indispensable

Olives and capers are essential seasoning ingredients for most of Italy's regional cuisines.

Olives

The fruit of the olive tree, one of the oldest cultivated plants in the Mediterranean, is mainly pressed for oil, although a substantial portion of the crop is sold as eating olives. Up to twenty varieties are offered at well-stocked market stands. Eating olives are usually bigger, fleshier, and lower in fat than those used for oil.

Cultivation

Few plants leave their mark on the whole of the Mediterranean landscape like this light evergreen tree, with its narrow leaves shimmering silvery-green in the sunlight. An undemanding tree, the olive can get by with little water, and live for several hundred years.

The olives ripen between October and December, and the various colors indicate how ripe they are. Unripe olives are green; they then slowly change to a purplish hue, until, completely ripened, they become dark, almost black. They taste different at the various stages: green olives are usually milder; the dark, strongly fermented olives are rather spicier, and sometimes also sharper tasting.

Inedible raw

Olives cannot be eaten fresh. If you were to pick a few from a tree and taste them, you would be bitterly disappointed: they have none of the expected flavor, only a bitter taste. Therefore, before olives can be served as an antipasto, or used to flavor various Italian, and in particular Sicilian, dishes, they must be soaked in an alkaline sodium chloride solution to extract the bitter substances. They are then transferred to a brine to preserve them.

Capers

These small, dark to olive-green morsels are the preserved flower buds of the caper bush, which flourishes throughout most of the Mediterranean on warm rock faces and walls. The thorny bush, with branches up to 3 feet long, grows wild and is cultivated in Sicily, on the Lipari Islands just offshore, and on Pantelleria, where the best *capperi* come from. The long-stemmed buds sit in the axils of the leaves and are carefully and individually picked before they open, for only tightly closed buds, rather than the showy, strong-scented pink-and-white flowers, are used in cooking. After they are picked, the buds are left to wither overnight.

Preserving

The flavor of capers varies according to the preserving method used. Capers preserved in vinegar, as they are most commonly available here, taste quite sour, and are unsuitable for Italian cooking. Instead, you need to use salted capers, which you might be able to find in delicatessens or Italian food stores. The most sought-after are the small buds, which are very flavorful and tender. Before using them, shake the salt off the buds, or soak them for 10–15 minutes, changing the water several times; otherwise, they will be too salty.

Capers are used as a

ANTIPASTI 27

If allowed, the caper buds develop into delicate, intricately patterned flowers whose splendor lasts for just one day. Clearly visible on the left are also the long-stemmed, still-closed buds, as well as the characteristic small, oval leaves.

seasoning in many dishes, including fish and veal, as well as pasta sauces and salads. Salted or in vinegar, they keep for a very long time in the refrigerator. The quality of salt-preserved capers can be determined by the color of the salt: if pure white, the capers are fine; if slightly yellow, the capers are a bit older, and a new jar should be bought.

Caper fruits

Capperone, which are also highly prized in the south of Italy, are really caper fruits. Developing from the flowers of the caper bush, they are sold preserved in vinegar or oil, and may be served as an antipasto.

Caper harvest on Salina, one of the Lipari Islands off the north coast of Sicily. From spring until midsummer, the closed flower buds of the caper bush are stripped off the plant every morning by hand, bud by bud — but only when they have reached the right size. Good-quality capers are hand-graded, and any buds that are already open or too large are discarded.

Caper fruits pickled in vinegar taste good with an aperitif. But use caper buds preserved in salt for cooking, since pickling in vinegar makes them too sour for many dishes.

Olive oil: Italy's liquid gold

Italian cuisine would be unthinkable without olive oil, but do not imagine that all olive oils are the same. Italy has many climatic zones, each of which gives the local oil a different taste. In addition, of course, the different varieties of olives, the nature of the soil, how far away the trees are from the sea, the age of the trees, and the time at which the harvest takes place are all important criteria for the development of the oil's flavor.

On the whole, the oils of the north are milder and lighter in color than the oils of the south. Among the olive-oil-producing countries, Italy ranks second worldwide, behind Spain. Within the country itself, it is the south, particularly Apulia and Calabria, that produces the greatest quantity of oil. There are several excellent oils produced there, although the ones from central and northern Italy have enjoyed a good reputation for longer. There are countless excellent Tuscan olive oils, among which those of the provinces of Lucca, Grosseto, and Arezzo are the most highly praised. Next come the Umbrian oils, which, like those from Latium, are very much in demand. Because of a favorable microclimate, the olive oils from the northern Italian lakes region are also much sought-after. The quantity yielded there, however, is very small, with the result that these oils are only very seldom exported. However, not only are the oils from Liguria prized for their lightness, but the yield is sufficient for export. Sicily and Sardinia also produce good oils.

Classification

In Italy the label "extra-virgin olive oil" (*extra vergine* in Italian) designates the best oil quality. By law, this oil must not contain more than 1 percent fatty acids, and must be produced by cold-pressing perfect olives without the addition of any chemicals. "Virgin olive oil" must also be cold-pressed, and may contain a maximum of 2 percent oleic acids. Bottles labeled "olive oil"

A long ladder is often needed to harvest the olives, especially in the case of old, tall trees like the ones here in Badalucco, in the Ligurian Valle Argentina near Imperia.

Small Taggiasca olives flourish at an altitude of between 900 and 2,300 feet above sea level. Mild and fruity in flavor, they are reddish-black when fully ripe.

Knocked from the trees with chestnut-wood poles — a task requiring great care — these olives are caught in a net.

To yield the best quality oil, the olives should be as free from damage as possible. They are usually harvested before they are fully ripe for better flavor.

ANTIPASTI

or "pure olive oil" generally contain a mixture of refined and cold-pressed oils. For the recipes in this book, and for Italian cooking in general, we recommend that you use only the best: extra-virgin olive oil.

Harvest and oil extraction

To make the highest-quality oils, olives are hand-picked and hand-graded. Harvesting with a "comb" or a sort of scissors, which "scrapes" the olives off the branches, is a particularly gentle method. Occcasionally the fruit is knocked off the trees with poles, which requires a certain amount of skill, as neither branches nor olives must be damaged. Once the olives are off the tree, they must be dealt with quickly, within 3 days, as shown below.

Nylon nets festooned like spiderwebs catch the harvested olives just above the ground, so that the fruit remains as undamaged as possible.

In the traditional manner, the whole olives are crushed by granite millstones for about an hour. The pulp is then spread about 1 inch thick on round mats.

Layer upon layer, the coir mats spread with the olive pulp are placed on top of each other, with a number of metal disks in between providing stability.

Through its own weight alone, the oil begins to drip out. This first oil is the most valuable and expensive of all olive oils.

Yellowish-green and viscous is the result of the pressing of the olive pulp and the subsequent centrifuging, which separates the oil and water.

30 ANTIPASTI

Tuscan-style beans Borlotti beans, with herbs, tomatoes, and mustard, marinated in oil and vinegar.

Porcini in olive oil Perfect young, mushrooms, cooked in vinegar and topped up with a good olive oil.

Garlic cloves, preserved in olive oil with sweet peppers, various herbs, and hot chile peppers.

Onions in balsamic vinegar Small onions, cooked, then marinated in good balsamic vinegar.

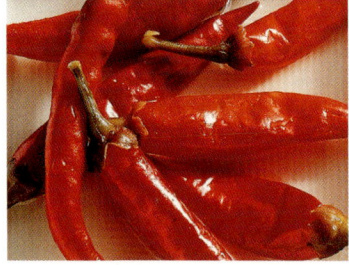
Moscardini Small, cooked octopus, marinated in olive oil with garlic, herbs, and salt.

Hot red peppers, pickled in a special brine. Popular for garnishes as well as antipasto.

Melanzane grigliate Broiled eggplant in oil and wine vinegar, with chile peppers, garlic, and parsley.

Cipolle borettane Onions, peeled and broiled, then marinated in oil, wine vinegar, salt, and sugar.

Broiled mushrooms, marinated in olive oil and seasoned with herbs, salt, pepper, and garlic.

Small white cannelini beans in a mild, delicately seasoned tomato sauce. Good with toasted bread.

Marinated *sepiolini* Tiny cooked cuttlefish marinated in olive oil with garlic and herbs.

Funghi di muschio sottolio Mushrooms cooked in vinegar, then salted and preserved in olive oil.

Grilled zucchini strips, in olive oil and wine vinegar, with chile peppers, herbs, garlic, and salt.

Peperoni in *bagna caôda* Bell peppers marinated in oil, vinegar, milk, anchovies, and garlic.

Cooked shrimp in olive oil, in a spicy marinade with plenty of parsley and chopped garlic.

Bell peppers preserved in wine vinegar, with salt, a pinch of sugar, and citric acid.

Shucked mussels in olive oil, seasoned with salt, pepper, and a pinch of paprika.

Carciofi grigliati Artichokes, boiled, then broiled, with chile peppers, vinegar, parsley, and garlic.

Large white beans, in a piquant oil marinade with tomatoes, garlic, parsley, salt, and pepper.

Sun-dried tomatoes, preserved in olive oil, with herbs and garlic, are eaten alone and used in many dishes.

Marinated, pickled, and preserved

Pickled peppers and mushrooms, marinated mussels and squid: Italians love such tidbits. Preserved in oil, they they are referred to as *sott'oli*, literally, "under oil." When the vinegar is dominant, they are *sott'aceti*. Herbs and garlic, and perhaps, capers or anchovies are often included.

Delicious antipasti

Spicy pickled or marinated morsels are served on their own or as an accompaniment to other antipasti. Sour, and in particular sweet-and-sour preserved fruit, are popular accompaniments to boiled or pickled meat in Italy. All of the products illustrated on these two pages can be bought ready-made. Be careful not to purchase cheap goods, however, as inferior oil and bad vinegar can spoil even the best ingredients.

Sott'oli

Preserving in olive oil suits many foods. Little artichokes, for instance, taste superb in oil, as do broiled zucchini and eggplant. And porcini in oil, or the little *chiodini* — young honey-fungus mushrooms — seasoned with garlic and parsley are a delicacy. It pays to keep a small supply of these delicious morsels on hand at home. If you want to be sure of quality, you can make your own *sott'oli*. To make the porcini in oil, you will need 2¼ pounds of small, young mushrooms. Trim and clean, but do not wash, them. Cook them for a few minutes in 4½ cups of white wine vinegar, drain, and leave to cool wrapped in a cloth. Place the dry porcini in a jar, add 1 teaspoon peppercorns, 2 bay leaves, and a little salt, and pour in extra-virgin olive oil to cover. The mushrooms keep for months. Other sorts of mushrooms and vegetables may also be preserved in this way.

Sott'aceti

To make *sott'aceti* first blanch the vegetable in boiling salted water — taking care that it remains *al dente*, and then pour a vinegar marinade over it. For 2¼ pounds of vegetables, you will need about 2¼ cups white wine vinegar. With their piquant note, *sott'aceti* are an ideal accompaniment to cold cuts. They make a less successful partner for very delicate-flavored hams such as Parma, San Daniele, or culatello, as their acidity would mask the hams' exquisite taste.

Another highly regarded antipasto are *cipolle in agrodolce*, sweet-and-sour onions. The onions are blanched in boiling water, then peeled and cooked in butter and water in a heavy-bottomed pot for about 20 minutes. When they are soft, about 1 tablespoon of vinegar is added to every 2¼ pounds of onions, along with 2 level teaspoons sugar, some salt, and freshly ground pepper. The onions are then left to simmer for about 1 hour, until they have become golden brown. They do not keep for very long.

Mostarda

Italian mostarda, of which there are a number of regional varieties, is a spicy hot, aromatic side dish of candied fruits preserved in a mustard syrup. Often partnered with pan-fried and boiled meat, it also goes well with game. Depending on the region, mostarda is also served as an antipasto, and has a particular affinity with prosciutto. While the *mostarda di Mantua* is generally produced from a single type of fruit, such as apple or quince slices, the mostarda from Cremona, which is the most famous, calls for a combination of several varieties of fruit: crunchy apples and firm pears, as well as figs, pumpkin, melon, cherries, peaches, and orange slices. It is important that the fruit be neither too ripe, nor too juicy, nor too sweet; hard, slightly tart fruit is best. The fruit is peeled, cut into pieces, and boiled in a syrup made from 2 parts sugar and 1 part water until soft, but not falling apart. Firm fruits such as apples and pears are given a 10-minute head start before adding softer fruits such as figs and melons. The fruit is then removed from the syrup and allowed to dry partially. Another syrup is made from 1 bottle white wine and 1 pound honey, into which 1 ounce of light mustard powder is stirred. The colorful fruit mixture is then placed in jars and the honey-and-wine syrup is poured over it. The condiment will keep for several weeks.

Assorted *mostarde*: Above left, *mostarda di Cremona*; above, **mostarda di Voghera**, with a mixture of figs, pumpkin, and melon; left, mostarda from the Veneto.

Green olive tapenade Made from pitted, puréed green olives mixed with salt, pepper, and oil.

Black olive tapenade Made from pitted black olives puréed with anchovies, pepper, and olive oil.

Prosciutto: Italian air-dried ham

Like ham in general, Italian prosciutto comes from the hind leg of a hog. With its delicate, incomparable flavor, it has justifiably achieved world fame. *Prosciutto crudo* (*crudo* means "raw" or "uncooked") is salted, then air-dried. The prosciutti of Parma and San Daniele are probably the best-known outside of Italy, although the hams from other regions are worth getting to know too.

The production technique is always similar: The salt draws out enough moisture from the meat to preserve it, and the slow air-drying imparts the desired mild flavor. Generally, the hams are not smoked, but there are a few exceptions, particularly in the north.

Prosciutto di Parma

The production of Parma ham (shown in the background of the picture above) is a lengthy, complicated process. Only pigs from certain regions may be used, and they must be specially reared; in some cases they are fed the whey that accrues during the process of making Parmesan cheese. The hogs must be over 10 months old when slaughtered, and weigh at least 310 pounds. The Consorzio del Prosciutto di Parma keeps a strict watch on quality. The coveted seal, the five-pointed ducal crown of Parma, is awarded only to hams produced strictly according to regulations. The rules stipulate that a ham weighing 15–20 pounds must be cured for at least 10 months, while heavy hams must age for 1 year, with the drying stage taking up to 2 years. After 7–8 months, and a weight-loss of about 25 percent, the ham is rubbed on the flesh side, usually with spiced lard, in order to prevent further drying. Tending a prosciutto during the curing period is a labor-intensive process. In addition, experts continually check up on its progress.

Parma ham is made in two

ANTIPASTI 33

Parma ham and Parmesan cheese are two of the splendid products of Emilia-Romagna that are sold in this shop in Ravenna.

Prosciutto cotto, cooked ham, is prepared in more than one way in Italy. Like *prosciutto crudo*, it is made from the hind leg of the hog, which is usually boned. Before it is cooked or steamed, *prosciutto cotto* is often flavored with herbs and spices. It is eaten as part of an hors d'oeuvre platter or in sandwiches.

styles: boneless and in various shapes; and on the bone, which is docked at the knee joint, giving the ham its plump appearance. Parma ham has a comparatively mild salt cure, and acquires its flavor from the hogs' feed (it is said that the whey is responsible for the slightly sweet note) as well as from the varying length of the cure. Understandably, the end result of this highly labor-intensive, lengthy production process does not come cheap, but a genuine Parma ham, aged for around 18 months, is a taste of perfection.

Prosciutto di San Daniele

This guitar-shaped ham from Friuli is every inch the equal of Parma ham, not only in terms of the time and effort lavished on its production, but also in aroma and flavor. In fact, thinly sliced (as in the foreground of the picture above, left) and served plain or with grissini, its delicate texture and flavor have led many a connoisseur to declare it the finer of the two. This prosciutto is made in the picturesque clifftop village of San Daniele del Friuli. Like Parma ham, it is salted before drying. It is then pressed between two wooden boards. This gives the ham its characteristic flat shape and makes it thinner, which means that it needs even less salt. Like Parma ham too, the production process is stringent, and regulated by law. Diet, age, weight, and manner of slaughter of the hogs are precisely stipulated. A consortium awards the appropriate quality seal to the hams after an optimal aging period of 14–16 months. In the past, the natural microclimate during drying — the meeting of the cold north winds with the moister Adriatic air — was exclusively responsible for the superb taste of this prosciutto: The drying houses, with their high, narrow windows through which the bora wind wafts, are in the northern part of the village. Today, however, owing to high demand and for the sake of better control, the hams are also hung to dry in chambers in which the alternation of dry and moist air is artificially generated.

Other prosciutti

There are many other fine Italian hams, including *prosciutto di Montefeltro* from the Marches; the particularly lean *aquilano* from Abruzzi; the Tuscan *casentino*; the *sauris* from Friuli; the prosciutto from the Veneto, and *culatello di Zibello*, described on pages 34–35.

Bresaola is a specialty of the Valtellina. The initial product is not pork, but lean beef, which is salted and air-dried. Bresaola remains tender and relatively moist in spite of these processes, but once sliced, it does not keep for as long. The village of Chiavenna between Maloja and Lake Como is famous for its bresaola.

until it is transformed into an artistic, pear-shaped weave. This handiwork requires great skill and a lot of strength. The culatello is not ready yet, though. Gradually drying in the air of the Po is crucial for its mild yet spicy flavor.

The moist air of the Po
At first, the ham needs moist, cool air: The temperature should be around 28–30°F at night, and 39–41°F during the day. For this reason, small companies (larger ones produce the required climatic conditions artificially) begin culatello production between November and February to take advantage of the natural conditions of the Bassa Parmense (Parma

The finest of the fine: culatello di Zibello

Whether culatello is the finest ham in the world is, of course, a matter of personal taste, but one thing is certain: it is one of the most expensive hams.

Carefully tied up
To make culatello, only the best part of the ham is used. The boned core of the haunch of a freshly slaughtered hog is rubbed with a little sea salt and covered with a natural casing. Next comes the *legatura*, the tying up — a difficult task. Culatello producer Roberto Mezzadri is pictured on the right getting the ham into shape. Using needle and string, he ties it up lengthwise, then crosswise,

Lowlands), the only area where culatello is produced.

Next the culatello must dry slowly in the moist air at 57–59°F for another 6 months to 2 years. It is the high humidity of 80–85 percent prevalent along the banks of the Po that gives the ham its uniquely mellow flavor. During the aging period the hams are checked repeatedly with a little hammer, whose sound reveals the extent to which they have dried, and with a *spillatura*, a horsebone needle used to prick the culatello in order to check the flavor, as the chef of the trattoria La Buca in Zibello is doing in the pictures on the far left. (This method is also used to judge the quality of Parma and other hams.) If the ham is found to be good, it is awarded the Culatello di Zibello seal.

A marvelous antipasto

Before it is eaten, the culatello is brushed off under running water, then left to marinate in dry red or white wine for 2–3 days. String, skin, and excess fat are then removed, and the meat is sliced wafer-thin and served as a delicious antipasto.

Delicate and spicy: sausage and bacon

Pork is very popular throughout Italy, especially in the form of sausages and bacon. Every region has its own specialties, which, unfortunately, are only seldom exported.

Mortadella
Pale pink pebbled with white, this sausage does credit to the reputation of Bologna, with its love of rich food. Consisting of 40 percent fat and 60 percent meat, mortadella is hardly what you would call a lean sausage. The best is made from 100 percent pork (*puro suino*, labeled with an "S"), but there are also mixtures of pork and beef, veal, lamb, or donkey meat. Finely chopped meat and long strips of bacon are stuffed into a natural casing and slowly steamed. Mortadella should always be sliced very thinly. Eaten with bread as an antipasto, it is sometimes also used as a stuffing ingredient. There are also varieties of mortadella with pistachios, and with liver.

Coppa
Coppa also belongs to the large family of *insaccati*, or "in-a-sack" sausages: those packed into a skin. Made from pork neck, the meat is salted, stuffed into a natural casing, bound tightly, and air-cured for 4–5 months.

Coppa di testa, a specialty from Emilia, is a type of brawn made from pig's head and tongue. The pieces of meat are cooked, seasoned, packed into a natural casing, and pressed. Similar products are *coppa umbra* and *soppressata*, a pig's-head brawn popular in various regions of Italy.

Speck from the Alto Adige. This bacon — here, a whole side with a piece of loin — is salted, spiced with juniper berries, and cold-smoked. Some *speck* is air-dried.

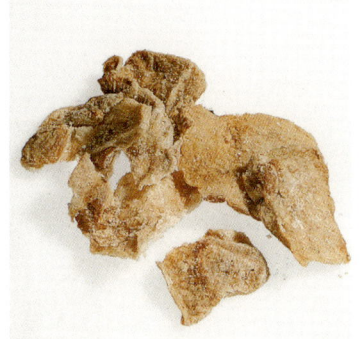   

The dark red meat streaked with white has a fine aroma. Sliced thinly, it is eaten as an antipasto. There are many regional variations. The central and southern Italian counterpart to coppa is capocollo, made from head and neck meat. Usually more strongly seasoned with pepper or cayenne pepper, it is sometimes also cold-smoked.

Pancetta, bacon, and *speck*

Pancetta is used in many Italian sauces, soups, and ragùs. This salted, but unsmoked, mild pork belly is sold rolled, usually without its rind, or flat and with the rind. Pancetta is salted, then rubbed with pepper and a series of other spices, such as cloves or juniper berries; the final flavor varies according to the spices used. After 14 days, it can be sliced thinly and served as an antipasto. There is also air-dried pancetta (*curata*), and occasionally smoked pancetta.

The back bacon of the pig, known as *lardo*, is also used a lot in cooking, particularly in sauces. Sometimes flavored with herbs, sometimes simply salted and hung, it adds substance and taste to a dish. In particular, the product from Colonnata in the province of Carrara has made a name for itself. When the bacon is rendered, it yields, in addition to lard, the popular *ciccioli*, or crackling, which is pressed and seasoned with salt, pepper, and bay leaf. Even beyond the borders of the Alto Adige, Italians are familiar with the *speck* of the southern Tyrol, which, either air-dried or smoked, is prized as an antipasto or an ingredient in ragù.

Salsicce

Salsicces are relatively coarse-textured sausages. Some are made exclusively of pork, others of pork combined with other meat. Some are fresh, some air-dried. Their culinary uses are also manifold: pan-fried, they can be eaten with pasta or rice, but they are also delicious boiled, broiled, grilled, and braised.

Italian sausage and bacon, from coppa to salsicce. Left to right: Different varieties of **coppa**, salted, air-dried neck of pork. **Coppata** is a coppa wrapped in rindless pancetta. **Coppa stagionata** must be air-cured for at least 3 months. The **ciccioli croccanti** are a sort of crackling from rendered pork fat, another specialty of Emilia-Romagna. **Pancetta** is a particularly mild bacon sold in various shapes, and used chiefly for cooking. **Arrotolata**, "rolled" bacon, as here, is also sliced and served as an antipasto. *Salsiccia fresca* is a coarse, fresh, pork frying sausage; and the long, thin *luganega* is a link sausage made of coarsely chopped pork.

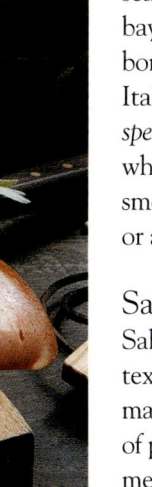

Mortadella, the big sausage from Bologna. This sausage can tip the scales at up to 110 pounds, although a weight of 10–33 pounds is usual. Even that is nothing to sneeze at: it still makes mortadella the largest of all Italian sausages.

To make *cicciolata*, pork trimmings are cooked for hours with rind, gristle, and a little salt. The mixture is then wrapped in muslin and pressed, which binds all the individual ingredients together into a solid mass.

Salami varieties pictured from left to right:
1 Bocconcino Modense, 2 Salamella,
3 Campotosto, 4 Stramilano, 5 Abruzzese,
6 Montanaro, 7 Vesurio.

Salami: flavor, pure and simple

All salamis are made from chopped meat — from pork alone, or from pork and beef, donkey, or horsemeat — that is packed into synthetic or natural casings, pressed, salted, and air-dried. During drying, which lasts 3–5 months, the salami loses up to 35 percent of its weight and a dry fungus establishes itself on the skin, producing the characteristic white color of the salami.

Generally, to make a good salami, you need good meat, to which you add salt, sodium nitrate, and seasonings. The more slowly the sausages are cured, the better their flavor. In Italy there are dozens of different sorts of salami. The differences lie in the ratio of meat to fat in the sausage meat, in the fineness of the sausage mixture, and in the seasoning. When you go into a *salumeria*, a specialty store for cured sausages and meats , the spicy aroma of the salamis immediately greets you. Some mild, some hot with chile, they never fail to surprise the palate with their splendid and varied flavors.

Huge variety

To introduce here all the types of salami in Italy would exceed the scope of this book. What follows, therefore, is a brief summary of the most common varieties. First, are those with fine-textured sausage meat. One of the best-known types in this category is the **salame di Milano**, made chiefly from lean, minced pork. As a rule, it is seasoned with coarsely ground black pepper, but sometimes too with white wine, or with red-wine-flavored garlic. It has a relatively large diameter and must be cured for at least 3 months before being sold. It should be served sliced very thinly. Also relatively fine is **salame ungherese**, highly prized for its slightly smoky flavor. It consists of one-third each pork, beef, and pork fat. After a curing period of 3 months, it, too, should be served thinly sliced. Among the best Italian salamis are the particularly delicate **salame gentile**, made from lean pork, and the medium-fine **salame di Felino** from the Parma area. Pieces of meat left over from Parma-ham production and pieces of pork shoulder are used to make the latter. This relatively small-diameter salami, which is generally sliced on the diagonal, is delicately seasoned with white wine and black peppercorns. Mild in taste, it is sold after a curing period of about 3 months. Similar varieties can be found around Verona and Genoa. Somewhat coarser-textured and more highly seasoned is the **salame di Varzi**, also called **salame piacentino**. Also fairly coarse in texture and prepared from equal proportions of meat and fat are numerous salamis from central and southern Italy. In Tuscany, **salame toscano** is made from very lean meat cured for 3–6 months, while the large **finocchiona**, made from coarsely chopped meat and seasoned with fennel seeds, is cured for up to 1 year, which is relatively long for a salami. Salami is often flavored with wild-fennel seeds in Apulia and Calabria too. Italians in the south like their food hot, and do not shrink from giving their salamis a chile-pepper kick. Finely chopped, the *pepperoncini*, and sometimes sweet peppers, are mixed into the coarse sausage meat, so that it is hardly surprising that varieties such as **salame di Napoli**, **salame abruzzese** and the coarse **salame calabrese**, whose red color comes from the peppers it contains, have a reputation for being quite spicy. In southern Italy salami is made mainly by small farmers. The small quantities produced mean that these delicious salamis are seldom seen outside the regions where they are made.

There are still many more specialty salamis worth mentioning, such as the spicy **spianata romana**, a specialty from Latium consisting of three-fifths lean meat and two-fifths firm bacon, and the smaller **salamella**, a mixture halfway between salami and salsiccia, especially popular in Mantua and Cremona. There is also the **cacciatore**, or "hunter's" salami, weighing about 7 ounces, which owes its name to its suitability as knapsack provisions; and the delicate Piedmontese **salam d'Induja**, a pork salami preserved in a pot of lard. Ferrara is known for its **salama da sugo**, "juicy" salami, which tastes absolutely superb cooked, cooled, and served with fragrant melon. That good salami need not always be made of slaughterhouse meats is amply proved by the **salame d'oca** from Novara, a goose salami that contains cubes of bacon. Lastly, there are various salamis made from game meat, such as hare and wild boar.

Salami varieties pictured from top to bottom: *salame ungherese; salame Montanaro gigante; salame Felina; salame stofelotto Mesola; Magyar salami filze.* The large, pear-shaped salami below on the right is a *salame Veneta*, and the flat, loaf-shaped one on the left in the foreground is a *salame Spianata*. The dark sausage without a white skin in the background is a *salsiccia Napoli forte*.

Antipasti

Start as you mean to go on: *affettato* and white beans in oil with warm shrimp

The Italians have an ancient precedent for the serving of assorted *antipasti* — a selection of little delicacies before the actual meal, to stimulate the appetite — since even the Romans were fond of their preprandial *gustationes*, which could be fruity and sweet, or hearty and piquant. Although the serving of a large selection of meat-based antipasti was for a long time chiefly an affair of the north, which produced the relevant sausages and ham on a larger scale, today *affettato*, or cold cuts, are enjoyed throughout Italy, in addition to vegetable-based antipasti. In the course of the growing nutritional awareness that places equal value on vitamins and flavor, these delicious tidbits have been accorded even greater honor. Here, as is so often the case, the simplest things are the best. Some slices of salami, a few good olives, and fresh bread are all that's

Cannellini beans are ideal for salads, as they become soft and mealy when cooked without falling apart. Warm shrimp make an excellent accompaniment.

needed — aside from a good wine to accompany them, of course. But the *affettato* also tastes superb with aromatic ham, as well as thin slices of pancetta; add a couple of little onions pickled in balsamic vinegar, some mushrooms in oil, or some marinated vegetables. There are no hard and fast rules; be guided by what you like. Taste is the only criterion. At most, therefore, you may only have difficulty in tracking down salami and ham as delicious as the Italian varieties, which are indisputably some of the best in the world.

WHITE BEANS WITH SHRIMP

Tender white beans, flavored with garlic and sage, and combined with diced tomatoes in olive oil, taste superb as an antipasto, especially when, as here, they are served with pan-fried shrimp. *Bruschette* — toasted

Classic antipasti: *affettato* and olives Sliced salami or ham are part of any good selection of antipasti, as are marinated olives.

slices of Italian bread with spiced tomatoes, oregano, and anchovies — are a popular accompaniment

Serves 4
¾ cup dried white beans
1 onion, halved
2 celery stalks, cut into 2-inch-long pieces
4 sage leaves
3 garlic cloves
14 oz tomatoes, peeled, seeded, and diced
½ cup olive oil
12 basil leaves, snipped
8 medium-size shrimp
salt; freshly ground white pepper
You will also need:
basil leaves

Place the beans in a bowl with cold water to cover and soak overnight. Drain and place in a pot with just enough fresh water to cover. Tie the onion halves, celery, and sage leaves together with kitchen string to make a bouquet garni. Add the bouquet garni and the garlic to the beans.

Simmer the beans over a low heat for 50–60 minutes, until they are soft. Pour off the water, fish out the bouquet garni, and transfer the drained beans to a large bowl. Mix in the tomatoes and basil.

Season the olive oil with salt and pepper, and mix all but 3 tablespoons of it into the beans and tomatoes. Leave to marinate for 1 hour.

Peel the shrimp down to the last joint and devein them. Heat the remaining seasoned oil in a skillet and pan-fry the shrimp briefly on both sides. Spoon the beans onto plates and arrange the shrimp on top. Garnish to taste with basil leaves and serve.

Crostini with olive paste, here garnished with diced tomatoes, make a superb-tasting antipasto. The smaller crostini are also popular with a topping of chicken livers, meat, or fish.

Bread with oil and flavorings
Bruschette, fettunta and crostini — sheer simplicity, but a taste to die for

The simplest antipasto, *bruschetta* can consist of nothing but white bread and the finest olive oil. This can be enhanced with the flavors of garlic plus tomatoes, olives, ricotta cheese, vegetables, or herbs. Originally grilled over charcoal embers, the slices of bread can also be browned in the oven or toaster — not quite the same, but still very good. In Tuscany, this hors d'oeuvre — which originated in Rome but is now found throughout central Italy — is called *fettunta*, and is eaten with nothing but olive oil, or an herb and garlic mixture.

CROSTINI WITH OLIVE PASTE

Serves 4

4 anchovy fillets in salt, 1 tablespoon salted capers

1 cup black olives, pitted

1 dried chile pepper, seeded

½ teaspoon fennel seeds, 5 tablespoons olive oil

1 tablespoon lemon juice

freshly ground black pepper, salt

12 slices Italian white bread with a strong crumb

1 cup diced seeded tomato

Briefly soak the anchovy fillets and the capers in water, then lift out, drain, and chop coarsely. Purée in a blender or food processor with the olives, chile pepper, fennel seeds, and oil. Season the paste with lemon juice and pepper, and salt to taste

Preheat the oven to 485°F and toast the slices of bread for 4 minutes until golden brown. Remove, spread with the olive paste, and serve garnished with diced tomatoes.

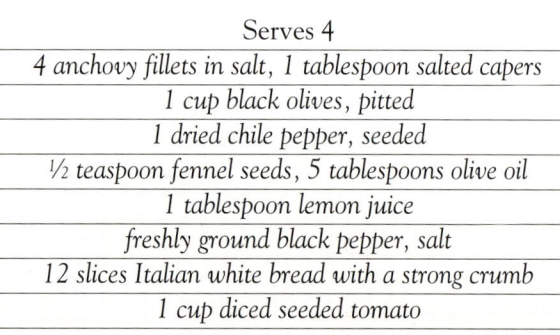

Tomato bruschette Instead of mixing the chopped garlic with the tomatoes, you could just rub the freshly toasted bread with a cut garlic clove, then spoon the tomatoes on top.

TOMATO BRUSCHETTE

If you like capers, add 2 teaspoons of finely chopped salted capers, and remember to go easy on the salt.

Serves 4
1 bunch basil
1 lb tomatoes, peeled, seeded, and diced
2 garlic cloves, finely chopped
2–3 tablespoons extra-virgin olive oil
12 slices Italian white bread
salt, freshly ground black pepper

Snip or slice all but a few leaves of the basil into strips. Combine the basil strips with the tomatoes, garlic, oil, salt, and pepper. Preheat the oven to 485°F and toast the slices of bread for about 4 minutes. Remove, and spoon the tomato mixture on top. Serve garnished with the whole basil leaves.

SALSA AL DRAGONCELLO

Serve this spicy tarragon sauce with fish or boiled meats; or blend the oil, garlic, tarragon, and vinegars, spread on bread, and serve as an antipasto.

Serves 4
4 thin slices Italian bread, ½ cup extra-virgin olive oil
3 garlic cloves, finely chopped
2 tablespoons chopped tarragon
2 tablespoons red wine vinegar
1 teaspoon balsamic vinegar, salt, freshly ground pepper

Place the bread in a container and add the olive oil. Sprinkle the garlic and tarragon on top. Seal the container with plastic wrap, and set aside for 1–2 hours. Add the vinegars, salt, and pepper, purée in a blender, and thin as required with meat or fish stock.

Slices of bread in fine olive oil, flavored with a mixture of tarragon, garlic, and two kinds of vinegar. In this bruschetta, tarragon takes the place of the frequently used arugula.

Pinzimonio Strips of raw vegetables, such as fennel, celery, carrots, peppers, Belgian endive, are dunked in fruity olive oil.

Beans, peppers, artichokes
Vegetable antipasti bring Mediterranean flavors to your table

Vegetable antipasti constitute a whole family, with market-fresh produce receiving treatment ranging from the plain to the sumptuous. The simplest, as with the bread, is the combination with olive oil alone, which is called *pinzimonio*. A good olive oil is also essential for marinating vegetables; it not only imparts flavor, but is also healthy and digestible. The high proportion of monounsaturated fatty acids in olive oil, in combination with the vitamins it contains, has a positive effect on metabolism, and helps to prevent cardiovascular diseases.

ARTICHOKES WITH TOMATOES

First prepare the artichokes, as shown on page 237. Here they are cooked in a special court bouillon.

Serves 4

6 artichokes with their stalks, juice of ½ lemon
⅓ cup finely diced shallot, ¼ cup extra-virgin olive oil
½ cup white wine, 1 sprig each thyme and rosemary
1 bay leaf, 1½ garlic cloves, 5 white peppercorns
2 tablespoons red wine vinegar, 1 teaspoon thyme leaves
14 oz beefsteak tomatoes, peeled, seeded, and finely diced
salt, freshly ground pepper

Halve the trimmed artichokes lengthwise and remove the choke. Brush the cut surfaces with lemon juice. Heat 1 tablespoon of the oil in a large saucepan and sweat the shallot until lightly colored. Deglaze with the wine and 1 tablespoon lemon juice. Pour in 6¼ cups water, add the herb sprigs, bay leaf, ½ garlic clove, salt, and peppercorns, and bring to a boil.

Three vegetable antipasti Far left, marinated artichoke halves with diced tomatoes. Center, sweet peppers with garlic, herbs, balsamic vinegar, and olive oil. Far right, a bean salad made with cannellini beans, which owes its spiciness to the heat of chile pepper and aromatic rosemary.

Preheat the oven to 425°F. Roast the peppers until their skins blister. Leave them to cool under a damp cloth or in a plastic bag, then peel, quarter lengthwise, and remove the stalk, seeds, and ribs. Strip the thyme leaves from their stalks, then combine with the garlic, vinegar, and oil. Season with salt and pepper, pour the dressing over the peppers, and leave to marinate for at least 30 minutes before serving.

BEAN SALAD WITH ROSEMARY

Serves 4

1½ cups dried white beans (e.g. cannellini)
1 teaspoon seeded red and green chile pepper strips
1 teaspoon finely snipped or chopped rosemary leaves
2 tablespoons red wine vinegar
1 generous pinch very finely chopped garlic
⅓ cup extra-virgin olive oil
salt, freshly ground white pepper

Add the artichokes and boil them for 10–15 minutes, taking care not to overcook them — they should still have some bite. Dice the remaining garlic clove and combine in a bowl with the vinegar, 1 tablespoon of the court bouillon, the thyme leaves, salt, pepper, and the remaining oil. Place the drained artichokes in a dish, add the tomatoes, pour over the dressing, and marinate for at least 30 minutes before serving.

SWEET PEPPERS WITH GARLIC

Serves 4

2 red, 2 green, and 2 yellow bell peppers
a few thyme sprigs, 1–2 garlic cloves, thinly sliced
2 tablespoons balsamic vinegar
⅓ cup extra-virgin olive oil, salt, freshly ground pepper

Soak the beans overnight in cold water to cover, then drain. Place in a pot with fresh water to cover and bring to a boil. Simmer the beans over a low heat for just under 1 hour, until tender. When they are almost done, salt them lightly. Drain the beans and combine in a bowl with the chile pepper and rosemary.

In another bowl, whisk together the vinegar, garlic, oil, salt, and pepper. Pour the dressing over the beans, and marinate for 1 hour before serving.

Broccoli aspic

A first course that owes a lot to neighboring Austria, like the cooking of Trento and Friuli in general

Serves 4
1 onion, unpeeled and halved
1¼ lb brisket of beef, 4 oz marrowbones
¾ cup coarsely chopped carrot
½ cup coarsely chopped celery root
1 bay leaf, 1 clove
1 bouquet garni, consisting of e.g. 3 parsley stalks, 1 lovage stalk, ½ celery stalk, ½ leek
2 small zucchini, ends trimmed
1 carrot, 4 oz celery root
3½ cups broccoli florets, 8 sheets gelatine
salt, freshly ground white pepper
For the remoulade sauce:
1 egg, ¼ teaspoon freshly ground white pepper
½ teaspoon salt, ½ teaspoon lemon juice
¼ teaspoon sharp mustard, ¾ cup vegetable oil
½ cup chopped gherkins, ¼ cup chopped capers
1 hardboiled egg, chopped
1½ tablespoons chopped herbs (e.g. chervil, parsley, and chives)
cayenne pepper
You will also need:
14-inch long, 1 quart mold

Slightly more than half-fill a large pot with water and bring to a boil. Caramelize the onion halves on a hot griddle or cast-iron skillet without fat. As soon as the water comes to a boil, add the brisket, marrowbone, caramelized onion, bay leaf, clove, bouquet garni, chopped carrot, and chopped celery root. Season with salt and pepper, reduce the heat, and cook, uncovered, for about 1½ hours.

Lift the meat from the broth and leave to cool. Pour the liquid through a strainer lined with cheesecloth. Reserve 2⅔ cups for the aspic, and use the rest in another recipe.

Cook the zucchini and the remaining carrot, celery root, and broccoli in boiling salted water until *al dente*, then lift out, chill in ice water, and drain thoroughly.

Cut the brisket, zucchini, carrot, and celery root into ½-inch-thick slices, then into ½-inch-wide strips. Leave the broccoli florets whole or halve them, depending on size.

Soak the gelatine in cold water. Heat the brisket stock and season to taste with salt and pepper. Squeeze out the gelatine well, add to the hot stock, and stir until dissolved. Place the mold in a container of ice water. Pour an even, ⅛-inch-thick layer of aspic onto the base of the mold. Top with a layer of meat and vegetables, taking care to leave an ⅛-inch edge free all around the sides of the pan. Pour some more aspic over this layer and allow to set slightly. Continue in this manner until all of the ingredients are used up. Finish with a layer of aspic, and leave in the refrigerator overnight to set completely.

To serve, dip the mold briefly in hot water, turn the aspic out onto a board, and return to the refrigerator to set again. Slice and arrange on a platter.

To make the remoulade, place the egg, pepper, salt, lemon juice, and mustard in a blender or food processor. Blend on the lowest setting, pouring in the oil in a steady stream. Stir in the gherkins, capers, hardboiled egg, and herbs, and season with cayenne pepper. Hand the sauce around separately to accompany the aspic.

Serve the sliced broccoli aspic with a piquant, spicy remoulade. Fragrant bread, fresh from the oven, and a glass of wine complement this appetizer nicely.

Roasting over an open flame is a simple way of peeling bell peppers. Turn the peppers slowly over the flame until the skin blisters and blackens all over, then leave to cool under a damp cloth or in a plastic bag. Rub off the burnt skin under cold running water.

Peperoni all'olio

From mild bell peppers to fiery-hot chiles, all capsicum varieties lend themselves to pickling or marinating

Antipasto di peperoni is quite delicious, and goes well with many dishes. It is therefore worth preparing a large supply, especially since these marinated vegetables will keep for several months in jars. Preparation is simplicity itself; only peeling the peppers takes a bit of time. The first step is to roast the peppers, which also imparts the desired smoky flavor. You can do this over a gas flame (see above), under a broiler, or in the oven. Oven roasting, shown in the picture sequence on the right, is especially suitable for a fairly large quantity of peppers. Large, thick-walled peppers may also be peeled using a vegetable peeler, but they will lack the roasted flavor.

MARINATED PEPPERS

Serves 4
about 2 red, 2 green, and 2 yellow peppers
1 small bunch thyme
1–2 garlic cloves, thinly sliced
4 teaspoons balsamic vinegar (optional)
⅓ cup extra-virgin olive oil
salt, freshly ground pepper

Prepare the peppers as shown in the picture sequence on the right. Cut the halved peppers into fourths, eighths, or large pieces, and layer in a shallow bowl. Strip the thyme leaves from the stalks, and combine with the garlic, vinegar, if using, oil, salt, and pepper. Pour the mixture over the peppers and marinate for at least 30 minutes.

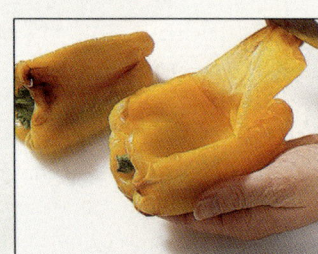

Oven-roasting peppers: Preheat the oven to 425°F and roast the peppers until their skins blister and blacken. Remove from the oven and leave to cool under a damp cloth or in a plastic bag. Pull off the skins from top to bottom. Halve the peppers lengthwise, taking care not to squash the soft flesh, then remove the stalks, seeds, and ribs.

Marinated peppers with wafer-thin slices of San Daniele prosciutto, finely shaved Parmesan cheese, and black olives, make an appealing appetizer plate. A few drops of balsamic vinegar lend it that certain something.

CHILE PEPPERS IN OIL

This appetizer can range from mild to highly piquant, depending on how hot the peppers are (not illustrated).

Serves 4

1 lb fresh chile peppers
2 garlic cloves, thinly sliced
1 rosemary sprig
4 teaspoons balsamic vinegar
¼ cup extra-virgin olive oil
salt

Larger chiles can be peeled in the same way as sweet peppers. For smaller ones, it is best to heat a skillet over a medium heat and dry-roast them until their skin is covered with brown blisters, then quickly transfer the chiles to a zip-lock bag, seal the bag, and let them "sweat" for about 10 minutes. Remove the chiles from the bag and rub off the charred skin under cold running water. Remove the stalk end, slit the chiles open lengthwise, scrape out the seeds, and rinse.

Steep the chiles in slightly salted water for 2–3 hours, then drain well. Combine the chiles in a bowl with the garlic, rosemary, vinegar, salt, and oil, and marinate in the refrigerator overnight.

It is best to have your butcher cut a pocket in the breast of veal, since this is no easy matter for the uninitiated. This dish tastes superb warm, although it is even more aromatic when cold, once the flavors have had a chance to develop. You can also flavor the aspic with ¼ cup Madeira wine, white port wine, or even with a robust muscatel.

Stuffed breast of veal

Cima alla Genovese, a Genoan specialty, served here with a basil sauce and delicate cubes of aspic

Serves 10–12
1 boned breast of veal with pocket (about 3 lb)
For the stuffing:
7 oz veal sweetbreads, 2 slices white bread, lukewarm milk
⅓ cup finely diced onion
1 garlic clove, finely diced
10 oz peas in the pod or 1½ cups frozen peas
¾ cup diced carrot, 2 tablespoons butter
10 oz boneless pork shank, 1 egg
1 teaspoon chopped herbs (thyme, marjoram)
3 tablespoons freshly grated Parmesan cheese
2 hardboiled eggs, peeled and chopped
salt, freshly ground pepper
For the broth:
1 cup finely diced onion, ¾ cup finely chopped celery
¾ cup chopped carrot, ¾ cup chopped leek, 1 bay leaf
10 black peppercorns, salt
For the aspic:
4 sheets gelatine
salt, freshly ground white pepper
For the basil sauce:
2 garlic cloves, finely chopped
2 teaspoons pine nuts
1 cup fresh basil leaves, 7 tablespoons olive oil
salt, freshly ground black pepper
You will also need:
1 square pan, about 8 x 8 inches

Soak the sweetbreads in a bowl under cold running water for about 2 hours, then remove any traces of skin and blood. Blanch the sweetbreads in gently boiling salted water for 5 minutes, lift out, drain, and cut into ¾-inch dice. Soak the bread in a little milk and squeeze dry.

Shell the peas, if using fresh, blanch in boiling salted water for 3 minutes, lift out, refresh under cold water and drain. Melt the butter in a skillet and sweat the onion and garlic without letting them color. Add the carrot and continue sweating over a low heat for 5 minutes. Add the peas and cook for a further 2 minutes, then season with salt and pepper, and leave to cool.

Using the fine blade on a meat grinder, grind the pork twice. In a bowl, combine the ground pork with the egg, bread, herbs, Parmesan, sweetbreads, vegetables, hardboiled eggs, salt, and pepper. Stuff the breast of veal with the mixture, leaving some room for expansion, then sew the pocket shut and season the outside of the meat with salt and pepper.

Fill a large saucepan with sufficient water to cover the breast of veal. Heat the water, add the vegetables and seasonings, bring to a boil, and reduce the heat. Wrap a cotton cloth around the breast of veal and secure. Simmer the meat in the broth for about 1½ hours, lift out onto a platter, weigh down, and leave to chill in the refrigerator overnight. Reserve 1¾ cups of the broth and leave to get cold; save the remainder for another recipe.

To make the aspic, soften the gelatine in cold water for about 10 minutes. Strain the chilled broth into a pot and heat. Dissolve the softened gelatine in the broth, season with salt and pepper, pour into the square pan, and leave to set in the refrigerator. Dip the pan briefly in hot water, unmold the aspic, and cut into ½-inch cubes.

To make the basil sauce, pound the garlic to a paste in a mortar with the pine nuts and salt. Add the basil, and pound until you have a creamy mixture. Transfer to a bowl and gradually stir in the oil, then season with salt and pepper.

Unwrap the breast of veal, slice, arrange on plates, and serve with aspic cubes and a little basil sauce, handing around the remaining sauce separately.

Mozzarella & friends
Vegetables in particular are superb in combination with this buffalo cheese

Insalata Caprese — tomatoes with mozzarella cheese, basil leaves, and olive oil — is regarded by many people as the quintessential Italian appetizer. Here, the basic recipe is embellished with onions, olives, and two other cheeses, making the light, summery hors d'oeuvre somewhat more piquant. Here, too, the quality of the ingredients is of the highest importance. Only fully ripe tomatoes, aromatic basil, and the finest cold-pressed olive oil should be considered. As far as the cheese is concerned, the mozzarella should be *mozzarella di bufala*, one made from buffalo, not cow's, milk; the Gorgonzola should be a spicy *piccante*; and the Parmesan should, of course, be shaved at the last minute. An alternative to this salad would be to arrange the mozzarella on plates with cherry tomatoes, black olives, fresh herbs, and a few green salad leaves, then serve it with balsamic vinegar and olive oil.

Tomatoes and fresh basil, both kissed by the sun, are unbeatable for flavor. They have their place in many Italian dishes, but taste especially delicious served fresh with cheese, as a Mediterranean salad.

TOMATOES AND CHEESE

Serves 4

1¼ lb tomatoes, thinly sliced
2 white onions, thinly sliced in rounds
¼ cup black olives, a few basil leaves
buffalo mozzarella cheese, Gorgonzola piccante cheese
freshly shaved Parmesan cheese
4–5 tablespoons extra-virgin olive oil
salt, coarsely crushed black pepper

Arrange the tomato slices on plates and top with the onion rings, olives, and basil leaves. Sprinkle with salt and pepper. Slice the mozzarella and Gorgonzola, and tuck in among the tomato slices. Top with shaved Parmesan to taste, and drizzle with olive oil.

EGGPLANT WITH MOZZARELLA

Serves 4 (Not illustrated)

9 oz eggplant, 12 slices tomato, 12 slices mozzarella cheese
¼ cup olive oil, 12 basil leaves
salt, freshly ground pepper

Trim the eggplant and cut crosswise into 12 slices about ½ inch thick. Salt the slices, place on a plate, cover with another plate, and let stand for 1 hour.

Pat the eggplant slices dry, brush lightly with olive oil, broil on each side for 2 minutes, then transfer to a baking sheet. Top each piece of eggplant with a tomato slice and a basil leaf, and season with salt and pepper. Finish off each stack with a slice of mozzarella, and gratiné briefly under a hot broiler.

Vitello tonnato
Thin slices of veal, coated with a fine tuna-fish sauce with anchovies and capers

Now popular as an antipasto throughout Italy, *vitello tonnato* originated in the north of the country, in Milan. Countless recipes describe its preparation. Usually, the veal is marinated in white wine, then simmered slowly in the marinade until done. By contrast, this recipe calls for the meat to be roasted — a must-try twist on the classic dish, which produces a really flavorful result. Although *vitello tonnato* is a typical summer dish, it can be served at any time of year.

Serves 4
2¼ lb boneless round of veal, 3 tablespoons olive oil
⅓ cup coarsely chopped leek
¼ cup coarsely chopped carrot
¾ cup coarsely chopped onion
⅓ cup coarsely chopped celery root
1 cup veal stock
salt, freshly ground pepper
For the sauce:
⅝ cup well-drained canned tuna fish
2 anchovy fillets in salt, 2 egg yolks
¼ cup salted capers, rinsed and drained
2 tablespoons white wine vinegar
1 tablespoon lemon juice, ½ cup olive oil
salt, freshly ground pepper
For the salad:
½ bunch arugula, a few leaves frisée
1 small head radicchio di Treviso
For the dressing:
1 tablespoon white wine vinegar
1 tablespoon balsamic vinegar
¼ cup finely chopped white onion
1 tablespoon chopped flat-leaf parsley, ¼ cup olive oil
salt, freshly ground pepper
You will also need:
aluminum foil, 1 lemon, sliced paper-thin
1 tablespoon salted capers

Preheat the oven to 350°F. Trim the veal to remove any skin and sinew, and season with salt and pepper. Heat the oil in a roasting pan. Add the vegetables and the meat trimmings and sauté briefly, then place the round of veal on top and roast for 1½ hours, basting frequently with veal stock and the pan juices. Remove the roast from the oven, wrap in foil, and leave to go cold. Strain the pan juices into a saucepan and reduce to about 3 tablespoons.

Place the tuna in a blender with the anchovies and the egg yolks, capers, vinegar, and lemon juice, and blend until smooth. Stir in the cold pan juices, and blend in the oil, adding it in a thin trickle. Season with salt and pepper.

Trim and wash the salad leaves, tear into bite-sized pieces, and spin dry. Make the dressing by combining the two vinegars, salt, and pepper in a bowl. Add the onion and parsley and stir in the olive oil.

Thinly slice the veal. Arrange the meat on plates with the lemon slices and capers, and pour over the tuna-fish sauce. Arrange the salad greens to the side and drizzle over a little dressing. Hand around the rest of the tuna-fish sauce separately.

Capers are not to everyone's taste, but are the crowning touch in this recipe. The salted buds are more suitable than those pickled in vinegar; although the latter are easier to get hold of, they are simply too sour for this dish. The slices of meat can be served plain, with just the tuna-fish sauce poured over them, or, as here, garnished with a few salad leaves and thin slices of lemon.

Stuffed anchovies are part of the curriculum for these students at the Istituto Professionale di Stato per i Servizi Alberghieri e della Ristorazione in Finale Ligure. As can be seen, the up-and-coming members of the catering trade are totally involved in the task at hand.

Sardelle & carpaccio

A recipe for stuffed sardines, followed by the classic antipasto from Harry's Bar in Venice

As you might expect from a country with such a long coastline, Italy boasts numerous fish and seafood antipasti. Two types of fish are especially popular for antipasti: anchovies and sardines. Anchovies are called *alici* when fresh, but are usually referred to as *acciughe* when preserved; sardines, on the other hand, which are used in this recipe, are variously called *sardelle*, *sarde*, or even *sardine*.

SARDELLE RIPIENE

Stuffing transforms sardines into a special delicacy. The different regions of Italy have their own recipes for *sardelle ripiene*. In Sicily, for example, the tiny fish are stuffed with bread crumbs, pine nuts, and raisins. In Liguria, they prefer to use basil on its own, and in Campania, oregano. Here is a spicy combination of both herbs and bread crumbs.

Serves 4
1 lb fresh sardines
For the stuffing:
1½ cups fine fresh bread crumbs (no crusts)
½ cup freshly grated Parmesan cheese
2 garlic cloves, finely chopped
1 tablespoon finely chopped basil
½ tablespoon finely chopped oregano
2–3 tablespoons extra-virgin olive oil
½ teaspoon salt
freshly ground white pepper

Slit open the bellies of the sardines. With your thumbnail, free the spine from the surrounding flesh, then carefully pull it out and detach it at the tail end. Cut off the head with the spine, and carefully remove the dorsal fin. Wash the sardines under cold running water, drain, and pat dry with paper towels.

To make the stuffing, combine the bread crumbs with the grated Parmesan, the chopped garlic, and the basil and oregano, and season with salt and pepper. Stir in enough olive oil to yield a relatively firm, but still malleable mixture.

CARPACCIO WITH BASIL SAUCE

This delicious antipasto, made of wafer-thin slices of raw meat, has achieved worldwide fame. The original version was dreamed up by Giuseppe Cipriani, the proprietor of Harry's Bar in Venice.

Serves 4

*7oz beef tenderloin, 1–2 tablespoons extra-virgin olive oil
a little salt, freshly ground white pepper*

Preparing carpaccio: Place the slices of meat between two pieces of plastic wrap that have been brushed with olive oil. Pound with the meat tenderizer until paper-thin. Arrange the beef slices on the oiled, seasoned plates so that they overlap slightly.

Preheat the oven to 350°F. Lay half of the sardines on a work surface, opened out flesh-side up, and spread the stuffing evenly over them. Top each with a second "butterflied" sardine, flesh-side down. Place the stuffed sardines on a lightly greased baking sheet and gratiné in the oven for 10–12 minutes.

An ideal accompaniment is a small, fresh salad, such as the combination of arugula, spinach, radishes, and olives pictured below, with a dressing of olive oil, wine vinegar, balsamic vinegar, garlic, oregano, seasoned to taste with salt and pepper.

*For the basil sauce:
1 tablespoon coarsely chopped basil leaves
1 tablespoon pine nuts, 1 small garlic clove
1 tablespoon grated Parmesan cheese
2–3 tablespoons extra-virgin olive oil
You will also need:
⅓ cup diced potato, 1 teaspoon butter
¼–⅓ each red, green, and yellow peppers
fresh herbs (basil, celery leaves, and chervil)*

Cut the carefully trimmed beef tenderloin into slices ¼ inch thick. Brush a thin layer of olive oil onto 4 plates, and sprinkle with salt and pepper. Pound the meat slices and arrange on the plates as shown above on the right.

To make the sauce, pound the basil leaves, pine nuts, and garlic in a mortar with a pestle. Add the Parmesan and olive oil, and stir to a smooth paste.

Blanch the potato in boiling salted water, and drain. Melt the butter in a skillet and sauté the potato cubes until golden brown, then drain on paper towels.

Peel the bell peppers with the potato peeler. Core, seed, and cut the flesh into small diamond shapes. Drizzle the meat with the sauce, and sprinkle with the fried potatoes and the peppers. Serve garnished with the herbs.

insalate
SALADS

Appetizing, light, and digestible, salad refreshes the palate, whether made with crunchy lettuce leaves, pleasantly bitter endive, or a composition of fresh wild herbs. Somewhat more sumptuous is *panzanella*, the bread salad from Tuscany. Further south, salads made with oranges, and fish and seafood salads are popular.

Red and white wine vinegars are frequently used in Italy. Here, in the foreground, an *aceto balsamico di Modena riserva* (6% acidity). Behind, an oak-cask-matured white wine vinegar (7.1% acidity); far left, a Barrique wine vinegar (7.45% acidity), which is matured for 1 year in a larch cask, then aged in oak casks.

Aceto

Vinegar has been used to flavor and conserve foods since ancient times. Today, it is used for dressing salads, for making *sott'aceti* — vegetables pickled in vinegar — and for marinating meat and fish. It, or lemon juice, is the sour component of *agrodolci*, a term that refers to sweet-and-sour preserved fruits and sauces.

How vinegar is made
Broadly speaking, vinegar is made when an alcoholic liquid comes into contact with air. Aerobic bacteria known as *acetobacter* settle on the surface of the liquid and multiply, producing a yeast residue, called the "mother of vinegar." If vinegar is left uncovered, this biochemical process will continue, especially if the vinegar has a relatively low acidity level, until the acetic acid itself is destroyed. This is why mild vinegars, with an acidity of up to 5 percent, do not keep as long as vinegars with a higher acidity.

Fruit and wine vinegars
Italian cooks generally use wine vinegar, but fruit vinegars also play a role in the kitchen. The latter are more complicated to produce, since the fruit must be fermented into wine before vinegar can be made from it, and they are correspondingly expensive. As a rule, fruit vinegars are relatively mild. Added sparingly, they lend a touch of refinement to sauces, and are good with broiled meat and grilled fish.

There are two kinds of wine vinegar, which according to Italian law must have a minimum acidity of 6 percent: *aceto di vino rosso*, red wine vinegar, and *aceto di vino bianco*, white wine vinegar. The latter is often made into an *aceto aromatico* with the addition of fresh herbs or seasonings such as dill, tarragon, or bay leaf, basil, chile peppers, or garlic.

Aceto balsamico
Aceto balsamico, balsamic vinegar, is produced chiefly in the area around Modena, in Emilia-Romagna, and in Calabria. A "genuine" *balsamico*, which is not synonymous with a *tradizionale*, has been aged for at least three years, and commands a correspondingly high price, since it only improves with age. Cheaper balsamic vinegars contain caramel coloring and flavoring agents, and are best given a wide berth.

Aceto balsamico tradizionale di Modena
The best, most famous, and most expensive vinegar is the *aceto balsamico tradizionale di Modena*. It has a syrupy consistency and a mild, sweet-sour taste. A *tradizionale* cannot be hurried: Its dark color and unique taste can be achieved only through a natural process of maturation in a series of casks. Two consortiums are responsible for quality assurances, one in Modena, the other in Reggio Emilia.

Production
In late fall, when their sugar content is highest, the Trebbiano grapes are hand picked and brought to the *acetaie*, the vinegar factories. The grapes are pressed to must, which is simmered outdoors over an open fire for about twenty hours to neutralize any

bacteria and fungal spores that might impede the maturation process. At the same time, the must is generally reduced by one- to two-thirds. When it has cooled down, it is transfered to special barrels.

The secret of the cask
The *tradizionale* acquires its characteristic flavors by slow maturation in barrels of different sizes and wood types, which have special ventilation hatches. In an *acetaia*, five

barrels stand together as a *batteria*, or set, of which there are countless numbers in the factory. The largest barrel, into which the young must is first decanted, has a capacity of about 60 liters (about 16 gallons), and is made of oak. Over the years, the must is decanted into ever-smaller barrels of chestnut, cherry, ash, and mulberry. It is important that the must is always allowed to "breathe," since it is only by contact with oxygen and natural temperature fluctuations that it is transformed into vinegar. Just what happens and when is a closely guarded secret of the *maestri acetii*, the master vinegar-makers.

Vinegar samples from the Acetaia Malpighi in Modena. The vinegar must pass over ninety tests before it can be called *aceto balsamico tradizionale di Modena*. It is then sold in its characteristic 10 deciliter bottle, rather than in containers such as these.

The *tradizionale* matures for years in "batteries" of five casks of differing size and wood-type. The monitoring of the maturation process demands great experience and instinctive feel; samples are taken repeatedly to check quality.

Use

This procedure, which may last up to twenty-five years, has its price. Thus, a 10-deciliter (3½ fl. oz.) bottle of twelve-year-old balsamico can easily run to $44–$50; the twenty-five-year-old costs about double that amount. However, with such a highly concentrated product, just a few drops will flavor a salad or meat dish. Balsamic vinegar is added to cooked dishes at the last minute, so that its flavor is not impaired.

Italian salads

L'insalata is not usually served as an appetizer in Italy, but accompanies the main course or, even more often, appears after it, to refresh the palate. Naturally, this sequence of courses is not always strictly observed, Italians on the whole being averse to hard and fast rules; just about anything goes, provided that the dish is appetizing, and tastes good.

It is essential for salads to be fresh and crunchy. When choosing salad leaves, Italian cooks let themselves be guided by what is in season. Moreover, in Italy many types of salad leaves, such as radicchio, that are eaten raw also taste wonderful fried or broiled.

Most salad leaves belong to either the lettuce family or the chicory family.

Head and loose-leaf lettuce

The tender loose-leaf lettuces such as oak leaf, lollo rosso, and lollo biondo, as well as the many varieties of head lettuce, belong to the lettuce family. Because of their delicate leaf structure, they do not stay fresh for very long, and if possible should be eaten on the day of harvest or purchase. Somewhat more robust is iceberg lettuce, which can easily be kept in the refrigerator for several days, ideally wrapped in damp paper towels, then plastic wrap. Other varieties of lettuce, for instance romaine, can also be kept fresh in this way

The chicory family

Members of the chicory family are distinguished by a certain bitter note, which is more or less pronounced depending on variety. Both escarole and its close relative endive are members of this family, as are the different varieties of radicchio, and the large-leafed chicories such as Catalogna and its relative, *puntarelle*.

Dandelion, arugula, and hops

Dandelion is another slightly bitter salad leaf. It can be eaten on its own, or mixed with other salad leaves. Many people find arugula too spicy and hot to eat "solo." Used in moderation, though, it adds relish to many dishes. Still largely unknown as a salad ingredient in this country, but popular in Italy, are the young shoots of the hop plant, which are always blanched.

Some of the numerous varieties of radicchio:
1 Radicchio di Chioggia. Forms firm, round heads, and is available year-round in white and red. **2** Radicchio Trevisiano. Long, narrow, closed heads. **3** This Radicchio di Chioggia is red-and-white speckled. Its color is reminiscent of Radicchio di Castelfranco, but the latter produces rosettes. **4** Rossa di Verona, with small, elongated heads.

Radicchio Lucia A new breed with a cone-shaped head and red-and-white-variegated leaves.

Radicchio di Treviso Elongated leaves with thick, white midribs; does not form a solid head.

SALADS

Escarole Large, flat rosette. The broad leaves with their thick ribs stay fresh for quite a while.

Red oak-leaf lettuce is commonly cultivated and exported. Tasty, but quite perishable.

Green Cicorino, *ceriolo verde* Slightly bitter rosette chicory, comes on the market in early spring.

Head lettuce Solid head with robust outer leaves. Prized for its fresh taste.

Yellow-hearted frisée Hemispherical rosette. The fullness of the inner leaves makes the heart slightly yellowish.

Batavia lettuce A variety of iceberg lettuce. Taste is between that of head and iceberg lettuce.

Red Cicorino, *ceriolo rosso* Bitter, even more popular than the green variety, especially in northern Italy.

Red head lettuce Increasingly popular, its leaves are even more tender than those of the green variety.

Green frisée It too has the slightly bitter endive taste. Stimulates the appetite.

Catalogna Large-leafed chicory with stalk and bunch of dandelion-like leaves. Very bitter.

Lollo biondo Loose-leaf lettuce. Tender, frilly leaves with a strong, slightly bitter taste.

Dandelion, *dente di leone* Cultivated variety with only slightly dentate leaves. Spicy.

Romaine Green, round variety. Grows upright, with robust outer leaves and a yellowish heart.

Green crisphead lettuce Forms firm heads, fleshy, crunchy leaves. Sold with its wrapping leaves still on.

Lollo rosso Except for color, does not differ greatly from lollo biondo. In season from May to October.

Wild arugula, *rucola selvatica* From the Mediterranean. Long, narrow leaves; hot, intense taste.

Romaine Oval variety, with yellowish. inner leaves . Slightly coarser than head lettuce, but keeps longer.

Red crisphead lettuce Tastes very similar to green varieties. Crunchy, stays fresh for a long time.

Young hop shoots, *bruscandoli* Popular in Italy; used blanched, for example in risottos.

Arugula, *rucola aromatica* Cultivated variety with round, tender leaves. An aromatic seasoning herb.

Mediterranean flavors: herbs and garlic

The seasoning combination of garlic and herbs is found in the cuisines of most Italian regions, with the possible exception of Venice, where garlic has never played a major role, and other seasonings have traditionally been emphasized.

Aglio ed erbe aromatiche: healthy and tasty

Seasoning foods with herbs and garlic has several advantages: first and foremost, the incomparable flavor they impart. Kissed by the Mediterranean sun, thyme, rosemary, oregano, and basil have a stronger scent than elsewhere, and their appearance alone is enough to whet the appetite. Whereas other seasonings are often expensive and must be imported, most of the herbs used in Italy's kitchens grow in the country itself, so the second advantage is that they are not expensive. Many Italian cooks also collect wild herbs or grow their own in the garden, on the balcony, or simply in a large pot outside their door. In this way, they always have the flavors they need to hand. Even if the sun shines less where you live, and the results are not quite as aromatic, it pays to grow your own kitchen herbs — they will taste better than forced greenhouse herbs. A third advantage is the positive effect herbs and garlic have on your health and metabolism: both are full of vitamins A, B, and C, for instance, and garlic can also lower cholesterol levels.

Parsley

One of the most universal kitchen herbs is parsley. Finely chopped, it is added to almost

all savory dishes. Italian cooks prefer the flat-leaf variety, which is more aromatic and milder than curly parsley. As healthy as it is tasty, parsley is high in provitamin A, and vitamins C and E, as well as the minerals iron and calcium.

Oregano

The oval-leafed herb oregano has a distinctive smell, an

aromatic, spicy, somewhat hot taste, and is indissolubly linked with the cooking of the Mediterranean region. Indigenous to southern Europe, oregano grows wild in all dry, warm locations, and is also cultivated in Italy. Oregano is the pizza herb *par excellence*, which is probably the reason for its popularity outside of Italy. It is also used to enhance the flavor of pan-fried and broiled veal and pork, and, with tomatoes and garlic, is a main ingredient in *pizzaiola*, a sauce served with fish and pan-fried meat. Unlike marjoram, oregano dries well, and the drying process intensifies its flavor.

Oregano in full bloom This is the right time for harvesting the herb, which is used both fresh and dried.

Marjoram
Marjoram is botanically closely related to oregano. It is popular mainly in Liguria, for instance as a seasoning for pasta sauces.

Thyme
One of the most typically Italian herbs, thyme leaves its mark chiefly on the cooking of the southern part of the country, where it grows wild. It has a very spicy taste, which goes superbly with garlic, tomatoes, sweet peppers, and zucchini. Legumes and potatoes also benefit from its strong flavor, and it is an ideal partner for braised beef, lamb, and game, and for broiled or grilled meats in general. Unlike many other herbs, its flavor is not detrimentally affected by heat, so it can boil or fry along with the other ingredients from the start. Often whole sprigs are added to the dish, which are then removed before serving. If you wish to substitute dried thyme for the fresh herb called for in a recipe, reduce the quantity given by two-thirds, as the herb is substantially stronger when dried.

Rosemary
Next to parsley, rosemary must be the most frequently used herb in Italian cooking. Its dark-green, leathery leaves, which resemble pine needles, are very aromatic, and have a pungent, bitter taste, for which reason they are used relatively sparingly in cooking. When fresh, the leaves can easily be cut up small; generally, though, whole sprigs are used, which are cooked with the other ingredients and then removed before serving. Rosemary is ideal as a spicy partner for white meats and for Mediterranean vegetables such as tomatoes or eggplant, just as it goes well with pasta dishes and white beans. It is also popular as an ingredient in marinades. And when you are grilling outdoors, a few rosemary sprigs tossed on the hot embers lend a splendid aroma and flavor to the food.

Thyme dried out in the field Thyme is usually harvested shortly before it flowers, when its leaves are most aromatic. It also dries well: ideally, as here, in whole sprigs, from which the leaves are then stripped off.

Rosemary Above, growing wild, as part of the *macchia* or "scrub," and below, cultivated in pots. In Liguria, several firms now specialize in the outdoor cultivation of good-quality culinary herbs.

Fresh and spicy

The quality of herbs can be checked by their very smell, as demonstrated here by the chef of the Ristorante 12 Apostoli in Verona. Wilted or dull-looking stalks are discarded.

Herbs should be harvested properly to ensure that they retain their flavor until use. It is important, for instance, to cut off whole shoots or shoot tips, not just individual leaves. This can be done as soon as the morning dew has evaporated and the flowers have opened. To store herbs for short periods after picking them, either seal them in an airtight plastic container, or spray them with water and pack them loosely in a plastic bag, taking care not to crush the leaves. Fresh herbs retain their flavor best over a longer period of time if frozen.

Dill and fennel

Although extremely similar in appearance, dill and fennel taste quite different. Dill is tangy and spicy, and should always be used fresh, or at most frozen, since the tender tips wilt quickly and lose much of their taste when dried. Herb fennel, with its sweet aniseed-like taste, is a popular salad ingredient in Italy. The seeds of the plant are also used as a spice.

Tarragon

Tarragon is used fresh in Italian cooking; only in this way can it impart its full flavor. When tarragon is dried, its volatile flavoring substances and, with them, its spicy, refreshing taste are lost. Used judiciously, tarragon is popular in salads, and harmonizes well with eggs, poultry, and fish. Tossed in butter, it lends a sophisticated touch to broiled meat. It is also a main ingredient in *salsa béarnaise*, the classic béarnaise sauce illustrated above.

Also popular in Italian dishes is tarragon vinegar — a couple of stalks of the herb are sufficient to flavor 1 quart of white wine vinegar — which is especially suitable for salads. Tarragon is prized not least of all for its digestive effect.

Sage

Sage, an evergreen semi-shrub, is native to the Mediterranean and is an indispensable culinary herb in the region, particularly in Italy. The feltlike, downy, green to silvery gray leaves are mostly used fresh. It is an integral part of *saltimbocca alla romana*, thin veal cutlets with a slice of prosciutto and sage; harmonizes beautifully with other white meat, such as chicken and pork; and is very popular with calf liver. Its flavor develops best when it is cooked with the other ingredients in a dish. Sage leaves sautéed in browned butter until appetizingly crisp are an ideal complement for fine stuffed pasta dishes. Sage can also be dried, but freezing is a better method of preserving the herb. Place the leaves to be frozen between waxed paper or aluminum foil thickly brushed with olive oil: in this way, they will stay supple and can be peeled off individually.

Dill has a slightly tangy flavor, which cannot really be compared with that of any other herb.

Herb fennel, with its distinctive aniseed note, tastes pleasantly aromatic and slightly sweetish.

The sage plant looks lovely in bloom, but the leaves are at their spiciest just before the plant flowers.

Tricolor An attractive sage plant with variegated leaves, with a slightly bitter but mild taste. Use with fish and meat.

Purple sage has a very intense sage flavor. Its leaves are also brewed to make a herb tea.

Chervil
Chervil, a typical spring herb, is botanically closely related to parsley, and is sometimes even confused with it. However, chervil leaves are lighter, lacier, and more delicate than those of parsley. Chervil goes well in fresh herb mixtures, soups, and vegetable dishes, and with potatoes, fish, and salads. Leaves, mainly young ones picked before the plant flowers, are used fresh; dried chervil is not worth using.

Watercress
Watercress is a perennial that grows in clear springs and slow-flowing waters. Eaten raw in spring, its peppery taste is well suited for salads.

Rue
The gray to bluish-green rue leaves are picked before the plant flowers. Only very small amounts of rue should be used at a time, since larger quantities have a toxic effect.

Bay leaf
The dark-green leaves of the bay tree are among the most versatile seasonings. Bay is used to season many pickled and preserved foods, in marinades and braised dishes, and is also suitable as a broiling and grilling seasoning. Use whole, dried leaves, as these have the most flavor but yield it only slowly, making long cooking or marinating times necessary.

Chervil's delicately spicy aniseed flavor harmonizes with fish, potatoes, and salads.

Watercress has a tangy, piquant to mustardy flavor. Good as a spring salad.

The leaves of the bay tree, with their spicy, tangy flavor, are a well-established ingredient in Italian cooking, used, for instance, in marinades and for stuffed sardines in Sicily.

Rue has a hot, slightly bitter taste. Goes well with cheese, game, egg dishes, and salad.

White lemon balm, a relative of lemon balm, has a pleasant, mild lemon scent. Also used for tea.

Balm
The different types of balm are distinguished by a more or less intense lemon flavor. Lemon balm is the variety chiefly used in cooking. It lends a fresh note to salads, as well as to fish and egg dishes. The leaves should never be cooked with the dish, but added at the last moment, ideally whole. Their refreshing, lemony flavor is also popular in beverages.

Knarled old sage stumps like this one bring forth their aromatic leaves year-round. Even snow cannot harm them.

The scent of the south

For many Italian dishes, basil and garlic are an absolute must. Mint, too, is essential for a number of specialties, particularly in the south.

Basil

Originally from the Indian subcontinent, basil, with it powerful fragrance and flavor, has been known in Italy since about the twelfth century, and has earned itself a permanent place in that country's culinary repertoire. Indeed, if tomatoes symbolize the red of the Italian flag, and mozzarella, the white, then basil stands for the green — a combination of ingredients teamed to ideal effect in the *insalata caprese*, among other dishes. There are many varieties of basil, the best-known one being the large-leafed sort pictured below. Red and green bush basil, illustrated below to the right, are also frequently available in Italy. Basil develops its seductive, appetizing aroma and taste best when fresh; the dried herb is no substitute in terms of taste. One way of preserving basil is to place the dry, unwashed leaves in olive oil. Otherwise, it is best to buy pot basil. The plants, which are highly sensitive to the cold, can be kept for a few days or weeks indoors, even in winter. Since the flavor of the delicate leaves suffers greatly if they are cooked, basil is as a rule added only at the end of the cooking process. This herb is used to season a wide range of dishes, including pasta sauces and pizzas. It is particularly unbeatable in combination with garlic — as in the famous pesto — with tomatoes, or with both; and it is superb in salads.

Mint

Of the many different varieties of mint, aside from the well known peppermint, it is chiefly the small-leafed Roman mint, mountain mint, and curly mint that are used in Italy. All have an aromatic to burningly spicy taste. Mints, and in particular mountain mint, grow wild in Italy, and play an especially important culinary role in the south. Mint goes well with lamb

Green bush basil This small-leafed, decorative variety has a good, strong flavor.

Mountain mint This slender, dainty plant has a pronounced mint flavor and a scent reminiscent of camphor.

Red bush basil in flower. Interesting red-leafed variety with compact growth habit.

Roman mint has plump, somewhat lighter-colored leaves than the better-known peppermint.

and fish, and with vegetables such as zucchini. It is excellent in teas and other beverages. It is usually used fresh, but sometimes dried in teas.

Garlic

Garlic, one of the most important flavorings in Italian cooking, is used in the vast majority of recipes. One consequence of eating raw garlic is "garlic breath." A remedy for this, supposedly, is to drink a glass of milk or red wine. Some people also swear by the eating of whole cloves (the spice) or sprigs of parsley. The smell and taste are less powerful if, for instance, you rub a salad bowl with a halved garlic clove or roast the cloves whole.

Preparing garlic

Garlic is usually peeled, except when it is to be roasted. It tastes strongest finely chopped and raw, or very briefly sweated. With longer cooking, it becomes milder. If you are using a great many cloves, it is best to crush them flat with the wide blade of a knife. You can use a garlic press, but it is not always the best option, since the garlic is so finely mashed that it burns easily when cooked. In general, it pays to be careful here; garlic must not be allowed to get too brown, or it can become unpleasantly bitter.

Garlic, fresh (above) and dried (below). Young, wet garlic is milder and more delicate tasting than dried.

After harvesting, the garlic is dried and woven into braids, then sold. Like this, it will keep for several months.

Huge garlic fields in Polesine near Rovigo in northern Italy. At harvest time, the plants are simply pulled from the ground with their up-to-3-foot-high, lanceolate leaves, then dried in the blazing sun for eight to ten days. Next, the garlic is conveyed to cold-storage depots, where it is stored at 36°F until needed, and then made into thick braids for selling.

Fritelle di borragine

Deep-fried battered herbs, and *torta fritta* and *sgonfiotti*, little pastries with and without a stuffing, to serve with aperitifs

If borage is unavailable, use sage leaves.

Serves 4
For the batter:
¾ cup all-purpose flour
2 eggs, 6 tablespoons milk, ½ teaspoon salt
¼ teaspoon freshly ground white pepper
For the dip:
2 red bell peppers, halved, cored, and seeded
1 small red chile pepper, seeded, and finely chopped
1 garlic clove, finely chopped
1 teaspoon lime juice, 1 teaspoon sweet paprika
salt, freshly ground pepper
You will also need:
7 oz borage leaves, vegetable oil, coarse salt

Make a smooth batter from the ingredients given, and strain if necessary to get rid of any lumps. Wash the borage leaves and drain very well.

To make the dip, preheat the oven to 425°F and roast the bell peppers until their skin blisters. Remove the peppers from the oven and leave in a plastic bag or under a damp cloth to cool. Peel off the skin.

Finely dice half the bell peppers, and purée the other half in a blender or food processor until smooth. Combine the diced and puréed peppers in a bowl with the remaining ingredients.

Heat the oil to 350°F in a saucepan or deep-fryer. Dip each leaf in the batter and deep-fry. Lift out and drain on paper towels, arrange on plates, then sprinkle with a little coarse salt, and serve with the dip.

SALADS 71

Using a pasta machine for practicality, Vincenzo, chef of an experimental kitchen in Parma, rolls out the dough to the desired thickness, one small batch at a time. Here, he places the stuffed sgonfiotti on a platter. The unstuffed torta fritta is prepared from the same dough, but is cut into larger pieces, usually 3-inch-a-side diamond shapes.

Making sgonfiotti:

Lay the sheet of dough out flat. Top with ¾-inch cubes of cheese, leaving at least 3 inches between each one, and fold the edge closest to you up over the cheese.

Using a 3-inch round, fluted cutter, cut out semicircles around each piece of cheese.

Press the edges of the sgonfiotti together tightly to seal, then heat the oil in a large saucepan or deep-fryer to 350°F and deep-fry until golden.

Whether plain (torta fritta) or stuffed with cheese (sgonfiotti), these pastries taste superb with antipasti such as ham, but are also ideal for rounding out a light salad.

TORTA FRITTA AND SGONFIOTTTA

Serves 4

4 cups all-purpose flour,
1½ teaspoons active dry yeast, ¾ cup lukewarm milk
1 egg, 2 tablespoons sunflower oil
1 pinch sugar, 1 pinch salt
You will also need:
cubes of cheese as desired (Mozzarella, Fontina, Bel Paese)
4½–6½ cups oil for deep-frying

Sift the flour onto a work surface and make a well in the center. Dissolve the yeast in the milk and pour into the well. Knead all of the ingredients together into a smooth dough. Cover, and leave in a warm spot to rise for 1½ hours. Finish making the pastries as shown in the picture sequence on the right.

SALADS

Salad of wild herbs with eggs and olives

A simple dish that brings a touch of spring to your table

For most of us, the business of procuring food is usually associated with a trip to the nearest supermarket. Those who are fortunate enough to have a farmer's market nearby may also pay it a weekly visit. Very few of us will actually hunt for our salad ingredients in the great outdoors. This is a pity, since the flavor of wild herbs can really add an extra dimension to everyday dishes. Besides, the gathering process is fun. The combination suggested here — *dente di leone* (dandelion) and *acetosa* (sorrel) — should present no difficulties, since both of these plants are easy to find outside of Italy, flourishing as they do in almost all climatic conditions. In Italy, people are also fond of combining wild fennel and asparagus, or nettles and arugula. In addition, you can mix in a few finely chopped anchovy fillets, which provide extra spiciness. When gathering your own wild herbs, bear in mind the location: busy roadsides and ditches are unsuitable, because of exhaust fumes and stagnant water respectively. You should also avoid patches of ground that have been treated with herbicides or heavy applications of fertilizers. Aside from these caveats, there are no restrictions. It is best to harvest the dandelions for this salad in the early spring, when the leaves are still tender and delicate, and not yet bitter.

Open-air market in Sicily. In the narrow maze of streets and alleys of Palermo, a great range of produce is offered for sale, including veritable mountains of the aromatic, small black Sicilian olives that lend a spicy note to this herb salad.

Dandelion and sorrel set the tone of this salad. You may, if wished, add a couple of leaves of wild bear's garlic, in which case the garlic clove can be left out of the dressing.

Serves 4
For the salad:
8 oz young dandelion leaves
4 oz sorrel
1/3 cup finely chopped onion
For the salad dressing:
3 tablespoons balsamic vinegar
2 tablespoons dry white wine, 1/2 level teaspoon salt
1 garlic clove
6 tablespoons olive oil
You will also need:
2 hardboiled eggs, coarsely chopped
1 cup pitted black olives, quartered lengthwise

Trim the dandelion and sorrel, or any other combination of wild herbs you like, then wash thoroughly and spin dry in a salad spinner. Tear the larger leaves in half. Toss in a large bowl with the onion, and arrange in a large, shallow bowl or on a large plate.

To make the dressing, whisk the balsamic vinegar, white wine, and salt in a bowl until the salt dissolves. Squeeze the garlic through a garlic press into the bowl. Pour in the olive oil in a steady stream, whisking to blend well. Using a tablespoon, drizzle the dressing evenly over the wild herbs, and leave for a few minutes to allow the flavors to develop.

Arrange the chopped eggs on top of the salad and sprinkle over the olives. Fresh Italian country bread or ciabatta goes well with this dish.

With bread and oranges
Juicy and refreshing specialty salads from Tuscany and Sicily

The following two salads are unusual in their combination of ingredients. The first recipe teams golden pan-fried croutons with crunchy vegetables; the second, oranges with onions and olives.

PANZANELLA

This very simple Tuscan bread salad is traditionally prepared in its native region with the saltless *pane sciocco* and the long, thin, Italian sweet peppers with a pointed tip, called bull's horn peppers here.

Serves 4
1 loaf day-old Tuscan or other Italian white bread
3–4 tablespoons olive oil
3 scallions, cut into rings
1 garlic clove, finely chopped
7 oz tomatoes, peeled, seeded, and diced
1 cup diced cucumber
2 yellow bull's horn peppers, cored, seeded, and cut into ¼-inch-thick rings
For the dressing:
2–3 tablespoons red wine vinegar
salt, freshly ground pepper
5–6 tablespoons olive oil, 1 tablespoon chopped parsley
You will also need:
frisée lettuce
8 anchovy fillets
2 teaspoons capers

Cut the bread into ¾-inch cubes. Heat the oil in a skillet and sauté the cubes on all sides until golden and crunchy.

Toss the bread, scallions, garlic, tomatoes, cucumber, and pepper rings in a bowl. Thoroughly whisk together the ingredients for the dressing, pour

For the best taste, make sure you use really ripe oranges for this salad. In Catania in Sicily, it is often also prepared with the somewhat sharper sanguinella, a variety of blood orange.

over the salad ingredients, toss to mix, and marinate in the refrigerator for 1 hour.

Meanwhile, trim and wash the frisée, spin-dry in a salad spinner, and tear into bite-sized pieces. Arrange the bread salad decoratively on plates with the frisée leaves, anchovies, and capers, and serve.

ORANGE SALAD

This distinctive salad is a Sicilian specialty. If red onions are not particularly to your liking, you may either leave them out entirely, since even in Sicily this salad is sometimes made without them, or you can first "pickle" them in salt, then rinse them and pat them dry, which will reduce their sharpness. If you like salad dressings to be tart, we recommend the one given below; purists, however, will content themselves with good olive oil and black pepper.

Serves 4
4 oranges (about 8 oz each)
1 red onion, thinly sliced into rings
¼ cup black olives, coarsely ground black pepper
For the dressing:
2 tablespoons lemon juice
5 tablespoons orange juice
6 tablespoons good olive oil, salt
You will also need:
lemon balm or mint leaves

Peel the oranges with a sharp knife, carefully removing the bitter white pith. Using a serrated knife, cut the fruit into even ¼-inch slices. Arrange the orange slices, onion rings, and olives on plates, and grind some pepper over the top. Whisk together the dressing ingredients, pour over the salad, marinate briefly, then garnish with the lemon balm or mint and serve.

When harvesting capers, the closed buds of the caper bush must be carefully picked by hand, one by one. Capers are sold graded according to size, and the rule of thumb is "the smaller the caper, the finer the quality."

Spring salad
With chicken, young dandelion leaves, and small artichoke hearts

Serves 4
1 chicken (about 1¾ lb)
½ cup chopped carrot, ¾ cup chopped onion
½ cup chopped parsley root
½ cup chopped leek, ½ cup chopped celery root
1 bay leaf, ½ teaspoon black peppercorns
5 oz young dandelion leaves, 2 hardboiled eggs, salt
For the artichokes:
15 small artichokes with their stalks (about 5 oz each)
salt, juice of 1 lemon
For the salad dressing:
1 tablespoon wine vinegar, 1 tablespoon lime juice
1 teaspoon hot mustard, ½ teaspoon salt
1 tablespoon chopped herbs (parsley, basil, and peppermint)

Trim off the prickly, quite bitter leaf tips with kitchen scissors.

Pull off the tough outer leaves until the tender, light-colored inner leaves are revealed.

Cut off the top third or so of the artichoke with a sharp or serrated kitchen knife.

Slices of white bread, toasted golden-brown in the oven or broiler, then rubbed with garlic and drizzled with best-quality olive oil, make a tasty accompaniment to this salad.

¾ cup finely chopped onion, 1 teaspoon chopped capers
¼ cup olive oil, freshly ground white pepper

Thoroughly wash the chicken inside and out under cold running water. Place the chicken and the chopped vegetables in a pot with cold water to just cover the bird. Bring to a boil and use a slotted spoon to skim off any scum as it rises to the surface.

Reduce the heat and add the bay leaf, peppercorns, and salt. Cook over a low heat for 40–50 minutes, then lift out the chicken and leave to cool. Pour the broth through a strainer lined with cheesecloth and reserve for use in another recipe.

Prepare the artichokes. Cut off the prickly leaves on the stalks, then proceed as shown in the picture sequence opposite. Break off the stalks of the artichokes. Bring a large saucepan of salted water to a boil with the lemon juice, and boil the artichokes for 10–15 minutes, taking care not to overcook them. Lift out and leave to cool. Halve them lengthwise and scoop out the choke with a small spoon.

Trim and wash the dandelion leaves, then spin dry in a salad spinner. Peel the eggs and slice crosswise. Skin the chicken, then strip the meat from the bones and cut into pieces. Carefully mix together the artichokes, eggs, and chicken in a bowl.

To make the salad dressing, whisk together the vinegar, lime juice, mustard, and salt until the salt dissolves. Whisk in the chopped herbs, onion, capers, olive oil, and pepper. Pour the dressing over the salad and toss. Refrigerate, covered, for 30 minutes to allow the flavors to develop. Arrange the salad on plates and serve.

With catalogna

Two summery salads: one made from the leaves, one from the shoots of this unusual leaf vegetable

Like Belgian endive, catalogna (large-leafed chicory) has a distinctly bitter flavor and quite tough leaves. For use in a salad, therefore, the leaves are blanched to make them more supple and remove some of the bitterness. Catalogna can then be served dressed with cold-pressed olive oil and lemon juice, or drizzled with melted butter. In addition to eating them raw in a salad, Italians also enjoy *puntarelle*, the sweetish shoots of Catalogna di Galatina, boiled or puréed.

CATALOGNA SALAD

Crunchy vegetables such as carrots and bell peppers go well with the blanched catalogna. Enriched with boiled eggs and mozzarella, this salad (pictured on p. 79) makes a delicious first course, or can be a meal in itself on hot summer days, when served with some crusty bread.

SALADS

Serves 4

1¼ lb catalogna, 2 cups diced carrot
¾ cup peeled, seeded, and diced sweet red peppers
2 tablespoons olive oil
1–2 zucchini (about 4 oz), sliced into ⅛-inch-thick rounds
4 eggs, 4 oz mozzarella, in little balls or cubed
salt, freshly ground pepper
For the dressing:
juice of 1 lemon, 3–4 tablespoons olive oil
1 garlic clove, finely chopped
1 teaspoon thyme leaves
salt, freshly ground pepper

Trim the catalogna, removing the thick stems. Wash the leaves and tear into bite-sized pieces. Blanch in boiling salted water for 2–3 minutes. Lift out and drain well. Cook the diced carrot in boiling salted water for 3–4 minutes; lift out and drain.

Heat the oil in a skillet and sauté the zucchini briefly on both sides, then season with salt and pepper. Boil the eggs for 6 minutes so that the yolks are set but still soft, then rinse under cold water and peel. Halve lengthwise and season with salt and pepper.

To make the dressing, whisk the lemon juice with the pepper and salt until the salt dissolves. Whisk in the olive oil, followed by the garlic and thyme, then adjust the seasoning.

Arrange the salad leaves, carrot, zucchini, and red pepper on plates. Garnish with the eggs and the mozzarella, drizzle with the dressing, and serve.

CATALOGNA DI GALATINA SALAD

The somewhat bizarre-looking shoots of this variety of catalogna, known as *puntarelle* ("little tips"), are particularly popular in Rome. There, among other things, they are served as a crunchy salad, as in the following recipe, usually dressed with a vinaigrette that is a garlic lover's delight. The larger outer leaves surrounding the *puntarelle* can be used in a salad, as in the preceding recipe.

Serves 4

1–2 heads catalogna di Galatina
For the dressing:
3–4 tablespoons white wine vinegar
6 tablespoons olive oil
4 garlic cloves, finely chopped
8 anchovy fillets, finely chopped
salt, freshly ground pepper

First, remove the *puntarelle* from the catalogna heads, and slice them as shown in the picture sequence on the right.

To make the dressing, whisk the vinegar with pepper and salt to taste in a small bowl, until the salt is completely dissolved. Whisk in the olive oil, garlic, and anchovies, then season to taste with salt and pepper.

Arrange the prepared *puntarelle* on plates, then drizzle with the garlic dressing and serve.

Preparing catalogna di Galatina: Separate the puntarelle from each head of catalogna and cut off the stalk. Wash the shoots, drain well, and slice lengthwise into thin strips.

In addition to the finely diced vegetables, little balls of mozzarella lend visual interest and flavor to this salad containing blanched catalogna.

With beans and pumpkin
Olives or sheep's cheese lends a spicy note to these salads

Pumpkins and squash in all shapes and colors. In Italy, they turn up in the widest variety of dishes, from salad to pasta, where they are used as a stuffing for tortellini.

Pumpkin and beans taste rather bland on their own, and are therefore especially suitable for combining with piquant dressings or other stronger-flavored ingredients.

BEAN AND OLIVE SALAD

Small white beans are especially recommended for this salad, but you could always use other varieties.

Serves 4
1¼ cups small dried white beans
10 oz green beans, ⅓ cup black olives, salt
For the dressing:
5 tablespoons olive oil
2 garlic cloves, finely chopped
1 cup finely chopped white onion
1 tablespoon lemon juice, zest of ½ lemon
2 tablespoons white wine vinegar
1 tablespoon chopped marjoram
salt, freshly ground pepper
You will also need:
a few marjoram or mint leaves

This colorful salad — yellow pumpkin, green peas, red tomatoes, white cheese, and shiny black olives — is a pleasure for both the eyes and the palate.

Soak the white beans overnight in cold water to cover. The next day, drain, transfer to a pot with fresh cold water to cover, bring to a boil, and cook until *al dente*. Drain and leave to cool. Cut the green beans diagonally into 1-inch-long pieces, and cook in boiling salted water for 10–12 minutes. Refresh under cold water and drain.

To make the dressing, heat the oil in a skillet and sweat the onions and garlic without letting them color. Stir in the remaining ingredients and let the mixture cool. Toss the white beans, green beans, and olives in the dressing, and leave in a cool place for about 2 hours to allow the flavors to develop. Serve garnished with marjoram or mint leaves.

PUMPKIN SALAD

If you like it hot, you can replace the sweet pepper in the dressing with finely chopped chile pepper to taste.

Serves 4

9 oz pumpkin, peeled
9 oz peas in the pod
½ cup finely chopped white onion
2 garlic cloves, finely chopped
1 green bell pepper, cored, seeded, and thinly sliced into rings
4 oz fresh sheep's cheese, crumbled into small chunks
4 oz cherry tomatoes, quartered
few leaves Romaine lettuce, ⅓ cup black olives, salt

For the dressing:
3 tablespoons mild white-wine vinegar
1 tablespoon lemon juice
6 tablespoons olive oil
1 small bull's horn pepper, cored, seeded, and finely diced
salt, freshly ground pepper

You will also need:
1 tablespoon mint leaves, cut into strips

Cut the pumpkin into almost paper-thin slices, then into strips about 2 inches long. Shell the peas. Blanch the pumpkin strips in boiling salted water for 1 minute, then refresh in ice water and drain well. Blanch the peas for 2 minutes, then refresh and drain.

To make the dressing, whisk together the vinegar, lemon juice, salt, and pepper until the salt has completely dissolved. Whisk in the oil and stir in the diced pepper. Adjust the seasoning. Arrange the pumpkin, peas, onion, garlic, bell pepper, cheese, tomatoes, Romaine leaves, and olives on plates, drizzle with the dressing, sprinkle with mint, and serve.

Fresh from the sea
Two choice salads with shellfish, shrimp, and squid

The first recipe combines clams and scallops with salad greens; the second is a medley of delicious seafood (not pictured).

SALAD WITH SCALLOPS AND CLAMS

Serves 4
2¼ lb small clams (vongole lubini)
1 tablespoon vegetable oil
¼ cup diced onion, ⅓ cup diced carrot
¼ cup diced celery, ⅓ cup diced leek
½ cup white wine, 1 bay leaf, 1 thyme sprig,
1 celery stalk, ½ apple
1–2 heads radicchio di Treviso (about 5 oz)
handful of salad greens (watercress, arugula, sorrel)
4 scallops, 2 tablespoons butter
4 oz cherry tomatoes, peeled, quartered, and seeded
¼ teaspoon pink peppercorns, salt, freshly ground pepper
For the dressing:
2 tablespoons apple-cider vinegar,
2 tablespoons walnut oil, ¼ cup sunflower oil
salt, freshly ground pepper

Scrub the clams under cold running water, discarding any open ones. Heat the oil and sweat the diced vegetables until lightly colored. Add in the clams, white wine, bay leaf, and thyme, and cook, covered,

for 5–6 minutes. Strain the liquid over a bowl and reserve 6 tablespoons. Shuck two-thirds of the clams.

To make the dressing, whisk together the vinegar, reserved clam liquid, salt, and pepper until the salt has dissolved, then whisk in both oils.

Cut the celery stalk into thin strips about 2 inches long. Core the apple and cut into strips. Strip the leaves off the radicchio head and halve them lengthwise, then wash and spin dry with the watercress, arugula, and sorrel.

Clean and open the scallops. Using a sharp knife, detach the scallop meat all around the gray edge. Pull this membrane off the white meat and the orange coral. Melt the butter in a skillet. Lightly salt the scallop and coral, season with pepper, and fry for about 1 minute on each side. Arrange the salad leaves, celery, apple, and tomatoes on plates with the scallops, shucked clams, and clams in their shells. Sprinkle with pink peppercorns, drizzle with the dressing, and serve.

SEAFOOD SALAD

Serves 4
14 oz cleaned and prepared squid
½ cup dry white wine, ¼ cup white wine vinegar
½ cup coarsely chopped onion
½ cup coarsely chopped carrot
1 bay leaf, 2¼ lb mussels, 8 oz boiled shrimp, peeled

For the dressing:
juice of 1 lemon, 6–8 tablespoons olive oil, salt
1–2 garlic cloves, finely chopped
2 small red chile peppers, seeded and diced
1 bunch flat-leaf parsley, finely chopped
You will also need:
1 lemon, cut into wedges

Wash the squid inside and out under cold running water and slice into rings. Pour the wine and vinegar into a saucepan, add the onion, carrot, and bay leaf, and bring to a boil. Add the squid, and simmer in this court-bouillon over a low heat for about 50 minutes, until the squid is tender. Remove the squid and drain. Reserve 1 tablespoon of the court-bouillon.

Scrub the mussels under cold running water, removing the beards and any barnacles. Discard any open mussels. Steam the mussels in 1 cup water for about 6–8 minutes, until they open. Discard any that remain closed and shuck the rest.

To make the dressing, whisk the lemon juice with the reserved tablespoon of court-bouillon and the salt until the salt has dissolved. Whisk in the olive oil and stir in the garlic, chiles, and parsley.

Combine the squid, mussels, and shrimp in a bowl. Drizzle with the salad dressing and refrigerate, covered, for 1 hour to allow the flavors to develop. Arrange on plates, garnished with the lemon wedges, and serve.

zuppe SOUPS

In Italy, *zuppe* or *minestre* are usually served as a *primo piatto*, or first course, after the antipasti. These are hardly light little dishes, however. Soupy but substantial is the motto, so all kinds of ingredients are used, with the soup not infrequently turning into a stew.

Vegetables play the leading role, as in the famous minestrone, with rice or pasta often being added, depending on the region where the recipe originates. Similarly indispensable for many soups are beans, which — like pancetta, prosciutto, or Parmesan cheese — contribute flavor, texture, and body.

Fresh or dried: peas and beans galore

In Italy all kinds of peas and beans are available by the sackful all year around. The range of choice is huge. Many kinds are sold fresh — and what could be more delicious than very young, tender peas, which, thanks to the warm Italian climate, can be harvested in early spring — or dried, but some varieties, such as lentils, are available dried only.

Legumi secchi — lentils, garbanzos, and dried beans — were a valued and indispensable source of protein for the poorer rural population of Italy until after the Second World War, since other protein-rich foods, such as meat, were often beyond their means. In addition, the drying of legumes provided, then as now, a welcome means of laying in stocks so that they would be available at any time of year, but especially when fresh vegetables were scarce. The combination of legumes with rice or products made from wheat flour, such as bread and pasta, is ideal from a nutritional point of view, as when the amino acids in each are brought together they form complete proteins. In addition, beans and peas contain plenty of carbohydrates and a high proportion of fiber.

From the *cucina povera*

Many of the Italian recipes containing legumes come originally from the simple "peasant" cooking of the various provinces. For a long time these dishes were not particularly well regarded by city dwellers, but attitudes and tastes have changed, and peas and beans enjoy great universal popularity. Today, the cooking of rural and urban central Italy — Tuscany, Umbria, and Latium — would be unthinkable without lentils and beans. Indeed, the extensive number of bean dishes of Tuscany explains why the Tuscans are teasingly nicknamed *mangiafagioli* — "bean eaters" — by the rest of Italy. The white kidney beans, called cannellini, are essential for so many Italian vegetable stews and soups.

SOUPS

Rich and creamy
Beans add richness and body to a soup. To add creaminess too, you can purée half or a third of the cooked legumes and stir the purée into the soup. When planning your meal, bear in mind that virtually all dried legumes must be soaked before cooking, ideally overnight. Always discard the soaking water, as it contains indigestible substances. Unlike lentils, beans and garbanzos are usually cooked separately from the rest of the dish, as they generally take longer to cook.

Peas — *piselli*
Peas (*Pisum sativum*) have been cultivated throughout southern Europe for thousands of years and thrive best in nutrient-rich, light, moist soils. They are intolerant to excessive heat, which is why the fresh-pea season is limited to the spring.

Shelled peas are used in numerous Italian dishes. Chiefly harvested unripe and eaten while still green and fresh as a vegetable, they also have their place when ripe and dried, in soups for example. The famous *risi e bisi*, one of the favorite dishes of the Venetians, is a sort of thick soup with rice and peas. It is traditionally eaten on April 25 in honor of St Mark, the patron saint of Venice. *Piselli alla fiorentina*, a delightful Florentine vegetable dish, is made by steaming young peas in oil with garlic, parsley, a bit of diced ham, and a little water. Tender snow peas, of course, do not need to be shelled, but can be eaten in their thin pod.

Lentils — *lenticchie*
The lentil (*lens culinaris*) is one of the oldest cultivated plants in the eastern Mediterranean. There are many varieties of lentils, which differ from one another in color and size. Colors range from yellow to red, and from brown to green. Italians are very fond of both the larger green lentils and the small brown lentils from Umbria, which are prized for their strong flavor. Those from the Castelluccio plateau have achieved particular fame, with, unfortunately, a price to match. The different sorts of lentils are always sold dried and podded, and as a rule must be soaked for several hours or even overnight before cooking; follow the instructions on the package.

Lentils are superb as a side dish with boiled sausage, such as cotechino, but also go well with the hearty, substantial zampone. Somewhat lighter are lentils dressed in a little olive oil and vinegar, and served either lukewarm or cold as a salad. Since lentils readily absorb different flavors from their cooking liquid, it is a good idea to add a sprig of rosemary, thyme, or oregano to the pot while they simmer, according to the desired final taste.

Garbanzos — *ceci*
Cultivated since very early times in the Mediterranean, the garbanzo, or chickpea (*Cicer arietinum*), thrives primarily in the hot, dry zones of the south in sandy soils. Its cream-to-ocher-colored, hazelnut-sized seeds, for which the plant is chiefly cultivated, are rich in protein and carbohydrate. Garbanzos are used in thick soups, sometimes with other legumes, to make them even more substantial and nourishing. In some places, the nutty-tasting seeds are also made into a purée or mash, which is served with grilled bacon. In Rome, garbanzos feature in a soup *al rosmarino*, for which the cooked legumes are mixed with finely chopped onions lightly browned in olive oil, and seasoned with rosemary and pepper, before being added to the soup.

Pasta e ceci is a dish teaming garbanzos with pasta, which has become famous in Apulia, Piedmont, and Lombardy.

Garbanzos are available either dried or ready-to-use in cans. Unlike most other legumes, garbanzos survive the canning process with their quality intact. If you buy them dried, soak them for 8–12 hours (they can be as hard as bullets), then cook them in salted water for 2–3 hours, until tender.

Preparing garbanzos: Soak in cold water for at least 8 hours. Pour off the soaking water, rinse thoroughly under cold running water, and cook in salted water for 2–3 hours until tender.

Navy beans, also known as small white beans, are mealy-textured when cooked. They are especially popular in soups and stews.

Cannellini beans, a soft-cooking, medium-size, mealy variety, is very popular in central Italy, particularly in Tuscany.

Flageolets have a delicate flavor that makes them especially popular, above all with lamb, and in salads.

Fava beans or **broad beans** are a large, mealy-cooking variety, often used in soups, also sometimes made into a purée.

Borlotti, cannellini, or fava — beans are indispensable

Among the legumes, the different varieties of beans or fagioli, dried or fresh, share top billing in many Italian dishes. They are eaten in soups, with pasta, or, seasoned generously with herbs, as a side dish or antipasto. The range of choice, however, has not always been as wide as it is today.

Once there was just the fava bean

For a long time fava, or broad, beans were the only type of bean known in all of Europe. What *Vicia faba* lacked in variety, it more than made up for in terms of antiquity. Made into a mash or purée, fava beans figured frequently on ancient Egyptian, Greek, and Roman menus. In Italy, they were most commonly eaten in southern and central parts of the country, and were hardly known in the north. The exclusive role of the fava bean began to change when explorers of the New World, such as Columbus, brought back tomatoes, corn, and the smaller varieties of beans from Central and South America. These foods were brought to Italy from Spain by Venetian merchants, and became the indispensable ingredients of Italian cooking.

Almost a staple food

White beans became popular in many regions of Italy, but are particularly associated with Tuscany. Tuscan cuisine is simply unthinkable without cannellini beans, for example, as a popular side dish with *bistecca alla fiorentina*, but also in dishes that can stand on their own. Cannellini taste particularly delicate simmered slowly, Florentine-style, in a pot-bellied wine flask, as *fagioli al fiasco*. The combination of white beans with bacon, pork rind, or pork sausage, is frequently found under the name *fagioli al forno*. Cannellini beans with olive oil, garlic, sage, and tomatoes, known in Tuscany as *fagioli all'uccelletto*, are also popular.

Beans are also eaten with gusto elsewhere in central Italy, in Umbria, Latium, and the Abruzzi. Even the Veneto, further to the north, has become famous for a bean dish: its *pasta e fagioli* is considered one of the classic Italian bean soups.

The different varieties

While beans are of great importance in the cooking of the different provinces, the

Fava beans fresh from the pod. Among the first delicate harbingers of spring, these green beans are on the market in Italy from April to June.

Black-eyed peas, *fagioli dell'occhio*, are so called because of the black spot near the embryo. They absorb seasonings and flavors well.

Large borlotti beans are an important ingredient in many Italian dishes. They are used mostly dried in minestrone and other soups.

Small borlotti beans cook up soft and are slightly bittersweet in taste. They are used chiefly in soups and stews.

Pinto beans are mealy but remain firm when cooked. Their name means "dappled."

same varieties are not used everywhere, nor is every variety suitable for every dish. A favorite in northern and central Italy is the borlotti bean, which is sold in different sizes. When fresh, both pods and seeds are pale yellow with dark-red speckles. When dried, however, the seeds are darker, and can range from pale pink to dark red. When cooked, borlotti beans turn dark red. They are used in various soups and stews, above all in minestrone.

The very popular smaller, white, elongate cannellini bean is to be found in summer — fresh, and still in its thin, yellowish pod — from about July onward in Italy's vegetable markets. Cannellini beans owe their good reputation to their rather refined taste and to their attractive, uniformly white color. They are seldom found fresh outside of Italy.

However, you may well find fresh fava beans, which are eaten raw in Italy in the early spring, accompanied only by a little pecorino cheese. Later in the season they are more likely to be eaten cooked, with olive oil, oregano, or rosemary, and a little garlic. If the fava beans are somewhat older, peel them before cooking. Cooking time can vary enormously: Fresh beans need just 10 minutes, whereas dried beans may require more than 2 hours even after soaking for 18–24 hours. Roman cuisine in particular boasts many fava-bean dishes, such as *zuppa di fave*, the typical Easter soup made with the tender beans, which ushers in the fava-bean season. Whereas the bittersweet fresh beans are used rather like fresh peas, the dried brown seeds are mostly made into nourishing and substantial winter soups, for example *favata*, which contains cabbage, pork, and pork sausage.

Buying beans
When buying fresh beans, bear in mind that the pods account for a considerable proportion of the total weight; always buy twice the amount used in the recipe. Although dried beans are in themselves a very simple, natural product, it is not easy tyo know what you are buying. Italians make sure that they purchase beans only from the previous year's harvest, so that when they are cooking, the beans are all done at the same time. Outside of Italy, dried beans of different ages are sold mixed together, which may become unpleasantly apparent: while half of the beans are disintegrating, the other half may still be as hard as bullets.

Preparing beans
Dried beans should always be soaked, with soaking times depending both on the variety and the age of the beans. As a rule of thumb, the older the beans, the longer the soaking period; follow the instructions on the package.

Cooking beans
Cooking dried beans is not difficult, provided that you follow a few basic rules. In the beginning, the beans should cook for several minutes (10 for kidney beans) at a rolling boil, after which the heat should be lowered, to prevent the skins from splitting. The ideal way to cook beans is slowly and gently in a *fagioliera*, a pot-bellied terracotta vessel in which the flavors — assuming that garlic or herbs, or both, are added — develop superbly. Add salt only when the beans are nearly done, or it can toughen them.

Soaking legumes:
Place the dried beans in a bowl and cover with cold water. Remove and discard any beans that float to the surface. After 8–12 hours, drain the beans, discarding the soaking water. Rinse the beans thoroughly with fresh water.

Bean soups
Hearty and substantial

Cooking times for dried beans vary according to age; the older the beans, the longer the cooking time. If you cannot find cannellini or borlotti beans, use other varieties of white beans and kidney beans respectively.

CABBAGE AND BEAN SOUP

Cavolo nero is a long-leafed winter cabbage that is popular in Tuscany. To make this soup even more substantial, place 2 slices of ciabatta, toasted and spread with garlic, in each bowl, and ladle the soup on top.

Serves 4

¾ cup dried cannellini or other white beans
1¾ lb cavolo nero, 3 tablespoons extra-virgin olive oil
2 garlic cloves, finely chopped
¾ cup finely chopped white onion
¾ cup diced carrot, ¾ cup thinly sliced celery
about 6¼ cups vegetable stock
9 oz tomatoes, peeled, seeded, and diced
1 teaspoon thyme leaves
salt, freshly ground pepper

Soak the beans overnight in plenty of cold water. The next day drain the beans. Remove the stalk from the *cavolo nero*, strip off the individual leaves, and cut out the leaf ribs. Wash the leaves and cut into strips.

Heat the oil in a pot and sweat the garlic and onion until translucent. Add the carrot and celery, and continue to sweat briefly. Add the beans and half of the stock. Season with salt and pepper, and

Cavolo nero, or "black cabbage," lends a spicy note to this soup. Presumably, it owes its name to its dark-green color.

simmer, covered, for 20 minutes. Add the tomatoes, cabbage, and the remaining stock, sprinkle in the thyme, and simmer, covered, for another 35–40 minutes .

BEAN SOUP WITH PENNE RIGATE

Serves 4
1¼ cups dried beans (borlotti or kidney, cannellini or other white beans)
2 bay leaves, 6–8 sage leaves, 1 sprig savory
2 garlic cloves, unpeeled and lightly crushed
9 tablespoons olive oil, ½ cup finely chopped onion
1 red bell pepper, cored, seeded, and cut into strips
1 green bell pepper, cored, seeded, and cut into strips
1 cup diced celery, ½ cup diced carrot
5½ oz tomatoes, peeled, seeded, and chopped
4½ cups chicken stock
1 teaspoon thyme leaves
2 tablespoons chopped basil leaves, 7 oz penne rigate
salt, freshly ground pepper
You will also need:
freshly grated Parmesan cheese

Soak the beans overnight in plenty of cold water. The next day drain them and transfer to a deep, wide skillet. Add the bay leaves, sage, savory, and the garlic cloves. Drizzle over 6 tablespoons of the olive oil and pour in enough water to cover the beans by 1–1½ inches. Cook the beans either over a low heat on the stove, or preheat the oven to 400°F and bake in a covered ovenproof pot, for about 1½ hours, until they are soft.

Meanwhile, prepare the vegetables. Heat the remaining oil in a pot and sweat the diced onion until lightly colored. Add the peppers, celery, carrot, and tomatoes, and sweat for 2–3 minutes. Pour in the chicken stock and simmer over a low heat for 30–40 minutes.

Drain the beans over a bowl and reserve ½ cup of the cooking liquid. Fish out the herbs and garlic, and pass half of the beans through a sieve. Mix the sieved beans with the cooking liquid, and stir this mixture and the remaining beans into the soup. Bring back to a boil. Season with salt, pepper, thyme, and basil. Cook the penne in briskly boiling salted water until *al dente*, then drain and mix into the soup before serving. Hand around the grated Parmesan separately.

Pasta e fagioli Pasta and beans is a familiar and popular combination, particularly in soups or stews, in many regions of Italy, but above all in Tuscany.

Campo dei fiori, the picturesque vegetable market in the center of Rome, offers a lavish selection of fresh produce all year. The market is busiest in the early hours of the morning.

Minestrone di verdura
A substantial vegetable soup based on a homemade chicken stock, served with grated cheese

Italy's abundant and varied supply of fresh vegetables is often made into soup. It may be a *minestra di verdura*, a light version frequently prepared with spring vegetables, but minestrone, the more substantial variety, is also very popular and has numerous regional variations. In addition to plenty of vegetables, this soup usually contains dried beans, pasta, or rice. Fresh Italian bread and a glass of light red wine are good accompaniments.

Serves 4–6
⅜ cup dried cannellini or other white beans
¼ cup butter
2–3 celery stalks, cut into julienne
1½ cups diced potatoes
5 oz zucchini, cut into rounds
1 small carrot, cut into rounds
1 small leek, cut into rings
2 cups cauliflower florets
7 oz fresh peas (½ cup shelled)
9 cups hot chicken stock
1 bay leaf
1 bunch parsley
⅓ cup diced pancetta
½ cup finely chopped onion
1 garlic clove, finely chopped
4 oz tomatoes, peeled, seeded, and diced
½ cup cooked rice
chopped basil
freshly ground white pepper
You will also need:
freshly ground Parmesan cheese

Soak the beans overnight in plenty of cold water. The next day drain the beans.

Melt the butter in a pot, add the celery, potatoes, zucchini, carrot, leek, cauliflower, and peas, and cook, stirring, for 2–3 minutes. Add the beans, stock, bay leaf, and parsley, and simmer partially covered for 15–20 minutes.

Place the pancetta in a hot skillet and cook until the fat is rendered. Add the onion and garlic, and sweat without letting them brown. Add to the soup, with the tomatoes and rice. Simmer for a further 5 minutes, stirring occasionally.

Before serving, fish out the bay leaf and parsley. Season the soup with basil and pepper. Sprinkle with Parmesan to taste at the table.

In Italy people are choosy about their fruit and vegetables: nothing but the best is good enough for *la cucina italiana*.

Minestrone from Campania

Hearty and nourishing, this version of the classic vegetable soup comes from the southwest of Italy

Unlike Tuscan minestrone, which is almost always enriched with dried beans or slices of bread, this variant from the *mezzogiorno* is made exclusively with fresh vegetables — hardly surprising, as an extremely wide variety of top-quality produce is available nearly all year in Campania, on the fertile slopes of Vesuvius. Depending on the season, an appropriate selection is made from this "vegetable garden." Substance is provided by waxy potatoes and ditali — hollow pasta that look very like short, macaroni. Whereas in northern Italy a minestrone is usually prepared with rice, the use of pasta is characteristic for the thick vegetable soups of the south. Either way, minestrone tastes delicious, especially when, as here, fresh basil and grated pecorino cheese are added. For even cooking, dice the root vegetables and the potatoes to the same size.

Heat a large pot and render the pancetta without the addition of fat. Add the garlic and onion rings, and sweat without allowing to color. Pour in the vegetable stock, bring to a boil, reduce the heat, and simmer for 20 minutes.

Trim the green beans and halve or cut into thirds, according to size. Halve and core the cabbage and slice the leaves into ½-inch-wide strips, and wash and drain in a colander.

Add the beans, carrot, celery root, and potatoes to the soup, and simmer for 10 minutes. Add the leek and cabbage, and simmer for a further 5 minutes. Finally, stir in the peas and pasta, and cook the soup for a further 10 minutes.

Sprinkle the parsley and basil into the soup, and season with salt and pepper. Garnish the minestrone with whole basil leaves and serve, sprinkled with a little grated pecorino if wished.

Fresh ewe's milk is essential for the production of pecorino. Made chiefly in central and southern Italy, this spicy hard cheese can add the crowning touch when freshly grated over pasta or a hearty soup.

Serves 4
½ cup diced pancetta
2 garlic cloves, sliced
1 onion, sliced into rings
9 cups vegetable stock
7 oz green beans
10 oz Savoy cabbage
1 cup diced carrots
1½ cups diced celery root
2¼ cups large diced waxy potatoes
1 leek, sliced into ½-inch-thick rings
½ cup fresh peas
¾ cup soup pasta (such as ditali piccoli rigati)
2 tablespoons chopped parsley
1 tablespoon basil, cut into strips
salt, freshly ground pepper
You will also need:
basil leaves for garnishing
¼ cup freshly grated aged pecorino cheese (optional)

With arugula and spinach
Thick soups with leafy green vegetables

CREAM OF ARUGULA SOUP

This fine, frothy soup owes its special taste to the pleasant, peppery-hot flavor of arugula, also known as rugola or rocket in English. For this soup the slender, serrated leaves are deep-fried, which gives them an even more distinctive nutty flavor.

Serves 4
7 oz arugula
1¼ cups extra-virgin olive oil
2 tablespoons butter
½ cup finely chopped shallots
1 garlic clove, finely chopped
1 tablespoon flour
½ cup white wine
2¼ cups chicken stock, 1 cup light cream
salt, cayenne pepper

Snip off the tough stalk ends from the arugula, wash the leaves, and spin dry in a salad spinner. Heat the oil in a large pot and deep-fry the arugula in batches until crisp. Remove and drain well on paper towels. Reserve a few arugula leaves for the garnish and cut the remaining leaves into small pieces.

Heat the butter in a large pot and sweat the shallots and garlic until the shallots are translucent. Sprinkle with the flour and cook, stirring, without allowing the flour to color. Deglaze the contents of the pot with white wine and stir until smooth.

Pour in the chicken stock, stirring constantly until smooth, and simmer for 10 minutes. Add the cream and simmer briefly. Season with salt and cayenne pepper. Stir in the deep-fried, cut-up arugula leaves.

Purée the soup in a blender until very smooth, then strain back into the pot. Bring to a boil once more, adjust seasoning, and blend with a hand-held blender until foamy. Ladle the soup into heated bowls and serve garnished with the remaining deep-fried arugula leaves.

SPINACH SOUP WITH RICE

This *minestra marià*, a light soup with rice popular in Piedmont and the Valle d'Aosta, does not require many different, or indeed unusual, ingredients, but those used must, of course, always be the best quality. (Not illustrated.)

Serves 4
1½ lb fresh spinach, thick stems removed
3 tablespoons butter, ⅜ cup finely chopped onion
1 garlic clove, finely chopped
½ cup long-grain rice, 4½ cups beef stock
1 egg, ¼ cup freshly grated Parmesan cheese
salt, freshly ground pepper
You will also need:
¼ cup freshly grated Parmesan cheese

Blanch the spinach leaves in a pot of briskly boiling salted water just until they wilt, then lift out with a slotted spoon. (Blanching makes the spinach nice and supple.) Drain in a colander and lightly squeeze out the water. Leave the spinach to cool, then chop coarsely.

Melt the butter in a large pot and sweat the onion and garlic, stirring frequently, without allowing them to color. Tip in the rice and sauté until translucent. Pour in the stock, bring to a boil, reduce the heat, and simmer the rice for 15–20 minutes. Add the spinach during the last 5 minutes of cooking time. Season the soup with salt and pepper.

Whisk the egg in a soup tureen. Work in the Parmesan, stirring. Ladle in a third of the hot soup and stir into the egg–cheese mixture. Stir in the remaining soup and serve at once. Hand around the cheese for sprinkling.

Deep-fried arugula leaves When preparing this unusual soup garnish, take care to dry the leaves very carefully before lowering them into the hot oil; otherwise, you run a very great risk of splashing yourself!

Zucchini soups

Ideal for the summertime, when zucchini plants are blossoming and fruiting simultaneously

ZUCCHINI-FLOWER SOUP

Serves 4

20–25 zucchini flowers, 2 tablespoons butter
2 scallions, sliced into thin rings
2 garlic cloves, sliced into rounds
1 green chile pepper, sliced into thin strips
10 oz zucchini, sliced into rounds
1 tablespoon chopped herbs (parsley, thyme, tarragon)
3½ cups chicken stock, 1 tablespoon crème fraîche
salt, freshly ground pepper
For the garnish:
7 oz skinless, boneless chicken breast
10 zucchini flowers, 2 tablespoons butter
2½ cups sliced button mushrooms
1 tablespoon chopped parsley, salt, freshly ground pepper,

If the zucchini flowers are open, snip out the pistils and stamens with kitchen scissors, and cut off the calyxes and the tip of the stalk. If the flowers are closed, twist out the calyx with the pistils and stamens. Cut all the flowers crosswise into thin strips.

Melt the butter and sweat the scallions and garlic without letting them color, then stir in the chile strips. Add the zucchini pieces and flowers and sweat briefly, then add the herbs and stock. Season with salt and pepper. Bring to a boil, reduce the heat, and simmer for about 15 minutes. Purée the soup in a blender, stir in the crème fraîche, adjust seasoning, and keep warm.

The hearty stuffing of the zucchini flowers creates a most interesting flavor counterpoint to this mild cream soup.

To make the garnish, cut the chicken breast into ½-inch-wide strips. Prepare the zucchini flowers as described above and cut into strips. Melt the butter and brown the chicken on all sides. Add the mushrooms and sauté for 1–2 minutes. Add the zucchini flowers, sautéing only briefly. Season with salt and pepper, and sprinkle in the parsley. Ladle the soup into warmed bowls, place some of the garnish in the center, and serve.

The fruits and flowers of the zucchini plant form the basis of this zucchini-flower soup. After sweating in butter with garlic and chile pepper, they are cooked in chicken stock, then puréed. To serve, ladle the soup into warmed bowls and arrange the garnish on top.

CREAM OF ZUCCHINI SOUP

Serves 4

1 lb zucchini, 3 tablespoons butter
1 garlic clove, finely chopped
¾ cup finely chopped white onions, 2⅔ cups veal stock
1 thyme sprig, ½ cup light cream
salt, freshly ground pepper
For the stuffed zucchini flowers:
8 zucchini flowers, 3 tablespoons olive oil
½ cup finely diced prosciutto
⅓ cup finely chopped white onion
1 garlic clove, finely chopped
½ cup finely chopped eggplant
1¼ cups finely chopped bell peppers (red, yellow, or green)
4 oz tomatoes, peeled, seeded, and diced
1 tablespoon chopped fresh herbs (sage, parsley, thyme, rosemary)
salt, freshly ground pepper,
You will also need:
thyme leaves

Make the garnish first. Remove the pistils and stamens from the zucchini flowers. Heat the oil and sweat the prosciutto, onion, and garlic until lightly colored. Add the eggplant and peppers, and sweat for a further 1–2 minutes. Stir in the tomatoes, reduce the heat, and stew for 10 minutes. Season with salt and pepper, and sprinkle in the herbs. Cool slightly, then using a teaspoon, stuff the flowers with the mixture. Twist the tips of the flowers together to seal.

Using a small melon baller, scoop balls from one of the zucchini and set aside. Cut the remaining zucchini into ½-inch pieces. Melt the butter in a pot and sweat the zucchini, garlic, and onions for 3–4 minutes. Pour in the stock, add the thyme, and season with salt and pepper. Simmer, covered, for 15 minutes. Fish out the thyme and blend the contents of the pot until very smooth. Stir in the cream. Simmer for a further 10 minutes, then adjust seasoning. Simmer the zucchini balls in lightly salted water for 3–4 minutes; lift out, drain, and add to the soup. Keep the soup warm.

Wrap the flowers in plastic wrap, tie with kitchen twine, and cook gently in simmering water for 5 minutes. Ladle the soup into bowls. Lift the zucchini flowers from the water, remove the plastic wrap, and arrange two flowers in each soup plate. Sprinkle the soup with thyme leaves and serve.

Hearty fare for chilly days
Cipollata and *ribollita*: two of the most delectable soups with bread

CIPOLLATA

Serves 4

1¼ lb tomatoes, peeled
⅔ cup diced pancetta
4 tablespoons olive oil, 1½ tablespoons butter
1 lb onions, sliced into rings
1 teaspoon sugar, 4½ cups vegetable or chicken stock
salt, coarsely ground black pepper

For the garnish:
1 loaf Vinschgauer bread (see p. 421)
2–3 tablespoons extra-virgin olive oil
2 eggs, 2 teaspoons butter
¾ cup freshly grated Parmesan cheese
1 tablespoon chopped herbs (parsley, basil)
salt, freshly ground pepper,

Quarter and core the tomatoes. Remove and strain the seeds, reserving the juice, then chop the tomato flesh. Heat a pot and render the pancetta without additional fat. Add the oil, butter, and onions, sprinkle the sugar on top, and sauté over a moderate heat for about 15 minutes, until golden brown. Pour in the stock and tomato juice, stir in the tomatoes, and season with salt and pepper. Bring to a boil, reduce the heat, and simmer for 15–20 minutes. If necessary, pour in a little more stock. Adjust seasoning.

Preheat the oven to 400°F. Cut the bread into ½-inch-thick slices. Place them on a baking sheet lined with waxed paper, drizzle with a little oil, and bake until golden. Just before you are ready to serve, whisk the eggs in a bowl and season them with salt and pepper. Melt the butter in a heavy-based skillet and pour in the eggs. As soon as they start to set, stir continuously with a pancake turner, pushing the mixture toward the center of the pan until the scrambled egg is uniformly creamy and still shiny and moist.

Ladle the soup into warmed soup plates. Place a piece of toasted bread in each bowl, sprinkle with Parmesan, top with scrambled egg, and season with coarsely ground pepper and the herbs. Serve at once.

RIBOLLITA

"Reboiled" is the literal translation of *ribollita*, a thick bean soup that, once made, improves in flavor with each reheating. The following recipe is recommended for people who wish to make and serve the soup on the same day. The thick consistency is achieved here by blending half of the soup. (Not illustrated.)

Serves 4–6

4 tablespoons olive oil, ¾ cup finely chopped white onion
1 garlic clove, finely chopped
1¼ cups dried cannellini or other white beans
5 oz prosciutto in one piece
1 small dried red pepper (peperoncino), 2 thyme sprigs
1 small rosemary sprig, ¾ cup diced carrot
2 celery stalks, sliced
3–4 young leeks, cut into thin strips
5 oz Swiss chard, cut into ½-inch-wide strips
salt, freshly ground pepper

You will also need:
4–6 slices Tuscan country bread, toasted
½ cup freshly grated Parmesan cheese

Soak the beans in plenty of cold water for 4 hours, then drain. Heat 2 tablespoons oil in a pot and sweat the onion and garlic until lightly colored. Add the beans and prosciutto, and pour in 9 cups water. Bring to a boil, reduce the heat, add the peperoncino, thyme and rosemary, and simmer, covered, for about 1 hour.

Heat the remaining oil and sweat the carrot, celery, and leek for 3–4 minutes, stirring. Stir these vegetables into the soup and cook for a further 40 minutes. Mix in the chard and cook for another 20–25 minutes. Lift out and dice the prosciutto. Purée half of the soup in a blender, stir back into the unblended portion, and stir in the cubed prosciutto. Season with salt and pepper. Place the toasted bread in soup plates and sprinkle with half of the cheese. Ladle the soup on top and sprinkle with the remaining cheese. Flash briefly under a hot broiler and serve immediately.

With fennel and tomatoes

Whereas the *zuppa di finocchio* is embellished with toasted bread, a little basil is the only garnish needed for the tomato soup

FENNEL SOUP

Serves 4

1 lb fennel, 2 tablespoons olive oil
⅓ cup diced pancetta
½ cup finely chopped white onion,
2½ tablespoons tomato paste, 4½ cups veal stock
1 tablespoon each chopped parsley and fennel leaves
salt, pepper
For the toasted bread:
4–8 slices Italian country bread
5 tablespoons extra-virgin olive oil

You will also need:
¼ cup freshly grated pecorino cheese
1 tablespoon chopped herbs (parsley, fennel leaves)

The typical fennel flavor, with its powerful aniseed note, is imparted to the soup not only by the fennel bulb itself, but also by the feathery green leaves, which are far too good to throw away.

waxed paper, drizzle with the olive oil, and bake for a few minutes until crunchy.

Ladle the soup into a tureen. Place the bread on top of the soup, sprinkle with the grated cheese and herbs, and serve immediately.

TOMATO SOUP

Eaten and enjoyed throughout Italy, this is a real summer soup. For a strictly vegetarian version, simply use vegetable stock instead of veal stock. (Illustrated on page 84.)

Serves 4
2 tablespoons olive oil, ¾ cup finely chopped onion
1 garlic clove, finely chopped
½ cup diced carrot
½ cup chopped celery
½ cup chopped parsley root
½ bunch parsley with stalks, coarsely chopped
1 lb ripe tomatoes, cored and coarsely chopped
3¼ cups veal stock, 1 thyme sprig, a few lovage leaves
salt, freshly ground pepper
You will also need:
a few fresh basil leaves

Heat the oil in a casserole and sweat the onion and garlic until lightly colored. Add the carrot, celery, parsley root, and parsley, and continue to sweat for 4–5 minutes. Add the tomatoes, simmer for 4 minutes, then pour in the stock. Add the thyme and lovage, and season with salt and pepper. Serve the soup garnished with a few basil leaves.

Trim the root tip and green stalks off the fennel bulbs, reserving the delicate, feathery green leaves. If necessary, remove the tough outer ribs from the bulbs. Quarter the fennel lengthwise, remove the core, and finely dice the bulbs. Finely chop the fennel leaves; you will need about 1½ tablespoons.

Heat the oil in a large pot and render the bacon. Add the onion and fennel, and sweat until translucent. Quickly stir in the tomato paste — do not let it catch on the bottom of the pot or it will become bitter. Pour in the stock and bring to a boil. Reduce the heat and simmer, covered, for 30 minutes. Season with salt and sprinkle in the parsley and fennel leaves. Bring the soup back to a boil, and season to taste with salt and pepper.

In the meantime, preheat the oven to 400°F. Place the slices of bread on a baking sheet lined with

Tomato paste is still prepared at home by many southern Italians, by spreading puréed tomatoes on a board and leaving them to dry in the blazing sun until the desired concentration is reached.

Tuscan vegetable soup with beans and artichokes

This traditional *zuppa garmugia* is served with freshly toasted croutons, which are added just before eating

In Italy this soup is made with brown borlotti beans, which are closely related, botanically and in shape and flavor, to red kidney beans. Whether you use dried or canned beans is more a question of time than taste. Dried beans must be soaked, boiled, and simmered for 1–2 hours until they are done. People who like their beans very soft should extend the cooking time accordingly. Canned beans need only to be rinsed under cold running water and stirred into the soup 10 minutes before the end of cooking time.

Serves 4
½ cup dried red kidney beans
10 oz small artichokes without stalks
3 tablespoons olive oil
⅓ cup diced pancetta
4 oz ground beef
1 leek, sliced diagonally into ¼-inch rings
1 onion, thinly sliced into rings
9 oz peas in the pod (about ¾ cup shelled)
4½ cups beef or vegetable stock
salt, freshly ground pepper

Some varieties of artichokes can be prepared and eaten whole when they are young and tender. In Italy, they are sometimes sold already cooked. Small, thorny artichokes are prepared like the large varieties.

For the croutons:
2 slices white bread, crusts removed
2 tablespoons olive oil, 1 garlic clove

Soak the beans overnight in plenty of cold water. The next day tip the beans into a colander, rinse well with fresh water, and drain. Boil the beans in a pot of lightly salted water for 10 minutes, reduce the heat, and simmer for at least 45 minutes. Strain and leave to drain.

In the meantime, prepare the artichokes. If necessary, strip off the small tough leaves around the base of the stalk. Snip off the tips of the leaves with kitchen scissors. Use a sharp knife to cut off evenly about one-third of the top portion of the artichokes. Quarter the artichokes and scoop out the fibrous, inedible "choke" with a teaspoon.

Heat the oil in a pot and brown the ground beef until crumbly, stirring frequently. Add the pancetta and continue to fry. Add the leek and onion, and sweat them until translucent. Pour in the stock and bring the contents of the pot to a boil. Add the beans and the artichokes, reduce the heat, and simmer for 10 minutes. Tip in the peas, season with salt and pepper, and simmer the soup for a further 10 minutes.

To make the croutons, cut the bread into ½-inch cubes. Heat the oil in a skillet. Squeeze the garlic through a garlic press into the skillet. Add the cubed bread and sauté, stirring frequently, until crunchy.

Ladle the soup into warmed bowls, sprinkle the croutons on top, and serve at once. If you prefer, the croutons can be handed around separately at the table for each person to add just before eating; that way, they stay crunchier for longer.

In the Mediterranean, fish and shellfish are usually caught with a trawl. Only small cutters that specialize in catching high-quality fish use a long line.

Minestrone with monkfish and jumbo shrimp
A puréed vegetable soup with a fine seafood garnish and shavings of mild cheese

If you are used to thinking of vegetable soups as substantial dishes containing a medley of different vegetables such as celery, carrots, leek, and white beans, rounded out by potatoes, noodles, bacon, or meat, this exquisite recipe with fish and jumbo shrimp might come as a bit of a surprise. This aristocratic soup tastes even better if you prepare the vegetable stock yourself from fresh ingredients.

Different types of Caciotta are made in central Italy, chiefly from cow's or ewe's milk, and less often from a mixture of cow's, ewe's, and goat's milk. Here, an aged Caciotta with a firm body is needed for its pleasantly mild, sweetish flavor.

Serves 4
1 lb tomatoes, peeled
½ cup olive oil
1 cup finely chopped onions
2 garlic cloves, finely chopped
2 cups diced yellow bell peppers
2 cups diced mealy potatoes
2 tablespoons tomato paste
about 4½ cups vegetable stock
salt, freshly ground pepper
1 lb skinned monkfish
4 jumbo shrimp, peeled and deveined
salt, freshly ground pepper
You will also need:
small basil leaves
½ cup freshly shaved aged Caciotta cheese

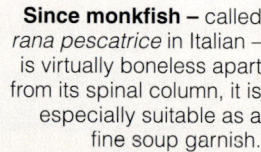

Since monkfish – called *rana pescatrice* in Italian – is virtually boneless apart from its spinal column, it is especially suitable as a fine soup garnish.

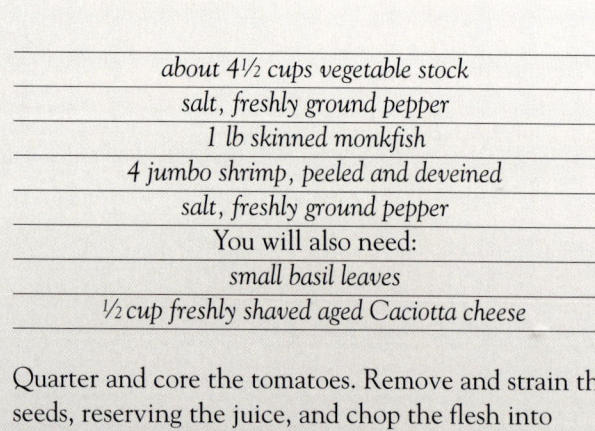

Quarter and core the tomatoes. Remove and strain the seeds, reserving the juice, and chop the flesh into small pieces.

Heat half the oil in a large saucepan and sweat the diced onions and garlic without letting them color. Add the tomatoes, peppers, and potatoes, and cook for

5 minutes. Stir in the tomato paste and continue cooking for 2 minutes. Pour in the reserved tomato juice and the stock, and season with salt and pepper. Bring the soup to a boil, reduce the heat, and simmer for 25 minutes. Purée with a hand-held blender or in a food processor until very smooth, then adjust the seasoning and keep warm.

Carefully wash the monkfish under cold running water, pat dry, and remove any remnants of skin. Cut the fish into rounds ½–¾-inch thick; you can slice through the spine easily with a heavy knife.

Heat the remaining oil in a large skillet. Season the monkfish medallions with salt and pepper, and sauté in the oil for about 2 minutes on each side. Add the shrimp and sauté for 1 minute more, turning to cook both sides.

Ladle the vegetable soup into warmed soup plates. Add the monkfish medallions and the shrimp. Serve garnished with the basil leaves and the shavings of Caciotta cheese.

Located on the southern tip of the lagoon, Chioggia, like Venice itself, has a branching network of canals at its disposal, though on a somewhat more modest scale. These enable the fishermen to bring their catch directly into the town to special market stalls.

Mussel soup

Mussels and vegetables aplenty, gently cooked in mussel and fish stock and white wine

It is hardly surprising that the cuisine of Venice and its surroundings excels at using maritime delicacies when fish and seafood are available fresh daily, and in great variety, from the local fish markets. The very popular black, broad-shelled mussels with their bright orange flesh are on sale here throughout the year, owing to large-scale mussel farming in the lagoon. The visible signs of this activity are the posts rising out of the water, on which the lines for the nets are hung. The mollusks grow in these nets for about 1½ years before they are harvested.

Serves 4
3½ lb mussels
3 tablespoons olive oil
1 white onion, halved and thinly sliced
3 garlic cloves, finely chopped
1 cup white wine
3½ cups fish stock
1 lb tomatoes, peeled
¾ cup thinly sliced carrot
coarse sea salt, coarsely ground black pepper
For the garlic toast:
5 tablespoons extra-virgin olive oil, 3 garlic cloves
4–8 slices Italian white bread

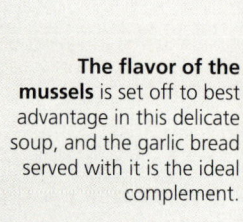

The flavor of the mussels is set off to best advantage in this delicate soup, and the garlic bread served with it is the ideal complement.

You will also need:
3 tablespoons chopped parsley

Thoroughly scrub the mussels under cold running water, remove the beards, and discard any open mussels.

Heat the oil in a large pot and sweat the onions and garlic until lightly colored. Add the mussels and pour in the wine. Cover the pot and cook for about 7–8 minutes, shaking the pot vigorously from time to time, until the mussels have opened. Discard any mussels that remain closed. Lift the mussels and onions out of the stock with a slotted spoon and set aside.

Strain the mussel stock through a strainer lined with cheesecloth, to remove any possible sand residue. Place this strained stock in a pot with the fish stock and bring slowly to a boil.

In the meantime, core the tomatoes. Strain the seeds, reserving the juice, and dice the flesh. Add the tomato juice to the stock. Stir in the tomatoes and carrots, and simmer for about 10 minutes.

Shuck two-thirds of the mussels and return the mussel meat and the reserved onions to the soup to heat through. Season with salt and pepper.

To make the garlic toast, preheat the oven to 400°F. Pour the olive oil into a small bowl. Squeeze the garlic through a garlic press into the oil, and stir to mix thoroughly. Place the slices of bread on a baking sheet and brush them with the garlic oil. Place the baking sheet in the oven and bake until the bread is golden brown.

When the bread is toasted, ladle the soup into warmed bowls and spoon in the unshucked mussels. Sprinkle with the parsley. Serve the soup immediately, handing around the hot garlic toast.

Pasta PASTA

Golden yellow and glossy, cooked *al dente*, coated in a well-seasoned sauce, and perhaps sprinkled with cheese is how perfect Italian pasta should be served. Whether the pasta dough is made from soft flour or durum semolina, with or without eggs, is a matter of personal taste as well as tradition. Here is an opportunity to discover a multiplicity of pasta types and shapes, learn which sauce tastes best with which variety, and try out the most exciting fillings for stuffed pastas.

All about pasta, and why it is usually served with cheese

A plate of pasta as a *primo piatto*, or first course, without cheese is almost unthinkable. In fact, Italians forgo the *formaggio* only if the sauce contains seafood, whose often very delicate flavor would be completely overpowered by the strong taste of cheese.

In Italy people combine cheese with pasta in various ways: grating it over the top, so that the noodles are uniformly seasoned; shaving it wafer-thin, to provide a flavor contrast; or letting it melt gently into the sauce. Particularly spectacular is a serving method sometimes used at the diners' table in Italian restaurants: A hollowed-out block of Parmesan is brushed inside with high-proof spirits and set alight. The flames are left to die down until the cheese is melting on the surface. The prepared hot pasta is then added and tossed in the Parmesan "bowl" until the noodles are completely coated with melted cheese. However *formaggio* and pasta are combined, before we can think of providing the finishing touch to a plate of pasta with cheese, we must prepare the pasta itself.

Fresh pasta

If you have a pasta machine, the preparation of *pasta fresca*, or fresh pasta, poses no real problems. Italian *pastaie* — professional pasta makers — however, often prepare their pasta by hand, equipped with nothing but a rolling pin, a board, and cutting utensils. Their practiced hands turn out the pasta so quickly that a machine would not speed up the process significantly. The *sfoglia*, or thinly rolled-out sheets of pasta dough, can be cut into long ribbon noodles in varying widths, or into fairly large, rectangular sheets such as lasagne, which are used flat, and cannelloni, which are stuffed and rolled into tubes. *Sfoglia* is also used for other *pasta ripiena*, or stuffed pasta, such as ravioli,

Bucatini in a Parmesan block This way of serving pasta is admittedly an expensive indulgence for smaller quantities, and so is more suitable for a fairly large pasta party or for a gourmet dinner.

Quality is crucial both in the choice of the appropriate variety of cheese and in the *pasta fresca*, which is prepared daily, in, for instance, Bologna. These noodles are for the most part destined for restaurant use, but smaller quantities are also sold to private households.

agnolotti, tortellini, and pansoti. The *sfoglia* can be cut into shapes that are folded over the stuffing; or the stuffing can be placed in little mounds on a sheet of pasta, covered with a second sheet, and the shapes cut out around the filling. Other sorts of pasta are shaped after being cut. For example, to make orecchiette, the pasta shaped like little ears, a thin roll of dough is divided into small, equal portions, and each piece is shaped by pressing it out on the work surface with one's thumb. Tubular pasta, such as garganelli, is made by hand by wrapping pieces of dough around wooden sticks; and corkscrew pasta, such as fusilli, is made by twisting thin strips of pasta in a spiral around the handle of a wooden spoon. Time and patience are essential, if every piece of pasta is to be shaped with the same care.

Where did pasta come from?

We do not know who created pasta, but the story that Marco Polo discovered it on his travels in China and brought the recipe back to Italy is a myth. Dried pasta that would today be described as a type of spaghetti is recorded in 1154 — long before Marco Polo was born — in the Arab geographer Al-Idrisi's description of the world, as a specialty manufactured in Trabia, a village near Palermo. Dried pasta became a staple food in Italy, as even poorer people could afford the ingredients, and the finished product could be stored for relatively long periods of time.

Dried pasta in all shapes

Even in Italy, the overwhelming proportion of dried pasta is manufactured industrially, rather than made at home. The quality of much of this *pasta secca*, prepared chiefly from durum semolina, is so good, that you can use it confidently if you do not feel like making your own, or if you are not sure of the quality of store-bought fresh pasta. Moreover, Italian *pasta secca* comes in every shape imaginable, which would be difficult to make at home, and in colors ranging from golden yellow to tomato-red and spinach-green to squid-ink black. Only stuffed pasta, such as tortellini, is best avoided as a ready-made dried product.

Making *pasta secca*

Long gone are the days in which pasta hung drying, like long curtains, on the streets in Italy. Modern standards of hygiene demand that noodles be handled differently, so now high-quality pasta is dried in factories at a constant temperature of 140–150°F for 15 hours. *Pasta lunga*, long noodles such as spaghetti, are hung next to each other for drying on long iron poles, as can be seen in several of the pictures on the opposite page. After drying, *pasta corta*, or short shapes, travel along a conveyor belt on which they are shaken about in order to separate the pieces from each another. Then are they packaged and sold throughout the world.

Harmony of shape and flavor

Italian cooks are seldom at a loss when it comes to choosing which of the seemingly endless varieties of pasta to cook with which sauce; in the country where pasta originated, people develop a flair for these things. They know that different pasta shapes are capable of absorbing different amounts of *sugo*, or sauce, with penne, for instance, having a greater "capacity" than spaghetti. The type of surface is also important; more sauce sticks to each piece of *pasta rigata*, or grooved pasta, than to *pasta liscia*, smooth pasta. Moreover, fresh egg pasta absorbs more *sugo* than dried durum wheat pasta. By contrast, the small shapes, for example short, round tubular pasta such as ditali, or letters of the alphabet, are especially suitable for soup garnishes.

A variety of *pasta secca* 1 Pipette; 2 Gnocchetti di zite; 3 Pastina all'uovo; 4 Mezze penne rigate; 5 Pennette rigate; 6 Elbow macaroni: plain, and colored with spinach and beet juice; 7 Conchigliette tricolori; 8 Strozzapreti

Cheeses with a quality seal

"Extra-hard" is the description applied to the three varieties of Italian cow's-milk cheese grouped together under the generic term *grana*, or grain: Parmigiano Reggiano, Grana Padano, and Grana Trentino. These three varieties are made in a very similar fashion, and produce a very similar result: an especially hard cheese with a slightly granular structure and only a few small holes, if any. Because of this structure, a well-ripened, perfect *grana* cheese is more easily broken into pieces with a stable, spatula-shaped knife than it is sliced. The surfaces of the break then have a leafy structure.

Parmigiano Reggiano

The most famous of the extra-hard cheeses, Parmigiano Reggiano should never be confused with those grated products sold as "Parmesan." Genuine Parmigiano, with its straw-yellow interior and its name stencilled all around the rind in dotted writing, is sold from the wheel. To preserve its full flavor, it should be grated or shaved into thin flakes just before use.

Cows whose milk is used for Parmigiano must be fed exclusively on grass or hay. The name Parmigiano Reggiano is a designation of origin (*denominazione di origine controllata*, or DOC) protected by law, and may be carried only by cheeses produced under the described conditions and in a precisely circumscribed area between the cities of Parma, Mantua, Reggio Emilia, and Bologna. Product quality is monitored by the Consorzio Tutela Parmigiano Reggiano, the Consortium for the Protection of Parmigiano Reggiano. Only impeccable cheeses are branded with the consortium's symbol, which includes its name, a registration number, and the month and year of production. Cheese that is to be exported also receives a special label.

Grana Padano and Grana Trentino

Grana Padano and Grana Trentino are also DOC cheeses. Grana Padano is produced in an area that mainly stretches north of the Po river, but extends

Grana Trentino (top) carries a quality seal consisting of a diamond with the inscription *trentino*, the symbol of the regional consortium. **Grana Padano** (above) can be recognized by its cloverleaf brand next to the diamond with its legend.

south to Ravenna. Grana Trentino comes from the province of Trento. Grana is spicy and aromatic in flavor, and its color may vary between whitish and straw-yellow, depending on the time of year at which it was produced. Local consortiums are also responsible for monitoring the quality of these cheeses.

Production

Taking Parmigiano Reggiano as an example, the picture sequence on the right shows the steps in manufacturing this type of cheese. Milk from the evening milking remains overnight in large vats. It is partially skimmed the next morning and mixed with skimmed milk. To encourage fermentation, whey from previous batches is added. Next, the liquid is heated to 91°F, after which the rennet, which causes the mixture to thicken, is added. In the meantime, the mixture, now called "curd," must be stirred constantly with a huge paddle in order to cut it into small granules: the finer the granulation, the harder the cheese ultimately becomes. The curd is heated to 131°F, after which the granular mixture settles at the bottom of the kettle. It is then transferred to a large linen cloth and rocked back and forth to produce a ball. The ball is cut up and each part is formed into a cheese, which is wrapped in linen, pressed into a ring, covered with a wooden disk, and weighed down with weights of up to 55 pounds. This pressing lasts about 20 hours, with the cheese being turned every hour. After 5–6 hours, the cloth is removed. Next, the cheese is placed in a brine bath for 20–24 days, depending on weight. The cheeses are then placed in a warm spot for a few hours, before they are stacked on shelves and left to ripen in air-conditioned storage rooms, where they are turned at intervals and have their surfaces cleaned regularly. Grana is ripened in this manner for at least 10 months, while Parmigiano takes at least 24. After a year's aging, the cheese is called *nuovo*; after 2 years, *vecchio*, after 3, *stravecchio*, and after 4 years, *stravecchione*.

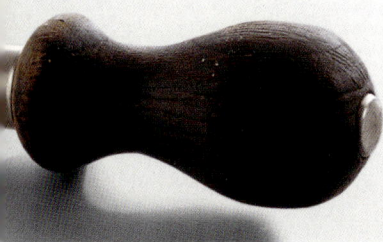

Sheep are important suppliers of milk, especially in southern Italy, where the barren soil is not suitable for rearing cattle. In many places the sheep are still milked by hand, and the milk is made into cheese using traditional methods.

Pecorino: sheep's-milk cheeses

In Italy they say there are *mille varianti*, a thousand variations, of the sheep's-milk cheese called pecorino. To distinguish between them, therefore, most varieties bear a reference to the cheese's place of origin in the name; some are even DOC cheeses. Not all pecorino cheeses are made from pure sheep's milk; some add small proportions of goat's or cow's milk, and some use calf, lamb, or kid rennet — and even an extract of artichoke flowers — to coagulate the milk. Pecorino Canestrato is distinctive because it is drained in basket, whose weave is then imprinted on the outside of the cheese.

Ripeness and taste

The purpose for which a pecorino can be used depends to a certain extent on its production method and its particular mixture of milk, but is above all a question of how long the cheese is ripened. Pecorino is sold fresh as pecorino *fresco*, or only slightly ripened, as pecorino *semifresco*. Just like the mild, only slightly salted pecorino *dolce*, these varieties are table cheeses, and are rarely used for cooking. More strongly salted varieties of pecorino can also be enjoyed as mild table cheeses in their first few months; but when the curd becomes harder and more piquant with increasing age, they are used chiefly for grating,.

Pecorino Romano

As its name implies, the original home of Pecorino Romano is the area around the capital of Italy; for historical reasons, however, it is also produced on Sardinia. At the beginning of the twentieth century, Roman salt companies established a number of cheese factories on the island because of the favorable production conditions there. That salt companies in particular should promote the production of Pecorino Romano is explained by the way this cheese is made. After a brief drying period, the fresh, pressed cheese is washed with salt water and then sprinkled all around with salt, a procedure to which every cheese is subjected repeatedly at regular intervals during the first 2 months of the ripening period. The rind is then washed with salt water for the last time, after which the cheeses are placed in special ripening rooms for at least 6 months before they are ready to be sold.

The white to straw-yellow curd of the 18–49-pound cheeses is then very firm — supple, in the case of full-fat cheese; granular, in the case of low-fat cheese — and interspersed with the tiny "cheese crystals" typical of fully ripened cheeses.

Pecorino Romano is an Italian cheese with a legally protected name. The dark rind and the light, somewhat crumbly body containing very few holes are characteristic of this cheese, which must ripen for at least 8 months.

Pecorino Toscano is a name applied to a number of widely differing cheeses produced in Tuscany. This is a *semi curato* or medium-ripe cheese. According to connoisseurs, the best comes from the hills around Pienza, Montalcino, and Montepulciano.

Pecorino Pepato, This pecorino is studded with crushed peppercorns, rather than the more usual whole black ones. Almost every pecorino in Italy is also made in a similarly spicy variation.

Pecorino Sardo This piece comes from a well ripened wheel of sheep's-milk cheese, has a relatively dark interior, and is so piquant it is almost hot. Relatively hard, it is excellent for grating.

Pecorino Sardo

Pecorino Sardo also comes from Sardinia. Resembling Pecorino Romano in both production method and flavor, Pecorino Sardo cheeses are a great deal smaller, weighing only 3–9 pounds. They are recognizable by their slightly convex rim. Pecorino Sardo ripens for a minimum of 9 months, and often longer.

Pecorino from Sicily

The most famous sheep's cheese from Sicily is Pecorino Canestrato Siciliano, still produced chiefly by hand in the mountains. This pecorino, too, is a DOC cheese. Full-fat sheep's milk is the sole raw ingredient used in its production, so the cheese has a high fat content. The milk for genuine Canestrato Siciliano must be coagulated only with lamb or kid rennet, for which purpose it is traditionally heatedin a copper kettle over a wood fire. As soon as the milk curdles, it is cut up. The curd is then ladled into baskets, as described above, in which they are pressed by hand. After the initial drying, the cheeses are salted — the amount of salt is 4–5 percent of the weight of the cheese — in order to improve their keeping qualities. This cheese can be eaten after only a few days, but it must ripen for 4 months before it can be sold as a table cheese; after 6–8 months' ripening it is hard enough for grating. On Sicily, the sort of Canestrato containing no further ingredients is also called a pecorino *bianco* or a pecorino *calcagno*. The Pecorino Siciliano Pepato or Canestrato Pepato are pecorinos into which black peppercorns are sprinkled at the time of production. Unlike other pecorino *pepati*, in which the spicy peppercorns are distributed evenly throughout the cheese, they usually lie in a layer next to each other in the Sicilian Pepato. Canestrato can be made into huge wheels weighing 45 pounds and more. These impressive cheeses, with their characteristic rind, are the main attraction of many a cheese stand at Sicilian markets. Ripe Canestrato is piquant and spicy-tasting, hence the Italian fondness for grating it and sprinkling it over risottos and pasta. Yet another variation of the Sicilian pecorino is the Piacintinu from Messina, which is sometimes dyed with saffron.

Pecorino Canestrato On the rind of this medium-aged cheese from Sardinia you can still see the imprint of the woven-reed basket in which the curds drained. The Sicilian Pecorino Canestrato also bears such a pattern. Two whole wheels of the latter can be seen below in the picture of a market stall in Palermo.

This Pecorino Toscano has ripened for 2 months, and is known at this stage as *giovane*, or young.

Pasta filata: cooked cheeses

The cooked, kneaded cheeses of Italy are referred to as *formaggi a pasta filata*. The best known are mozzarella, caciocavallo, and provolone. They have a common curd structure but differ in other respects. According to variety, they are sold fresh or ripened, soft or firm, and smoked or unsmoked.

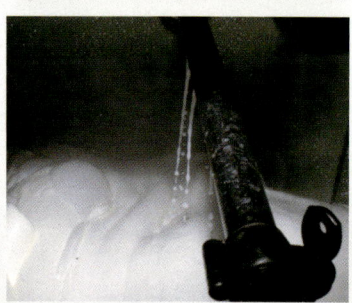

How provolone is made

To make provolone, and other cooked and kneaded cheeses, the curd — in this case, peanut-sized — is first allowed to draw together into a cake. The cake is cut into thick slices, as can be seen in the first picture below on the left, which are heaped on top of each other to acidify further, until the fibrous structure has developed in the body of the cheese. Then the curd is cut up, usually mechanically, as can be seen in the second picture on the left, and cooked in hot water. This produces a cohesive, elastic, malleable dough. The dough is repeatedly drawn out into ropes and cut into suitable-sized pieces. In the first picture above, the two cheesemakers are filling a mold with such a piece. When the mixture has solidified in the mold, the cheese is removed, tied up, and immersed in a salt bath. It is then dipped in paraffin or wax if the cheese is meant to be eaten young. Provolone left to ripen longer generally does not receive this treatment. The cheeses are suspended by strings from a special apparatus to ripen. A distinction is drawn in terms of taste between the mild provolone *dolce*, a popular table cheese sold after a 2–3-month ripening period, and the considerably spicier provolone *piccante*, whose flavor, is determined not only by its longer ripening period (6–12 months), but also by the kid rennet added to the cow's milk. As can be seen in the pictures above on the right, this cheese comes in a number of very different shapes. Well known is the classic truncated cone, 14–18 inches long. Smaller cheeses in the same shape are sold under the name of Calabresi and Silani. If the cheeses are cylindrical and weigh more than 13 pounds, the Italians call them *giganti*. Smaller cylindrical shapes are also available, and are called *pancettoni*, *pancette*, or *salami*, depending on size. A spherical provolone is known as a *mandarine* or *melone*. The smaller, pear-shaped provolone with the tied-off "head", available both smoked and unsmoked, is also well known.

Provola or Cicillo

Provola is a small, spherical *pasta filata* cheese, similar to provolone, but with a slightly shorter ripening period and greater moisture content. It is made from water buffalo's milk or cow's milk, or from a mixture of the two.

Caciocavallo

A cow's-milk cheese from the south of Italy, caciocavallo is extremely popular in the south. As a table cheese it is consumed young, after a ripening period of just 2–3 months. After 6–10 months' ripening, it is used as a spicy grating cheese, like a provolone *piccante*. Caciocavallo is made like provolone. Plump to spindle-shaped, it has a thin, golden-yellow rind. Inside, it is white to yellowish in color. Caciocavallo are sold in pairs, bound together with string. In Sicily, a variation of caciocavallo is the cuboid Ragusano, named after the town of Ragusa, and once suitably ripened, used by Sicilians just like pecorino or Parmesan.

Ripened provolone The layers in the curd formed through kneading are scarcely still visible.

Provolone *piccante* After a ripening period of 6 months, it is a spicy, highly esteemed grating cheese.

Mozzarella *di bufala*. A *pasta filata* cheese made from water-buffalo milk, with a mild but distinctive flavor.

Burrata A specialty cheese from Apulia, with fresh cheese and cream between the *filata* layers.

Treccia pugliese affumicata is a firm, unusually shaped, smoked mozzarella type from Apulia.

Mozzarella

Mozzarella is one of Italy's best known *pasta filata* cheeses, if not the most famous of all. Originally made exclusively from water buffalo's milk, mozzarella was available only where these creatures were raised: in southern Latium, and in Campania and Molise. Although water buffalo herds are still found there, the amount of milk they produce falls far short of satisfying the demand for mozzarella *di bufala*, which continues to rise even though buffalo-milk mozzarella is much more expensive than the cow's-milk version. Italians pay the additional cost gladly, however, since only genuine mozzarella *di bufala* has the coveted pleasantly fresh, slightly sweetish and delicately spicy taste. A cow's-milk mozzarella, sometimes also called Bocconcino or Fior di Latte, is simply less aromatic.

Mozzarella is made in a similar way to provolone. The milk, particularly the buffalo milk, is usually processed right after the morning milking; the milk is first coagulated, and then the curd is cut into walnut-sized pieces. After the balls are cooked and shaped, they are placed in cold water for 10 minutes, to cool and firm up. Next, they go into a salt solution. Mozzarella is intended to be eaten fresh, but can be stored in brine for a couple of days. Depending on where it is produced, mozzarella is sold in different shapes, and even with additional designations or under different names, for instance, Ciliege, Nociolini, Nodini, or Ovaline. Scamorza is a slightly ripened *pasta filata* cheese from the Abruzzi made according to the mozzarella method, and it is often eaten smoked. Burrini, or Butirri, is another mozzarella-type specialty cheese in which a piece of butter is worked into the *pasta filata* curd, an old method of preserving butter in very warm places.

◀ **Ragusano** A Sicilian *pasta filata* cheese — more precisely, a caciocavallo — ripens over a long period into a good grating cheese. Even spicier is the Ragusano Pepato in the background of the picture on the left, which is studded with whole peppercorns.

▶ **Cow's-milk mozzarella** is often used as a substitute for mozzarella *di bufala*, since demand for the latter far outstrips market supply.

The pulling apart into strands, *filare* in Italian, gave this family of cheeses its name, and makes the cooked cheese curd easy to shape.

Finished Asiago wheels A semi-hard cheese from the Veneto. The main difference between the various is their fat content. Asiago is marketed with a DOC quality seal branded onto its rind.

Making Montasio The curd and whey mixture runs into a vat, where the curd is evenly spread and the whey drains off. After the curd is lightly pressed, appropriate-sized pieces are cut, placed in molds, and pressed for 24 hours. After 1–2 days in a salt bath, the cheeses are placed in the storage room to ripen further at a temperature of 57–60°F and a relative humidity of 80-85 percent.

Semi-hard or sliceable cheeses

Semi-hard, or sliceable, cheeses, are distinguished from hard cheeses by their round-hole formation. They also contain less dry matter and more moisture than had cheeses, which is why they require less ripening time. During storage, however, semi-hard cheeses can become hard cheeses or extra-hard grating cheeses, as is the case with Asiago for instance.

Asiago and Montasio

Asiago and Montasio are two similar cow's-milk cheeses, but while the former is a typical product of the Veneto region, Montasio is produced chiefly in the provinces of Udine and Gorizia. Common to both is the fact that their production is entrusted chiefly to cooperative cheese factories. There are three different types of Asiago: Asiago D'Allevo (or d'Allievo), with a medium fat content, has a reddish-yellow rind, with a light straw-colored interior interspersed with small holes. As the it ripens, the cheese becomes darker and spicier. The ripest form, the hard Asiago *piccante*, is used as a grating cheese. Asiago *pressato*, on the other hand is usually eaten fresh, at about 4 weeks old. It has a somewhat higher fat content, as well as being softer and having considerably more holes. Asiago Grasso di Monte has the highest fat content of the three. It is produced in summer from full-fat milk in the Alps of the Altopiano.

Caciotta

Caciotta refers to various soft cheeses that may differ from one another both in the type of milk used and their degree of ripeness. Caciotta is produced in

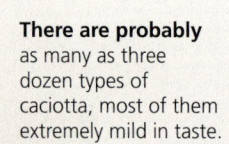

There are probably as many as three dozen types of caciotta, most of them extremely mild in taste.

A selection of the best-known semi-hard Italian cheeses (top to bottom): The cuboid **Taleggio** from northern Italy is named after the eponymous valley north of Bergamo. Traditionally, it is made from raw cow's milk, and ripens for 40-45 days in alpine-valley caves at a temperature of only 41–43°F. It has a spicy flavor and is one of the most popular cheeses in Italy, and is also exported. Another of the most popular cheeses in Italy is **Bel Paese**, which means "beautiful country," and which owes its unmistakable character to its soft, elastic, and straw-colored curd. Made in the shape of a disk, it weighs about 4½ pounds and has a delicate and slightly tart flavor. Because the original producer had the poetic name trademarked, other cheeses in this group are marketed under the name Italico. Also belonging to the group of semi-soft cheeses made from unpasteurized cow's milk is **Robiola Valsassina,** which is available in both a mild and piquant version. The one pictured on the right is a mild *tipo dolce* with a sparse red surface flora. Robiola is produced mainly in Lombardy, but also in Piedmont. Smaller versions are referred to as Robiolina. **Bambolo** is a cheese made from a mixture of cow's and sheep's milk. The impression left by the cheese mold is still visible on its surface. Generally speaking, the slightly tart-tasting Bambolo is sold after little ripening, with a hint of mold and a supple interior. **Marzolino,** a Tuscan cheese sold in small, plump wheels, is also produced from a mixture of sheep's and cow's milk, although it may also be made from sheep's milk only. Characteristic of this cheese is its light, straw-colored interior, which becomes yellower from the edge inward as it ages. Marzolino is mild to slightly piquant in taste. **Quartirolo,** a Lombardian specialty made from raw cow's milk in the area from Como to Milan, is pictured bottom right. It resembles Taleggio in structure, and is tart to aromatic and mild depending on age. The cuboid cheeses, weighing about 3 pounds, are marketed at different stages of ripeness. The one shown here is still young, and has only a light surface mold.

the main from sheep's or cow's milk, or a mixture of both; but the small, round wheels can also be made from goat's milk. Caciotta is known mainly in central Italy, and is eaten fresh or only slightly ripened.

Fontina from the Valle d'Aosta, a raw cow's-milk cheese, and the related Fontal are important in the cuisine of northern Italy. Their mild flavor means that they harmonize well with many dishes.

Montasio *fresco* (top) A raw-milk cheese that is either eaten at the age of 4 weeks, when mild and scarcely ripened; or enjoyed as **Montasio mezzano** (above) when medium-aged, after 2–4 months ripening. The one pictured here is 6 months old and is almost suitable as a piquant grating cheese.

The name **Fontina** (top) may be used in Italy only to designate a raw-milk cheese produced in the Valle d'Aosta. It has a spicy, pleasantly mild flavor and is well suited to cooking, as it melts very easily. **Fontal** (above) is made in the same style as Fontina, but from pasteurized milk. A mild table cheese, it has a white to straw-yellow curd.

Gorgonzola, a classic among blue-veined cheeses, is known worldwide. Two types are distinguished: the mild Gorgonzola *dolce*, in the foreground of the photo on the left; and the very spicy *piccante* behind it.

Blue-veined cheeses and fresh cheeses

Mold is an essential ingredient in some cheese. The mold *Penicillium gorgonzola* is deliberately added to the milk during production of Gorgonzola. Later, the wheels of cheese are pierced with needles so that the air can circulate through the channels created and mold formation will be as even as possible. The shaped, salted cheeses are still ripened in the grottos and caves of Valsassina. After 20–30 days' ripening, mold formation begins, and after another 20–30 days the Gorgonzola is ready — streaked with blue-green veins, and pleasantly spicy in taste. In addition to the two types shown here, there is also the extra mild Gorgonzola *dolcelatte*, and a version layered with mascarpone.

Fresh cheeses

"Fresh cheese" is a term applied to unripened products that are ready to eat immediately after manufacture. Among them are cottage cheese, the different types of ricotta, mascarpone (also called mascherpone), and

Panerone, also known as **Pannarone** or Gorgonzola *bianco*, is a raw-milk cheese without veining. This cheese ferments strongly during the ripening process.

Fresh table cheeses with a soft, supple interior are referred to in Italy as **Formaggini** (top), which means "little cheeses." Sometimes they are ripened for several weeks, during which time their flavor changes from tart to mild and aromatic. Also displaying this wide range of flavors is **Stracchino** (above), a fresh cheese with a delicate paste that nonetheless holds its shape. Produced in Lombardy and Piedmont, it is marketed fresh or after up to 2 weeks' ripening.

Robiola Osella (top) is a creamy, mild fresh cheese from Piedmont with a high fat content. The best-known fresh cheese of Italy, however, is **mascarpone** (above), which is made from fresh cream. It is manufactured by heating the cream to 194°F, then adding citric acid or another acid to make it curdle. Owing to its pleasantly mild flavor and its aroma of fresh milk, mascarpone is also the ideal basis for many desserts.

Ricotta production in Emilia-Romagna Ricotta is made from cow's-milk whey, to which more cow's milk is usually added. The whey and milk mixture is heated to 176–203°F to precipitate the protein, then ladled into little baskets or containers (in which the cheese is then generally sold) to drain.

robiola, which are various round cheeses with a creamy, slightly tart taste.

Ricotta

In Italian *ricotta* means "cooked again," and this is precisely the principle behind ricotta production: the whey left over from the cheesemaking process is heated and the protein contained in the whey is precipitated, producing the ricotta. Ricotta is made from both cow's-milk and sheep's-milk whey. Ricotta di Pecora can be subdivided into three types: *tipo dolce* is neither salted nor ripened; *tipo moliterno* is somewhat firmer and salted; while the *tipo forte* is ripened in wooden containers.

Goat cheeses

Goat cheeses, or *formaggi caprini*, come in firmer and softer versions. Raw, and sometimes pasteurized goat's milk is used in making them. Some sorts are made from mixtures of milk — either of cow's and goat's milk, or of cow's, sheep's, and goat's milk. Goat cheeses are produced chiefly in southern Italy and on the islands, but also in other areas where the climate or the nature of the land makes dairy farming impossible. Their manufacture lies for the most part in the hands of artisans working in fairly small businesses. Like fresh cheeses in general, goat cheeses are intended for speedy consumption, and most of it is bought where it is made. In Liguria and Piedmont, smaller goat cheeses are preserved in oil and vinegar. Riper goat cheeses usually have a yellower rind, but remain white on the inside.

These easy-going goats are superb milk producers. Goat cheese is still produced for the most part on smallholdings in the traditional manner.

Creamy, fresh goat cheese The type shown here is only lightly salted, and is mild and slightly tart tasting.

Ricotta di Pecora (top), a special fresh cheese, is produced from the whey that accumulates when sheep's-milk cheeses are made. The whitish, fine, supple curd is typical of sheep's-milk ricotta. **Ricotta di Vacca** (above), also called **Ricotta Vaccina**, on the other hand, is manufactured from the whey left over from making cow's-milk cheeses, to which more cow's milk is usually added. This fresh cheese, which is shaped in small baskets, is known chiefly in the north of Italy, while sheep's-milk ricotta is more common in the south.

Ricotta *salata* (top), is somewhat firmer than ricotta *tipo dolce*. Salt is sprinkled over the mixture while it is still in baskets; when the cheeses are removed, they are salted an additional 2-3 times. **Ricotta *salata al forno*** (above) from Sicily or Sardinia, is a salted ricotta that is baked, thereby acquiring a brown crust; sometimes it is even smoked.

Fresh goat's-milk whey Though it is not to everyone's liking, there are people who rate this completely fresh goat cheese very highly either slightly salted on a piece of bread, or sweetened and served with fruit as a dessert.

Making fresh pasta dough:

Sift 2¼ cups all-purpose flour onto a worktop, make a well in the center, and add ½ teaspoon salt, 3 eggs, and 1 tablespoon olive oil.

Using a fork or spoon, first mix the ingredients in the well together, then stir in a little flour from the edge.

Continue stirring, incorporating more and more flour from the edge, until you have a paste in the center.

Using both hands, carefully heap the remaining flour at the outside over the paste in the center.

First squeeze the flour into the paste, then work it in thoroughly with both hands.

If the dough is still too tough and crumbly, add a little water (about 1 tablespoon) so that all the flour can be worked in.

Thoroughly work in the water with both thumbs. The dough should be uniformly moist all over.

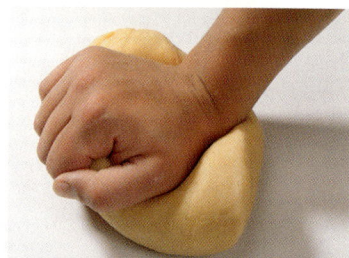

Now the actual kneading begins. Push out the dough with the heels of the hands, then form it back into a ball.

Knead until you have a smooth, firm dough. Wrap in plastic wrap, and let rest in a cool place for about 1 hour.

Making spinach dye:

Gradually process 7 oz cleaned, trimmed spinach to a smooth purée.

Place the purée in a piece of cheesecloth, and wring the juice out into a saucepan.

Heat the spinach juice to 150°F, and skim off the chlorophyll as it rises to the surface.

Homemade pasta

Once you have tasted *pasta fresca*, you'll never want to eat anything else, as the taste is heavenly. It is easy to make if you follow the simple directions. In addition to the right flour, all you need are fresh eggs, fine-grained salt, and, for the basic recipe given here, 1 tablespoon of olive oil. All ingredients should be at room temperature so that they can be worked effortlessly into a smooth, firm, even-textured dough. Also helpful when making pasta are a solid wooden board and a long rolling pin, or a pasta machine. If there is not enough room in your kitchen to lay out the finished pasta to dry, a wooden Italian pasta stand, or your own homemade construction consisting of cooking spoons laid between chairs, will solve the problem.

Making green pasta

Making homemade green pasta is not simply a matter of mixing puréed spinach into the dough, as one might assume. This would make the pasta far too wet and difficult to work with. Instead, you need to extract the chlorophyll from the spinach, as shown in the second picture sequence on page 126. You then add this dye to the well in the flour along with the eggs. Continue to make the pasta in the same way as plain fresh pasta.

Rolling out pasta dough by hand:

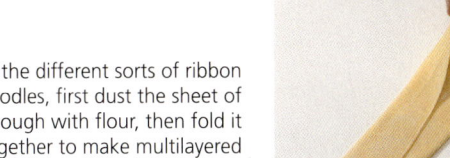

Dust the work surface with flour and roll out the dough into a sheet, rolling from the center alternately in both directions.

Cutting pasta by hand:

For the different sorts of ribbon noodles, first dust the sheet of dough with flour, then fold it together to make multilayered strips.

Rolling out pasta dough by machine:

Put the individual strips of dough through the machine's smooth rollers several times, narrowing the setting each time, until the desired thickness is achieved.

Cutting pasta by machine:

Make pappardelle and lasagnette by cutting the pasta into strips ½–¾ inch across with the appropriate attachment, then dust the noodles in flour and curl them into loose nests.

Cut tagliatelle and fettuccine ¼ inch and ⅓ inch wide, respectively. If they are not to be cooked immediately, curl them into loose nests and let dry a little.

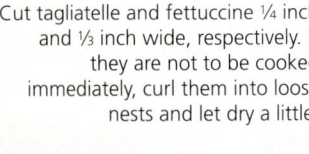

Tagliolini or taglierini are very narrow ribbon noodles. Make them using a cutting roller with a width of ⅛ inch.

For pappardelle or lasagnette, cut the dough into strips ½ ¾ inch across. Unfold immediately so they do not stick together.

For tagliatelle, cut the dough into strips ¼ inch across. Fettuccine, also called fettucce, are ⅓ inch across.

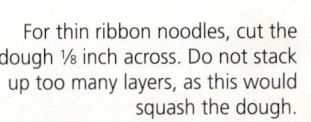

For thin ribbon noodles, cut the dough ⅛ inch across. Do not stack up too many layers, as this would squash the dough.

Cooking pasta properly

To cook your pasta properly you must have a saucepan or kettle of high quality that lies flat on the burner and is large enough to hold sufficient water. The rule of thumb is 5 cups of water to 4 ounces of pasta as a minimum. Increasing the amount of water by 25 percent is advantageous, as it makes it easier to maintain as constant a temperature as possible. You should use about 2 teaspoons of salt to 5 cups of water. Oil, however, is added to the water only in the case of large strips of pasta such as lasagne, or with fresh, thin noodles, which would otherwise stick together. The water must be at a rolling boil before you add the pasta. Long varieties of pasta such as spaghetti should be placed in the water; short noodles should be tipped in all at once. Stir briefly so that the pasta does not stick together. Now put a lid on the pot so that the water comes back to a boil quickly. As soon as this happens, either leave the pot one-third uncovered, so that the steam can escape, or else remove the lid; this uses more energy but lets you monitor the cooking process closely. Adjust the heat so that the surface of the cooking water ripples slightly, but no longer bubbles — in this way, the pasta will cook evenly at a constant temperature. Although the pasta will be moving about by itself in the cooking water, stir it from time to time with a wooden spoon or fork, so that it cooks evenly. Determining when the pasta is *al dente*, or firm to the bite, can be done only by testing. The pasta should feel soft, but offer a slight resistance when you bite it. Once this stage has been reach, tip the pasta into a colander and drain it. The pasta is now ready to serve. If the pasta is to be served as a side dish, it should be rinsed under cold running water in order to arrest the cooking process and remove the starch, which would cause it to stick together. Before serving, you can pour a little hot cooking water over it to warm it.

Tomato sauces

The most suitable tomatoes for a *sugo* are vine-ripened plum tomatoes. If fully ripened fresh ones are not available, use canned peeled Italian tomatoes. The first of the two picture sequences on this page is for a sauce made from fresh tomatoes, which really should be made only in summer from fully ripe tomatoes, since, in the absence of both onions and garlic, the tomato flavor is of paramount importance. If no first-class tomatoes are available, follow the second recipe on this page shown on the right. This puréed sauce can be used as the basis of many other *sughi*, or sauces, and, once made, keeps for several days in the refrigerator. In Italy, the tomato crop is frequently turned into such *sughi*, which are packed into jars and then sterilized, providing the household with adequate supplies for the entire winter. In this way, there is no need to forgo the delicious flavor of tomatoes out of season.

Making fresh tomato sauce:

Finely dice the flesh of 1¾ lb fully ripe, peeled tomatoes. Wash 20 basil leaves, drain well, and tear up coarsely. Melt ½ cup butter in a stew pan and briefly sweat the tomatoes. Simmer for several minutes. Season with salt and freshly ground pepper. Lastly, stir in the fresh basil and serve the *sugo* immediately. If you prefer, this sauce can be made with olive oil instead of butter.

Preparing a basic tomato sauce:

Wash and core 1¾ lb ripe plum tomatoes. Using a sharp knife, quarter the tomatoes, then cut them into small pieces.

Tip the tomatoes and ½ cup finely diced carrot into a saucepan. It is important for the tomatoes to be on the bottom of the pot, since they will exude liquid.

Add 1 cup each diced onion and celery. Cover the pan, and simmer on a low heat until soft, about 40 minutes.

Transfer the vegetable mixture to a large-mesh strainer in batches, and press through with the back of a tablespoon.

At first, the sauce will be quite thin, so scrape all the pulp from the strainer and add it to the sauce. Pour the sauce into a pot.

Heat the sauce, then season with 1 teaspoon salt and ground pepper. Add 4 tablespoons extra-virgin olive oil to the sauce a tablespoonful at a time, stirring to blend after each addition. Stir in 1 tablespoon chopped basil.

Bolognese meat sauce
This *ragù bolognese* is perhaps the most famous of all the Italian pasta sauces with meat

In Bologna, ragù is often served with homemade fresh tagliatelle, while in many other places it is usually eaten with spaghetti.

Gigina's, 1 via Stendhal, Bologna, serves a superb-tasting *ragù bolognese*. The eponymous chef prepares big pots of the sauce fresh daily. Fine quality ingredients are essential, of course, beginning with the choice of meat, which ideally should be bought in one piece and put through the grinder oneself. Whether beef or pork should predominate, or even lamb should be included, is a question of personal taste, as is the addition of ½ cup of red wine. What is important, though, is to simmer the sauce for a sufficient length of time, to give the flavors a chance to blend thoroughly.

Serves 4
8 oz prosciutto
2 x 14-oz cans whole tomatoes
10 oz round of beef, 7 oz boneless pork
¼ cup olive oil, 1¼ cups finely diced carrot
1¾ cups finely diced yellow onion
2 garlic cloves, finely chopped
1½ cups finely diced celery
¼ cup chopped parsley, 6 tablespoons butter
1¾ lb fresh tomatoes, peeled, seeded, and diced
6 tablespoons tomato paste, 1 cup meat stock
1 teaspoon salt
freshly ground pepper, ½ teaspoon sugar (optional)

Finely dice the prosciutto. Dice the canned tomatoes, draining and reserving the juice, and set aside. Grind the beef and pork. Heat the oil, sweat the carrots, and proceed as shown in the picture sequence below and to the right.

Add the ground beef and pork and brown lightly, stirring and breaking up the meat until crumbly.

Add the prosciutto to the meat and vegetable mixture, and cook 5 minutes, stirring constantly.

Add half of the butter, followed by the fresh tomatoes.

Add the canned tomatoes and stir all the ingredients together thoroughly. Simmer briefly, uncovered.

Add the tomato paste a tablespoonful at a time, stir in carefully, then simmer a little to reduce the sauce slightly.

Pour in the meat stock, season, and simmer gently for 1 hour, leaving the pot slightly uncovered.

Add the onions and garlic to the carrots and sweat, stirring.

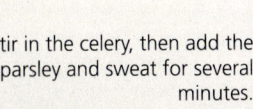
Stir in the celery, then add the parsley and sweat for several minutes.

Pesto and co.
Here, herbs or olives season the sauce; there, cheese adds the piquant note

The following two recipes are not so much sauces in the literal sense as spicy pastes, which are always used at room temperature. Sometimes they can be so concentrated that they have to be mixed with a few spoonfuls of pasta cooking water to achieve a saucelike consistency. This is true for *pesto alla genovese*, a Ligurian specialty that has become famous far beyond the boundaries of its native province.

PESTO

To improve the shelf life of pesto, do not add the grated cheese to the mixture, but sprinkle it over the pasta just before serving.

Makes about 2 cups
4 garlic cloves, coarsely chopped
⅓ cup pine nuts
2½ cups fresh basil leaves, snipped or cut into fine strips
½ cup freshly grated pecorino cheese
¾ cup freshly grated Parmesan cheese
pepper, salt to taste
½–⅔ cup extra-virgin olive oil

Making pesto:

Using a mortar and pestle, pound the garlic with the pine nuts. Add the basil and crush to a fine paste.

Add the grated cheese gradually, working each addition in carefully. Season with pepper, adding salt only if necessary.

Add the oil in a thin trickle, as if making mayonnaise, and stir well so that it blends the herb mixture.

TAPENADE

Tapenade, a blend of olives and anchovies, makes a tasty sauce for pasta and can be used unthinned as a spicy topping for *crostini* or toasted bread. With very few ingredients, you can conjure up one of the Mediterranean's most delicious spicy sauces. You do, however, need a little patience, since the garlic oil needs to cool before you proceed with the recipe.

Makes about 1¼ cups
3 garlic cloves, finely chopped
½ cup extra-virgin olive oil
⅔ cup black olives, pitted and chopped
2 anchovy fillets, finely chopped
salt, freshly ground pepper

SAUCE MORNAY

Coating a dish with béchamel sauce, scattering grated cheese over the top, and baking it in the oven until the cheese is melted and bubbling produces a delicate, golden-brown crust. Stirring grated cheese directly into the hot béchamel sauce, rather than sprinkling it on top of the dish, gives you a Sauce Mornay, which owes its spiciness to the cheese. In this recipe two cheeses, fontina and Parmesan, are used. The sauce can also be made with just one type of cheese, as long as it is not an extra-hard variety, such as Parmesan. Though sufficiently spicy, Parmesan is too low in fat to impart the desired creaminess to the sauce.

Makes about 2¼ cups
2 tablespoons butter, ¼ cup flour
2¼ cups milk, white pepper, salt
freshly grated nutmeg, 1 egg yolk, ½ cup heavy cream
You will also need:
¼ cup each freshly grated Parmesan and fontina cheese
1–2 tablespoons whipped cream

Preparing a sauce Mornay:

Melt the butter in a saucepan, add the flour, and cook, stirring, for 1–2 minutes without browning.

Pour in the milk, whisk until smooth, and season to taste with the salt, pepper, and nutmeg. Simmer for 20 minutes, stirring constantly.

Making tapenade:

Sweat the garlic in half of the oil. Strain the oil and leave to cool.

Whisk together the egg yolk and cream. Remove the saucepan from the heat and add the egg–cream mixture.

Bring the sauce to a boil, stirring. Strain, then heat through again.

Using a mortar and pestle, pound the olives, anchovies, and remaining oil to a fine paste.

Gradually stir the cooled garlic oil into the olive and anchovy mixture. Season with salt and pepper.

Stir the cheeses into the sauce until melted. Only then fold in the whipped cream.

Buckwheat pasta dough
Sift the buckwheat and wheat flours together into a bowl and mix with salt. Stir in the water quickly and briskly with a fork.

Pizzoccheri

Robust-tasting noodles made from a mixture of buckwheat and wheat flours are a specialty of the southern side of the Alps

Buckwheat (*Fagopyrum esculentum*) is not actually a cereal grain, but its ground seeds are used in the same way. Rich in protein, vitamins, and minerals, this member of the knotgrass family is popular in the United States and Canada, but it has fallen into oblivion throughout large parts of Europe. In Italy, there are only a few areas where it is still used. Buckwheat flour contains no gluten, which is why wheat flour must always be added to buckwheat pasta doughs.

BUCKWHEAT PASTA

When preparing the dough, it is important to sift both kinds of flour together, so that they are evenly mixed and properly aerated. The water can then be worked into the flour quickly, thus avoiding the formation of any hard lumps. If, contrary to expectations, the dough turns out tough and crumbly, work in an egg.

Makes about 1 lb
2½ cups buckwheat flour
1¼ cups all-purpose flour
½ teaspoon salt, 1¼ cups water

Prepare the dough as shown in the picture sequence on the left. Start by mixing the buckwheat flour and the all-purpose flour together.

PIZZOCCHERI WITH SAGE

Instead of casera, the cheese traditionally used in this recipe, another "mountain" cheese can be used, although a mixture of equal quantities of delicate fontina and spicy Gruyère would make a good substitute too.

As soon as the water is absorbed, place the paste on a floured work surface and knead into a smooth dough.

Divide the dough into 4 equal pieces. Roll out each piece into a disk ⅛ inch thick, dusting it frequently with flour while rolling.

Dust the disks with buckwheat flour and let them dry slightly. To make noodles, cut the first disk into strips 2 inches wide.

Stack the cut strips on top of each other so that the edges are flush. Then cut the strips across into short noodles about ¼ inch wide.

Place the cut noodles on a clean dish towel. Cut the remaining disks into noodles in the same way.

Since *grano saraceno*, as buckwheat is called in Italy, contains no gluten, this pasta dough is made with buckwheat and wheat flours in a ratio of 1:2.

Serves 4

1 recipe buckwheat pasta dough (see p. 134)
8 oz potatoes, peeled and cut into ½-inch cubes
8 oz Swiss chard leaves, cut into strips
¾ cup butter
2 garlic cloves, thinly sliced
8 sage leaves,
12 oz casera cheese, cut into ½-inch cubes
1 cup freshly grated Parmesan cheese

Hearty enjoyment is promised by this traditionally meatless, yet very nourishing dish from the Italian Alps.

Prepare a batch of noodles according to the recipe on page 134. Bring plenty of salted water to a boil, add the potatoes, and cook for 10 minutes. Add the noodles and cook for 8–10 minutes. Finally, add the Swiss chard and cook for 2 minutes, then drain.

Melt the butter, sweat the garlic until lightly colored, and add the sage leaves. Transfer half of the noodle-and-potato mixture to a bowl, arrange the cubes of cheese on top, and cover with the remaining noodle-and-potato mixture. Pour the sage butter over the top, sprinkle with Parmesan, and serve.

Simple pasta dishes with bacon

With air-dried pancetta and a little spicy cheese, well-flavored pasta dishes can be conjured up almost effortlessly

The *chitarra* is a wooden frame strung with wires that resemble the strings of a guitar. The sheet of dough is laid on top of the wires, and a rolling pin is rolled over the top, cutting the noodles.

Pasta, pancetta, and Parmesan: These three complementary ingredients even sound good together. Of course, the best results will be achieved by making the pasta yourself, by always freshly grating the cheese yourself, and by taking care to buy genuine air-dried Italian pancetta.

SPAGHETTI ALLA CHITARRA

This spaghetti, with its square cross section, is made on a special cutting device called the *chitarra* ("guitar"), from which it gets its name. To make this type of spaghetti fresh without the aid of a *chitarra*, you can cut it by hand with a knife. Some pasta machines also have the appropriate attachment. You might find dried *spaghetti alla chitarra* in an Italian delicatessen, or you can use ordinary spaghetti.

Serves 4
1 lb spaghetti alla chitarra
For the sauce:
8 oz pancetta, ¼ cup olive oil

Pancetta and tomatoes set the tone in this very simple pasta dish, which is especially delicate tasting prepared with homemade spaghetti. The whole is rounded out with spicy pecorino cheese and a couple of basil leaves.

1 onion, sliced into rings
2¼ lb ripe plum tomatoes, peeled, seeded, and diced
salt, freshly ground pepper
You will also need:
1 cup freshly grated pecorino cheese
30 small basil leaves

To make the sauce, cut the pancetta first into slices, and then into short strips. Heat the olive oil in a saucepan and sweat the pancetta and the onion until lightly colored. Add the tomatoes, reduce the heat, cover the pan, and simmer for 15 minutes. Remove the lid and simmer the sauce for a further 45 minutes. Season with salt and pepper.

Cook the spaghetti in briskly boiling salted water for 8–10 minutes, until *al dente*. Drain, and mix immediately with some of the sauce. Serve the pasta on warmed plates, spooning over the rest of the sauce. Sprinkle with the grated pecorino and serve garnished with basil leaves.

SPAGHETTI ALLA CARBONARA

Opinions differ as to who actually invented this pasta dish, the classic version of which is always made with spaghetti, bacon, and a cheese-and-egg sauce. Some people interpret the name of the dish as "spaghetti cooked over a charcoal burner," but that does not explain its origins. In the opinion of one Italian researcher, this specialty was developed towards the end of the Second World War when American GIs stationed in Rome brought some eggs and bacon to the Italian friends they had made there and asked them to cook them something. Whatever the truth of this story, everyone agrees that this delicious dish is a Roman specialty. Romans make spaghetti carbonara with smoked bacon, or with the milder flavored salted bacon, *guanciale*, and in some cases with lightly smoked pig's cheek. You can, of course, also make it with pancetta. Experiment to discover which type of bacon is most to your liking. The important thing is to season the eggs generously with pepper and whisk them with the cheese while the spaghetti is cooking, so that the resulting sauce can be added to the pasta as soon as it has been drained and is still hot.

Serves 4
1 garlic clove, unpeeled
2 tablespoons olive oil
8 oz pancetta, finely diced
4 eggs
¾ cup freshly grated Parmesan cheese
1 lb spaghetti
salt, freshly ground pepper
2 tablespoons chopped parsley (optional)

Lightly bruise the unpeeled garlic clove with the flat of a knife blade so that the skin splits slightly, and proceed as shown in the first two steps of the picture sequence below.

Bring some lightly salted water to a boil in a large pot. Add the spaghetti and cook for 8–10 minutes, until *al dente*. Drain the pasta in a colander and return to the pot. Finish making the dish as shown in the last picture below. After the sauce has been stirred in, arrange the spaghetti carbonara on warmed plates and serve immediately.

Heat the olive oil in a saucepan and fry the pancetta and garlic until the pancetta is crispy and browned.

Break the eggs into a large bowl. Add the cheese and whisk vigorously. Season with salt and pepper.

Mix the spaghetti with the pancetta and with the parsley, if using. Remove the pot from the heat, add the egg and cheese mixture, and mix thoroughly.

Hot and spicy

Depending on the number of *peperoncini* used, the heat index of these dishes ranges from pleasantly piquant to hellishly hot

That even dishes consisting of the simplest ingredients can taste superb if properly prepared is proved yet again by the following three recipes, which are all quick and easy.

PENNE ALL' ARRABIATA

Serves 4

4 oz pancetta, 1 lb ripe plum tomatoes
2 teaspoons butter, ½ cup finely chopped onion
2 garlic cloves, finely sliced
2 red chile peppers
1 lb penne rigate
½ cup freshly grated Parmesan cheese
1 small bunch flat-leaf parsley, cut into thin strips
salt, freshly ground white pepper

Slice the pancetta into thin strips. Peel and dice the tomatoes, and push them through a strainer. Bring plenty of salted water to a boil in a large pot, add the pasta, and cook for about 8 minutes, until *al dente*. Meanwhile, prepare the sauce. Melt the butter in a skillet, and briefly sweat the onion, garlic, and whole chile peppers. Stir in the strained tomatoes, simmer briefly over a low heat, and season with salt and pepper. Drain the pasta and mix with the sauce, fishing out the chile peppers. Sprinkle with Parmesan cheese and parsley, and serve.

SPAGHETTI CON AGLIO, OLIO E PEPERONCINO

The following version of this famous recipe is fairly innocuous in terms of heat. If you like it hotter, simply increase the number of chile peppers.

Serves 4

1 lb spaghetti, ¼ cup olive oil
3 garlic cloves, halved
1 dried chile pepper
1 tablespoon finely chopped flat-leaf parsley
salt, freshly ground white pepper
Parmesan cheese (optional)

Cook the spaghetti in plenty of boiling salted water for 8–10 minutes, until *al dente*. Meanwhile, heat the oil in a large skillet and sweat the garlic and chile pepper over a low heat. Drain the spaghetti thoroughly. Remove the garlic and chile pepper from

Hot, hotter, hottest Whether in Penne all' Arrabiata (above) or Spaghetti con Aglio e Olio (below), the little red chile peppers certainly pack a punch!

the oil, and reserve. Sprinkle the parsley into the oil, add to the spaghetti and mix well. Season with salt and pepper. Arrange the spaghetti on warmed plates, garnish with the garlic and chile pepper, sprinkle with a little freshly grated Parmesan cheese if wished, and serve at once.

SPAGHETTINI WITH CAPER SAUCE

The distinctive flavor of capers harmonizes well with garlic and olives. All the ingredients in this pasta sauce, which can easily take a bit of heat, originate in southern Italy.

Serves 4
3 heaping tablespoons salted capers
½ cup black olives
12 anchovy fillets in salt
6 tablespoons olive oil
2 garlic cloves, finely chopped
2 shallots, finely chopped
1 lb ripe plum tomatoes, peeled, seeded, and diced
2 large red chile peppers, seeded and finely chopped
1 teaspoon salt, 1 lb spaghettini
You will also need:
2 oz aged pecorino cheese, freshly shaved

Tip the capers into a strainer and shake off the salt. Pit the olives and chop finely with the capers. Soak the anchovy fillets in water for a few minutes, then drain and cut into small pieces.

Heat the olive oil in a skillet and sweat the garlic and shallots until lightly colored. Add the capers, olives, and anchovies, and sweat for 2–3 minutes, stirring constantly. Add the tomatoes and chile peppers, and braise all the ingredients for a further 15 minutes.

Meanwhile, cook the spaghettini in briskly boiling, lightly salted water until *al dente*. Drain the pasta and mix with the sauce. Arrange the spaghettini on warmed plates, sprinkle with shaved pecorino, and serve at once.

Only capers preserved in salt are suitable for this sauce; capers pickled in vinegar would completely change the character of the dish.

Garganelli in brodo
Served *con rigaglie*, with a ragout made from the giblets of a guinea hen

At the Palazzo Tesorieri in Bagnacavallo, all the necessary components of this simple yet refined dish are prepared fresh. These are, firstly, a good, substantial chicken broth, which needs to simmer for a long time: two-and-a-half hours is about right for it to contribute sufficient flavor to the dish, the success of which stands or falls with the broth. Next come the garganelli, the fresh, homemade tubular pasta "turned" from flat squares of dough. Last, but not least, is a ragout made from the giblets of guinea hens. If these variety meats do not appeal, however, the ragout can be prepared instead with the meat of a guinea hen or another fowl, cut into small pieces. Take the time to follow the recipe below carefully and you will be rewarded with a light, eminently digestible, and splendid pasta dish.

Serves 4
For the chicken broth:
1 boiling fowl weighing 3 lb
1 lb veal bones, cut in pieces
10 peppercorns
1 garlic clove, unpeeled and bruised
1 small onion studded with 2 cloves
For the bouquet garni:
1 carrot, 1 young leek, 1 celery stalk
1 bay leaf, 1 thyme sprig
3 parsley stalks
For the pasta dough:
2½ cups all-purpose flour
2 eggs, 4 egg yolks, ⅓ teaspoon salt
For the guinea-hen ragout:
7 oz guinea-hen giblets
2 tablespoons olive oil
½ cup finely chopped onion
1 garlic clove, finely chopped
salt, freshly ground pepper
⅓ cup white wine

Rinse the boiling fowl thoroughly inside and out under cold running water, and cut into quarters. Place the fowl and the veal bones in a pot with hot water to cover. Bring to a boil, skimming off the foam that rises to the surface. Pour off the water, then rinse the chicken and the veal bones with warm water. Cover with fresh water, bring back to a boil, and skim again.

After skimming twice, bring the chicken to a boil with 9 cups of water, turn down the heat to low, and keep just below boiling point. Tie the ingredients for the bouquet garni together with string. After 1½ hours, add the bouquet garni, peppercorns, garlic, and onion to the pot, topping up with a little water if necessary.

Cook for 1 hour more, lift out the chicken quarters and reserving the meat for another use. Pour the broth through a strainer lined with a dish towel into a saucepan, and let cool. Using a pancake turner, skim the fat from the surface of the cooled broth and discard.

In the meantime, make the dough for the garganelli. Sift the flour onto a work surface and make a well in the center. Add the eggs, egg yolks, and salt to the well and stir together with a little flour from the sides. Knead the ingredients to a smooth dough, wrap in plastic wrap, and rest in the refrigerator for 1 hour. Form the pasta dough into garganelli, as shown in the first four photos of the picture sequence on the right, and leave for a little while to dry out slightly before cooking.

To make the ragout, remove any sinews and fat from the giblets, then wash, pat dry, and dice finely.

Meanwhile, reheat the chicken broth. In a separate saucepan, bring plenty of salted water to a boil; add the pasta, cook until *al dente*, and drain.

Finish preparing the ragout. Heat the oil in a saucepan and sweat the onion and garlic until lightly colored. Add the giblets, and fry for 1–2 minutes. Deglaze with the white wine, simmer for 1 minute, and season with salt and pepper.

Drain the pasta. Ladle the broth into warmed soup plates, add the garganelli, top each portion with 2 spoonfuls of ragout, and serve at once.

Roll out the dough for the garganelli with a long rolling pin.

Roll out the sheet of dough thinly, then cut into 2-inch squares.

Wrap these around a wooden dowel ¼ inch in diameter, and roll over a grooved board.

Carefully pull out the dowel without pressing the pasta together.

The hand-turned, hollow pasta shapes are served in the hot chicken stock with a little ragout.

Fettucine with white truffles
Homemade noodles with wafer-thin shavings of white truffles make this a truly luxurious dish

Even with nothing but butter and plenty of freshly grated cheese, fettucine make a special meal. The addition of this most expensive of all truffles, however, transforms the pasta into an exquisite delicacy. The extremely strong flavor of the white truffle is, admittedly, not to everyone's taste, but once you have succumbed to the scent and taste of the coveted *tartufi*, you will not be deterred by their steep cost, and will look forward to treating yourself to this dish every year during the truffle season, in the late fall and winter.

Wafer-thin slices of truffle are shaved over the fettucine. Ideally, this task is performed with a special truffle shaver. It is difficult to give exact quantities for the truffle — it is largely a matter of cost — but a few slivers per portion should be about right.

Judging truffle quality from the outside is not easy. Tartufi should feel heavy for their size and firm, never spongy. Ask for larger specimens to be cut in half crosswise for inspection, as these sinfully expensive fungi are not infrequently full of maggots.

Serves 4
For the pasta dough:
2½ cups all-purpose flour, 2 eggs, 4 egg yolks
⅓ teaspoon salt, 1 tablespoon water as needed
For the sauce:
1 cup light cream
2 red chile peppers, seeded and cut into thin strips
1 teaspoon truffle oil
salt, freshly ground white pepper
You will also need:
about 2 oz white truffle
1 tablespoon basil, snipped or sliced in thin strips
freshly grated Parmesan cheese (optional)

Heap the flour onto a work surface and make a well in the center. Add the eggs, egg yolks, and salt to the well, and mix with a fork, working in the flour from the edges. If the dough is too firm, add up to 1 tablespoon water. Knead by hand to a smooth dough, roll into a ball, wrap in plastic wrap, and rest in the refrigerator for 1 hour.

Using a pasta machine, roll out the dough to the desired thickness and cut into fettucine about ⅛-inch wide. Leave the noodles to dry out slightly.

Pour the cream into a saucepan and reduce by half, then lower the heat and stir in the chile strips and the truffle oil. Season with salt and white pepper.

Just before you are ready to shave the truffle, brush it very briefly under cold running water and dry it immediately; under no circumstances must it absorb any water. Remove any ingrained dirt or damage with the point of a sharp knife, taking care not to waste any of this expensive delicacy.

Cook the fettucine in briskly boiling salted water until *al dente*, then drain well. Arrange the pasta on warmed plates, pour over the sauce, and shave wafer-thin slices of truffle over the top. Sprinkle with basil and Parmesan, if using, and serve at once.

With pumpkin and zucchini

Whether black spaghetti *alla chitarra*, or tortelli, ravioli's round cousin, pasta tastes simply wonderful with squash

SQUID-INK PASTA WITH ZUCCHINI

This distinctive pasta dish needs nothing else except perhaps a glass of dry white wine to accompany it — perhaps a Pinot Grigio or a Vermentino from Liguria.

Serves 4
For the black pasta dough:
2½ cups all-purpose flour
2 eggs, 1 tablespoon olive oil, ½ teaspoon salt
4 teaspoons liquid, or 1 tablespoon dried, squid ink
For the tomato sauce:
1¼ lb ripe tomatoes, ⅓ cup finely chopped onion
1 garlic clove, finely chopped
2 tablespoons olive oil
salt, freshly ground pepper
You will also need:
10 oz zucchini, 2–3 tablespoons olive oil
1 tablespoon basil, snipped or sliced in strips
a few whole basil leaves
salt, freshly ground pepper

Sift the flour onto a work surface and make a well in the center. Add the eggs, oil, salt, and squid ink to the well, and stir with a fork, gradually working in more and more flour from the sides. Using both hands and working from the outside inwards, work in the remaining flour. If this becomes difficult, add a little water. Knead the pasta dough until it is smooth and firm, then roll it into a ball, wrap in plastic wrap, and rest in the refrigerator for 1 hour.

To make the sauce, peel and seed the tomatoes. Strain the seeds and reserve the juices. Dice the tomato flesh. Heat the oil in a saucepan and sweat the onion and garlic without letting them color. Add the tomatoes and sweat briefly, then season with salt and pepper. Pour in the reserved tomato juices, and simmer the sauce for 10 minutes.

Meanwhile, wash the zucchini and cut lengthwise into ⅛-inch-thick slices. Halve the zucchini slices lengthwise again. Heat the oil in a skillet, salt and pepper the zucchini, and brown briefly on both sides.

Using a pasta machine, roll out the dough to the desired thickness, then cut into square spaghetti. Cook in boiling salted water until *al dente*, then drain well. Arrange the spaghetti on warmed plates with the zucchini, spoon on the tomato sauce, sprinkle with the basil strips, and garnish with whole basil leaves.

TORTELLI WITH PUMPKIN STUFFING

With their piquant filling, these round dough pockets should win over even those who think that pumpkin is suitable only for pie.

Serves 4
For the pasta dough:
1¼ cups all-purpose flour, 1 cup cornmeal
2 eggs, 3 egg yolks, 1 tablespoon olive oil
½ teaspoon salt, freshly grated nutmeg
For the stuffing:
2 oz amaretti, 1¾ cups pumpkin purée (see p. 242)
1¾ cups freshly grated Parmesan cheese
salt, freshly ground white pepper
1 egg white
You will also need:
1½-inch round cutter
a little freshly ground pepper
6 tablespoons butter, 1 handful sage leaves

Sift the flour and cornmeal onto a work surface, make a well in the center, and pour in the remaining ingredients for the dough. Proceed as shown in the first picture on the right. Using your hands, work in the flour from the outside inwards, then knead to a smooth dough with the heels of your hands. Roll the dough into a ball, wrap in plastic wrap, and rest in the refrigerator for about 1 hour. Place the amaretti in a bag and crush them with a rolling pin. In a bowl, stir together the pumpkin, amaretti, and Parmesan, then season with salt and pepper. Mix well, then spoon the mixture into a pastry bag with a round tip. Using a pasta machine, roll out the dough to the desired thickness as shown on the right. Mark circles on half of the pasta sheets with the cutter, and proceed as shown below.

The dough for the tortelli is rolled out in the pasta machine to the desired thickness. It should not be too thin, however, or it might tear.

Stir the ingredients in the well with a fork, working in more and more flour from the sides.

Pipe a blob of filling in the center of each circle. Brush the surrounding dough with egg white.

Lay a second sheet of dough on top of the pumpkin mounds, and gently but firmly press down the dough in between.

Cut out circles with the cutter. Press the edges together well to seal in the filling.

Cook the tortelli in briskly boiling salted water. They are done as soon as they rise to the surface.

Spoon the well-drained tortelli onto plates, grind over some pepper, and drizzle with lightly browned sage butter.

A light, summery pasta dish, which beckons appetizingly from the plate. The fruity red tomato sauce is not only visually attractive, but also harmonizes brilliantly with the taste of the squid-ink pasta.

Tortelli with oxtail stuffing

One of the very finest fall recipes: homemade pasta with a delicious, delicate stuffing, topped off with fresh chanterelles

Making your own *pasta ripiena*, or stuffed pasta, is somewhat time-consuming, but worth the effort. For this recipe, you'll also have to allow a couple of hours to make the stuffing, since the oxtail must be braised in the oven until tender before you can proceed. Your labors will be rewarded with a true delicacy.

Serves 6–8
For the dough:
2½ cups all-purpose flour
2 eggs, 4 egg yolks, ⅓ teaspoon salt
For the stuffing:
1 garlic clove, unpeeled
3 celery stalks, 2 small leeks
1 oxtail weighing about 3½ lb
¼ cup vegetable oil
¾ cup diced carrot, ¼ cup diced parsley root
5 juniper berries, 1 bay leaf, 5 sage leaves
2 tablespoons tomato paste, 2¼ cups Chianti
1 tablespoon flour
1 tablespoon chopped herbs (parsley and lovage)
1 egg yolk
salt, freshly ground pepper
You will also need:
egg white
1 lb chanterelle mushrooms, 3 tablespoons butter
salt, 2 tablespoons chopped parsley

To make the dough, sift the flour onto a work surface and make a well in the center. Add the eggs, egg yolks, and salt to the well. Stir the ingredients in the well with a fork, then gradually mix in more and more flour from the sides. Knead to a smooth dough. Roll into a ball, wrap in plastic wrap, and rest in the refrigerator for about 1 hour.

To make the stuffing, bruise the garlic clove with the flat of a knife blade. Trim the vegetables. Cut the celery into small disks and the leek into thin rings.

Preheat the oven to 350°F. Prepare the oxtail as shown in the first three pictures on the right. Cover

A chanterelle sauce, spooned over the tortelli just before serving, rounds out the dish beautifully. Make sure you try this recipe sometime during the mushroom season.

A dry Chianti makes a splendid foil for the oxtail stuffing, and is just the right partner for the hearty, spicy tortelli.

Heat the oil in a roasting pan and sear the oxtail sections. Add the garlic and all the vegetables.

After about 10 minutes, add the juniper berries, bay leaf, sage leaves, and tomato paste. Pour in the red wine.

After about 2 hours, take out the oxtail pieces, which should be meltingly tender. Remove the meat from the bones and chop finely.

Strain the sauce, pressing down lightly on the vegetables so that some vegetable purée is forced through into the sauce.

Distribute the stuffing evenly at well-spaced intervals over one sheet of thinly rolled-out dough. Brush some egg white on the dough around each portion of stuffing.

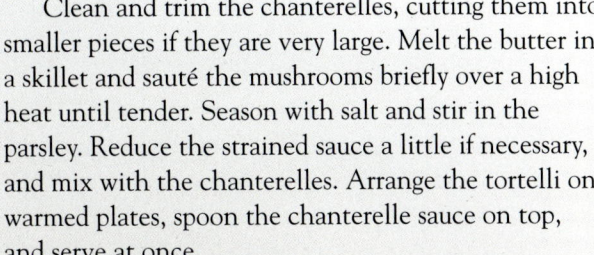

Lay the second sheet of dough on top. Cut out tortelli using a fluted 2¼-inch round cutter.

Locate the joints in the oxtail by feeling with your fingers, then cut across into its natural sections (or ask the butcher to do this). Season with salt and pepper.

the roasting pan and place in the oven for about 2 hours, stirring occasionally. Halfway through the cooking time, dust the meat with the flour.

Follow the directions in the fourth and fifth pictures. Mix the finely chopped meat with the herbs and the egg yolk. Add a few spoonfuls of the sauce to moisten the stuffing.

Divide the dough in half, and roll out both pieces into thin sheets on a lightly floured surface. Prepare the tortelli as shown in the last two steps on the right. Cook in briskly boiling salted water until they rise to the surface, then lift out with a slotted spoon and keep warm.

Clean and trim the chanterelles, cutting them into smaller pieces if they are very large. Melt the butter in a skillet and sauté the mushrooms briefly over a high heat until tender. Season with salt and stir in the parsley. Reduce the strained sauce a little if necessary, and mix with the chanterelles. Arrange the tortelli on warmed plates, spoon the chanterelle sauce on top, and serve at once.

With tomato and eggplant

Light vegetarian fare: pasta and vegetables *au gratin*, and pasta mixed with vegetable sauce

Drizzle this delicate vegetable gratin with melted butter from time to time as it bakes to give it an appetizing, shiny crust.

VEGETABLES AND PASTA AU GRATIN

Serves 4
10 oz tubular pasta (pennoni, rigatoni, macaroni)
For the vegetables:
¼ cup olive oil, ½ cup finely chopped onion
1 garlic clove, finely chopped
9 oz eggplant, unpeeled and diced
7 oz zucchini, thinly sliced; 2 celery stalks, sliced
10 oz tomatoes, peeled, seeded, and diced
1 teaspoon chopped thyme, 1 teaspoon chopped sage
½ teaspoon salt, freshly ground black pepper
½ cup dry red wine
For the cheese sauce:
1 cup freshly grated pecorino (sardo or toscano)
1 cup light cream, 3 egg yolks
1 tablespoon chopped herbs (parsley, marjoram, rosemary)
salt, freshly ground pepper, freshly grated nutmeg
You will also need:
¼ cup butter, melted

Heat the oil in a large skillet and sweat the onion and garlic until lightly colored. Add the eggplant, zucchini, and celery, and stir-fry over a high heat for 4–5 minutes. Add the tomatoes, seasonings, and wine. Stew uncovered over a fairly high heat until the vegetables are tender and the wine is reduced by half.

Cook the pasta in briskly boiling salted water until *al dente*, then drain and mix with the vegetables. Butter a gratin dish and spoon in the mixture.

In addition to the tubular pasta, both of these recipes require top-quality fresh vegetables. It is the flavor of the tomatoes, above all, that determines the success of both dishes.

Pasta alla Norma An opera by Vincenzo Bellini was the inspiration for the name of this dish, which is also called pasta catanese alla Norma after Catania, the home town of the composer.

Preheat the oven to 400°F. Mix together the cheese, cream, and egg yolks. Add the herbs, salt, pepper, and nutmeg. Spoon the cheese sauce evenly over the pasta. Place the gratin dish in the oven and bake for 20–25 minutes, every so often drizzling the dish with melted butter while it bakes.

PASTA ALLA NORMA

Serves 4

1 lb penne rigate, 1 lb eggplant

For the tomato sauce:

5 tablespoons olive oil, ½ cup finely chopped onion

2 garlic cloves, finely chopped

2½ lb plum tomatoes, peeled, seeded, and diced

salt, freshly ground pepper

You will also need:

fresh basil leaves, ¾ cup freshly grated pecorino cheese

Heat ¼ cup olive oil in a large saucepan, and sweat the onions and garlic until lightly colored. Stir in the tomatoes, season with salt and pepper, and simmer until the liquid is almost completely evaporated.

Slice the eggplant into ½-inch-thick rounds and season with salt and pepper. Heat the remaining oil in a skillet and fry the eggplant on both sides until crisp and brown.

Cook the penne rigate in briskly boiling salted water until *al dente*, drain, and mix with the tomato sauce. Spoon the pasta and eggplant onto warmed plates, sprinkle with basil and pecorino, and serve.

Bucatini ai carciofi
Tubular pasta with baby artichokes, a typical dish from southern Italy

Bucatini look like thick spaghetti, except that they are hollow in the middle. (Hence, their name, derived from *buca*, the Italian word for "hole.") This means that they are easier to cook, as well as cooking more quickly. In addition to good artichokes, you will need a superb oil for this dish: a cold-pressed extra-virgin olive oil. Olive oil is sometimes stored in small cans; the one shown above is a modern version of the traditional Italian oil can.

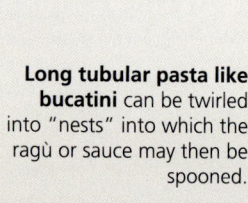

Long tubular pasta like bucatini can be twirled into "nests" into which the ragù or sauce may then be spooned.

Artichokes, the unopened flower buds of a thistle-like plant, are one of the most popular vegetables in southern Italy. With their slightly bitter flavor, the tender bottoms of the large artichokes and the hearts of the small ones are an ingredient in many dishes.

Serves 4
10 oz bucatini
For the artichokes:
12 small artichokes, juice of 1 lemon, ½ teaspoon salt
For the tomato sauce:
2 tablespoons olive oil
¾ cup finely chopped onion
1 garlic clove, finely chopped
1¼ lb tomatoes, peeled, seeded, and diced
½ cup diced carrot, ½ cup diced celery
½ cup vegetable broth, salt, freshly ground pepper
You will also need:
fresh thyme leaves

Cut off the stem of the artichokes right below the flower head, and strip away the small, tough leaves around the base of the stem. Snip off the tips of the outer leaves with kitchen scissors, and slice off the tip of each artichoke with a sharp knife. Halve the artichokes lengthwise, scrape out the choke, then quarter the globes and place at once in a bowl of water acidulated with half the lemon juice. To cook, place all the artichoke quarters in a large saucepan with just enough water to cover; add the remaining lemon juice and the salt, and boil for about 15 minutes.

To make the sauce, heat the oil in a skillet and sweat the onion and garlic. Add the tomatoes, carrot, and celery, and stew briefly. Pour in the stock, season with salt and pepper, and simmer for 10 minutes.

Cook the bucatini in boiling salted water until *al dente*, then drain. Lift the artichokes out of their cooking liquid and mix into the sauce. Serve the pasta topped with the sauce and sprinkled with thyme.

Ziti, zitoni, and macaroni (from top to bottom) are rather thick tubular pastas of fairly large diameter. Bucatini are somewhat thinner. They all originated in southern Italy and Sicily, and are usually eaten with a fairly dry ragù or sauce.

Here in the Ristorante Al Palazzo Tesorieri in Bagnacavallo, the impressive trick of packing a maximum of stuffing into a minimum of dough wrapper is pulled off with great dexterity and at breathtaking speed.

Two ways to serve cappelletti

Pasta stuffed with cheese: one in a fine broth; the other in a cream sauce, gratinéed till crisp

Both recipes serve 4–6. If wished, either stuffing can be flavored with grated lemon zest to taste.

CAPPELLETTI IN DUCK BROTH

For the pasta dough:
2⅔ cups all-purpose flour, 3 eggs, salt
For the stuffing:
1¾ cups freshly grated Parmesan cheese
⅓ cup ricotta cheese, 1 egg, 1 egg yolk
freshly ground pepper; salt (optional)
For the duck broth:
1 duck (about 4½ lb), 1 tablespoon vegetable oil
¾ cup coarsely chopped celery
¾ cup coarsely chopped carrot
5 oz tomatoes, seeded and chopped
¾ cup chopped onion, caramelized
salt, freshly ground pepper
You will also need:
1 egg white, freshly grated Parmesan cheese, truffle (optional)

To make the broth, remove all visible fat from the duck. Wash the duck inside and out under cold running water, then cut into quarters. Heat the oil in a large pot and sweat the celery and carrot. Add the duck quarters, pour over 6–9 cups of water, add the tomatoes and the onion, and season lightly with salt and pepper. Bring to a boil and simmer for about 3 hours. Remove the duck quarters and reserve the meat for another recipe. Pour the broth through a strainer lined with cheesecloth; there should be about 5½ cups remaining. Leave the broth

A summery version of stuffed pasta in broth. Prepare tortellini according to the recipe for cappelletti, and float them in a strong beef consommé with diced red and yellow tomatoes. Garnish with chive tips and serve.

The prepared soufflé molds are lined with the large squares of dough, and a portion of cappelletti is placed in each. A teaspoon of heavy cream and a little grated Parmesan per serving complete the "stuffing." The molds are then placed in a preheated 400°F oven and gratinéed for 10 minutes. To serve, the pasta is turned out of the molds and arranged on plates with the cream sauce. Thin slices of truffle may be shaved over the top if desired.

to cool, then skim the fat from the surface.

To make the pasta, knead the flour, eggs and salt to a dough, working in a little water if necessary. Wrap in plastic wrap and rest in the refrigerator for 1 hour. Cut the dough into 1½-inch squares.

To make the stuffing, stir together the Parmesan, ricotta, egg, and egg yolk. Season with pepper, and add salt to taste. Place a little stuffing on each square and brush the edges of the square with egg white. Fold the squares into triangles. Join up the points of each triangle, forming the pouches of dough into a ring, and pinch tightly to seal.

Heat the duck broth and season to taste with salt and pepper. Cook the cappelletti in batches in lightly salted boiling water for 5 minutes. Lift out, drain, and arrange on warmed soup plates. Ladle the broth over the pasta, sprinkle with Parmesan, and serve garnished with truffle slices if desired, as shown in the large picture above.

CAPPELLETTI CROCCANTE

Pasta dough as in the previous recipe
For the filling:
1¼ cups freshly grated Parmesan cheese
¼ cup ricotta cheese, 1 egg
freshly ground pepper, salt (optional)
For the cream sauce:
2 thin slices of truffle
1 cup light cream, ¼ cup freshly grated Parmesan cheese
freshly ground pepper, salt (optional)
You will also need:
1 egg white, 6 x 2-inch diameter soufflé molds
butter and fine white breadcrumbs for the molds
2 tablespoons butter, melted; 6 tablespoons heavy cream
⅓ cup freshly grated Parmesan cheese, truffle (optional)

Prepare the pasta dough as described in the preceding recipe. To make the stuffing, combine the Parmesan, ricotta, and egg, season with pepper, and salt to taste. Roll out the dough thinly and cut out six 4-inch squares. Cook in lightly salted boiling water until *al dente*, lift out, and spread out on a damp dish towel.

Cut the remaining dough into 1½-inch squares and brush the edges with egg white. Stuff and shape the cappelletti as described in the previous recipe. Cook in batches in lightly salted boiling water for about 5 minutes. Lift out and drain. Butter the soufflé molds and dust with bread crumbs. Line with the larger sheets of pasta and stuff with the cappelletti as shown in the first two photos of the picture sequence above on the right.

Meanwhile, prepare the sauce. Add the truffle slices to the cream and reduce the cream by half. Sprinkle in the Parmesan and simmer for 5 minutes. Season with pepper, adding salt if necessary. Unmold the pasta as described above on the right, spoon the sauce on top, and serve.

To clarify a game stock pour it through a strainer lined with cheesecloth.

Stuffed pasta in broth

A good broth is an absolute must here: only then do the spinach-stuffed ravioli or the tortelloni with pheasant taste perfect

RAVIOLI IN A CLEAR BROTH

Serves 4

For the pasta dough:
2½ cups all-purpose flour
1 egg, 7 egg yolks, 1 tablespoon oil, ½ teaspoon salt

For the tomato broth:
1 large carrot, 3 celery stalks, 1 leek
1 white onion; 1 lb beef tomatoes, peeled
1 lb whole canned tomatoes, 10 oz beef shank
2 garlic cloves, crushed
2 egg whites, whipped to soft peaks
1 bay leaf, 5 juniper berries, sea salt
5 crushed peppercorns, 9 cups meat stock

For the stuffing:
9 oz leaf spinach, ½ cup rye bread crumbs
2 tablespoons milk
1 egg, 2 tablespoons chopped herbs (parsley and thyme)
½ tablespoon finely pounded juniper berries
1 pinch each cinnamon and ground cloves
salt, freshly ground pepper

You will also need:
1 egg white, 1 small carrot, ½ leek, 1 small celery root

To make the dough, sift the flour onto a work surface and make a well in the center. Add the egg, egg yolks, oil, and salt to the well. Stir the ingredients with a fork, gradually working in more and more flour from the sides, then knead to a smooth, firm dough. Roll the dough into a ball, wrap in plastic wrap, and rest in the refrigerator for 1 hour.

To make the tomato broth, cut all the vegetables and the beef into pieces. Put the carrots, celery, and beef through the medium disk of a meat grinder. Mix in the remaining vegetables, egg white, and seasonings. Heat the stock, add the meat and vegetable mixture, and bring to a boil, stirring. When a white foam forms and the meat rises to the top, reduce the heat and simmer for 15 minutes without stirring. Pour the broth through a strainer lined with cheesecloth. Bring to a boil again and skim off the fat.

To make the stuffing, blanch the spinach, squeeze it dry, and chop finely. Soak the bread crumbs in the milk and squeeze out the excess moisture. Mix the bread crumbs with the spinach, egg, parsley, thyme, and juniper berries. Season with cinnamon, ground cloves, salt, and pepper.

Roll out the dough thinly. Cut out circles with a 1½-inch fluted cutter. Place a little stuffing in the center of each circle, brush the edges with egg white, fold over into half-moon shapes, press firmly to seal, and let dry briefly. Cut the vegetables into julienne. Cook the ravioli in boiling salted water, and serve with the vegetable julienne in the hot tomato broth.

TORTELLONI WITH PHEASANT

Serves 4

For the pasta dough:
2½ cups all-purpose flour, 2 eggs, 4 egg yolks
⅓ teaspoon salt, 1 tablespoon water as needed

For the pheasant stock:
½ pheasant; ½ leek, 1 small carrot
½ onion, 2 tablespoons oil, 1 bay leaf

For the pheasant stuffing:
1 oz dried morels, ¼ cup white port, 2 tablespoons butter
¼ cup diced shallot; 1 garlic clove, crushed
½ cup diced celery, ½ teaspoon salt, pepper
2 teaspoons chopped herbs (thyme and sage)

For the game broth:
3½ cups game stock, ½ leek
1 small carrot, a few celery leaves

You will also need:
1 egg white

Prepare a pasta dough from the ingredients above, wrap it in plastic wrap and chill for 1 hour.

To make the pheasant stock, bone the pheasant and set the meat aside. Cut the leek and carrot into pieces, and quarter the onion. Heat the oil in a saucepan, and brown the pheasant bones, skin, and sinews on all sides. Add the vegetables, onion, and bay leaf, and sauté for 2–3 minutes over a high heat. Pour in 2¼ cups of water. Simmer, uncovered, for about 1 hour. Strain the stock as shown in the picture on the opposite page, boil down to ½ cup, and leave to cool.

To make the stuffing, soak the morels in port and the cold pheasant stock. Purée half of the reserved meat and dice the remaining meat very finely. Melt the butter and sweat the shallot, garlic, and celery until lightly colored. Add the diced meat, and sear over a high heat. Remove from the heat and mix with the puréed meat, salt, pepper, and herbs. Remove the morels from their soaking liquid, dice, and mix into the meat stuffing. Strain the soaking liquid through a cheesecloth and add enough to the meat mixture to form a paste. Add the remaining liquid to the stock.

To make the game broth, reduce the stock by half. Meanwhile, make the tortelloni. Roll out the dough thinly, and cut out circles 2 inches in diameter. Place a little of the cooled stuffing on each circle, brush the edges with egg white, fold over into half-moon shapes, and press down firmly to seal. Cook the tortelloni in boiling salted water for 6–8 minutes.

Cut the leek, carrot, and celery leaves into julienne, and simmer briefly in the game stock just before serving. Arrange the drained tortelloni in warmed soup plates and ladle the game broth on top.

Ravioli stuffed with seafood

Whether filled with shrimp, or — the height of sophistication — rock lobster, these ravioli make a delicate first course

RAVIOLI WITH A SHRIMP STUFFING

Serves 4
For the dough:
2½ cups all-purpose flour, 1 egg
7 egg yolks, 1 tablespoon oil, ½ teaspoon salt
For the stuffing:
2 tablespoons butter, ¼ cup diced celery
⅓ cup diced carrot, ⅓ cup chopped leek
¼ cup diced white onion, 1 garlic clove, finely chopped
8 oz raw shrimp, peeled, deveined, and chopped
1 small or ½ large chile pepper, halved, seeded, and finely chopped
salt, freshly ground pepper, 1 tablespoon chopped parsley
You will also need:
1 egg white, rock-lobster sauce (see following recipe)

To make the dough, sift the flour onto a work surface and make a well in the center. Add the egg, egg yolks, oil, and salt to the well. Mix the ingredients with a fork, gradually working in more and more flour from the sides, then knead into a smooth, firm dough. Roll the dough into a ball, wrap in plastic wrap, and rest in the refrigerator for 1 hour.

To make the filling, melt the butter in a skillet and sweat the diced vegetables for 4–5 minutes. Add the shrimp and the chile pepper, and sweat for a further 2 minutes. Season with salt and pepper, stir in the parsley, and let the mixture cool.

Roll out the pasta dough thinly and cut out circles with a 2½-inch fluted cutter. Place a little stuffing in the center of half of the circles. Brush the edges with egg white, top with the remaining circles of dough, and press the edges down firmly to seal.

Cook the ravioli in briskly boiling salted water for 6–8 minutes. Lift out with a slotted spoon and drain well. Arrange the ravioli on warmed plates, spoon over the rock-lobster sauce, and serve.

These ravioli, whose color comes from squid ink, are not only eye-catching; with their sumptuous filling and delicate lobster sauce, they also taste sensational.

BLACK RAVIOLI STUFFED WITH ROCK LOBSTER

Serves 4–6
1 rock-lobster tail (about 10 oz), cooked
For the black pasta dough:
2½ cups all-purpose flour, 2 eggs
2 teaspoons oil, ½ teaspoon salt, 4 teaspoons squid ink
For the rock-lobster sauce:
2 tablespoons olive oil, ½ cup diced celery
½ cup diced carrot

1¾ cups rock-lobster, or lobster, stock
½ cup light cream, salt, freshly ground pepper

For the stuffing:
1½ tablespoons butter, ¼ cup diced celery
¼ cup chopped scallion, ½ cup diced carrot
4 oz tomatoes, peeled, seeded, and chopped
salt, pepper

You will also need:
1 egg white, 10 oz zucchini, 1 tablespoon oil
1½ tablespoons butter
a little beurre noisette *(lightly browned butter)*
salt, freshly ground pepper

Make a pasta dough from the ingredients given. Roll the dough into a ball, wrap in plastic wrap, and rest in the refrigerator for 1 hour. Crack open and devein the rock-lobster tail and refrigerate the meat. Thoroughly clean the shell and trimmings, and cut up small.

Heat the oil in a roasting pan and brown the shells and trimmings. Add the vegetables and sauté for 5 minutes. Pour in the stock and cream, and reduce by half over a low heat. Pour through a very fine strainer, then season with salt and pepper.

To make the stuffing, finely dice the lobster meat. Heat the butter in a skillet and sweat the celery, scallions, and carrot for 3–4 minutes, then add the tomatoes and sweat for a further 2 minutes. Add the lobster meat and sauté for 1 minute, then season with salt and pepper. Mix the stuffing well and let cool.

Roll out the pasta dough thinly and cut out 40 circles with a 2½-inch fluted cutter. Place a little stuffing on half of the circles, brush the edges with egg white, top with the remaining circles of dough, and press down firmly to seal. Cook the ravioli in boiling salted water for 6–8 minutes.

Cut the zucchini lengthwise into ⅛-inch-thick slices, then halve the slices lengthwise. Heat the oil and butter in a skillet, sauté the zucchini, then season with salt and pepper. Reheat the sauce and purée with a hand-held blender. Arrange the ravioli and zucchini on warmed plates, drizzle with a little *beurre noisette*, and pour the lobster sauce all around.

Ravioli *di magro*

Pasta with a vegetarian stuffing of ricotta and spinach or herbs, drizzled with *beurre noisette*

Di magro, or "lean," ravioli is the name given to this pasta in the Bologna area, since it was originally a meatless Lenten dish.

Serves 4
For the dough:
2½ cups all-purpose flour
2 eggs, 4 egg yolks, ⅓ teaspoon salt
For the stuffing:
10 oz young leaf spinach, salt, 1 cup ricotta cheese
freshly ground pepper, freshly grated nutmeg
1 cup freshly grated Parmesan cheese, 2 egg yolks
You will also need:
1 egg white, 6 sage leaves, 6 tablespoons butter
freshly grated Parmesan cheese

Sift the flour onto a work surface and make a well in the center. Add the eggs, egg yolks, and salt to the well, and stir with a fork, gradually working in more and more flour from the sides. Knead to a smooth dough, adding a little water if necessary. Wrap the dough in plastic wrap and rest in the refrigerator for 1 hour.

To make the stuffing, blanch the spinach in lightly salted boiling water for 1–2 minutes. Drain, plunge into a bowl of ice water, then drain well and squeeze out as much of the remaining water as possible. Chop the spinach coarsely and proceed as shown in the first step of the picture sequence below.

Lightly dust a ravioli mold with flour. Roll out the dough into two thin sheets, and line the mold with one of the sheets. Stuff the ravioli as illustrated in the last two steps of the picture sequence.

Carefully remove the stuffed ravioli from the mold. Cook in briskly boiling salted water for 4–5 minutes, then lift out and drain well. Cut the sage leaves into strips. Melt the butter in a skillet, add the sage leaves, and toss briefly. Spoon the pasta onto warmed plates, drizzle with the sage butter, and serve sprinkled with Parmesan.

Place the spinach, ricotta, ½ teaspoon salt, and the remaining ingredients for the stuffing in a bowl, and mix together to a smooth paste.

Put some stuffing in each indentation. Moisten the dough around the stuffing with a little egg white if necessary.

Place the second sheet of dough on top and carefully roll over the top with a rolling pin, taking care not to disturb the stuffing.

PANSOTI WITH WALNUT SAUCE

This stuffed pasta from the coastal province of Liguria, is not only spelled *pansoti, pansooti, pansotti,* or even *panzotti,* but is also prepared in numerous variations.

Makes about 60
For the dough:
1¼ cups semolina flour, 1¼ cups all-purpose flour
2 eggs, 1 egg yolk, ⅓ teaspoon salt
For the herb stuffing:
3 cups mixed fresh herbs (parsley, sage, thyme)
3 cups fresh basil, 1½ cups fresh borage (or another herb)
1 egg, 1 garlic clove, finely chopped
¼ cup ricotta cheese
¼ cup freshly grated Parmesan cheese
salt, freshly ground pepper
For the walnut sauce:
1¼ cups walnut pieces, ¾ cup white bread crumbs
3 tablespoons olive oil, ¼ cup light cream, salt
You will also need:
1 egg white, *a little* beurre noisette
1 tablespoon chopped herbs (parsley, basil, thyme, sage)
¾ cup freshly grated Parmesan cheese

To make the dough, mound the semolina and the all-purpose flour on a work surface and make a well in the center. Place the eggs, egg yolk, and salt in the well, and stir the ingredients together with a fork, gradually stirring in more and more flour from the edge, until you have a sticky dough. Leaving the fork to one side, work in the remaining flour with both hands, kneading until the dough is smooth and firm. Roll the dough into a ball, wrap in plastic wrap, and rest in the refrigerator for about 1 hour.

To make the stuffing, blanch the herbs. Refresh in cold water, squeeze out all excess water, dry in paper towels, and chop very finely. Mix the herbs and garlic with the egg, ricotta, and Parmesan, then season with salt and pepper. Blend all ingredients briefly in a food processor and set aside.

Make the sauce. Using a mortar and pestle, pound the walnuts coarsely. Soak the bread crumbs in 1 tablespoon water and squeeze out well. In a food processor, blend walnuts and bread crumbs to a fine purée. Transfer to a bowl. Alternately work in the oil and cream until smooth. Season with salt to taste.

Roll out the pasta dough thinly and cut out 2-inch squares. Place a teaspoonful of stuffing on each square, then brush the edges with egg white. Fold the squares over into triangles, pressing the edges together firmly.

Cook the pansoti in briskly boiling salted water for 6–8 minutes, then lift out and drain. Arrange on warmed plates, drizzle with the *beurre noisette*, and sprinkle with the herbs. Serve with the walnut sauce and the grated Parmesan.

In Liguria, pansoti are served in a wide variety of shapes: triangles, as shown here, and half moons, squares, and tortellini-like rings.

Truffle fazzoletti with seafood

Truffle slices are the highlight of this dish, with a delicious mixture of rock lobster and porgy between the layers of pasta

Serves 4
1¼ cups all-purpose flour, 1¼ cups cornmeal, 3 eggs
3 egg yolks, 1 tablespoon olive oil, ½ teaspoon salt
freshly grated nutmeg, 1 summer truffle (about 1 oz)
For the stuffing:
2 boiled rock-lobster tails (about 14 oz each)
1 lb porgy fillet, 6 tablespoons butter
½ cup finely chopped onion
8 oz yellow tomatoes, peeled, seeded, and diced
8 oz red tomatoes, peeled, seeded, and diced
salt, freshly ground pepper
You will also need:
1 summer truffle (about 1 oz), 3 tablespoons butter
salt, pepper, fresh basil leaves

Knead the flour and cornmeal together with eggs, egg yolks, oil, salt, and nutmeg. Wrap the dough in plastic wrap and rest in the refrigerator for 1 hour.

Using a brush, carefully clean off any earth clinging to the truffles. If deep cracks in the body make this impossible, peel the truffles sparingly with a sharp knife. Wash briefly under running water only if absolutely necessary. Shave the truffles for the pasta into thin slices.

Using a pasta machine, roll out the dough for the fazzoletti into ¼-inch-thick sheets. Cover half of the sheets with the truffle slices, placing 2 in each row, and proceed as shown in the first three steps of the picture sequence opposite. Allow the pasta to dry briefly before further use.

pepper. Arrange the fried truffle slices on the pasta with a spoonful of the remaining seafood and fish mixture, add with a few basil leaves, and serve at once.

Summer truffles are the somewhat less expensive version of the black or white tartufo. Their flavor is not quite as intense, but this can be compensated for by the large quantity used.

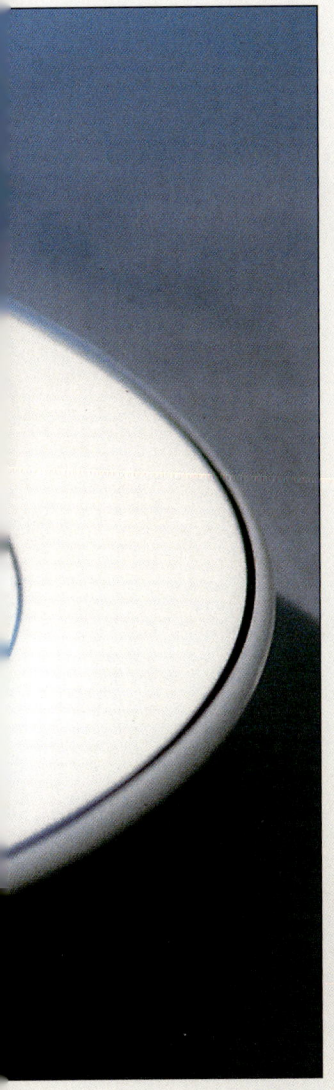

Although a bit time-consuming and complicated to prepare, these truffle fazzoletti are sure to be a success at a dinner party, as they are simply perfect in appearance as well as taste.

To make the stuffing, carefully crack open and devein the rock-lobster tails and slice the meat. Halve the porgy fillet lengthwise and cut into strips. Melt the butter in a skillet and briefly sauté the lobster meat on both sides. Season with salt and pepper and lift out. Sauté the fish strips briefly on both sides, then season with salt and pepper and lift out. Sweat the onion in the remaining butter until translucent, then add the tomatoes and sweat for 3–4 minutes. Return the rock-lobster and the fish to the skillet, carefully sauté all the ingredients until they are heated through, then season with salt and pepper to taste.

Cook the truffle fazzoletti in briskly boiling salted water until *al dente*, then lift out and drain well. Arrange them on warmed plates as shown in the last two steps of the picture sequence. To finish, place a third sheet of pasta on top, and garnish it.

Shave the truffle for the garnish into slices. Melt the butter in a saucepan and sauté the truffle slices very briefly on both sides, then season with salt and

Position the second sheet of dough exactly on top, and roll over it with a rolling pin so that the sheets of dough are firmly stuck together.

Put this length of dough through the pasta machine again, then cut crosswise into strips, with 2 truffle slices in each strip.

Cut through the middle of each strip between the truffle slices to make squares of about 4 inches.

Place 1 pasta sheet on each warmed plate, and spoon some of the seafood and fish stuffing on the top.

Place the second sheet of pasta on top, then cover this too with a spoonful of stuffing, reserving a little stuffing for the garnish.

Tagliatelle with seafood

Pasta *con frutti di mare* and fresh herbs is a popular dish not only in coastal areas

Top-quality shrimp and squid are needed for this recipe. Thanks to modern transportation and refrigeration systems, supplying fresh fish and seafood to inland areas is no longer a problem, but you can also use frozen products. Fresh pasta tastes better too, so if you have a bit of time, it is worth making the tagliatelle yourself, following the basic recipe on pages 126–7.

Almost all of the sea's bounty goes well with pasta — bivalves of all kinds, fish, even squid and cuttlefish — but the addition of freshly caught shrimp, like those this Sicilian fisherman is busy sorting, makes the dish particularly delicious.

A thoroughly Mediterranean medley of shrimp, squid, and fresh tagliatelle. With a soupçon of garlic and fresh herbs, this is the ideal meal for a fine summer's day.

Serves 4
10 oz squid
1 lb tomatoes, peeled, seeded, and diced
12 oz tagliatelle, 1 tablespoon butter
¼ cup olive oil
⅓ cup finely chopped shallot
1 garlic clove, finely chopped
½ teaspoon salt
1 tablespoon chopped herbs (basil, thyme, parsley)
8 raw shrimp, peeled and deveined
12 black olives, freshly ground pepper

Wash the squid and pull off the skin. Pull the tentacles out of the body sac and cut them off just above the eyes so that they remain joined together by a narrow band. Remove the beak and quill, and wash out the inside of the body. Poach the tentacles and body sacs briefly in boiling salted water. Cut the body sacs into ½-inch-wide rings; leave the tentacles whole.

To make the sauce, heat the olive oil in a large saucepan and sweat the shallots and garlic until lightly colored. Add the tomatoes and season with salt and pepper. Stir in the herbs and sweat for about 5 minutes.

In the meantime, bring plenty of salted water to a boil in a large pot. Add the tagliatelle and cook until *al dente*.

Melt the butter in a large skillet and briefly sauté the shrimp and the squid rings and tentacles. Add the olives to the tomato sauce.

Drain the noodles, refresh under cold water, and drain again. Toss gently with the shrimp and squid, and the tomato sauce. Arrange the tagliatelle on warmed plates and serve immediately.

Mushroom cannelloni

A dish for late summer and fall, when chanterelles and porcini mushrooms are in season

The regions of rainier northern Italy, especially Trentino and the southern Tyrol, are reputed to provide the richest pickings for mushroom hunters, and the southern slopes of the Alps boast a wide range of edible fungi. Just which varieties to choose for this aromatic stuffing depends on what you've managed to collect on your foray, what's on offer at the market, and your personal preferences. The cannelloni can be baked either in a large casserole dish or in individual gratin dishes, as shown opposite.

Serves 4
For the dough:
¾ cup semolina flour, ¾ cup all-purpose flour
1 egg, 1 egg yolk, salt
For the stuffing:
5 oz spinach, 2 tablespoons butter
¾ cup chopped onion
1 garlic clove, finely chopped
10 oz mixed wild mushrooms
⅓ cup diced leek, ½ cup cream
½ teaspoon salt, 1–2 leeks
freshly ground white pepper
For the sauce:
1 cup cream, 1 egg yolk
salt, freshly ground white pepper
1 tablespoon chopped parsley
You will also need:
4 small gratin dishes; butter

Blanched leek leaves add a pleasant note to the mushroom cannelloni. They are placed on the strips of pasta, topped with the stuffing, and then rolled into cannelloni.

To make the pasta dough, mix the flours together well and knead to a smooth dough with the remaining ingredients. Wrap the dough in plastic wrap and rest in the refrigerator for 1 hour.

Wash the spinach, removing the stems, then drain well, and chop finely. Melt the butter in a skillet and sweat the onion and garlic until translucent. Tip in the mushrooms and fry for 3 minutes, then add the spinach and the diced leek, and sauté until the spinach wilts. Pour in the cream, season with salt and pepper, and reduce for 3–4 minutes. Remove from the heat and leave to cool.

Trim the whole leeks and cut off a piece about 4–5 inches long from the white part. Carefully peel off 8 leaves from it, and cook them in boiling salted water for 4 minutes. Lift out, refresh under cold water, and drain well.

Roll out the dough thinly on a floured surface and cut out into 8 rectangles measuring 3½ x 5½ inches. Cook the pasta in briskly boiling salted water for 2 minutes, then lift out and spread out on a damp dish towel. Top each piece of pasta with a leek leaf, spread some of the mushroom stuffing over it, and roll up into cannelloni.

To make the sauce, pour the cream into a saucepan and simmer until the liquid is reduced by a third. Whisk the egg yolk in a small bowl and stir in 1 tablespoon of the hot cream. Stir the egg-yolk mixture into the hot cream, taking care not to let the sauce boil. Season with salt and pepper and sprinkle in the parsley.

Preheat the oven to 400°F. Place 2 cannelloni in each buttered gratin dish, pour over the cream sauce, and bake for 12 minutes. Place under the broiler for the final minute of cooking to brown the cannelloni.

Topped with a fine cream sauce, then baked, the cannelloni remain moist while browning appetizingly.

Fresh porcini mushrooms taste delicious. Their season is short, however, so if you happen to come across them at a market or on a walk in the woods, take advantage of the opportunity and set aside several to be sliced and dried. They can be stored this way for a long time, and you can be sure of having high-quality wild mushrooms to hand.

Porcini pasta
Served with a sauce made from fresh, aromatic tomatoes, these noodles are a special delicacy

Pounded to a powder and mixed into the dough, intensely flavored dried porcini mushrooms are an ideal flavoring agent for pasta. The simple trick of boiling a handful of dried porcini in the cooking water before adding the pasta enhances the mushroom taste even further.

Serves 4
For the porcini pasta dough:
2 cups all-purpose flour, 2 eggs, 1 egg yolk
½ teaspoon salt, 2 tablespoons oil
⅓ oz dried porcini mushrooms, pounded in a mortar
1 tablespoon finely chopped parsley
water as needed
For the tomato sauce:
½ cup butter, ¾ cup finely chopped shallots
1¼ lb ripe tomatoes, peeled, seeded, and coarsely chopped
8 medium-sized sage leaves, cut into strips
½ teaspoon salt

Thanks to dried porcini and canned tomatoes, this dish can easily be prepared throughout the year, but it tastes best made in late summer, when tomatoes are at their most flavorful and fresh wild mushrooms are — with luck — available.

A rather special pasta Here, the porcini are added directly to the pasta dough, rather than to the accompanying sauce.

You will also need:
4 oz Parmesan cheese

To make the pasta dough, mound the flour on a work surface and make a well in the center. Add the eggs, egg yolk, salt, oil, powdered mushrooms, and parsley to the well. Start off by mixing with a fork, then knead all the ingredients to a smooth dough with both hands, working in a little water if necessary. Wrap the dough in plastic wrap and rest in the refrigerator for 1 hour.

To make the sauce, melt the butter in a large saucepan and sweat the shallots until translucent. Add the tomatoes and stew for 10 minutes. Lastly, stir in the sage, season with salt, and remove the sauce from the heat.

Roll out the pasta dough on a floured surface, cut into sheets, and roll these out to the desired thickness by putting them through the pasta machine several times. Cut into strips ½-inch wide. Place on a lightly floured dish towel and allow to dry slightly.

Cook the noodles in briskly boiling salted water until *al dente*, then drain. Toss the pasta with the sauce, then arrange on warmed plates, shave a little Parmesan over the top, and serve.

Pasta con porcini

The regal porcini, or cèpe, is to be found in many regions of Italy, even in southerly Sicily and in Sardinia

PENNE RIGATE WITH PORCINI IN CREAM

The superb flavor of fresh porcini mushrooms harmonizes perfectly with pasta. Served *alla panna* — in a fine cream sauce — the mushrooms are set off to best advantage.

Serves 4
1 lb fresh porcini mushrooms, 1 cup cream
4 oz prosciutto, cut into ¼-inch dice
2 tablespoons butter, ½ cup finely chopped onion
¼ cup finely chopped parsley root
1 lb penne rigate
2 tablespoons finely chopped parsley
salt, freshly ground pepper
You will also need:
freshly grated Parmesan cheese

Carefully clean and trim the porcini, and slice them lengthwise. Boil the cream over low heat to reduce by about half.

Melt the butter in a skillet and sweat the onion and parsley root until lightly colored. Add the mushrooms and prosciutto, and sauté briefly, stirring constantly. Pour in the reduced cream, sprinkle in the parsley, and simmer over a low heat for a few minutes until the porcini are tender.

Cook the pasta until *al dente*, then drain. Mix immediately with the sauce, then season with salt and pepper. Spoon onto warmed plates, sprinkle with Parmesan, and serve.

PAPPARDELLE CON FUNGHI

In Italy people know how to treat fine mushrooms, slicing them thinly and mixing them in with pappardelle, wide ribbon noodles, for example. In the fall, pasta dishes with fresh porcini figure on the menus of restaurants specializing in regional cuisine. Porcini are also prized by Italian home cooks browsing around the market in search of ingredients for a pasta dish. Depending on the quality of the porcini, it might be advisable to buy a larger amount than that given in the recipe, to make sure that you'll be left with the desired quantity after trimming.

Serves 4
14 oz trimmed porcini mushrooms
1 cup meat stock, 1 lb pappardelle
3 tablespoons fine olive oil
¾ cup finely chopped onion
1 garlic clove, finely chopped
2 oz prosciutto, cut into thin strips
7 oz tomatoes, peeled, seeded, and diced
salt, freshly ground white pepper
2 tablespoons chopped parsley
You will also need:
freshly shaved Parmesan cheese

Slice the porcini lengthwise, keeping the original shape wherever possible. Bring the meat stock to a boil and reduce to about a third of its original volume. Cook the pasta in briskly boiling salted water for about 8 minutes, until *al dente*, then drain.

Heat the olive oil in a skillet and sweat the onion and garlic until lightly colored. Add the prosciutto and sauté briefly. Add the mushrooms and tomatoes, season with salt and pepper, and braise for 4–5 minutes. Pour in the reduced meat stock and simmer over moderate heat for 20 minutes, until the liquid is almost completely evaporated.

Add the pasta and the parsley, and reheat until piping hot. Serve with freshly shaved Parmesan.

Even rustic penne rigate taste brilliant with a delicate porcini-cream sauce. To enhance the mushroom flavor yet further, soak a small amount of dried porcini for 30 minutes, then chop it finely and mix it into the sauce.

Macaroni and spinach au gratin

Delicious pasta dishes can be conjured from simple ingredients: spinach, noodles, tomatoes, herbs, and cheese

We recommend that you use a fairly thin tubular pasta, such as bucatini or perciatelli, for a gratin such as this, but the somewhat thicker long macaroni is also suitable. Make sure that you buy really fresh, young spinach with unwithered leaves — firstly, because it still contains most of its valuable vitamins, and secondly, because it is a good deal more tender and better tasting.

Serves 4
14 oz young spinach, 12 oz long macaroni or bucatini
3 tablespoons olive oil
¾ cup finely chopped onion
2 garlic cloves, finely chopped
10 oz tomatoes, peeled, seeded, and diced
1 cup cubes piquant, firm cheese
salt, freshly ground pepper
You will also need:
butter for the baking dish
½ teaspoon chopped rosemary leaves
½ teaspoon chopped thyme
3 tablespoons butter, in curls

Sort through the spinach, removing the hard stalks, then wash thoroughly and drain.

Cook the pasta in briskly boiling salted water until *al dente*, then drain well.

Meanwhile, heat the olive oil in a skillet and sweat the onion and garlic until lightly colored. Add the spinach, and cook until just wilted. Season with salt and pepper. Add the tomatoes and sweat briefly with the other ingredients. Tip in the pasta and the cheese, and toss gently.

Preheat the oven to 400°F. Butter a baking dish, and spoon in the spinach and pasta mixture. Sprinkle with rosemary and thyme, dot the top with butter curls, and bake for about 20 minutes.

The cheese should impart plenty of flavor to this dish. We recommend a well-ripened Corsica, Bambolo, or even the piquant Taleggio. If Italian cheeses are not available, you could also use another spicy, semi-soft cheese, such as Tomme de Savoie.

Striped fazzoletti with quail ragout

The highly coveted little birds, *quaglie*, are served here as a *ragù* and accompanied by spicy chanterelle mushrooms

Serves 4
For the light pasta dough:
1¼ cups all-purpose flour, 1 egg, 1 egg yolk
½ tablespoon olive oil, ¼ teaspoon salt
For the green pasta dough:
8 oz spinach, 1¼ cup all-purpose flour
5–6 egg yolks, 1 tablespoon olive oil
½ teaspoon salt, 3 tablespoons butter
freshly grated nutmeg
For the quail ragout:
4 oven-ready quails (about 6 oz each)
2 tablespoons oil, ½ cup finely chopped shallots
½ cup diced celery, ¼ cup diced parsley root
¼ cup diced carrot, ⅓ cup diced pancetta
2 garlic cloves, finely chopped
1 teaspoon flour, 1 cup chicken stock
2 tablespoons chopped parsley
salt, freshly ground pepper
For the tomato sauce:
1¼ lb ripe tomatoes, peeled, seeded, and diced
15 small basil leaves, coarsely torn
5 tablespoons butter, salt, freshly ground pepper
You will also need:
5 teaspoons butter
4 oz small trimmed chanterelle mushrooms
salt, freshly ground pepper

Make a light pasta dough from the given ingredients, adding a little more water if necessary. Wrap the dough in plastic wrap and rest in the

Somewhat time-consuming and complicated to prepare, but the result is quite special. The striped fazzoletti are served with a fresh tomato sauce and chanterelle mushrooms sautéed in butter.

refrigerator for 1 hour.

Make a green pasta dough from the given ingredients, as described on pages 126–7. Wrap the dough in plastic wrap and rest in the refrigerator for 1 hour.

Carefully wash the quails inside and out under cold running water, then drain and pat dry with paper towels. Cut off the legs and wings, and then cut out the breast. Season the quail pieces lightly with salt and pepper, then cover and refrigerate.

Heat the oil in a skillet and sweat the shallots until lightly colored. Add the diced vegetables and sweat for 2–3 minutes, then lift out and set aside. Brown the pancetta in the skillet, add the quail pieces and brown them on all sides over a high heat. Mix in the garlic and sprinkle the contents of the pan with flour. Sauté for a further 3–4 minutes, deglaze with the stock, and braise uncovered until the meat is done and the liquid is reduced by half. Stir in the parsley and season to taste.

In the meantime, melt the butter in a saucepan and sweat the tomatoes, then simmer for 5 minutes. Season with salt and pepper, stir in the basil leaves, and set aside.

Using a pasta machine, roll out both doughs somewhat thicker than the intended final thickness of the fazzoletti. With the help of a ruler and a plain pastry wheel, cut the sheets of dough into ½-inch-wide strips. Moisten the long edges of the strips with a little water. Line up alternating light and green pasta strips side by side, overlapping slightly, and roll out into sheets of dough of the desired thickness, then cut the striped pasta dough into 12 rectangles measuring 3 x 4 inches. Cook the fazzoletti in briskly boiling salted water for 3–4 minutes, then lift out with a slotted spoon and drain well.

Melt the butter in a small skillet and sauté the chanterelles for several minutes, then season with salt and pepper. Reheat the tomato sauce.

To serve the fazzoletti, place 1 sheet of pasta on each warmed plate and spoon a quarter of the tomato sauce over it. Place a second pasta sheet on top, followed by a quarter of the quail ragout. Top with a final sheet of pasta, and spoon some of the chanterelles on top. Arrange a few mushrooms next to the stuffed fazzoletti, drizzle with a little ragout sauce, and serve at once.

Buckwheat dumplings

These hearty dumplings are another culinary contribution from the southern Tyrol

There are two main culinary styles in the southern Tyrol. The heavier, country style originated in the Alps, and the fresher, lighter style is from further south in Italy. These bread dumplings, served with a warm tomato salad, are a fine example of the two cuisines.

Serves 4
For the dumplings:
3–4 day-old crusty rolls
⅔ cup lukewarm milk
5 teaspoons butter
1 garlic clove, finely chopped
½ cup chopped onion
½ cup thinly sliced leek rings
2 eggs
½ cup buckwheat flour
2 tablespoons chopped herbs (parsley, chives, lovage)
½ teaspoon salt, freshly ground white pepper
1 generous pinch freshly grated nutmeg
6 oz cubes Emmental cheese
For the tomato salad:
3 tablespoons olive oil
⅓ cup finely chopped shallots
3 celery stalks, cut into thin strips
1¼ lb tomatoes, peeled, seeded, and diced
2 tablespoons red wine vinegar
salt, freshly ground pepper
1 tablespoon chopped celery leaves
You will also need:
about 6 tablespoons butter

To make the dumplings, cut the rolls into thin slices, place in a bowl, add the milk, and soak for at least 15 minutes.

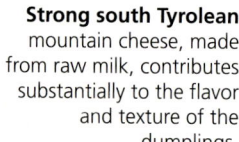

Strong south Tyrolean mountain cheese, made from raw milk, contributes substantially to the flavor and texture of the dumplings.

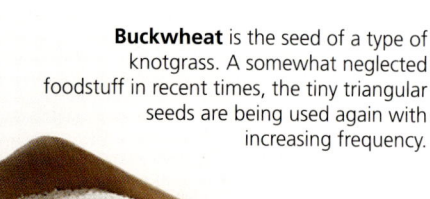

Buckwheat is the seed of a type of knotgrass. A somewhat neglected foodstuff in recent times, the tiny triangular seeds are being used again with increasing frequency.

Melt the butter in a skillet and sweat the garlic, onion, and leek until lightly colored. Stir into the soaked bread. Add the eggs, flour, herbs, and seasonings, and mix to a loose dough. Leave to rest for 15 minutes. Knead the cheese into the dough.

Shape the dough into 12 small dumplings. Bring a pot of salted water to a rolling boil, then add the dumplings. Reduce the heat at once and simmer the dumplings — do not allow them to boil — for 12–15 minutes, until done.

To make the salad, heat the oil in a skillet and sweat the shallots until lightly colored, then add the celery and tomatoes, and cook for 3 minutes. Season with vinegar, salt, pepper, and celery leaves.

Heat the butter in a skillet until light brown and foaming. Lift out the dumplings with a slotted spoon and drain. Arrange the dumplings on warmed plates, drizzle generously with the *beurre noisette*, and serve with the warm tomato salad.

Gnocchi with spinach or cheese

Drizzled with *beurre noisette* and sprinkled with Parmesan, these gnocchi never fail to please

Spinach and cheese gnocchi are prepared at home throughout northern Italy, and are usually served accompanied only by brown butter and freshly grated cheese.

SPINACH GNOCCHI WITH HARE RAGOUT

These spinach dumplings also make an excellent side dish, since they are more than capable of standing up to the strong flavor of the wild hare.

Serves 4
For the hare ragout:
2¼ lb wild hare (saddle or whole hare)
1 red onion, quartered
1 garlic clove
10 juniper berries
1 teaspoon white peppercorns
2 bay leaves
6 fresh sage leaves
2¼ cups red wine
¼ cup olive oil
⅓ cup chopped carrot
½ cup chopped onion
½ cup chopped celery
1 lb tomatoes, quartered
2 tablespoons tomato paste
1 cup game stock
salt, freshly ground pepper

For the spinach gnocchi:
1 lb fresh spinach
9 slices day-old white bread
½ cup milk
2 eggs, ¾ cup flour
salt, pepper, freshly grated nutmeg
You will also need:
¼ cup butter, 8 sage leaves
½ cup freshly grated Parmesan cheese

To make the hare ragout, remove all skin and sinew, and place the meat in a bowl. Add the red onion, garlic, juniper berries, peppercorns, bay leaves, and sage, and pour over the wine. Cover the bowl with plastic wrap and marinate in the refrigerator for 12 hours. Lift the meat from the marinade and pat dry with paper towels. Bone the meat, cut it into ½-inch cubes, and set aside. Reserve the marinade.

Finely chop the bones. Heat half the oil in a skillet and brown the bones well on all sides. Add the onion, carrot, and celery, and sauté, stirring constantly. Add the tomatoes and tomato paste, and sauté briefly. Deglaze with the stock and 1 cup of the reserved marinade, and season with salt and pepper. Braise, covered, for 2–3 hours, gradually adding the remaining reserved marinade. Strain the sauce.

Heat the remaining oil in a skillet and brown the meat. Pour over the sauce and braise, covered, for about 20 minutes, until the meat is tender.

To make the spinach gnocchi, blanch the spinach in boiling salted water. Squeeze out as much moisture as possible and chop finely. Remove the crust from the bread, cut into small cubes, pour over the milk, and mix thoroughly. Add the spinach, eggs, flour, and seasonings, and mix well. Using a tablespoon, mold dumplings the size of eggs in your wet hand.

Drop the dumplings into boiling salted water, reduce the heat, and simmer for 5–7 minutes until done. Lift out with a slotted spoon and drain. Melt the butter in a casserole dish and sauté the sage leaves. Place the gnocchi in the dish, spoon over the sage butter and sprinkle with the Parmesan. Serve with the hare ragout.

CHEESE GNOCCHI

Traditionally, these light dumplings from the southern Tyrol are prepared with Graukäse, a Tyrolean sour-curd cheese. However, since Graukäse is not universally available, we recommend that you use Emmental cheese.

Serves 4
1 cup lukewarm milk
9 slices day-old white bread
2 teaspoons butter
1 onion, finely chopped
8 oz Emmental cheese, finely diced
1½ tablespoons flour
2 eggs, 1 egg yolk
2 tablespoons chopped herbs (parsley and chives)
salt, freshly ground pepper
1 generous pinch freshly grated nutmeg
You will also need:
6 tablespoons butter
½ cup freshly grated Parmesan cheese

Pour the milk over the bread and leave to soak.

Melt the butter in a skillet and sauté the onion until golden. Add the onion and cheese, flour, eggs, and egg yolk to the softened bread and combine well. Stir the herbs into the mixture, and season with salt, pepper, and nutmeg. Using a tablespoon, mold dumplings the size of eggs in your wet hand.

Bring a large pot of salted water to a boil, drop in the cheese gnocchi, and cook for 12–15 minutes until done. Lift out the dumplings and drain on a dish towel or on paper towels. Meanwhile, melt the butter in a skillet and allow to turn light brown.

Transfer the cheese gnocchi to warmed plates, sprinkle with the Parmesan, drizzle with the browned butter, and serve.

Enjoying life through all one's senses has been a tradition in Rome since ancient times. Even nowadays, for example, Romans appreciate the sight of a well-proportioned building as much as a perfectly prepared and seasoned dish.

Gnocchi alla romana

Served with a piquant tomato sauce, these dumplings make a delicate main course

The gnocchi best known outside of Italy are the ones made from a mixture of boiled potatoes and flour. In Rome, however, gnocchi are traditionally prepared from cornmeal, and served, drizzled with herb butter, as a *primo piatto*.

Serves 4

For the piquant tomato sauce:
5 tablespoons olive oil
¾ cup finely chopped onion
1 garlic clove, thinly sliced
2 tablespoons chopped parsley
1 tablespoon chopped herbs (oregano, sage, rosemary)
1 small sweet red pepper, cored, seeded, and finely chopped
½ cup meat stock
1 lb ripe, juicy tomatoes, peeled, seeded, and diced
⅛ cup ricotta cheese
salt

For the polenta:
1 teaspoon salt, 1¼ cups medium cornmeal

For the herb butter:
7 tablespoons butter
1 garlic clove, crushed
2 tablespoons chopped herbs (parsley, oregano, rosemary)

You will also need:
butter
⅓ cup freshly grated Parmesan cheese

Heat the olive oil in a saucepan and sweat the onion and garlic until lightly colored. Add the parsley and other chopped herbs, the red pepper, and tomatoes.

Gnocchi are usually prepared in the north of Italy in the shape of little dumplings. Only Roman-style gnocchi are cut from cooled polenta in an oval shape.

Cut out oval disks with a 2½-inch cutter. Layer in a buttered casserole dish, overlapping the gnocchi like roof tiles, then sprinkle with Parmesan and drizzle evenly with the melted herb butter.

Pour in the stock and braise, covered, over a low heat for 20 minutes.

Meanwhile, prepare the polenta. In a large saucepan, bring 2¼ cups water to a boil with the salt. Slowly trickle the cornmeal into the water while stirring vigorously with a wooden spoon to prevent

lumps from forming. (Lumps tend to occur chiefly when the water temperature falls below boiling point, which is likely to happen if the cornmeal is added all at once.) Until the polenta thickens, it tends to spray in all directions, so you might want to place a dish towel over the top of the pot. Keep stirring the polenta clockwise for about 20 minutes, until it comes away from the sides of the pot. Tip the polenta onto a wet board, spread with a palette knife to a thickness of ½ inch, and leave to cool.

To make the herb butter, melt the butter in a small saucepan and sweat the garlic briefly. Stir in the herbs and remove the pan from the heat.

Cut out oval gnocchi shapes as shown in the picture sequence on the left.

Preheat the oven to 425°F. Place the casserole dish in the oven and bake for 11 minutes, then place under the broiler for 1 minute. Before serving, stir the ricotta into the sauce, season with salt to taste, and hand around the tomato sauce separately to accompany the polenta gnocchi.

Gnocchi au gratin can be served with a tomato sauce, as suggested here, and also taste very good with a game ragout.

Gnocchi with boar ragout
These little dumplings can take a lot of the hearty, spicy sauce

To make the gnocchi dough, mound the mashed potatoes on a work surface with the flour and the eggs.

The potato dough is made supple by the addition of flour and egg yolk, and is very easy to mold. Each little piece of dough is pressed with a finger against a grater and rolled over it, producing gnocchi with a lattice pattern at the front and a concave shape at the back.

Working as quickly as possible, knead the ingredients to a smooth, supple dough.

Roll the dough into ropes ¾-inch thick. Place these side by side and cut into pieces 1¼ inches long.

Roll each piece of dough over a grater to give it a lattice pattern.

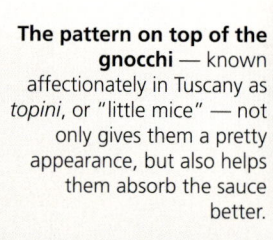

The pattern on top of the gnocchi — known affectionately in Tuscany as *topini*, or "little mice" — not only gives them a pretty appearance, but also helps them absorb the sauce better.

Serves 4
For the wild boar ragout:
3 lb boar haunch, bone in
1 tablespoon juniper berries, 2 bay leaves
6 fresh sage leaves
2⅔ cups dry red wine, 6 tablespoons olive oil
1 onion, finely chopped
1 garlic clove, crushed
¾ cup chopped carrot, ¾ cup chopped celery
1½ lb plum tomatoes, peeled and chopped
3 tablespoons tomato paste, 1¾ cups game stock
salt, freshly ground white pepper
For the gnocchi:
3 lb mealy potatoes
1⅔ cups all-purpose flour, 2 egg yolks

Place the meat in a large dish. Sprinkle the juniper berries and the bay and sage leaves over the top, and pour over the red wine. Cover with plastic wrap and marinate in the refrigerator for 12 hours.

Lift the meat out of the marinade and pat dry with paper towels. Remove the bone and set the meat to one side. Strain the marinade, reserving the liquid and the seasonings separately.

Heat half of the olive oil in a large saucepan and brown the bone over medium heat for 10 minutes. Add the onion, garlic, carrot, and celery, and cook over low heat for 2 minutes, stirring constantly, until the vegetables take on some color. Add the tomatoes, the reserved marinade seasonings, and the tomato paste, and reduce until the liquid has evaporated. Add 1 cup of the reserved marinade, and the game stock to the pot, and braise for about 3 hours, gradually adding the remaining marinade. Season the sauce with salt and pepper and strain. Cut the boar meat into small cubes and sear in the remaining olive oil. Pour the sauce in with the meat, deglaze the pan, and braise for about 20 minutes.

To make the gnocchi, boil the potatoes in their skins for 30 minutes, then peel and mash them while still warm. Prepare the dough and shape the gnocchi as shown in the picture sequence. Bring some salted water to a boil in a large pot, then reduce the heat. Add the gnocchi to the water in batches. As soon as they rise to the surface, lift them out with a slotted spoon, drain, and keep warm.

Arrange the cooked gnocchi on a warmed platter, spoon the ragout on top, and serve.

Gnocchi in tomato sauce

Potato dumplings, topped with a tasty *sugo*, sprinkled with spicy pecorino sardo cheese, and baked till browned and bubbling

In this recipe, the potatoes for the gnocchi dough are not boiled, but baked slowly in the oven. Although this takes a bit longer, it ensures that the potato dough stays drier and that the gnocchi turn out beautifully light in texture.

Serves 4
For the gnocchi:
2 lb mealy potatoes
1¼ cups all-purpose flour, 2 egg yolks, salt
For the tomato sauce:
1¾ lb plum tomatoes, peeled, seeded, and diced
½ cup finely diced carrot
1 cup finely chopped celery
1 cup finely chopped onion
1 teaspoon salt, freshly ground black pepper
1 pinch sugar
¼ cup olive oil
1 tablespoon snipped purple basil
1 teaspoon thyme leaves
You will also need:
⅓ cup freshly grated pecorino sardo cheese
¼ cup freshly grated Parmesan cheese
5 teaspoons butter, in curls
purple basil for garnishing

Lightly flatten the ropes of dough and cut into ½-inch pieces with a sharp knife.

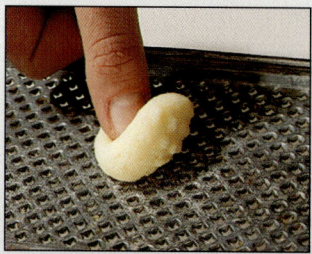

Roll the gnocchi one at a time over a grater to decorate them with a lattice pattern.

Preheat the oven to 400°F. Wash and dry the potatoes, wrap individually in aluminum foil, and bake for about 1 hour.

To make the tomato sauce, place the tomatoes in a saucepan with the carrot, onion, and celery, and simmer, covered, over a low heat for about 40 minutes, until the vegetables are soft.

Use a spoon to help push the cooked vegetables, in batches, through a coarse-mesh stainer into a saucepan. Scrape off the purée clinging to the strainer and stir it into the mixture in the saucepan.

To make the gnocchi, peel the baked potatoes. Mound the flour on a work surface and make a well in the center. Add the egg yolks and salt to the well. Put the still-warm potatoes through a potato ricer in a ring around the edge of the flour, and quickly knead all of the ingredients to a smooth dough.

Roll the dough into 2 ropes each ¾ inch in diameter, and dust with flour. Proceed as shown in the picture sequence on the left.

Drop the gnocchi in batches into briskly boiling salted water, then reduce the heat. Lift out the gnocchi with a slotted spoon soon as they rise to the surface, and drain well.

Briefly reheat the tomato sauce and season with salt, pepper, and sugar. Stir in the olive oil a spoonful at a time. Sprinkle in the basil and thyme.

Preheat the oven to 400°F. Mix the gnocchi into the sauce and spoon into a buttered casserole dish. Sprinkle with the pecorino sardo and the Parmesan, and dot with curls of butter. Bake, uncovered, for 15–20 minutes, until browned and bubbling. Garnish the gnocchi with the basil leaves and serve.

Don Alfonso uses only, herbs, tomatoes, and other vegetables that are freshly harvested on his farm on the picturesque Sorrento peninsula — and you can taste the difference.

Gnocchetti Don Alfonso

Celebrity chef Alfonso Iaccarino serves the best *gnocchetti di patate* far and wide at his restaurant

Although his gnocchi recipe scarcely differs from other standard recipes for potato dough, Don Alfonso makes his gnocchi particularly small, and does not give them the typical gnocchi shape. He rolls the dough into thin ropes about ¼-inch in diameter, then cuts these into ½-inch-long pieces. What makes his gnocchi outstanding is the *sugo*, which he prepares only from fully ripe tomatoes harvested on his farm. In the fall, he cooks and bottles enough of this tomato sauce to last the entire year. His very special olive oil, cold-pressed from the fruit of his own groves, rounds out the flavor of the *sugo* beautifully. In this way, a simple pasta dish is transformed into a true delicacy. By adding other ingredients, he can vary the gnocchi — freshly cooked shellfish, for example, add a touch of sophistication, and the Bay of Naples provides Don Alfonso with a good supply of top-quality seafood.

Serves 4
For the potato dough:
1¼–1½ lb mealy potatoes
2 cups all-purpose flour
1 cup semolina flour
salt, 1 egg yolk
For the tomato *sugo*:
½ cup olive oil
½ cup chopped shallots
1 garlic clove, finely chopped
1½ lb tomatoes

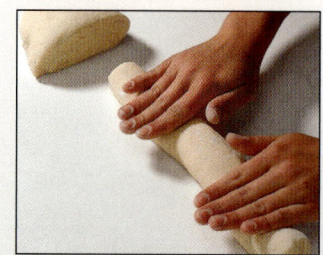

Mound the flour on a work surface and make a well in the center. Add the semolina flour, salt, and egg yolk to the well. Put the still-warm potatoes through a potato ricer in a ring around the edge of the flour, and knead all the ingredients to a smooth dough. Rest the dough briefly, then roll out into ropes about ¼ inch in diameter and dust with flour. Cut into ½-inch-long pieces.

| 1 rosemary sprig, 1 tablespoon chopped basil |
| 1 teaspoon salt, freshly ground pepper |

Preheat the oven to 400°F. Wash and dry the potatoes, wrap them in aluminum foil, and bake them for 1 hour. Remove them from the oven and peel them while they are still hot. Prepare the potato dough and shape the gnocchetti as described in the picture sequence on the left.

Add the gnocchetti to a pan of briskly boiling salted water, lower the heat, and cook until done. As soon as they rise to the surface, carefully lift them out with a slotted spoon and keep them warm.

In the meantime, heat the olive oil in a saucepan and sweat the shallots and garlic until lightly colored. Add the tomatoes, rosemary, and basil, and sweat briefly with the other ingredients. Season with salt and pepper. Spoon the gnocchetti onto warmed plates, pour over the tomato sauce, and serve.

Pasta dishes with arugula

Whether fresh, blanched, or deep-fried, this spicy-tasting salad leaf comes into its own when teamed with pasta

Arugula goes particularly well with the more compact pasta shapes like stringoli from southern Italy, or orecchiette from Apulia.

STRINGOLI WITH TOMATO SAUCE

Serves 4
For the pasta dough:
2½ cups all-purpose flour, 1 cup semolina flour, 2 eggs
2 tablespoons chopped parsley, 1 teaspoon salt
2 tablespoons olive oil
For the tomato sauce:
1 oz arugula, 3 tablespoons olive oil
½ cup finely chopped white onion
1 garlic clove, finely chopped
1¼ lb plum tomatoes, peeled, seeded, and diced
salt, freshly ground pepper
For the garnish:
½ bunch arugula, vegetable oil for deep-frying
2 tablespoons mascarpone, 1 tablespoon cream

Knead all the pasta dough ingredients together, wrap the dough in plastic wrap, and rest in the refrigerator for 1 hour. Roll the dough into thin ropes about 4 inches long, and let them dry slightly on a floured surface for 15 minutes.

To make the sauce, remove the stems from the arugula, wash the leaves, spin them dry, and chop finely. Heat the oil in a skillet and sweat the onions and garlic until lightly colored. Add the tomatoes and simmer over a low heat for 10 minutes, then season with salt and pepper, and stir in the arugula.

To make the garnish, prepare the arugula as described above, then deep-fry in batches in the hot

To serve, spoon the stringoli onto plates and top with the sauce. Mix the mascarpone and cream together, stir in the deep-fried arugula leaves, and arrange on top of the pasta.

Orecchiette, or "little ears," are often still made at home in Apulia and the Abruzzi from an eggless pasta dough. Their distinctive shape is achieved by making an indentation with one's thumb in the center of a little ball of dough.

Serves 4
12 oz orecchiette
For the sauce:
¼ cup olive oil
¾ cup finely chopped onion
1 lb fully ripe tomatoes, peeled, seeded, and diced
½ cup black olives, salt, freshly ground pepper
For the arugula–prosciutto mixture:
4 oz arugula, 2 tablespoons olive oil
3 garlic cloves, thinly sliced
5 oz prosciutto, finely chopped
salt
You will also need:
1¼ cups freshly grated aged pecorino cheese

oil and drain on paper towels. Cook the pasta in briskly boiling salted water for 10–15 minutes, until *al dente*, then drain. Serve as described in the caption to the picture above.

ORECCHIETTE WITH ARUGULA AND PECORINO

In spring, you can vary this recipe by replacing the arugula with young dandelions that you have picked yourself.

Heat the olive oil in a saucepan and sweat the onion until lightly colored. Add the tomatoes, season with salt and pepper, and simmer over a medium heat until they have almost disintegrated. Mix in the olives and set the sauce aside.

Cook the orecchiette in briskly boiling salted water for 12–15 minutes, until *al dente*.

Remove the stems from the arugula, wash the leaves, and carefully spin them dry. Heat the olive oil in a second saucepan and briefly sauté the garlic and prosciutto, stirring constantly. Add the arugula and sauté for 1 minute, still stirring, then remove from the heat. Stir the pasta into the arugula and prosciutto mixture. Spoon onto plates and top with the sauce, then sprinkle with the grated pecorino, and serve immediately.

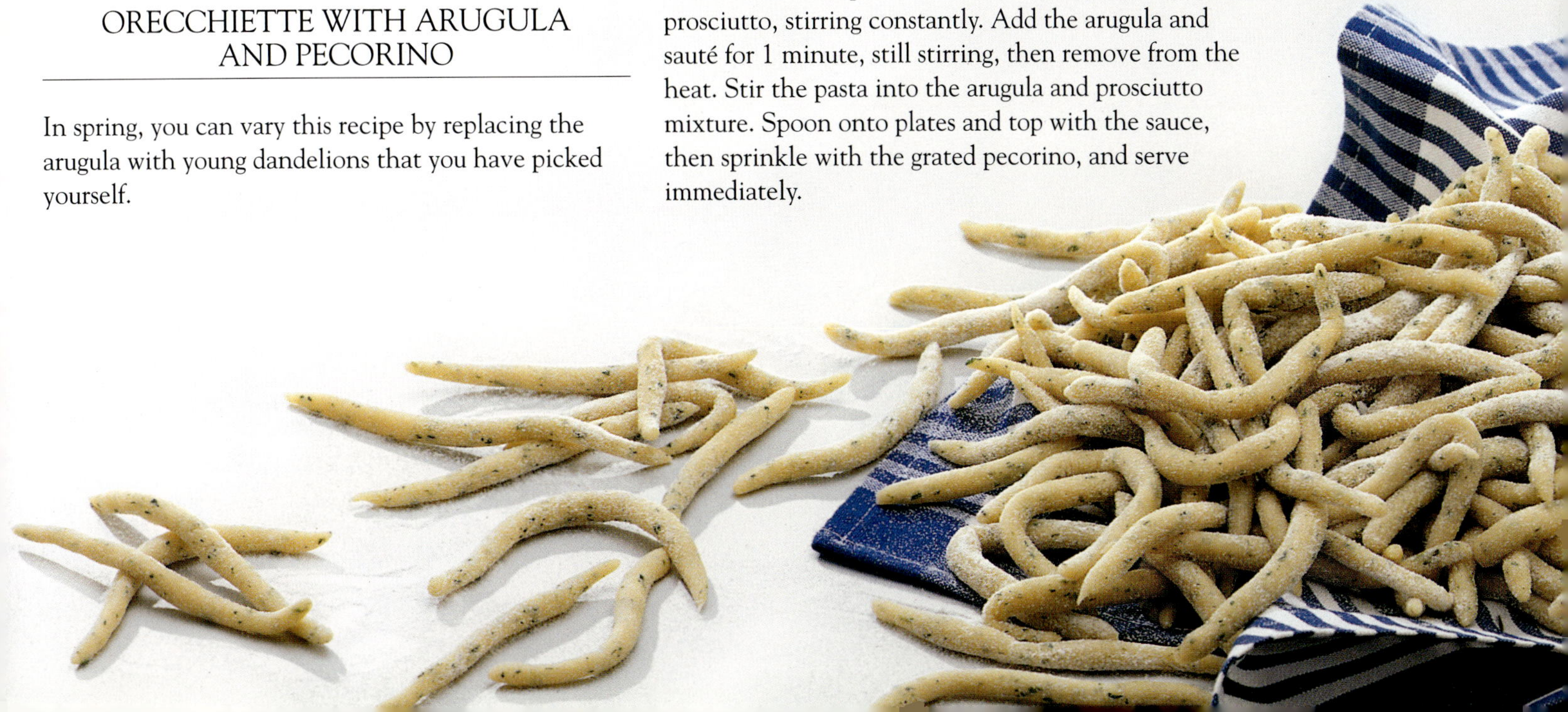

Bigo'li with quail
This hearty whole-wheat spaghetti is a Venetian specialty

Far from being a modern whole-food invention, bigo'li have long been served on fast days such as Ash Wednesday and Good Friday, with a sauce of salted anchovies, onions, and olive oil. In this recipe, however, the robust-tasting pasta becomes a veritable delicacy served with braised quail.

Serves 4
For the dough:
2¼ cups whole-wheat flour, 3 eggs, ½ teaspoon salt
For the braised quail:
4 oven-ready quails (6 oz each)
2 tablespoons oil
½ cup finely chopped shallots
⅔ cup finely chopped celery
¼ cup finely chopped parsley root
¼ cup finely chopped carrot
⅓ cup diced pancetta
2 garlic cloves, unpeeled and bruised
1 teaspoon flour, 1 cup chicken stock
2 tablespoons chopped parsley
salt, freshly ground pepper,

To make bigo'li, the relatively thick spaghetti, many housewives in the Veneto use a heavy, stable press with a perforated copper disk, through which the dough is extruded. On the other hand, the noodles can be made using a pasta machine with angular cutting rollers; like the pasta shown here, they will look more like *spaghetti alla chitarra*

Sift the flour onto a work surface and make a well in the center. Add the eggs and salt to the well and gradually work into the flour, adding a little water if needed, until you have a firm dough. Knead vigorously and slap down onto the work surface until the dough is smooth and elastic. Roll into a ball, dust with flour, wrap in plastic wrap, and rest in the refrigerator for 20 minutes. Roll out the dough thinly using a pasta machine and cut into 1/8-inch-wide spaghetti. Spread the pasta onto a dish towel and let dry briefly.

In the meantime, wash the quails inside and out, pat dry, and halve them lengthwise. Remove the legs and wings. Season the quail lightly with salt and pepper and set aside. Heat the oil in a skillet and sweat the shallots until lightly colored. Add the other vegetables and sauté over a high heat for 2–3 minutes, then lift out and keep warm. Render the pancetta in the skillet, add the quail pieces, and sear over a high heat. Add the garlic cloves. Sprinkle the contents of the pan with flour, sauté for 3–4 minutes, and deglaze with the stock. Braise, uncovered, until the meat is done and the liquid is reduced by a little less than half. Stir in the parsley and adjust the seasoning.

Cook the spaghetti in briskly boiling salted water until *al dente*, then drain. Serve with the braised quail.

Bologna is nicknamed *la grassa* — "Bologna the Fat" or "the Prosperous" — because the inhabitants of this city have always favored a rich, but undeniably delicious, style of cooking. When prepared with love and patience, the city's specialties taste too good to resist.

Lasagna bolognese
An Italian culinary classic that never fails to please

Even with classic Italian dishes such as this one, there are numerous variations. Many cooks prefer to use lamb, or even game, in their *ragù* instead of beef. There are no hard and fast rules here; just follow your own taste, and use the freshest, highest-quality produce on offer for the best results. Fresh lasagne sheets taste best, but dried ones can be used.

Serves 4–6
1 recipe fresh white lasagne (see pp. 116–XX) or 16 dried lasagne noodles
For the bolognese meat sauce:
3 tablespoons oil, 3 tablespoons butter
1 lb lean ground beef
½ cup finely chopped onion, ½ cup chopped carrot
⅓ cup chopped parsley root
¾ cup chopped celery, 2 tablespoons tomato paste
1¼ cups peeled canned tomatoes with their juice
salt, freshly ground pepper, 1 tablespoon chopped parsley
1 teaspoon chopped thyme leaves, 1 teaspoon chopped basil
½ cup strong meat stock, ½ cup red wine
For the béchamel sauce:
2 tablespoons butter, ¼ cup flour, 2¼ cups milk
salt, freshly ground white pepper
1 generous pinch freshly grated nutmeg
You will also need:
8 x 12-inch baking dish
butter, ¾ cup freshly grated Parmesan cheese

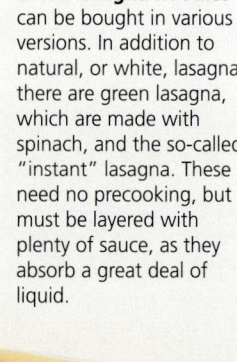

Dried lasagna noodles can be bought in various versions. In addition to natural, or white, lasagna, there are green lasagna, which are made with spinach, and the so-called "instant" lasagna. These need no precooking, but must be layered with plenty of sauce, as they absorb a great deal of liquid.

Spoon half of the meat sauce onto the first layer of pasta and spread evenly. Top with another 4 lasagna noodles, overlapping them slightly. Spread half of the béchamel sauce over this layer. Repeat the entire process, finishing with a layer of béchamel sauce, then sprinkle with the Parmesan.

To make the meat sauce, heat the oil with the butter in a large saucepan, then add the ground meat and fry until brown and crumbly. Add the carrot, parsley root, celery, and tomato paste, and sweat until beginning to soften. Stir in the tomatoes with their juice, the seasonings and herbs, and the stock and wine. Simmer for 50 minutes.

To make the béchamel sauce, melt the butter in a saucepan. When it is foaming, stir in the flour, and cook for 1 minute without letting it color. Pour in the milk, stir until smooth, and bring to a boil. Season with salt, pepper, and nutmeg, and simmer over a low heat for 20 minutes, stirring constantly. Remove from the heat and strain.

Cook dried lasagna noodles for 5 minutes, or fresh lasagna for 3 minutes, in briskly boiling salted water. Carefully lift out, lay each noodle flat, and cover with a damp dish towel.

Preheat the oven to 350°F. Butter the base of the baking dish and cover with 4 lasagna noodles slightly overlapping. Proceed as shown in the picture sequence on the left. Bake the lasagna for about 40 minutes, until the top is lightly browned. Cut into squares and serve on warmed plates.

A lasagna bolognese is an ideal dish for when you have company. Not only does the recipe make enough for 4–6 portions, but it can also be prepared in advance.

Line the base of a buttered baking dish with 3 lasagna noodles. Top with the vegetable filling, tomato strips, and cheese. Repeat this procedure twice more, finishing with a layer of pasta.

Swiss chard and kohlrabi lasagna
A vegetarian lasagna that looks especially effective made with layers of green pasta

Serves 4–6
12 green lasagna noodles
For the vegetable filling:
4 kohlrabi (8 oz each)
¼ cup butter
freshly grated nutmeg
1 tablespoon flour, 2¼ cups milk, 1 cup cream
1 lb Swiss chard
2 shallots, chopped
10 oz tomatoes, peeled, seeded, and cut into strips
salt, freshly ground white pepper
You will also need:
butter for greasing, 7 x 11-inch baking dish
2 cups freshly grated aged Provolone cheese
¼ cup crème fraîche, 1 egg yolk

Peel the kohlrabi and cut off their woody ends. Slice the bulbs into rounds ⅛-inch thick and the tender leaves into strips. Melt half of the butter in a pot and sweat the sliced bulbs with the leaves. Season with salt, pepper, and nutmeg, and sprinkle with flour. Pour in the milk and cream and simmer for 10 minutes. Transfer to a bowl and leave to cool.

Separate the Swiss-chard stalks from the leaves, trim them, and cut into pieces ¾-inch long. Melt the remaining butter in a skillet and sweat the shallots and the chard stalks. Remove the midribs from the chard leaves, slice the green part into wide strips, then blanch, refresh, and drain. Mix the chard stalks and leaves with the kohlrabi.

Cook the lasagna noodles in briskly boiling salted water for 5 minutes, then drain and refresh under cold water. Spread them out flat on a damp dish towel, and cover with another damp dish towel.

Preheat the oven to 350°F. Butter the baking dish. As shown in the picture sequence, spread a third of the vegetable mixture on top of the first layer of pasta. Top with a third of the tomato strips and sprinkle with a third of the cheese. Repeat the process twice more, finishing with a layer of pasta. Mix the crème fraîche with the egg yolk and brush it over the top.

Bake the lasagna for 40–45 minutes. Cut into squares and serve on warmed plates.

Kissed by the sun
Tomatoes that are fully ripe and aromatic, but firm, contribute their fine flavor to this *lasagna verde*. A mixture of milk and cream provides the creamy texture.

Pasticcio di maccheroni
The macaroni casserole is a popular dish throughout Italy

Once upon a time, a *pasticcio* was taken to mean a pie. Nowadays, the term is commonly used to describe a casserole similar to a lasagna, with various ingredients arranged in layers. When the Italians speak of *un bel pasticcio*, however, they are not praising someone's culinary skills, but rather speaking of "a fine mess."

Serves 4–6
For the pasta dough:
1 ⅔ cups all-purpose flour, 2 eggs, 1 teaspoon oil, salt water as needed
⅓ cup chopped herbs (sage, thyme, parsley)

Rabbit liver and meat give the filling its distinctive taste. Other ingredients are mushrooms, chopped parsley, and freshly grated Asiago, a cheese from northern Italy.

Clearly visible on these wheels of Asiago cheese is the protected quality seal burned into the rind. Asiago piccante, ripened for up to 1 year, is especially suitable for grating.

For the filling:
7 oz rabbit liver, 9 oz prepared rabbit meat
2 tablespoons olive oil, ¾ cup chopped onion
½ cup chopped carrot, ½ cup chopped celery root
½ cup red wine
1 tablespoon tomato paste
1 cup veal stock, ½ bunch parsley
⅓ cup chopped black olives
2 tablespoons butter
2 cups thinly sliced mushrooms
10 oz long macaroni
1¼ cups freshly grated Asiago cheese
salt, freshly ground pepper
You will also need:
2 tablespoons butter, in curls

Stir together the first five ingredients and knead into a supple dough. Wrap in plastic wrap and rest in the refrigerator for 1 hour.

To make the filling, trim the rabbit liver and cut into small pieces. Put the rabbit meat through the medium blade of a meat grinder.

Heat the olive oil in a saucepan and sweat the onion, carrot, and celery root until lightly colored. Add the meat and brown quickly. Deglaze with the wine and reduce the liquid slightly. Stir in the tomato paste. Pour in the stock, sprinkle in the parsley, and season with salt and pepper. Braise over a low heat for 20 minutes. Add the olives and continue to braise for 5 minutes. Melt the butter in a skillet, briefly sauté the mushrooms and the liver, and add to the meat sauce at the last minute.

Cook the macaroni in boiling salted water until *al dente*, then drain and refresh under cold water. On a floured surface, roll out the dough into 3 thin sheets of about 7 x 10 inches. Cook one at a time in boiling salted water for about 2 minutes, then lift out and drain well.

Preheat the oven to 400°F. Butter a baking dish and line with a sheet of pasta dough. Cover with a layer of macaroni, followed by half of the meat mixture, and then a third of the cheese. Repeat this process, finishing with a sheet of pasta dough. Sprinkle with the remaining cheese and dot with the butter. Bake for 30 minutes, cut into squares, and serve.

riso RICE

Not all rice is the same. This is true everywhere, but particularly in Italy, a major rice-producer and consumer. And although only short-grained rice should be used to make a risotto, there is still the question about when it is best to use a Carnaroli or a Baldo, a Vialone or an Arborio.

It is only at first glance that the wide range of rice on offer can be confusing. Once you have gained an overview of the varieties available, and are aware of the differences in their preparation, you will find that rice lends itself splendidly to experimentation, and that the sky is the limit for the creative risotto cook.

Short-grain rice for risottos

Italy, land of rice

Rice was first brought to Italy, via Sicily, by Arab traders as early as the eighth or ninth century, but it was planted there, chiefly in the north, only in the thirteenth or fourteenth century. Rice cultivation began in the Vercellese, that region of Italy, and of Europe, that even today produces the most rice. Canals were dug, and marshes were transformed into valuable agricultural land. In about 1600 the local populace, unaware of the real causes, blamed epidemic diseases on rice, but even their opposition did not stop its progress. Many more canals and irrigation channels were dug, with the result that the area around Vercelli today largely resembles a chess board on which the changing seasons are imprinted. Silvery reflections from the flooded fields in spring give way to the bright green of the young rice plants in summer, until the ripening grain turns the fields shimmering gold in the fall. In between the fields are dikes and rows of poplars, and herons pose like slender chess pieces before taking flight.

The Canale Cavour, finished in 1863, which brought water to Novara and the Lomellina, decisively improved rice-growing conditions in northern Italy. The main areas of cultivation lie in the Po Valley along the river, and extend from Piedmont via Lombardy up to the Veneto. There, the rice flourishes mainly on alluvial, sandy, or clay soils.

Rice cultivation is labor-intensive

In Italy, it is chiefly the japonica type rice that is grown. Distinguished by oval-to-short, thick grains, it is classified as a short-grain rice. The climatic conditions of the Po Valley are ideal for its development: sufficient warmth — about 86°F is optimal — plenty of sun, and enough water. Depending on the region, the growing cycle, from sowing to harvesting, takes between seven and eight months.

Before sowing, however, the fields must be prepared. In Italy, the subsoil is generally "dry-compacted," that is, the rice fields are plowed and harrowed before being flooded. Working

Ripening rice As the fields change from green to gold, the time of the harvest draws nearer. Gauging the proper time to harvest the crop is vital for the subsequent quality of the rice.

Harvesting by hand Until just a few decades ago, harvesting the rice with a scythe was an extremely arduous affair for which, as for the tending of the rice fields, women were often employed. Today a type of combine harvester performs this task.

Short-grain rice This is what the proper rice for Italy's No.1 rice dish looks like when cooked plain, rather than made into a risotto. The Italians have every reason to be proud of their rice, since in the case of short-grain rice and risotto, rice type and style of preparation complement each other uniquely well.

Rice seed that is sown directly into water must be germinated first, because it requires a great deal of oxygen in the beginning. The grains are soaked, then washed, then left to germinate for about two days. Before being sown, they may be disinfected to protect them against possible diseases. The rice grains are either sown thickly in special seedbeds, or broadcast straight into the fields.

An Italian rice farmer planting out the seed In Italy, hand-sowing is widespread even to this day. The pregerminated rice grains are strewn as evenly as possible over the flooded field.

the soil in this way is essential to keep the loss of nutrients and water to a minimum. In order to ensure optimum growth of the rice, the fields must also be absolutely level, so that the height of the water is the same everywhere, 2–6 inches. Leveling the subsoil, which used to be very difficult, is nowadays made much easier by the use of laser technology.

Sowing
The ability of rice to thrive in water as well as in dry conditions is a great advantage. It means the farmers can flood the fields before sowing, in order to suppress weed growth in the earliest growing stage. Late spring, from April to May, is reckoned to be the best time for sowing, which is done either by hand or by machine. If the young rice plants have been raised in a seedbed, they must be thinned out later. A period of intensive care then begins in the summer.

Weeding
From June to mid July, there is a constant need for weeding and pest control. In the past, battalions of female workers were employed not only for the thinning out of the seedlings, but for the weeding and the removal of pests. The so-called *mondine* — the Italian name for the seasonal female workers from the south — had a hard job, working through the fields two or three times a day, their backs bent the entire time, as they waded through the water with the sun beating down relentlessly from above. *Bitter Rice*, the classic 1948 movie starring Silvana Mangano, made a lasting impression in its portrayal of the hard life of these workers. Gone, now, however, is this vision of long rows of women moving across the fields: The use of special modern machines and pesticides has made the work substantially easier. And the use of insecticides has largely been replaced too, by environmentally compatible methods. What carp were for the Chinese, frogs are for the Italians: welcome, helpful and, what's more, edible aids for pest-control.

The harvest
The flowering of the rice plants in August heralds the approach of the harvest season. In September or October the rice panicles, now yellow but not yet fully ripe, are cut, either by hand with a scythe, or, as is overwhelmingly the case nowadays, by machine. In the case of hand harvesting, there is a several-day-long period in which the rice is dried in the sun before threshing. With machine harvesting, however, threshing generally takes place immediately in the field.

White or brown?

How people prefer their rice — with the bran layer intact or milled white — is first and foremost a question of taste, although there are a number of differences in terms of nutritional content and cooking time. Whether white or brown, though, the rice grains must be husked before they can be cooked and eaten.

From field to mill

After the harvest has been brought in, the raw rice — known as "paddy" in English, and referred to as *riso greggio* in Italy — is shipped to special warehouses. There it is dried further if necessary, and then stored in conditions that ensure the moisture content remains constant at 13–14 percent until processing. Next, the rice is sent to a mill for refining. This may be a large, modern, high-capacity plant, or a traditional mill that can handle only relatively small quantities.

Husking

Since the hull (the lemma) is inedible, it must be removed from the grain. Traditionally, the way rice has been prepared for centuries, the grains are tipped into round stone troughs and pounded rhythmically with large pestles, causing the grain and the hull to separate. In addition to it being very time-consuming, the chief drawback of this method is the large proportion of broken rice that it produces. The method generally used nowadays is considerably gentler and yields a higher proportion of high-quality rice. The raw rice is separated by being rubbed between two rubber rollers running at different speeds, and then sorted according to grain size. In this stage of processing, the rice, now referred to as brown or whole-grain, and in Italian as *riso semi-greggio*, can be cooked and eaten.

Milling

In Italy, risotto rices are usually milled, a further stage of processing. A rice grain is composed of several layers. On the inside lies the starchy white endosperm, which is surrounded by the various darker layers of bran: the peel and seed coat, and the protein-rich aleurone layer. Milling removes these outer layers; the grain becomes lighter and lighter, until only the white endosperm is left. There are two methods of milling. The first involves rubbing the rice grains against stone, an age-old method producing less broken rice but leaving the grains with a somewhat rough surface; the second, more recent, method involves rubbing the grains against each other, which yields a smooth surface but more broken grains. Both methods remove the germ, or embryo, as well as the outer bran layer, either partially or completely.

Rice is good for you

All rice is healthy. It is reputed to be especially digestible and is used in both special diets and reducing diets, being low in sodium, but high in potassium, which is responsible for the body's water balance. However, brown rice has a higher nutritional content than white rice. The unmilled grain retains both the outer bran layer and the nutritious, oil-bearing germ, which together contain the lion's share of minerals, trace elements, and vitamins. In particular, the B-complex vitamins and vitamin E are present in generous amounts in the outer layers. Because of the bran left, the percentage of fiber in brown rice is also a good deal higher than in white rice.

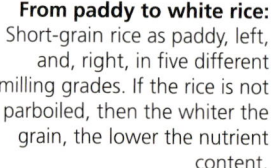

From paddy to white rice: Short-grain rice as paddy, left, and, right, in five different milling grades. If the rice is not parboiled, then the whiter the grain, the lower the nutrient content.

Milling the rice, as it used to be done in the Pila Vecia1 The rice is tipped into troughs known as *pile* and rhythmically pounded with pestles. Although brown rice contains the most nutrients, for the sake of appearance and a shorter cooking time, the rice is usually processed further, with the grains becoming increasingly white at each stage. Sifting separates the bran from the grain, and we are left with the finished product.

Provided that you use one of the short-grain varieties, brown rice is suitable for risottos, even when it is not specified. Because the bran layer forms a sort of barrier against heat and moisture, brown rice needs to cook a little longer than white rice (allow 40–50 minutes) and requires more liquid. It also has a higher fat content, and so does not keep indefinitely; any stores should be used up within a year.

Parboiled short-grain rice

Parboiling, a hydrothermic method using steam and pressure, restores up to 80 percent of the nutrients extracted when the rice is milled. In simple terms, it works like this: All the air is removed from the rice by low pressure in vacuum containers. Next, the rice is soaked in lukewarm water to dissolve the nutrients. Then the grains are treated with steam at high pressure, which forces vitamins and minerals back into the rice grain.

Repeated treatment with hot steam toughens the starch on the surface of the grain, so that grains do not stick together. It is very difficult to make a typical risotto with such rice since it is the starch released during cooking that produces the creamy consistency. Gabriele Ferron, the proprietor of the famous Antica Riseria Ferron, recommends that, instead of a pure-white rice, you use a darker one, in which less of the surrounding layers has been removed.

Rice north and south

Rice is eaten a good deal more often in northern and central Italy than in the south, where pasta is preferred. When rice is cooked in the north, it is almost always a risotto, a dish cooked chiefly in the winter. In Isola della Scala, a village not far from Verona, people wait with bated breath every year to see who will prepare the best risotto in the *Palio del risotto* competition. But rice dishes are also known in the south, such as the Sicilian *arancini*, consisting of rice balls the size of oranges — hence their name — with ground meat and peas, and the Roman *supplì*, rice croquettes with mozzarella and prosciutto. And it is in the south that the sweet rice dishes are a specialty.

Inside the Pila Vecia: Today this old mill, now owned by the Ferron family, is slightly more modern. The rice is milled mechanically in these pressure cylinders, where the rubbing of rice grain against rice grain removes the bran layer.

Vialone nano
Cooking time: 15–18 minutes

Vialone nano semifino, brown rice.
Cooking time: 30–35 minutes

Loto
Cooking time: 17–20 minutes

San Andrea
Cooking time: 18–20 minutes

Arborio
Cooking time: 15–18 minutes

Originario
Cooking time: 12–15 minutes

Roma
Cooking time: 15–18 minutes

Carnaroli
Cooking time: 18–20 minutes

Baldo
Cooking time: about 18 minutes:

Ribe
Cooking time: 15–18 minutes

Padano
Cooking time: 15–18 minutes

Ribe, parboiled.
Cooking time: 18–20 minutes

Ideal varieties for risottos

Risottos require a rice with very special cooking qualities. On the one hand, part of the starch from the grains must dissolve to produce the creamy thickness of the dish; on the other hand, the grains must be able to absorb liquid as they cook while remaining firm in the center, or *al dente*. Only Italian short-grain rice ideally fulfills these prerequisites. Here, rice variety and preparation method determine and complement each other optimally. But there are still considerable differences between one variety of risotto rice and another. These can sometimes be seen in the size of the grain, and in its shape and color. The Italian classification into four groups refers to the size of the rice grain. Thus, *commune* or *originario* are short, small grains (under 5.2 mm); *semifino* are medium-length grains (5.2–6.4 mm); *fino* are large, long grains (over 6.4 mm); *superfino* are also large, long grains over 6.4 mm, but only of particular varieties (for example, Arborio, Baldo, Carnaroli). It is chiefly the different starch composition that determines the quality of the variety.

Different types of starch

There are two types of rice starch. First, there is amylopectin, which is responsible for the swelling of the grains and their tendency to stick together; then there is amylose, the water-soluble part of the endosperm, which dissolves out of the grains when the risotto is stirred. As a rule, the higher the amylose content, the better the rice variety. Carnaroli, for example, has one of the highest percentages of amylose (24.1%), closely followed by Vialone nano, a classic risotto rice (23.9%). Arborio (19.6% amylose) and Baldo (20.5% amylose) are slightly stickier, but are also excellent risotto rices.

Stirring risotto — a must?

According to the classic Lombardian method, the risotto is always stirred in an open pot while small amounts of liquid are added repeatedly, as part is absorbed by the rice, and part evaporates. Thus the rice starch becomes a thickening agent, which makes the risotto beautifully creamy. In the Piedmont, however, the rice is risotto). The amount of liquid needed to keep the risotto moister during cooking varies. For this reason, the quantities given in the following recipes are meant as guidelines only. If a risotto threatens to become too dry, simply add a little more heated stock or hot water. The liquid used for the risotto should not be too salty, since the flavor and seasonings become more concentrated as the liquid evaporates, and the cheese — usually Parmesan — that is stirred into many risottos just before the end of the cooking time is also salty.

Cooking rice

There are Italian dishes other than risotto in which rice plays a role. For these, the rice is often cooked by the absorption method illustrated below.

not stirred after it is sweated. This causes an exquisite crust to form on the base of the pot. In both cases, the risotto remains relatively compact. In the Veneto, by contrast, the people are fond of a more liquid *risotto all'onda* (literally, a "wavy"

Cooking rice by the absorption method:

Measure a sufficient quantity of water for the volume of rice and pour into a suitable-sized pot. Tip in the rice.

Bring the rice and water to a full boil, reduce the heat to low, and simmer the rice.

If there is any water left when the rice is done, pour it away. Otherwise, allow excess steam to evaporate, fluffing the rice lightly with a fork.

The basic way to prepare risotto:

Melt 1½ tablespoons of butter in a large pot, add ½ cup diced onion, and sweat, stirring, without letting the onion color.

Tip in 2 cups short-grain rice all at once over a moderate heat and stir immediately so that the grains do not catch on the base of the pot.

Sweat the rice, stirring, until the grains start to become translucent. Neither the rice nor the onions should take on any color.

Pour in ⅔ cup white wine. Continue stirring over a moderate heat until the rice has absorbed most of the liquid.

Gradually add 4½–5½ cups hot meat stock, stirring constantly. Add more stock only when the liquid in the pot has been largely absorbed.

Cook the risotto for 12–15 minutes, until done. Season with salt and stir in 2 tablespoons butter and freshly grated Parmesan to taste.

Thoroughly classic risottos

First saffron-yellow, then green with herbs — and always a sheer delight

Probably the most famous dish of its kind — and for good reason — is *risotto alla milanese*. This classic specialty from Lombardy is simple yet refined. The essential ingredients are beef marrow and saffron, the right variety of rice, and a good, flavorful broth.

RISOTTO ALLA MILANESE

Serves 4
1–2 tablespoons beef marrow
5 tablespoons butter
½ cup finely diced onion
½ garlic clove, finely diced
2 cups Arborio rice, ⅔ cup white wine
salt, about ¼ teaspoon saffron threads
4½–5½ cups hot meat stock
freshly ground white pepper
⅔ cup freshly grated Parmesan cheese
You will also need:
curls of butter for the top
¼ cup freshly grated Parmesan cheese

Soak the marrow in cold water for 10 minutes, then drain and dice.

In a large pot, render the marrow in 2 tablespoons of the butter. Add the onion and garlic, and sweat until lightly colored. Tip in the rice and stir until the grains are slightly translucent.

Deglaze with the white wine and reduce slightly. Stir in the salt and the saffron threads. Gradually add the stock and cook the risotto for 15–18 minutes or until done, stirring constantly. Season with salt and pepper and stir in the grated Parmesan and the remaining butter. Remove from the heat and allow the flavors to mingle for a few minutes. Spoon the risotto onto warmed plates, top each portion with butter curls, and hand round the grated Parmesan separately.

Tinted yellow with saffron, the world's most expensive spice. This is how a *risotto alla milanese*, which tastes equally good as an appetizer or an accompaniment, should look. The flavor of the dish may be further refined by substituting veal marrow for the beef marrow.

HERB RISOTTO

This risotto tastes best in the early spring, when nettles, dandelion, and bear's garlic (also known as ramson) are still young and tender. The herbs must be added to the pot right after the rice to retain their vivid color. *Rocambole*, known in English as sand leek or giant garlic, or sometimes "gourmet" garlic, also lends a special touch to the dish.

Serves 4
4 tablespoons vegetable oil
½ cup finely chopped rocambole (with leaves)
1 garlic clove, finely chopped
4 oz young spinach, finely chopped
4 oz wild herbs (nettles, dandelion, bear's garlic), finely chopped
2 tablespoons white wine
2 cups Arborio rice, 6¼ cups hot veal stock
½ teaspoon salt, freshly ground white pepper
¾ cup freshly grated Parmesan cheese
3 tablespoons butter
You will also need:
¼ cup freshly grated Parmesan cheese

Heat the oil in a pot and sweat the rocambole and garlic until lightly colored. Stir in the spinach and herbs. Deglaze with the white wine and stew for 1–2 minutes. Tip in the rice. Gradually add the stock, and cook the risotto for 15–18 minutes or until done, stirring constantly. Season with salt and pepper. Mix in the grated Parmesan and the butter. Remove from the heat and allow the flavors to blend for a few minutes. Spoon onto warmed plates and hand around the Parmesan separately.

RISOTTO WITH BASIL

Since cooking basil for too long would impair its taste, it is added only when the rice is almost done. (Recipe not pictured.)

Serves 4
2 tablespoons beef marrow, 2 tablespoons olive oil
⅓ cup chopped shallots, 2 garlic cloves, crushed
2 cups Vialone rice, ½ cup dry white wine
6 cups hot chicken stock
½ teaspoon salt, freshly ground pepper
2 cups finely chopped basil
½ cup each freshly grated aged pecorino and Parmesan cheese
¼ cup butter, flaked

Soak the marrow in cold water for 10 minutes, then drain and dice. Heat the oil in a pot with the marrow, then add the shallots and garlic, and sweat until lightly colored. Tip in the rice and stir until the grains start to become translucent. Deglaze with the wine and allow it to evaporate almost completely. Gradually add the stock and cook the rice for 15–18 minutes, until done, stirring constantly. When the risotto has reached the desired consistency, season with salt and pepper. Mix in the basil with the grated cheeses. Top with the butter, remove from the heat, allow the butter to melt, and serve.

Piquant, ripened hard cheeses, such as pecorino, Parmigiano Reggiano, grana padano, and even Gouda, are superbly suitable for grating, and hence for seasoning rice dishes.

With seafood

Risottos become a sophisticated appetizer — first with shrimp, then with a trio of shellfish

SHRIMP RISOTTO WITH SAVOY CABBAGE

Serves 4
For the risotto:
3 tablespoons butter; ½ cup finely chopped onion
1½ cups Arborio rice
½ cup dry white wine, 4½ cups fine meat broth
½ teaspoon salt, freshly ground white pepper
You will also need:
½ small Savoy cabbage, ⅓ cup finely diced pancetta
½ cup finely chopped onion, 1 garlic clove, crushed
10 oz shrimp, shelled and deveined
2 oz pecorino cheese, salt, freshly ground white pepper

Melt the butter in a pot, add the onion, and sweat until lightly colored. Tip in the rice and sauté over a high heat, stirring constantly, until the grains are translucent. Pour in the wine and allow to reduce. Gradually add the broth, stirring constantly. Cook the risotto for about 12 minutes, adding a little extra broth if necessary. Season with salt and pepper.

Meanwhile, core the cabbage and slice into ½-inch wide strips. Fry the pancetta with the onion and garlic for a few minutes. Add the cabbage and cook for about 6 minutes, turning frequently. Add the shrimp, season with salt and pepper, and stir this mixture into the nearly cooked risotto. Cook for about 5 minutes while you use a vegetable peeler to shave the pecorino. Stir in the cheese and serve.

An unusual combination of ingredients that works surprisingly well: The smoked bacon is slightly unexpected in a risotto, the Savoy cabbage even more so, but they harmonize well with the shrimp.

Three varieties of shellfish — hard-shell clams, mussels and scallops — are featured in this risotto, which also includes chunks of monkfish. The mollusks are shucked and mixed into the rice, except for a few that are left in the shell for a garnish.

RISOTTO WITH SEAFOOD

Serves 4
1½ lb monkfish, 1 lb clams, 1 lb mussels
2 carrots, 2 celery stalks, 1 bay leaf
5 white peppercorns, 8 scallops, 3 tablespoons butter
1 garlic clove, finely chopped
½ cup finely chopped onion
1½ cups Vialone nano rice, ½ cup white wine
1 tablespoon chopped parsley, salt, freshly ground pepper

Bone the monkfish and slice into 1-inch pieces. Wash and scrub the clams and mussels well under running cold water, discarding any open ones. Remove the beard from the mussels. Peel the carrots, trim the

celery, and cut both into small dice. Bring 5½ cups water to a boil in a pot with the bay leaf, vegetables, some salt and the peppercorns. Reduce the heat, add the monkfish and simmer for 5 minutes. Lift out the fish and set aside. Bring the court-bouillon back to a boil, add the clams and mussels, and cook until they open. Lift out the shellfish, discarding any that remain closed. Strain the court-bouillon and reserve 3 cups.

Clean the scallops thoroughly. Holding each one firmly in a cloth, slice through the inner muscle with a sturdy, pointed knife and lift off the flat upper shell. Slide the knife along the gray edge of the scallop flesh to release the meat. Remove the gray sac and carefully separate the white meat from the orange roe, or coral. Cut the white meat in half crosswise. Melt the butter in a casserole, and sauté the scallops and corals for 1 minute on each side. Lift out and set aside. Sweat the onion and garlic in the butter until the onion is translucent. Tip in the rice, and sauté until it, too, has become translucent. Add the white wine and reduce, stirring. Season with salt and pepper, and gradually add the reserved court-bouillon, stirring constantly. The rice will be done in 15–18 minutes. Shuck the clams and mussels, leaving a few in their shells.

Mix the fish, the shucked clams and mussels, and the scallop meat and coral into the risotto in the last few minutes of cooking to warm them through. Sprinkle in the parsley, adjust the seasoning, garnish the risotto with the reserved clams and mussels in their shells, and serve from the casserole.

With tomatoes and zucchini

Summery, light risottos with young zucchini and really ripe tomatoes

RISOTTO CON ZUCCHINE FIORITE

Serves 4

7 oz zucchini, 10 zucchini flowers

6 tablespoons butter, ¾ cup finely chopped onion

2 cups Arborio rice, ⅔ cup white wine

4½–5½ cups hot vegetable stock, salt

⅓ cup freshly grated Parmesan cheese

You will also need:

¼ cup freshly grated Parmesan cheese

Trim the zucchini, then cut into sticks about 1 inch long and ⅓ inch wide. Remove the stalk and pistil from the flowers and cut the petals into small pieces. Melt 4 tablespoons (¼ cup) of the butter in a pot and sweat the onions without allowing them to color. Add the rice and sauté, stirring, until translucent. Pour in the wine, reduce, and cook the risotto for 15–18 minutes, stirring constantly and adding the stock gradually. The rice should remain barely covered with liquid. About 8 minutes before the end of cooking time, mix in the zucchini sticks. Add the flowers only in the last minute and simmer. Season with salt and stir in the remaining butter and the cheese. Hand round the Parmesan cheese separately.

TOMATO RISOTTO

Serves 4
3 tablespoons olive oil, 1½ cups finely chopped onion
2 garlic cloves, finely chopped
1¾ lb ripe, aromatic tomatoes, coarsely diced
6 tablespoons butter, 1½ cups Arborio rice
⅔ cup white wine, 3 cups hot veal stock
⅔ cup freshly grated Parmesan cheese
salt, freshly ground white pepper

You will also need:
¼ cup freshly grated Parmesan cheese
1 tablespoon chopped herbs (parsley, basil)

Heat the oil in a pot and sweat half the onion and half the garlic until lightly colored. Add the tomatoes. Season with salt and pepper, cover, and simmer over a moderate heat for about 15 minutes. Push the tomatoes through a strainer, scrape off the purée clinging to the strainer and use it too. Stir the tomato purée and season to taste with salt and pepper.

Melt half the butter in a large pot and sweat the remaining onion and garlic until the onion is translucent. Tip in the rice and stir until it, too, is translucent. Season sparingly. Pour in the wine and cook until it is reduced by half. Add the stock gradually, stirring constantly. The rice should remain barely covered with liquid. Cook the risotto for 15–18 minutes until done, continuing to stir. Five minutes before the end of cooking time, stir in the tomato purée, and a little more stock if necessary. The risotto should have a relatively liquid consistency. Season to taste. Stir in the grated Parmesan and the remaining butter. Spoon the risotto onto warmed plates, sprinkle with Parmesan and chopped herbs, and serve.

Risotto with spinach and Gorgonzola
A traditional combination, and one of the best risottos of all

Gabriele Ferron, rice-mill owner in the Verona area and risotto chef *par excellence*, makes his risottos relatively dry, but it's not a rule — everyone is free to prepare their risotto with the consistency they like best.

The cheese is meant to melt appetizingly on the risotto before it is stirred in briefly at the end. The risotto should be still fairly liquid before the cheese is added so that it can simmer for a bit while the cheese is melting.

To ensure the success of this dish, we recommend that you use tender young spinach, a high-quality cold-pressed olive oil, and, of course, a good rice, such as Vialone nano semifino. Remember, the term "semifino" does not refer to the quality of the rice, but to the size of the grain. Equally well suited for a risotto is the somewhat larger-grained Carnaroli superfino, which, however, absorbs less liquid, resulting in a rice with a bit more "bite" when cooked.

Serves 4

14 oz spinach, 3 tablespoons olive oil
⅓ cup finely chopped onion
2 garlic cloves, finely chopped
2 cups Vialone nano semifino rice
4½ cups hot vegetable stock
¼ cup freshly grated Parmesan cheese
7 oz Gorgonzola piccante
salt, freshly ground pepper

Blanch the spinach in boiling salted water. Lift out with a slotted spoon and refresh under cold running water. Drain well, squeeze out the water, and chop the spinach finely.

Heat the oil in a pot and sweat the onion and garlic until the onion is translucent. Tip in the rice and sauté, stirring, until translucent. Stir in the chopped spinach and sauté briefly with the other ingredients. Pour in the stock gradually and simmer the risotto for 15–20 minutes, until done, stirring constantly.

Remove the risotto from the heat, stir in the Parmesan, and season with salt and pepper. Slice the Gorgonzola and arrange on the top of the rice. Cover the pot, and allow the cheese to melt. Remove the lid, stir in the melted cheese, and serve at once.

Risotto with brown rice

Brown rice is especially high in vitamins and minerals

It is chiefly in whole-food cuisine that brown rice plays an important role. Nutritionally, whole-grain rice is very valuable, as the bran layer still adhering to the grain, which is removed in processing to make white rice, contains large amounts of vitamins, minerals, and fiber. When short-grained brown rice is used for risotto, it needs to cook for longer than milled rice — about 40–50 minutes in all — and also needs more liquid because the bran forms a sort of shield against heat and moisture.

Other sorts of brown rice and other varieties of rice are less well suited to this preparation method, as they do not have the typical risotto characteristics. Thus, for example, red rice from the Camargue and Canadian wild rice must be soaked overnight or they will not cook through at all. Even then, they have a much longer cooking time than long-grain brown rice; you should allow at least 2 hours. This means that a great deal of liquid — especially veal or vegetable stock— must be used, and that, despite vigorous stirring, the grains will not produce that creamy thickening typical of the Italian short-grain varieties, and characteristic of a risotto.

The nutty taste of short-grain brown rice harmonizes perfectly with the flavors of all sorts of vegetables, so it is particularly well suited to vegetarian risottos. The best example of this is the Savoy cabbage risotto given below.

SAVOY CABBAGE RISOTTO

A gutsy risotto with plenty of flavor: smoked bacon and spicy *salsiccia*, or, failing this, a coarse salami, go very well with the hearty Savoy cabbage, which should be as young and tender as possible for this dish.

Serves 4
10 oz Savoy cabbage
4½ tablespoons butter
½ cup finely chopped onion
1 garlic clove, finely chopped
2 slices smoked bacon, cut into small dice
2 cups short-grain brown rice
½ cup white wine
about 7 cups hot veal stock

5 oz salsiccia
salt, freshly ground black pepper
You will also need:
¼ cup freshly grated Parmesan cheese

Quarter and core the Savoy cabbage. Remove the dark-green outer leaves, slicing only the light leaves into thin strips.

Melt half of the butter in a casserole and sweat the onion, garlic and bacon until the onion is translucent. Tip in the brown rice and stir until translucent. Pour in with the white wine and reduce until most of the liquid is gone. Ladle in a little hot veal stock — the rice should always be barely covered with liquid — and season with salt and pepper. Reduce the heat and simmer the rice for 30–40 minutes, stirring constantly, and adding the remaining stock gradually. Mix in the cabbage and cook for a further 20 minutes.

Meanwhile, skin the *salsiccia* and cut into rounds. At the end of the cooking time, stir the sausage into the rice and heat through, and season to taste. Dot the hot risotto with the remaining butter and serve at once, passing around the Parmesan separately.

VEGETABLE RISOTTO

Serves 4
6 tablespoons butter, ½ cup finely chopped onion
2 cups short-grain brown rice
about 7 cups hot vegetable stock
¾ cup diced carrot, 1 cup chopped leek
2 celery stalks, finely chopped
freshly grated nutmeg, salt, freshly ground pepper
You will also need:
½ cup freshly shaved Parmesan cheese
1 tablespoon chopped flat-leaf parsley

Melt half of the butter in a casserole and sweat the onion until translucent. Add the rice and sauté, stirring, until it too is translucent. Pour in a little stock and allow to reduce. Reduce the heat and cook the rice for 30–40 minutes, stirring occasionally and adding the remaining stock a little at a time so that the rice remains just covered with liquid. Season with salt, pepper, and nutmeg.

Meanwhile, melt the remaining butter in a frying pan. Add the carrot, leek, and celery, and sweat briefly. Remove from the heat and set aside. At the end of the cooking time for the rice, stir in the vegetables and cook together for a further 20 minutes. Remove the vegetable risotto from the heat, adjust the seasoning, sprinkle with shaved Parmesan cheese and chopped parsley, and serve.

Risotto with mushrooms
The distinctive flavors of porcini and truffles are incomparable with rice

Although porcini (also called cèpes) and truffles grow only in the wild, for some mushroom dishes it is not absolutely necessary to wait for the brief, quite weather-dependent season in late summer or fall when these coveted fungi are finally available at affordable prices, or, better still, are there for the picking on woodland walks.

PORCINI RISOTTO

This recipe is easily prepared throughout the year since it uses dried porcini mushrooms. None of the taste of the dish is sacrificed, as the flavor of porcini intensifies with drying. Butter, used here to sauté the rice as well as to fry the mushrooms, also contributes to the exquisite taste. In order not to overwhelm the delicate flavor of the mushrooms, the cheese is, for once, left out.

Serves 4
2 oz dried porcini
6 tablespoons butter
½ cup finely chopped onion
1½ cups Carnaroli rice
⅔ cup white wine, about 3½ cups hot veal stock
½ teaspoon ground saffron
salt, freshly ground pepper
You will also need:
1 tablespoon chopped parsley

Soak the dried porcini in lukewarm water for about 10 minutes. Drain them, squeeze them out well, and chop half of them very finely.

Melt 3 tablespoons of the butter in a casserole and sweat the onions and the chopped mushrooms until lightly colored. Tip in the rice and stir over a high heat until the grains are translucent, taking care that neither the rice nor the onion browns. Pour in the wine and reduce slightly, stirring. Add the stock gradually, stirring constantly and vigorously.

Season with saffron, salt, and pepper, and cook the risotto, stirring constantly, for 15–18 minutes, until done. Stir in half the remaining butter and remove the risotto from the heat.

Heat the remaining butter in a skillet and briefly fry the remaining mushrooms. Season with salt and pepper. Spoon the finished risotto onto warmed plates with the fried porcini, sprinkle with the chopped parsley, and serve.

If you can get hold of fresh porcini, try this variation: Prepare the risotto with just ⅓ oz dried mushrooms. Trim 10 oz fresh porcini, slice thinly and sauté with ½ cup finely chopped onion in 2 tablespoons olive oil. Sprinkle in the parsley. Serve over the rice.

RISOTTO WITH WHITE TRUFFLES

Tartufi bianchi, also called Alba truffles, are the most sought-after of all truffles. The highest quality specimens come from Piedmont and can fetch quite substantial prices — every fraction of an ounce is valuable. Attempts to cultivate these fungi have met with only limited success so far, and demand for them far outstrips supply, especially in years with dry weather — hence the high prices they command. Despite being exceedingly expensive, however, white truffles are a delicacy many Italians indulge in again and again. The very scent of the fungi, which, in fact, are not white but brownish with light marbling inside, is bewitching. For this reason, Gabriele Ferron, owner of the famous rice mill of the same name near Verona, from whom we have this delicious recipe, flavors the rice for his exquisite truffle risotto with the strongly scented fungi even before cooking. He does this by first trimming the truffles and then, only if necessary, cleaning them very briefly under running water; under no circumstances must they become saturated. He removes any furrows in which dirt is embedded sparingly with a sharp, pointed knife. Then he places the rice and truffles in an airtight container for 24–28 hours. As a final touch, Signor Ferron lavishly strews shaved truffles over the finished risotto. The recipe does not call for a precise amount of truffles; just adjust the quantity according to your own taste — and pocketbook.

White gold Rare white truffles from Alba are an extremely expensive delicacy, and therefore are packed carefully for sale, for example in little baskets.

Serves 6
½ cup finely chopped onion
6 tablespoons butter
3 cups Vialone nano rice
5½ cups vegetable stock
4 oz Parmesan cheese
white truffle
salt

Proceed as shown in the first three steps of the picture sequence opposite.

Slowly pour in the hot stock, stir, and allow the rice to simmer without further stirring for about 15 minutes. In the meantime, grate the Parmesan and proceed as shown in the final two pictures opposite.

Melt ¼ cup of the butter in a pot and sweat the onions until translucent.

Tip in the rice. For this fine risotto, Ferron chooses a Vialone nano. Add salt to taste.

Sweat the rice, stirring, for 2–3 minutes, until the grains are slightly translucent. In a separate pot, bring the stock to a boil.

Gabriele Ferron grates the cheese directly over the risotto, but less experienced cooks may prefer to grate it beforehand. Mix in the cheese and the remaining butter.

Finally, using a truffle shaver, shave paper-thin slices of white truffle over the finished risotto and serve.

Fennel risotto
With spicy Gorgonzola cheese — sheer poetry

Spicy Gorgonzola is a superb foil for the aniseed flavor of fennel. This refined combination comes from northern Italy, the home of the blue cheese in question, and works best with a Gorgonzola *dolce*, as the spicier Gorgonzola *piccante* would overpower the taste of the fennel. High-quality fresh fennel is available throughout the year. In Italy, as throughout the Mediterranean, it is cultivated chiefly as a winter vegetable. In spring, wild fennel, which has a substantially more intense flavor and grows in the arid karst areas of southern Italy and Sicily, also appears on the market. The bulbs of this plant are smaller and more elongate, and have plenty of roots and feathery green leaves. If you are lucky enough to find some wild fennel during the spring months, try it in this risotto recipe.

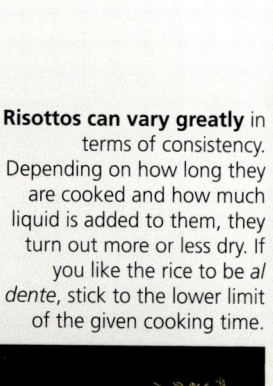

Risottos can vary greatly in terms of consistency. Depending on how long they are cooked and how much liquid is added to them, they turn out more or less dry. If you like the rice to be *al dente*, stick to the lower limit of the given cooking time.

The freshness of fennel can be judged by the state of the green leaves, which should be feathery and shiny. In addition, the places where the stalks are cut should not be dried up.

Serves 4
1 lb fennel bulbs
6 tablespoons butter
⅓ cup finely chopped shallot
1¾ cups Avorio rice
⅔ cup dry white wine
3½–4½ cups hot vegetable stock
salt, freshly ground white pepper
You will also need:
4 oz Gorgonzola cheese
1 tablespoon freshly chopped fennel leaves

Cut the root end and the green stalks off the fennel bulbs. Remove any tough outer ribs. Quarter the bulbs lengthwise and cut crosswise into thin strips.

Melt the butter in a large saucepan and sweat the shallots and the fennel until translucent. Tip in the rice all at once and sauté, stirring, until it too is translucent. Season sparingly with salt and pepper, and deglaze with the wine.

Cook, uncovered, until the wine is reduced by about half. Pour in enough stock to just cover the rice. Simmer, uncovered, for about 15–20 minutes, stirring constantly so that the rice doesn't catch on the base of the pan. While the rice is cooking keep adding enough stock to keep it barely covered, and stir frequently. Adjust the seasoning.

Cut the cheese into 4 slices. Spoon the risotto onto warmed plates, top each portion with a slice of Gorgonzola, and sprinkle with chopped fennel leaves.

Just a small quantity of the highly aromatic truffle oil is sufficient to give a considerable flavor boost to the risotto.

Saffron risotto with summer truffles

These "stepsisters" of the famous black and white are also true delicacies, but much better value for money

Summer truffles grow in Spain, the countries of the former Yugoslavia, and North Africa as well as in Italy. The more reasonable price of summer truffles means that they are used more lavishly than the exceedingly expensive black or white truffles from the Piedmont. Thus, quantity compensates for their perhaps slightly less intense flavor. You will need at least 3½ ounces for this recipe, but you can use more if you like. A delicate variation of this dish can be made by adding grated pecorino toscano cheese to the risotto.

Serves 4
3–4 oz summer truffles
6 tablespoons butter
½ cup finely diced shallots
¼ cup finely diced celery
2 cups Vialone rice
⅔ cup white wine
4½–6¼ cups hot vegetable stock
½ teaspoon ground saffron
¾ cup finely diced onion
2 teaspoons truffle oil
salt, freshly ground white pepper
1 tablespoon chopped parsley

Carefully brush the summer truffles under running water until the last remnants of soil are flushed out. Where deep furrows make this impossible, thinly pare the truffles.

Melt ¼ cup of the butter in a medium-sized pot and sweat the shallots and celery. Tip in the rice and sauté, stirring, until the grains are translucent. Add the white wine, stir, and reduce slightly. Gradually pour in the stock, season with the saffron, salt, and pepper, and cook the rice for 15–18 minutes, until done, stirring constantly. Just before the end of the cooking time, stir in half the truffle oil.

Heat the remaining butter and truffle oil in a skillet and sweat the onion until translucent. Pat the truffles dry, if necessary, and shave into thin slices. Add to the skillet and sauté briefly, until they begin to frizzle. Season with salt and pepper.

The truffles can be mixed into the risotto or passed around separately, as preferred. Sprinkle with the parsley and serve at once.

Risotto is an undemanding dish, as far as the quantities of ingredients used, but there can be no concessions in terms of quality. Another essential: time to stir!

Pumpkin and dandelion
Less familiar as risotto ingredients, but nonetheless exquisite

An undemanding crop, pumpkins and squashes flourish worldwide in countless varieties, in a huge range of colors, shapes, and sizes. The species belonging to the genus *Cucurbita* range in color from light yellow through a rich dark green to a reddish orange. Of culinary importance are the widespread robust summer squash *Cucurbita pepo* and the warmth-loving giant pumpkin *Cucurbita maxima*, as well as the smaller winter squash *Cucurbita moschata*. The Hokkaido pumpkin belongs to the latter species and is used in the recipe on page 221, where its glowing yellow flesh adds optical highlights to the rice.

Also used to color the risotto yellow are the petals of the dandelion, a flower once known as the saffron of the poor. *Risotto ai fiori di tarassaco* (risotto with dandelion flowers) is even today a popular specialty in the Piedmont region. When picking the dandelion flowers, choose plants that do not grow too close to busy roads or on heavily manured meadows.

Such a wide selection of pumpkins makes a decision difficult. The small, orange Hokkaido pumpkin has dark yellow, especially tasty flesh, which makes it a good choice for a pumpkin risotto.

RISOTTO WITH DANDELION FLOWERS

Serves 4
2 tablespoons olive oil
¼ cup finely chopped onion
½ garlic clove, finely chopped
¼ cup finely chopped young leek
1 bay leaf, 1 small sprig rosemary
1¼ cups Arborio rice, 2¾ cups hot veal stock
1 tablespoon dandelion petals stripped from stalks
salt, freshly ground white pepper
You will also need:
⅓ cup freshly shaved Parmesan cheese (optional)

Heat the olive oil in a pot and sweat the onion, garlic, and leek without allowing them to color. Add the bay leaf and rosemary sprig, tip in the rice, and sauté, stirring, until the grains are translucent. Add ½ cup of the veal stock and allow to reduce, stirring. Mix in the dandelion petals. Add the remaining hot stock a little at a time, simmering for a further 15–20 minutes, and stirring occasionally. Continue adding just enough stock to keep the rice barely covered.

Take the pot off the heat, season the risotto with salt and pepper, and mix well. Allow to rest briefly so that the flavors can blend, then spoon the dandelion risotto into heated shallow bowls. Sprinkle with shaved Parmesan cheese if wished, and serve.

PUMPKIN RISOTTO

Serves 4
1 lb Hokkaido pumpkin
2 tablespoons olive oil, 1 cup finely chopped onion
6 tablespoons butter
2¼ cups Arborio rice
salt, freshly ground white pepper
4½–5½ cups hot veal stock
½ cup freshly grated Parmesan cheese
You will also need:
¼ cup freshly shaved Parmesan cheese
1 tablespoon chopped flat-leaf parsley

Cut the Hokkaido pumpkin (or the same size of a different variety) into sections. Scoop out the seeds and the fibrous center with a spoon, peel the pumpkin, and cut the flesh into ¼-inch cubes.

Heat the olive oil in a pot with 4 tablespoons (¼ cup) of the butter. Add the onion, and sweat until translucent. Add the pumpkin cubes, and sweat over a moderate heat, stirring, for 5 minutes.

Tip in the rice and stir until the grains are translucent. Season sparingly with salt and pepper, and moisten with a little hot stock. Simmer the pumpkin risotto, uncovered, for 15–20 minutes, stirring frequently and adding just enough hot stock to keep the rice barely covered. Stir in the remaining butter and the grated Parmesan, mix well, and season to taste. Spoon the pumpkin risotto onto warmed plates, sprinkle with shaved Parmesan cheese, garnish with parsley, and serve.

Parmesan cheese, ideally a ripened Parmigiano Reggiano or a Grana Padano, lends just the right spiciness to the pumpkin risotto, which is actually rather mild on its own. For optimum flavor, grate or shave the cheese just before use.

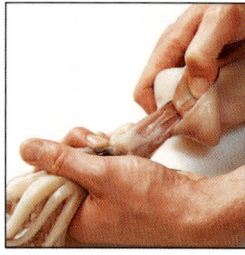

Grasp the tentacles of the squid and pull them out of the body sac. Cut off the tentacles just above the eyes so that they remain joined by a narrow band.

Calamari risotto
The ink lends not only color, but a certain sea flavor to this dish

This recipe may be prepared with squid, cuttlefish, or octopus. However, the flesh of large octopus is tough, and must be precooked or beaten so that it becomes really tender during the relatively short cooking time of the risotto. If you buy the squid right on the coast, the ink sac may still be intact. If, on the other hand, you buy it ready-prepared, you can buy cuttlefish ink separately in small quantities. It is often available in Italian or Spanish delicatessens, labeled *nero di seppia* and *tinta de calamar*, respectively.

Grasp the tentacles from below and pop out the beak with your index finger. Remove the transparent quill.

With a flick of the wrist, pull the fins off of the body, taking care not to damage it.

Leave the briefly scalded tentacles whole and cut the body into rings ⅓-inch wide.

A visually striking dish
Cheese sprinkled over the seafood risotto is not to everyone's taste, so try just a little at first.

Serves 4
1¼ lb squid
6 tablespoons butter
¾ cup finely diced onion
1 garlic clove, finely diced
1½ cups Arborio rice
⅔ cup red wine
4 teaspoons cuttlefish ink, diluted in a little fish stock
about 4½ cups hot fish stock, salt
You will also need:
parsley
⅓ cup freshly grated Parmesan cheese

Melt ¼ cup of the butter in a large pot and sauté the onions and garlic without letting them color. Tip in the rice, and sweat over high heat until translucent, stirring constantly. Pour in the wine and allow it to reduce slightly. Stir in the diluted cuttlefish ink. Pour in about one-third of the fish stock, and when it has been almost completely absorbed by the rice, add a further third.

In the meantime, wash the squid under cold running water. Grasp firmly with one hand and pull off the skin with the other. Proceed as shown in the picture sequence.

Add the tentacles and the squid rings to the rice. Pour the remaining stock into the rice, add salt, and cook the risotto over a moderate heat until done. If the liquid is used up before the rice is tender enough, add a little more stock or water. Adjust the seasoning.

Distribute the remaining butter evenly over the risotto, remove the pot from the heat, and cover. After a few minutes, carefully mix the melted butter into the rice. Garnish the risotto with parsley and serve at once, handing the Parmesan around separately.

Bell peppers are rich in vitamin C. Widely available, they are also rewarding to grow yourself, thriving in sunny, sheltered spots in home gardens or on warm balconies.

Risotto with sweet peppers
A delightful, light vegetarian dish that is rich in fiber and vitamins

For many Italians, risotto is not just a dish, but also a philosophy of life. It is therefore only natural that people argue vehemently over the "right" way to prepare it: How liquid should a risotto be? Is it best cooked with the lid on, or should it be stirred in an open pan? Whichever method you choose, the amount of liquid — in this case, white wine and vegetable stock — will vary according to the length of cooking time and the variety and dryness of the grains. That is why exact quantities are not given in these recipes. The guiding principle is that the rice should always be just covered by liquid while it simmers.

Serves 4
For the risotto:
¼ cup butter, ¾ cup finely diced onion
2 cups Arborio rice
⅔ cup white wine
4½–5½ cups hot vegetable stock
salt, freshly ground white pepper
For the red-pepper mixture:
1¼ lb red bell peppers
2 tablespoons oil, ½ cup finely diced shallot
½ teaspoon salt
½ cup white wine
1 tablespoon tomato paste
1 teaspoon sweet-pepper paste
1 tablespoon chopped herbs (basil, parsley, rosemary, thyme)
freshly ground white pepper
You will also need:
⅓ cup freshly shaved or grated pecorino sardo cheese

To make the risotto, melt the butter in a large pot and sweat the onions until translucent. Add the rice and sauté until it too becomes translucent, stirring constantly.

Add the white wine and allow it to reduce. Pour in half of the stock and cook the rice over a moderate heat, stirring constantly, until the liquid has evaporated almost completely. Add the remaining stock and continue to simmer, stirring, for about 18 minutes, until done. Season to taste.

Meanwhile, preheat the oven to 425°F. To make the red-pepper mixture, bake the peppers until their skins blister and brown slightly. Remove from the oven and place them under a damp cloth or in a plastic bag until cool. Skin the peppers, halve lengthwise, remove the seeds and core, and cut the flesh into ½-inch squares.

Heat the oil in a skillet, and sweat the shallots until lightly colored. Add the peppers and continue to cook for 2–3 minutes, stirring. Season with salt and pepper. Pour in the wine, stir in the tomato and pepper pastes and cook for 2–3 minutes, until done.

Sprinkle in the herbs. Arrange the risotto on warmed plates, spoon the pepper mixture on top, and serve, handing around the cheese separately.

Red vegetables on white rice
The dish is visually more appealing when the peppers are not mixed in with the risotto, which also presents the exquisite flavor of the sweet-pepper mixture to even better advantage.

Deluxe risottos

Exquisite in taste and color, risottos with jumbo shrimp or rock lobster are a Venetian favorite

JUMBO SHRIMP RISOTTO

Serves 4
16 jumbo shrimp, weighing about 3 oz each
3 tablespoons olive oil
For the stock:
3 tablespoons olive oil; 2 garlic cloves, chopped
¾ cup finely diced onion, ½ cup chopped fennel
⅓ cup chopped carrot, ½ cup chopped celery
1 tablespoon tomato paste, 4 oz tomatoes
1 red chile pepper, seeded; 1 cup white wine
1 bay leaf, salt, freshly ground pepper
For the risotto:
1 garlic clove, finely diced
½ cup finely diced onion, 3 tablespoons olive oil
1½ cups Baldo or Vialone nano rice, ½ cup white wine
2 tablespoons butter, salt, freshly ground pepper

Twist the tails off the shrimp and refrigerate. Wash out the heads and drain the shells. Heat the oil in a pot and stir-fry the shells. Add the garlic, onion, fennel, carrot, and celery, and continue to sauté, then stir in the tomato paste. Halve the tomatoes, and add to the pot with the chile pepper, and sauté briefly. Add the wine and simmer for 5 minutes. Add the bay leaf, pour in 5½ cups water, and bring to a boil. Reduce the heat and simmer for 20–25 minutes. Pour through a strainer lined with cheesecloth and reserve 1 quart of stock.

To make the risotto, heat the oil in a pot and fry the garlic and onion until lightly colored. Tip in the rice and stir until translucent; do not allow to brown. Pour in the wine and continue stirring over a moderate heat until the rice has absorbed almost all of the liquid. Add the hot stock a gradually and cook the risotto for 15–18 minutes until done, stirring constantly. Season with salt and pepper, and stir in the butter. Halve the shrimp tails lengthwise, devein, and season with salt and pepper. Heat the oil in a skillet. Place the shrimp in the skillet cut-side down and fry for 1–2 minutes on each side. Serve with the risotto.

HERB RISOTTO WITH ROCK LOBSTER

The right rice, fresh herbs, and fine rock lobster make a delicate combination; no cheese is added to this risotto, as it would overwhelm the flavor of the lobster.

Serves 4

2 rock-lobster tails weighing about 14 oz each
6 tablespoons olive oil, ¼ cup finely diced onion
1¼ cups Carnaroli rice, ½ cup white wine
2⅔ cups fish stock, 2 tablespoons butter
4 tablespoons chopped herbs (parsley, chives, chervil, tarragon)
salt, freshly ground pepper
You will also need:
chervil and parsley leaves, chives

Halve the rock-lobster tails lengthwise with a serrated knife, and remove the innards. Heat half the olive oil in a pot and sweat the onion until lightly colored. Tip in the rice and sauté over moderate heat, stirring, until the grains begin to become translucent, but do not let them brown.

Pour in the wine. Continue to stir until the rice has absorbed most of the liquid. Add the stock a little at a time, stirring constantly, and cook the risotto for 15–18 minutes, until done. Season with salt and pepper, and stir in the butter and the chopped herbs. Remove the risotto from the heat and allow the flavors to blend.

Heat the remaining oil in a skillet. Season the rock-lobster tails with salt and pepper, place cut-side down in the pan and sauté, turning frequently, for 6–7 minutes, until done.

Jumbo shrimp add their delicate flavor to risotto in two ways. The halved tails are sautéed in olive oil for 1–2 minutes on each side before being spooned onto a delicious risotto, which is permeated with the same wonderful flavor by being cooked in a stock made from the shrimp shells.

The shells of shellfish are simmered with root vegetables and tomatoes to make a stock that serves as the flavorful basis for some of the very best risottos of all.

Arrange the rock-lobster tails with a little herb risotto, then sprinkle with the chervil and parsley leaves and the chives.

Asparagus risotto
White and green asparagus are fine ingredients for a risotto

The difference between green and white asparagus lies in their respective cultivation methods. White asparagus grows in mounds of soil, with all light excluded until harvest time, while green asparagus grows above ground and absorbs sunlight, which gives it its color. Green asparagus is stronger-tasting, and can hold its own better than the white variety with the Parmesan cheese used in this recipe. When making a risotto with white asparagus, use a different cheese; a mild Fontina, for example, partners it superbly, and should be cubed and mixed into the rice, not grated.

Fresh green on a white background. This risotto is a "must" to try during the asparagus season in spring. A glass of dry white wine, perhaps a Chardonnay or a Sauvignon blanc, goes well with this dish.

During the asparagus season, many different varieties of the vegetable are sold in the markets in northern Italy, from pure white through violet to green. Wild asparagus is found only in the south of the country, and it is precisely this type that is ideally suited for a risotto.

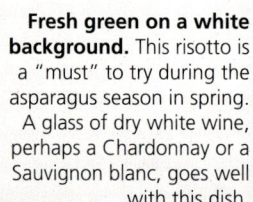

Serves 8 as a side dish or 4 as a main course
14 oz green asparagus, dash lemon juice
3 tablespoons butter, ½ cup finely diced shallot
1½ cups Arborio rice
1 cup dry white wine (Chardonnay)
2¼ cups hot veal stock
salt, freshly ground pepper
You will also need:
¼ cup butter, flaked
⅔ cup freshly grated Parmesan cheese

Cut off the stalk-ends of the asparagus, peel the lower third of the spears if necessary, and cut the spears into pieces 1–1½ inches long. Bring some lightly

salted water to a boil with the lemon juice and add the asparagus. Cook, covered, over a moderate heat for 10–12 minutes. Lift out the asparagus, drain well, and set aside. Strain the cooking liquid and reserve 2⅔ cups.

Melt the butter in a large pot and sweat the shallots until translucent. Tip in the rice and sauté, stirring, until it too is translucent. Pour in the wine, and cook, uncovered, until the liquid has evaporated. Add half of the veal stock and simmer over a moderate heat until the liquid has reduced almost completely. Stir the rice frequently as it cooks so that it does not stick to the bottom of the pot. Pour in the remaining stock and allow the liquid to reduce slowly in the uncovered pan, stirring constantly.

Add the asparagus and fold in gently so that they do not break up. Pour in the asparagus cooking liquid and continue simmering over a low heat until the rice is as tender as you like it. If necessary, add more liquid. The risotto should be neither dry nor runny in consistency.

Season the risotto with salt and pepper. Sprinkle with the cheese, dot the top with the butter, and replace the lid. After several minutes, gently stir the melted cheese and butter into the risotto, and serve at once. Sprinkle with more cheese according to taste.

Risotto with radicchio
An intriguing combination that is sure to win many fans

Typically Italian, this member of the chicory family has mostly dark- to wine-red leaves and glowing white leaf ribs. In Italy, it is grown mainly in the province of Venice. Indeed, the largest radicchio-growing area in Italy lies near Chioggia, at the southern end of the lagoon. Also typically Italian is the combination of this vegetable with rice, as the slightly bitter tang of radicchio is shown off to best advantage in a risotto. In principle, all red-leaved varieties that are not too bitter can be used; but the following recipe tastes particularly marvelous made with *radicchio di Treviso*, a long-leaved variety that forms an open leaf rosette rather than a head. Incidentally, this risotto turns out best when made in a metal-lined copper pan, which distributes the heat particularly well. To slightly vary the recipe below, instead of cooking the radicchio with the rice, sauté it separately in a little butter or oil and mix it into the rice just before serving. You could also add 3 ounces of pancetta, cut into thin strips and sautéed with the shallot and garlic.

Serves 4 as a side dish or 2 as a main course
7 oz radicchio
2 tablespoons butter,
1 shallot, finely chopped,
¼ garlic clove, finely chopped
1 cup risotto rice
⅔ cup white wine, 3¼ cups hot chicken stock
⅓ cup freshly grated Parmesan cheese, salt
You will also need:
4 pats butter

Trim the radicchio and cut up small. Melt the butter in a pot and sweat the shallot and garlic until translucent. Proceed as shown in the picture sequence. Lastly, spoon the finished risotto onto serving plates and top with the pats of butter. Hand around the remaining Parmesan separately

Add the rice to the sweated shallots and garlic, and sauté, stirring, until the grains become translucent. Salt sparingly.

Pour in the wine and simmer, uncovered, until the liquid has been reduced by half.

Pour in a little stock. Simmer, uncovered, for about 15 minutes, adding enough stock, a little at a time, to keep the rice slightly covered with liquid.

Add the radicchio and heat until it wilts. Stir in half of the Parmesan.

verdure
VEGETABLES

Nature has a soft spot for the boot of Italy: Almost everywhere in the country — from Chioggia, the "garden" of Venice, to the fertile fields of Campania, down to Sicily — climate and soil together favor the cultivation of an amazing variety of vegetables. This abundance is used to the fullest in Italy's kitchens, and Italian vegetable dishes are justly famous for their tastiness because Italians insist on using only the freshest market produce for their preparation.

Tomatoes, *numero uno* among vegetables

Few vegetables are so closely bound up with our conception of Italian cooking as the tomato. All the more surprising,

Cultivation
Since the eighteenth century, however, tomatoes have occupied an uncontested first place among

Round tomato varieties are juicy and contain a lot of seeds, making them less suited for cooking and better suited for eating raw. They are sometimes sold on the vine.

Plum tomatoes are ideal for sauces. The variety pictured here, "San Marzano," named after a town near Naples, is used chiefly for the production of *pomodori pelati*, or canned peeled tomatoes.

Yellow plum-shaped cherry tomatoes are not as commonly available as their small, red relatives. Italy is one of the main growing areas for these aromatic fruits.

Pomodorini, "little tomatoes," is the Italian name for these small, thick-skinned fruits. Tied together by their stalks, they are hung in whole bunches in shady, well-ventilated spots, as in the picture above, to provide a supply for the winter months.

therefore, that the species is actually a relative newcomer to Europe. Although mention is made of the *pomo d'oro*, or "golden apple," in Italian cookbooks as early as the sixteenth century, the first recipes were not especially varied. In general, the tomato was viewed with skepticism and thought to be poisonous, and was cultivated, if at all, as an ornamental plant. This attitude remained unchanged in Italy for two hundred years.

the most popular vegetables and have been grown in the widest range of varieties, shapes, and colors. Today, Italy is one of the biggest producers of field-grown tomatoes in Europe, and many Italians grow their own.

The different varieties
Not every variety is equally suitable for every purpose, and there are regional preferences. While southern Italians, for example, will choose fully ripe, sweet fruit not only for sauces,

but for salads too, northern Italians prefer tomatoes that are slightly underripe for salads, typically using strongly ribbed, aromatic, and firm-fleshed varieties such as *cuore di bue*. However, for a sauce, fully ripe tomatoes must be used, otherwise the *sugo* will turn out excessively sharp, and adding sugar will not help. The best varieties for this purpose are the plum tomatoes, which contain very little liquid around the seeds in proportion to flesh.

Pomodorini, the small, round tomatoes prized in southern Italy, offer the same advantage. If you are not quite sure whether the fresh tomatoes available are up to scratch, use canned ones.

Jar, can, carton, or tube?
Since Italians have always been reluctant to forgo their tomatoes out of season, they soon developed ways of preserving them. Very broadly speaking, there are two basic processes: canning or bottling, and drying.

Peeled plum tomatoes, often seasoned and flavored with basil, are placed close together in jars and preserved. *Pelati*, whole, peeled tomatoes heated in their own juice, are canned commercially according to a similar principle.

Polpo di pomodoro, chopped peeled tomatoes, are sold in jars and cartons. If these are strained, the result is *passato di pomodoro*, or passata, a thick, homogeneous sauce.

Drying tomatoes concentrates their flavor. For *pomodori secchi*, plum tomatoes are halved or quartered, salted, then dried in the sun until all their liquid has evaporated, a process that extends their shelf life almost indefinitely. Re-plumped in water, then preserved in oil, they are served as an antipasto or used to flavor sauces. If tomato purée is dried, it yields *concentrato di pomodoro*, or tomato paste, which is sold in small jars, cans, and tubes.

Cuore di bue, "ox heart," is the name given in Italy to this strongly ribbed tomato. In the north, people like to use it slightly underripe, or even while still green, for salads.

During the season, market stalls in southern Italy groan under the weight of ripe tomatoes. This stallholder in Palermo offers both round and plum tomatoes for sale.

Artichokes and lemons belong together. If the cut surfaces of artichokes are not brushed with lemon juice, they will turn brown.

Artichokes and cardoons

Artichokes and cardoons are both cultivated forms of thistles, and so closely related that the cardoon is thought to be the ancestor of the artichoke.

Artichokes: delicate flower buds

Artichokes — *carciofi* in Italian — are thought to be native to Arabia, Turkey, or Iran. The only edible portions of the plant

Small, tender artichokes are commonly available in southern Italian markets, and can be prepared and eaten whole.

are parts of the still-closed flower buds: the fleshy outer leaves and the base of the globe, or heart. Globes that are still small and tender can be eaten whole, with the top portion of the stalk. Most of the artichokes sold in Italy come from Liguria, the Veneto, Tuscany and Latium, Apulia and Campania, and Sicily and Sardinia. Not all artichokes are the same, however, and clear preferences emerge regarding cultivation and use of the different varieties. In Liguria and Sardinia, for example, people prefer to grow and eat *Spinoso Sardo*, a variety distinguished by a medium-sized, conically shaped head and yellowish leaves tapering to a point tipped with a long thorn. The people

Ripe for the picking A splendid specimen of the "Romanesco" variety, which develops round flower buds.

in central Italy, on the other hand, tend to prize plump, spineless artichokes, such as

Romanesco with its large, spherical globes and green leaves tinged with purple, the tips of which are notched; or the smaller, quite decorative *Violetto di Toscana*, with deep purple outer leaves and green inner leaves. Finally, Sicily is home to the *Catanese*, an artichoke with medium-sized, pointed, conical flower buds and long tapering leaves only slightly tinged with purple. All of these varieties are raised on a large scale for export as well as the domestic market, and there are also many varieties of only local importance.

Cardoons: the hunchbacked vegetable

The official Italian name of the cardoon (see p. 258 for pictures and recipe), which is very similar in taste to the artichoke, is *cardo*. It owes its nickname *gobbo*, "hunchback," to the peculiar bowed shape it develops during cultivation: When the leaves are large enough, they are tied up high to protect the fleshy stalks, the only edible part of the vegetable, from the light. Both prickly and smooth green and reddish varieties of cardoon are cultivated. When buying cardoons, look for firm, crunchy stalks and fresh leaves.

Preparing artichoke hearts:

Break off the stem from the base of the globe. Rub some lemon juice into the base to prevent discoloration. Cut away two-thirds of the outside leaves of the globe with a heavy knife.

The remaining outside leaves around the base of the globe can now be easily removed with the knife, exposing the so-called choke.

Using a small, sharp vegetable knife, remove any traces of leaf buds and hard spots from the underside of the artichoke heart.

The fibrous, inedible choke inside the heart is most easily removed with a melon baller or a grapefruit spoon.

Cook the hearts for 5–10 minutes in water acidulated with lemon juice or vinegar, then drain them and use them as desired.

Cooking whole young artichokes:

Remove the prickly leaves on the stem, and trim the stem back to about 4 inches in length. Trim the prickly leaf tips with scissors.

Remove the outer leaves, which are usually too tough and bitter to eat, until the light inner leaves are exposed.

Cut off the upper leaf tips with a heavy, sharp chef's knife; their toughness would spoil the dish.

Thickly peel the remaining portion of the stalk with a vegetable knife; it is tender and tasty.

Cook the prepared artichokes in water acidulated with vinegar or lemon juice for 10–15 minutes, depending on size. They should be tender, but not too soft.

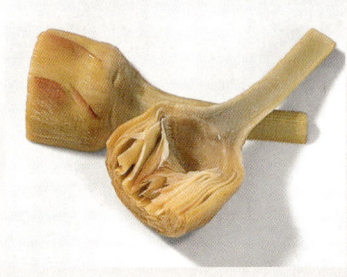

Either refresh the cooked artichokes under cold water, or leave to cool slightly, then halve them. Remove the choke with a teaspoon.

Peas

Peas — *piselli* in Italian — are among the oldest of all cultivated plants. They are normally a spring vegetable, since the plant must be protected from excessive heat in order to produce seeds, which are stripped from the pod and eaten while they are still young, tender, and green, after boiling or at least blanching. In Italy, cooked peas, onions, and ham or pancetta are a classic combination, for example in pasta sauces, but also in the famous Venetian rice dish *risi e bisi*, and in *piselli con le uova*, a sort of scrambled eggs with peas. Snow peas, on the other hand, can be eaten pod and all, hence, the expressive Italian name for this vegetable, *piselli mangiatutto* — literally, "peas that can be eaten in their entirety." Their other American name, "sugar peas," also alludes to a typical feature of this species: Both the peas and the pods have a high sugar content, and hence a sweet flavor. Snow peas are simply blanched in boiling salted water, since they are meant to remain crunchy. Like other green peas, the Italians usually serve snow peas with meat dishes.

There is very little waste when trimming *fagiolini*, or green beans, provided that they are still young and tender with no tough strings.

Beans

Fagiolini — fresh green beans — are a typical summer vegetable in Italy. They can be classified into two types: climbing pole beans and non-climbing bush beans. Green beans are eaten pod and all, and are boiled or steamed, or at the very least blanched, before eating. In Italy, they are also popular *in umido* — braised with tomatoes, in *minestroni*, and as a salad.

Green or white? Here at the Rialto market in Venice, the different varieties of asparagus, tied in firm bundles, stand side by side. Whether it is better to choose one or the other depends on the recipe in which they are to be used — both types are delicious.

Buck's horn plantain

Barba di frate, literally "monk's beard," is the Italian name of the grasslike buck's horn plantain — not to be confused with the plantain that is a member of the banana family. Buck's horn plantain grows wild throughout most of Italy in the spring. The slightly bitter leaves are blanched and mixed into salads, or dressed with lemon juice, oil, and salt, and served as a vegetable.

Barba di frate leaves grow to about 4 inches in length and resemble chive leaves. The plant is usually sold with the roots still attached.

Only the thicker asparagus spears need to be trimmed and peeled. Trimming is usually limited to cutting off the ends if they are woody. Only blanched asparagus is peeled along its entire length — as thinly as possible, to keep wastage to a minimum. With green asparagus, it is often enough simply to pare the bottom ends sparingly.

Asparagus

Green, purple, and white *asparago*, or asparagus, are grown in Italy. The different colors are a result of the different methods of cultivation. If asparagus spears are exposed to light as they grow, they turn green or purple; if not, they remain white. Colored asparagus has a stronger flavor and higher vitamin C content. When buying asparagus, choose uniform, straight, fresh stalks, characterized by closed buds, light-colored cut places, and the "squeak" heard when they rub against one another. Very fresh asparagus can be stored for a few days in the refrigerator, wrapped in a damp cloth. Ideally, though, they should be prepared without delay. Olive oil or melted butter, and a little prosciutto are the only accompaniments required. However, Italians also like asparagus with pasta, in risottos, soups, omelets, or served *au gratin* with Parmesan cheese. A unique delicacy are the thin, green, pleasantly bitter and particularly aromatic spears of wild asparagus, *asparago selvatico*. In Sicily, where it is called *sparico di spagna*, or "Spanish asparagus," it is stewed with onion, bacon, and parsley.

This asparagus, which takes on a strong purple color as soon as the spears come out of the ground, comes from Liguria.

The mighty cabbage family

Despite the fact that Italians scornfully refer to a none-too-bright person as a *cavolo*, or "cabbage head," there can be few families of vegetables as versatile as the cabbage.

Broccoli and cauliflower

Closely related botanically, broccoli and cauliflower are also similar in taste and methods of preparation. It is mainly the buds, or florets, that are eaten, while the leaves and the stems are consumed only if they are very young and tender. Broccoli — in Italian *broccolo* and, the diminuitive, *broccoletto* — should be prepared as soon as possible after it is picked, since even at low temperatures it will soon start to flower — you will see the florets turning yellow — and lose flavor. Fresh broccoli has closed buds tinged dark bluish-green or purple, depending on the variety.

Preparing broccoli First remove the lower stalk end and cut off the side shoots. Separate into florets. Slice or chop the peeled stalk and the leaves, and add them to soups or stocks.

Purple broccoli, a very popular variety in Italy, forms large, closed heads.

Although cauliflower, *cavolfiore* in Italian, is not as rich in vitamins as broccoli, it is a more robust plant, developing compact heads of firm florets that keep for longer. The white cauliflower popular in this country owes its pale color to its large leaves, which protect the florets from the sun. An attractive variant of green cauliflower is Romanesco, whose florets look like miniature minaret turrets.

Colorful cabbages

White, red, and Savoy cabbages form more or less firm round heads from densely packed leaves. This healthy and inexpensive vegetable is much prized in Italian cooking. In the southern Tyrol, Friaul, and the Veneto especially, where

Cavolo nero, kale or borecole, is easily recognized by its long, dark, somewhat ruffled leaves.

White cabbage, *cavolo cappuccio* in Italian, is a popular ingredient in substantial vegetable soups in Italy.
Red cabbage, *cavolo cappuccio rosso,* is served chiefly in the northeast of the country.

Austrian cuisine has left its distinct mark, red and white cabbage are popular in the winter, and the latter is sometimes made into sauerkraut. Indeed, *würstel con crauti,* bratwurst with

sauerkraut, is popular throughout the whole of Italy, even finding its way onto many a menu in the more southerly regions of the country. Fresh white cabbage is also often added to hearty soups and stews, and the Sicilians prepare a vegetable dish, as simple as it is tasty, by cutting white cabbage into strips and braising it in white wine with garlic and tomato paste.

Savoy cabbage — *cavolo verza* or *cavolo di Milano* in Italian — is also more a harvest, however, is a more relevant distinction for the cook, determining the most suitable method of preparation. Early and main crop varieties, which are harvested in the spring and summer, have small, tender leaves that cook in no time at all and are also suitable for eating raw. Late varieties, on the other hand, have dark, robust leaves that must be cooked. In Italy, the appropriate varieties of Savoy cabbage are cut into fine strips and served raw as a salad, or braised with

Left, from top to bottom: **green Savoy cabbage,** here a tender spring variety, and **violet-green Savoy cabbage,** a less common variety grown in the area around Verona. Right, from top to bottom: **Romanesco,** a chartreuse-colored variety of cauliflower with pointed florets; **purple cauliflower,** popular in southern Italy; and **green cauliflower,** more aromatic and richer in nutrients than the white variety.

specialty of the north, grown mainly in Piedmont, Lombardy, and the Veneto. Not all Savoy cabbage is the same. There are green and violet-green varieties, the latter being a specialty from the Veneto. Their time of red wine, tomatoes, and garlic, with the optional addition of small meatballs. In Piedmont, a type of stuffed cabbage is made with the larger Savoy leaves, which are wrapped around roast meat and baked.

Cavolo nero and *cima di rapa*

As with broccoli, the names of these typically Italian vegetables have been adopted unchanged into English and other languages, although "broccoli rabe" is a frequently used synonym for *cima di rapa*. Both are seldom grown or used outside of Italy, but they may occasionally be on sale in well-stocked produce or specialty stores. *Cavolo nero* — "black cabbage" or "borecole" in English — is planted chiefly in the south of Italy and in Tuscany, which is why it is also known as *nero di Toscana*. Its narrow dark-green leaves are non-heading, and have a strong, slightly bitter flavor, which makes them especially suitable for heartier recipes. In Tuscany, it is teamed with white beans — in soups, for example — or sautéed in a little lard, then braised in stock. *Cavolo nero* is prepared by peeling the leaves off the stalk and cutting out the thick midribs. The leaves are then cut into strips.

Cima di rapa (see p. 254 for picture and recipes) is rather similar to broccoli in appearance, hence its other Italian name, *broccoletto di rapa*. It, too, develops long, sturdy stems bearing dark-green leaves and lighter inflorescences that are eaten. The latter are distinctly milder tasting than the leaves, which have a strong cabbage flavor. *Cima di rapa* is best flattered by brief stewing with a fairly generous amount of seasoning, for example garlic, or even chile pepper.

Pumpkin and zucchini

As different as they may be in color, shape, and size, pumpkins and zucchini are closely related botanically, both belonging to the large family Cucurbitaceae. The varieties of pumpkin grown for consumption can be divided into the species *Cucurbita maxima*, giant pumpkins, and *Cucurbita moschata*, winter crooknecks or cushaws, which are distinguished by their intense flavor and brightly colored flesh. Both species are used when fully ripened; they then have a relatively thick shell and, uncut, can usually be stored for a very long time; once cut up, however, they should be cooked as soon as possible.

Cooking with pumpkin

In Italy, pumpkin, or *zucca*, is a popular ingredient, used in a wide range of sweet and savory dishes. In Sicily, for example, the flesh is candied and used in the famous cassata. Diced pumpkin flesh is added to risottos and soups, and whole pumpkins are baked in the oven and their flesh scooped right out of the shell. *Cappellacci* and *tortelloni* are pasta stuffed with a sweet and piquant pumpkin mixture. The basis for both of these dishes is pumpkin purée, which can easily be made in quantity and frozen for later use.

A colorful assortment of pumpkin and zucchini Left, different varieties of pumpkin; below left, the splendid *zucche a turbante*, or turban squash. Right, along basket edge: different-colored varieties of zucchini; at the very bottom, a round, green zucchini.

Stocking up on pumpkin purée

To make the purée, quarter the pumpkin or cut it into wedges, depending on the size, and scoop out the stringy interior, as shown in the first two steps of the picture sequence on page 243. Place the pumpkin pieces in a roasting pan and pour in water to a depth of ¾ inch. Preheat the oven to 350–400°F. Cover the roasting pan with aluminum foil and bake for 40–50 minutes, until the flesh is soft. Remove and leave to cool somewhat. Scoop the flesh from the shell with a spoon and pass it through a fine sieve. This should yield a smooth, dry, neutral-tasting, and hence versatile purée.

VEGETABLES

Light-green zucchini at a Sicilian market. Although the color is different, the taste is the same as that of darker varieties.

Zucchini like these, with dark-green skin speckled with yellow — here, the variety "Elite" — are the most common type on sale worldwide.

Pumpkin flowers come on the market less often — it pays to grow your own. They can be deep-fried or stuffed, just like zucchini flowers.

Round zucchini can be prepared like other varieties, but their shape makes them especially well suited for stuffing.

The lovely yellow flowers of the pumpkin can also be used, following the same recipes as for zucchini flowers. And, of course, pumpkin seeds make a delicious snack.

Many ways to treat zucchini

Zucchini belong to the species *Cucurbita pepo*, which, in contrast to the pumpkin, does not develop a tough shell, and is harvested while unripe. For this reason, the small, soft seeds can be eaten with the rest of the vegetable. Whether dark green, light green, yellow, or cream colored, and long or round, zucchini are the same in terms of taste and use. Italians prepare zucchini in the most varied ways: as a vegetable side dish, braised in olive oil with chopped onion, garlic, and herbs; sautéed or broiled, then marinated in vinegar, oil, and garlic; deep-fried in batter, or *au gratin* with other vegetables; and as an antipasto or main course, stuffed with ground meat, polenta, or even — quite simple, but delicious — bread crumbs, grated cheese, beaten egg, and possibly a few cubes of prosciutto. Zucchini are fairly straightforward to prepare; wash thoroughly, and, unless you wish to stuff them, cut off both ends. When buying zucchini, choose firm, shiny specimens with unblemished skin. Stored at low temperatures, but not below 50°F, they will keep for up to three weeks, provided that they are not stored near tomatoes or fruit, as they are sensitive to the ethylene these foods exude.

Zucchini flowers

In early spring zucchini often appear on the market in Italy with their yellow flowers still attached (see picture on left); the male flowers, borne on long stalks, are also sold in bundles. Zucchini flowers can be stuffed, and are also often dipped in batter, deep-fried, and — depending on whether they are to be served as a first course or a dessert — sprinkled with salt or confectioner's sugar. Even the tips of the tender shoots can be used as an ingredient in vegetable soups.

Preparing pumpkin: Cut the pumpkin into smaller segments or wedges. Scoop out the fibrous interior, together with its seeds. Peel off the shell in strips with a sharp knife, and prepare the flesh according to your recipe.

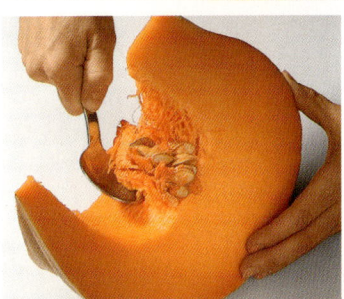

From mild to piquant and spicy

Capsicums

Like most other fruits of the nightshade family, the capsicum, or pepper, arrived in Europe only after the discovery of the New World, and like its relative the tomato, started its career as an ornamental plant. The Italians did not begin to appreciate its culinary merits until the nineteenth century, but recipes from that time for stuffed peppers, peperonata, and antipasti with preserved peppers show how successful they were at incorporating the formerly alien food into their diet. In Italian, a distinction is drawn between the larger *peperoni*, or sweet peppers, and the smaller *peperoncini*, or chile peppers (for the latter, see also p. 417).

Sweet peppers come in the most widely varying shapes, colors, and degrees of heat. *Quadrato d'Asti* from Piedmont, and the thick-fleshed *carnoso di cuneo*, which is also called *quadrato di Voghera* in Lombardy, are, for example, block-shaped, sweetish, mild tasting varieties. They may be green, red, or yellow; the green is not actually a particular variety, but simply the unripened pepper. The *quadrati* are especially well suited to stuffing. More elongated and angular is *lungo Marconi*, which is green or red. Finally, thin peppers tapering to a point are called *corni di bue*, "ox horns," there, but bull's horn peppers here, owing to their shape. Some varieties of pointed peppers can be quite hot; if in doubt, carefully taste a bit of the pepper before using it. The chile peppers are grown in southern Italy and used most often there. Elongated, pointed, red or green peppers, are called *a sigaretta*; small, round, red ones, are known as *peperoncini a cerasella* or "cherry chiles"; and small, conical ones are dried and ground into *pepe di Cayenna*, cayenne pepper.

Mild sweet peppers Above, green, thin-walled, and tender, ideal for stuffing; below, lemon-yellow and elongated, available in both a mild and a spicier version.

Red and green chile peppers Small, but hot! To tone down their heat a little, carefully remove the seeds and ribs.

Eggplants: curvaceous beauties

The eggplant, another member of the nightshade family, originated in India. Brought to the Mediterranean by the Arabs as early as the thirteenth century, it was not popular in many places because of the bitter substance in its flesh. However, eventually someone hit upon the idea of slicing and salting the vegetable, weighing

Eggplant, from flower to marketplace Although these vegetables (botanically, berries) can grow to quite a size, they always develop from relatively small flowers (only 1¼–2 inches), which are usually light purple, or less frequently, white (right). One or two berries form at each inflorescence of the approximately 3-foot-tall plant (right, center); depending on variety, these can vary greatly in color (purple, white, yellow, or green) and shape (egg-shaped, elongated oval, long and slender, or spherical). Typically Italian is the purple variety *violetta di Firenze*, with a white band around the calyx and a furrowed skin, like the ones on sale at this market stall in the Old Town of Palermo (extreme right).

it down with a plate, and leaving it for about 30 minutes; this removes excess water and the bitter juices. The eggplant not only tastes better, but also absorbs less oil when fried. Although new strains of eggplant may be free of bitter substances, it is still advisable to salt the vegetable for the latter reason.

Calabria boasts a delicious eggplant dish known as *polpa di melanzane*. The eggplant is roasted or char-grilled until soft, then puréed and seasoned with salt, finely snipped basil leaves, and garlic, and then combined with enough olive oil to yield a paste the consistency of mayonnaise. Though rather unprepossessing in appearance, the *polpa* is unsurpassed as an antipasto on Italian bread, and as an accompaniment to fish.

Fennel, wild and cultivated

The wild form of fennel (*Foeniculum vulgare*) can be found almost everywhere in southern Italy. Called *finocchio selvatico* or *finocchiella*, it has a stronger, spicier flavor than cultivated Florence fennel, which is known as *finocchio*. The white bulbs, the feathery green leaves, and the aromatic seeds of both the wild and cultivated forms are used in Italian cooking. The bulbs of Florence fennel are an essential ingredient in *pinzimonio*, but they are also braised, gratinéed, or — in a Sicilian recipe jokingly called *pisci di terra*, "land fish" — first cooked *al dente*, then quartered, dipped in beaten egg, dredged in flour, and fried until golden.

Lampascione, the wild onion

Lampascione, *muscari*, *cipollaccia*, *lampagione*, and *lampasciuolo* are all names given in Italy to this bulb, which grows in fields, vineyards, and olive groves. The bulbs, which are bitter and inedible raw, are soaked in water, then boiled until soft. They can be dressed with a vinaigrette, pickled, gratinéed, or breaded and deep-fried.

Florence fennel is in season in Italy from October to May. Depending on the variety, the bulbs can be almost spherical, as here, or thinner and more elongated.

Wild fennel, here displayed at a market in Sicily, has elongated bulbs with lots of feathery green leaves. These fronds, and the seeds, are used as a seasoning.

Culinary treasure: truffles, porcini, and other fungi

The *funghi* so beloved of the Italians grows on the southern slopes of the Alps and the Appenines, and on the plateaus of Calabria. The greatest number of species, however, flourish in the Veneto, Alto Adige, and Trentino. During the season, about a hundred varieties can be found in local markets. In November, when the mushroom season is largely over, the most exquisite of all fungi, the *tartufi*, or truffles, come on the market.

Truffles, rare and expensive

Although truffles must be one of the most costly culinary pleasures, most Italians treat themselves to this luxury from time to time. Truffles, whether white or black, cost what they do because no one has succeeded in cultivating them. The fungi, which grow under the surface of the soil, must be hunted out with great difficulty by pigs or specially trained dogs. In late fall and winter, special markets or stock exchanges are held in the truffle centers of Italy, which attract buyers from all over the world

White truffles

The most sought-after truffles are the *tartufi bianchi d'Alba* (*Tuber magnatum* Pico). One pound of class 1 truffles costs well over $1,000. Fortunately, you need only a very little to make an impact on a dish, and this helps to explain why truffles are sold by the gram ($\frac{1}{28}$ ounce). This mushroom, whose white-marbled flesh is reputed to have an aphrodisiac effect, is best shaved raw over warm dishes. Its bewitching smell and taste are superbly showcased with scrambled eggs or risotto, and pasta is irresistible with a couple of slivers of white truffle.

Black truffles

Central Italy is the place of origin of the black truffles, *tartufi neri* (*Tuber melanosporum* Vittadini). They occur relatively frequently in the area around Norcia, and are also called Norcia truffles. Black truffles are somewhat less expensive than

White truffles from Alba in the Piedmont. A special truffle shaver is used to cut wafer-thin slices of this exquisite, extremely aromatic mushroom.

Black truffles from Norcia in Umbria are also in great demand, though somewhat less expensive than the white ones. They, too, are sold by the gram.

VEGETABLES

Mushrooms galore From left to right: **Caesar's mushroom, *ovolo*** (*Amanita caesarea*), one of the most delicious edible mushrooms. When young, the mushrooms are completely encased in a bag-like veil. A member of the large boletus family is the **red-cracked boletus, *boleto dal piede rosso*** (*Xerocomus chrysenteron*), a moderately good edible mushroom. Behind it, an **orange birch bolete, *Porcinello grigio*** (*Leccinum scabrum*) a very good boletus. The **honey mushroom, *chiodino*** (*Armillaria mellea*), usually grows in bunches. In front, a **chanterelle, *cantarello*** (*Cantharellus cibarius*), and **cèpe** or **porcini** (*Boletus edulis*). Behind, the light-colored **hedgehog mushroom, *steccherino dorato*** (*Hydnum repandum*). Next to it a **bay boletus, *boleto baio*** (*Xerocomus badius*) and a **winter** or **funnel chanterelle** (*Cantharellus infundibuliformis* or *C. tubaeformis*). Far right: again, a chanterelle and a porcini.

Mushrooms in the kitchen

The undisputed king of mushrooms is the cèpe, or porcini. Fried, it goes superbly with pasta or meat, but is also great in a risotto. Very young specimens can be served as a salad, thinly sliced and drizzled with oil and a little lemon juice. Also excellent is a mushroom salad made from white truffle and Caesar's mushroom, both raw and sliced wafer-thin. Mushroom dishes in which different varieties are sautéed together are also delicious. In southern Italy in particular, the *pioppino*, or *Pholiota aegerita* (see picture on p. 304), is a must.

white ones, but still quite costly. Their flavor is not impaired by cooking, which is why they are frequently used to flavor sauces, pâtés, and similar dishes. One of the simplest and best Umbrian truffle recipes calls for chopping the mushroom finely, sweating it in butter, and then drizzling this sauce over fresh pasta.

Summer truffles

The *scorzone*, or summer truffle, *Tuber aestivum* Vittadini (see picture on p. 219), is less expensive than white or black truffles, but has much less flavor, a drawback that can be partially compensated by quantity. Summer truffles flourish from summer right into winter.

Truffle oil

People who cannot bear to forgo the flavor of truffles can use either white or black truffles preserved in brine, or truffle oil. *Olio al tartufo*, usually sold in small quantities, harmonizes brilliantly with meat and egg dishes. It is not exactly cheap, but even a couple of drops add an extraordinary flavor to foods.

Hunting for mushrooms

Without a pig or trained dog, you will never locate a truffle in the wild, but you have a sporting chance of finding many other mushrooms in fields and woods. However, only people who know their mushrooms should pick them in the wild. Even those who know their fungi should consult an expert in case of doubt, especially since the risk of confusing some of the best edible fungi with highly poisonous species is great. Less dangerous is buying mushrooms at a market. The only risk you run here is of paying too much for wormy or older specimens. For this reason, always buy young, firm mushrooms, and, in case of doubt, particularly with truffles, have the seller cut them open for you.

Preserving mushrooms

Italian cooks know various ways of preserving mushrooms: preserving in oil, pickling in vinegar, drying, and freezing. The last method preserves the flavor but changes the texture of the mushroom. Drying is especially suitable for the porcini, intensifying the flavor.

Basics of vegetable cooking

Dicing onions:

Halve the peeled onion and place flat on the work surface. Make a number of close parallel cuts from top to bottom.

Make one or two horizontal cuts, stopping just short of the root end so that the onion still holds together.

Cut thin slices crosswise from top to bottom, which will then fall naturally into fine dice.

Dicing carrots:

Carefully scrub or peel the carrot and cut lengthwise into thin slices.

Stack the slices exactly one on top of the other, and slice into thin strips with a large knife.

Place the carrot strips next to each other, hold firmly in place with your fingertips, and cut crosswise into fine dice.

Italian cooks have a huge selection of ultra-fresh produce available at markets and stores, and will not be satisfied with anything less than perfection.

Buying and storing

Except for those lucky people who can harvest vegetables from their own garden, we do not always have it quite so easy. Although many varieties of vegetables are available throughout the year, they are often grown in greenhouses or have to travel fairly long distances to their final destinations. For this reason, it is important to look for optimum quality and freshness when buying. The peel of vegetables such as tomatoes and sweet peppers should be undamaged and show no signs of pressure. Zucchini and eggplants should also feel heavy for their size. Withered leaf vegetables or cabbage whose outer leaves are yellowing should be rejected, as should asparagus or fennel that shows signs of drying where it has been cut. Vegetables should be stored in the appropriate refrigerator compartment. Many vegetables — for example, beans and peas, corn, spinach, Swiss chard, and even sweet peppers and leeks cut into strips — can be blanched and deep-frozen.

It's all in the knifework

Preparing vegetables for cooking or eating raw is not difficult if you have a selection of good, sharp knives at your disposal. A small vegetable or kitchen paring knife with a smooth blade is sufficient for many purposes. For larger vegetables, such as eggplants, a fairly long, heavy chef's knife is helpful; it is also useful for slicing or chopping onions and finely dicing carrots, as shown in the picture sequence on the far left.

For slicing tomatoes, use a knife with a serrated edge,

For a *soffritto*, cut onion, carrot, and celery into even-sized dice and sweat them in butter or oil.

which will allow you to breach the firm skin without squashing the soft insides too much. To give the vegetables an attractive shape, you can use a crenelated decorating knife, which gives a wavy or crinkle-cut surface. Delicate-textured vegetables such as zucchini can be crinkle-cut when raw, but harder ones, like carrots and beets, should be cooked first. A turning, or bird's beak paring, knife is marvelous for cutting vegetables into decorative shapes. It has a curved blade, which prevents round or oval pieces from falling apart when being cut.

The *soffritto*

When an Italian recipe calls for a *soffritto*, there is no escaping the *battuto*. Baffled by the kitchen Italian? Fear not, both terms are easily explained. *Battuto* is the name given to finely chopped or sliced ingredients that are sweated before further ingredients are added. A *battuto* usually consists chiefly of onions, carrots, and celery, with the possible addition of parsley, parsley root, leek, bay leaf, thyme, and garlic. Generally, the proportions used are 2 parts onion and carrots to 1 part celery, but the relative amounts of the individual ingredients may be varied according to taste. When all these ingredients are tipped into the pot and sweated, the result is a *soffritto*. Traditionally, vegetables and herbs are sautéed in rendered pancetta, but lard, butter, and olive oil are also used for this purpose in Italy. A *soffritto* is the starting point for myriad Italian braises, from *sugo* and *ragù* for pasta, to meat dishes such as *osso buco*.

Vegetable stock

A stock can be prepared from almost the same basic vegetables can be added, such as leek, or a halved, unpeeled onion whose cut surface is caramelized on a griddle or in a cast iron skillet without the addition of fat. The browning provides both color and flavor. Tomatoes and carrots also add color to stock. The trimmings that accumulate when vegetables are cut into shape are excellent in a stock too. Go easy on celery root and cabbage, however; they could overpower the more delicate flavors of other vegetables and dominate the stock. By contrast, asparagus and mushroom peelings are ideal. The recipe in the picture sequence below gives an example of the ingredients to combine for a strong vegetable stock.

Preparing vegetable stock:

Melt 2 tablespoons butter in a pot and sweat 2 onions, sliced into rings, until translucent.

Add and sweat the following coarsely chopped vegetables: 2 cups broccoli stalks, 2 cups leek, 2 cups carrots, 1¾ cups celery, and 1¼ cups zucchini.

Pour in 3½ quarts water and 1 cup white wine. Add ½ unpeeled, caramelized onion, 1 sprig each thyme and rosemary, 1 garlic clove, 2 cloves, and 2 bay leaves.

Bring to a boil over medium heat, and simmer for 30–40 minutes, skimming off foam with a spoon at regular intervals.

Pour the vegetable stock through a strainer lined with cheesecloth, reheat, and let reduce to 6 cups.

White beans with peppers

Delicious cold or warm, as an hors d'oeuvre or side dish, with Italian bread and a glass of wine

The idea of preparing cannellini beans *al fiasco* — in a bottle — originated in Tuscany. In the past, cooks would make it in the heat of the hearth fire — which, of course, was never allowed to go out completely during the cold winter nights — by placing a pot-bellied Chianti bottle partially filled with soaked white beans in the hot ashes for a few hours. This gentle cooking method suits the beans particularly well, as the protein they contain, if heated too long at too high a temperature, could cause them to become tough and dry. With this method, they stay tender and retain all their flavor. Of course, you do not really need a fireplace for *fagioli al fiasco*; the beans can equally well be cooked in the oven or in a water bath — at a moderate heat, lest a broken bottle render your beans a fiasco in the other sense!

Serves 4
For the beans:
2 cups cannellini beans, 3 garlic cloves
2–3 sage leaves
4½ cups lukewarm meat stock
¼ cup olive oil, freshly ground white pepper
For the sweet-pepper accompaniment:
3 mixed red and yellow bell peppers
¼ cup olive oil
½ cup chopped seeded tomato flesh
2 garlic cloves, sliced paper-thin
8 anchovy fillets, coarsely chopped
¼ cup meat stock
salt, freshly ground pepper
You will also need:
1 large, empty Chianti bottle (1.5 litre)
2–3 leaves each sage and basil, chopped

Soak the beans overnight in cold water, then drain them and pour them into the clean bottle until the bottle is no more than two-thirds full. Add the garlic and sage leaves. Pour in the stock. Stop up the mouth of the bottle with a clean linen cloth.

Place the bottle in a large pot and add water to come about three-quarters of the way up the bottle. Bring the water slowly to a boil, reduce the heat, and cook the beans just at boiling point for 2½–3 hours, until done. Remove the bottle from the water and let cool slowly. Drain off the excess stock and remove the sage leaves and garlic. Pour in the olive oil, season lightly with pepper, and shake gently.

To make the sweet-pepper accompaniment, preheat the oven to 425°F and roast the peppers until their skin blisters, then leave them to cool under a damp cloth or in a plastic bag. Peel the peppers and cut them into wide strips, removing the seeds and ribs.

Heat the olive oil in a saucepan and briefly sweat the garlic and anchovies. Add the tomatoes and stew with the other ingredients for 2 minutes, then add the peppers. Pour in the stock and season with salt and pepper. Stew for 8–10 minutes, until the pepper strips are soft. Spoon onto plates with the beans and serve sprinkled with herbs.

Actually, there are two dishes here: *fagioli al fiasco* and *peperoni alle acciughe*. They can, of course, be served separately, but they complement each other so well that you really should try them together at least once.

Cavolo nero and peperonata
Italian cooks have a real knack for preparing tasty dishes with a few simple ingredients

In this recipe two varieties of cabbage are combined with anchovies to make a wonderfully gutsy stew, while the sweet peppers lend a Mediterranean flavor.

CAVOLO NERO WITH ANCHOVIES

Serves 4

1¼ lb cavolo nero, 1 lb white cabbage
2 garlic cloves
10 anchovy fillets
3 tablespoons olive oil, 1 cup vegetable stock
salt, freshly ground pepper

You will also need:
small parsley leaves

Prepare the *cavolo nero* as shown in the picture sequence on page 253. Cut the white cabbage into fourths, cut out the core, and slice the leaves into ¾-inch-wide strips.

Heat the olive oil in a saucepan and sweat the garlic cloves without letting them color. Pour in the stock, add the *cavolo nero*, and cook for 10 minutes over a medium heat. Add the white cabbage, and stew for another 25 minutes. Then add the anchovies and

PEPERONATA

Cold, this tomato-and-pepper medley makes a marvelous hors d'oeuvre served with fresh Italian bread. Straight from the braising pan, it is the ideal complement for a wide variety of meat, poultry, and fish main courses. To lend a special touch to the peperonata, prepare it with skinned bell peppers and sprinkle over some toasted pine nuts before serving.

Serves 4
¼ cup olive oil
10 oz onions, sliced into thin strips
2 red and 2 green bell peppers, quartered, cored, and seeded
1 garlic clove, finely sliced
1 lb tomatoes, peeled, seeded, and coarsely chopped
¼ cup balsamic vinegar
1 pinch cayenne pepper, 1 pinch sugar
salt, freshly ground pepper
You will also need:
1 tablespoon fresh thyme leaves

Heat the oil in a large skillet and sweat the onions until translucent. Add the peppers and garlic, and sweat for 5 minutes. Stir in the tomatoes and deglaze with the vinegar. Season with cayenne, sugar, salt, and pepper. Braise, covered, over a low heat for 30–40 minutes. Sprinkle with thyme and serve.

Preparing the *cavolo nero* Cut off the stalk and pull off the individual leaves. Cut out the midribs and slice the washed leaves into ¾-inch-wide strips.

Cavolo nero, black cabbage, is a variety of kale. In this recipe, it is combined with *cavolo bianco* — white cabbage — and anchovies.

continue to cook over a low heat for 5 minutes until done, at which point the liquid should have evaporated.

After a total cooking time of 40 minutes, season with pepper, and add salt very carefully, since the anchovies are already very salty.

Garnish with parsley leaves, and serve with crusty Italian bread.

Broccoli rabe is cultivated chiefly in Campania and Apulia. With its somewhat bitter flavor and its slightly hot taste, it is a much prized vegetable.

Cima di rapa

With its distinctive flavor, broccoli rabe combines well with a variety of ingredients, as these recipes show

If you have difficulty in obtaining broccoli rabe, a type of brassica that unfortunately is not available everywhere, you can use broccoli instead, although it is somewhat milder in flavor.

BROCCOLI RABE WITH PROSCIUTTO

Prosciutto, pan-fried, lends zip to the greens in this recipe. You can, of course, use one of the other superb varieties of northern Italian ham instead of the admittedly very expensive culatello — San Daniele, for example, or Parma ham.

Serves 4
2¼ lb broccoli rabe, 2 tablespoons butter
4 oz prosciutto (e.g. culatello), cut into fine strips
1 cup finely chopped onions
4 garlic cloves, halved
5 tablespoons olive oil
⅔ cup veal stock
freshly grated nutmeg, salt, freshly ground pepper
You will also need:
freshly shaved Parmesan cheese (optional)

Prepare and cook the broccoli rabe as shown in the picture sequence opposite. Heat the butter in a skillet and fry the prosciutto until crisp. Serve the broccoli rabe with the prosciutto and top with Parmesan shavings if wished.

Remove the large outer leaves, and detach the inner leaves and the florets from the stalk.

Place the leaves and florets in a colander and rinse thoroughly under cold running water.

Transfer the broccoli rabe to a pot. Top with the onions and garlic, drizzle over the oil, and pour in the stock.

Cook the broccoli rabe over medium heat, covered, for 10–15 minutes. Season with salt, pepper, and nutmeg.

BROCCOLI RABE WITH CROUTONS

Garlic devotees might wish to flavor the croutons as well as the tangy broccoli rabe with the pungent herb. To do this, peel a garlic clove, squeeze it through a garlic press into the skillet with the bread cubes, and fry them together. Anyone afraid of overindulgence in garlic can reduce the quantity given below, or omit the garlic altogether. The croutons turn out best made with day-old bread, which is also then easier to dice. (Not illustrated.)

Serves 4

1½ lb broccoli rabe
2 tablespoons olive oil
2 shallots, finely sliced into rings
3–4 small garlic cloves, finely sliced
3 tablespoons veal stock
3 slices day-old white bread
2 tablespoons butter
salt, freshly ground white pepper
⅓ cup freshly shaved Parmesan cheese

Prepare the broccoli rabe as shown in the first two steps of the picture sequence on page 254. Heat the oil in a skillet and sweat the shallots and garlic without letting them color. Add the broccoli rabe and season with salt and pepper. Pour in the stock and braise the greens over a low heat for about 10 minutes.

In the meantime, remove the crust from the bread, and cut it into ¼-inch cubes. Melt the butter in a skillet and sauté the bread cubes until they are golden. Spoon the broccoli rabe onto warmed plates, sprinkle over the croutons and the Parmesan shavings, and serve immediately.

Simple to prepare, broccoli rabe with strips of crisp-fried prosciutto. is delicious. The dish can also be topped with shaved Parmesan cheese.

Try a non-vegetarian version of this dish. With a well-seasoned meat ragout and pan-fried zucchini slices, you can ring the changes quite successfully with a casserole like this.

Melanzane alla parmigiana
A delicious casserole of pan-fried eggplant, fruity tomato sauce, and mozzarella cheese

Although it is chiefly Campania that is famous for this dish, also called *parmigiana di melanzane*, it is prepared throughout southern Italy. There are many ways to vary this recipe. You could, for example, slice the unpeeled eggplants lengthwise, or coat each layer of eggplant and mozzarella with a little tomato sauce. (If you do this, start by spreading just a few spoonfuls of sauce over the base of the baking dish.) You could also sprinkle the top with Parmesan cheese, which makes the dish even spicier. The casserole can be made more substantial with the addition of thinly sliced hardboiled eggs. As for the cheese, it should ideally be a genuine buffalo-milk mozzarella.

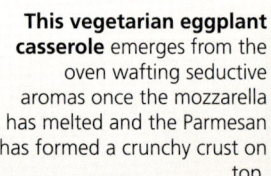

This vegetarian eggplant casserole emerges from the oven wafting seductive aromas once the mozzarella has melted and the Parmesan has formed a crunchy crust on top.

Serves 4
For the pan-fried eggplant:
1½–1¾ lb eggplant, salt
flour for dredging, ½ cup olive oil
For the tomato sauce:
2 tablespoons olive oil, ½ cup finely chopped onion
1 lb canned tomatoes, chopped, with their juice
2 tablespoons tomato paste, 1 pinch sugar
salt, freshly ground pepper
1 tablespoon finely snipped basil leaves
You will also need:
olive oil
8 oz mozzarella cheese, sliced
½ cup freshly grated Parmesan cheese
chopped flat-leaf parsley

First prepare the tomato sauce. Heat the olive oil in a large pan and sweat the onion until lightly colored. Add the tomatoes and their juice. Stir in the tomato paste, and season with sugar, salt, and a few grindings of the pepper mill. Simmer the sauce, covered, over a low heat for 30 minutes, then pour through a fine strainer. Stir in the basil and season to taste with salt and pepper.

Meanwhile, wash the eggplant and trim off both ends. Peel the eggplant thinly and cut crosswise into ½-inch-thick slices. Sprinkle the slices with salt and let sit for 10 minutes to draw out any bitter juices.

Pat the eggplant dry with paper towels, then dredge each slice in flour, gently tapping off any excess. Heat the oil in a skillet and fry the eggplant slices on both sides until golden. Lift out and drain on paper towels.

Preheat the oven to 400°F. Grease an ovenproof dish with a little olive oil. Spoon in the tomato sauce. Layer alternating slices of eggplant and mozzarella on top, overlapping them like tiles, and sprinkle with the grated Parmesan. Bake for 20–25 minutes. Remove from the oven, sprinkle with the parsley, and serve.

Cardoon with tomato sauce
A vegetable dish that could hardly be simpler, and yet is full of flavor

In Italy, baking the boiled vegetable, *au gratin*, with béchamel sauce or with a grated hard cheese, *alla parmigiana*, is the classic way of preparing cardoon. In this recipe the vegetable is combined with Parmesan cheese and a tomato sauce that adds an even spicier note. Although cardoon stalks resemble celery in appearance, their affinity with the artichoke is revealed by two of their characteristics: their slightly bitter taste and the fact that their cut surfaces quickly turn dark, for which reason the stalks must be acidulated immediately after they are trimmed, either by brushing them with lemon juice or placing them in vinegar water.

Cut off the stalk of the cardoon plant with a sharp knife.

Completely remove the remains of the leaves as well as the prickly edges.

Pull off the tough, inedible strings, and halve the stalks lengthwise.

The cardoon, a relative of the artichoke, adapts beautifully to Mediterranean-style seasonings — tomato sauce, olives, and Parmesan cheese.

Serves 4
1 cardoon plant (about 14 oz)
For the tomato sauce:
2 tablespoons oil
¾ cup finely chopped onion
1 garlic clove
1 lb tomatoes, peeled, seeded, and diced
1 bay leaf
You will also need:
vinegar water, 10 black olives
1 teaspoon chopped rosemary
1 teaspoon chopped parsley
⅓ cup freshly shaved Parmesan cheese

Prepare the cardoon as shown in the picture sequence on page 258. Place the stalks in vinegar water immediately to prevent discoloration. Cook the cardoon stalks in briskly boiling salted water for about 30 minutes, then remove any stringy bits.

Meanwhile, make the sauce. Heat the oil in a saucepan and sweat the onion and garlic until lightly colored. Add the tomatoes and the bay leaf, and simmer for about 15 minutes.

Cool the sauce slightly and strain. Pour all but 3 tablespoons of the sauce in a gratin dish, and place the cardoon stalks on top. Sprinkle over the olives. Spoon the remaining tomato sauce over the stalks, sprinkle with the rosemary and parsley, top with the Parmesan, and serve immediately.

VEGETABLES

Wafer-thin zucchini slices, swiftly produced on a vegetable mandolin, are ideal for salads. Prepared like this, the zucchini needs no cooking; just drizzle it with a spicy olive oil and white wine vinegar dressing.

Zucchini — delicious baked or marinated

These three dishes, simple to prepare and completely vegetarian, show just how versatile this summer squash can be

ZUCCHINI AND TOMATO GRATIN

Serves 4

6 tablespoons olive oil, 1½ cups finely chopped onion

2 garlic cloves, finely chopped

¾ cup diced carrot, 1 thyme sprig

2 teaspoons sweet paprika

1¾ lb tomatoes, peeled, seeded, and diced

2 lb zucchini, cut into ½-inch dice

¼ cup flour

salt, freshly ground pepper

You will also need:

oil, 1 cup freshly grated Montasio fresco cheese

a few thyme leaves

Heat half of the oil in a skillet and sweat the onions and garlic until lightly colored. Add the carrots and sweat for 3–4 minutes, then season with the thyme sprig, paprika, salt, and pepper. Add the tomatoes and braise over a medium heat for 10–12 minutes.

Season the zucchini with salt and dredge in flour. Heat the remaining olive oil in a separate skillet and pan-fry the zucchini until golden brown, stirring constantly.

Preheat the oven to 400°F. Grease a baking dish with oil. Spoon in half of the zucchini cubes and top with half of the tomato mixture. Spread over the remaining zucchini cubes and finish with the rest of the tomato mixture. Sprinkle this mixture with the

This summery zucchini gratin tastes especially good when accompanied by a fresh, crusty baguette.

cheese, and bake for 15–20 minutes, until the top is browned and bubbling. Remove the gratin from the oven and serve sprinkled with thyme leaves.

MARINATED GREEN ZUCCHINI

Serves 4
1¼ lb small zucchini, 4–5 tablespoons olive oil
For the dressing:
2 tablespoons lemon juice, 1 tablespoon balsamic vinegar
6 tablespoons olive oil, ¼ cup chopped white onion
2 garlic cloves, thinly sliced
1 small sweet red pepper, thinly sliced into rings and seeded
1 tablespoon fresh herbs (thyme, oregano, basil)
salt, freshly ground pepper

Trim off both ends of the zucchini and cut on a slight diagonal into oval slices about ¼ inch thick. Heat the olive oil in a skillet and sauté the zucchini slices in batches on both sides until golden brown. Lift out and leave to cool.

To make the dressing, whisk together the lemon juice, vinegar, salt, and pepper in a bowl and stir in the oil, onion, garlic, red pepper, and herbs. Spoon the zucchini onto a platter, drizzle with the dressing, and leave to marinate for about 15 minutes.

MARINATED YELLOW ZUCCHINI

Serves 4
1 lb yellow zucchini
¾ cup white wine vinegar, 1 teaspoon salt
For the marinade:
thinly pared zest of 1 lemon
3 tablespoons red wine vinegar
3 garlic cloves, thinly sliced
6 tablespoons olive oil
salt, freshly ground pepper
You will also need:
1 tablespoon small peppermint leaves

Trim off both ends of the zucchini and cut into ¼-inch-thick rounds. Bring the vinegar to a boil in a saucepan with 2¼ cups water and add the salt. Add the zucchini slices to the pan and simmer for 2 minutes, then remove and drain well.

To make the marinade, cut the lemon zest into thin strips. Whisk together the vinegar, salt, and pepper until the salt has dissolved. Stir in the garlic, lemon zest, and olive oil. Add the zucchini slices to the dressing and marinate for 20 minutes. Season to taste with salt and pepper, spoon onto a platter, and serve sprinkled with mint.

A melon baller is perfect for hollowing out the zucchini halves, but a small sharp-edged spoon will also do the job.

Zucchini with a polenta stuffing
Baked in vegetable stock with a spicy golden-brown topping of pecorino cheese

Quick, good, and delicious. Neither the initial preparations for, nor the cooking of, this dish are particularly time-consuming or complicated. If you cannot get hold of pecorino toscano cheese, you can use pecorino romano, but not its too-strong Sardinian cousin pecorino sardo. Polenta is usually made with water in Italy, but a vegetable stock makes for a fuller-flavored dish. The dried porcini as well as the celery and carrots contribute additional flavor to the stuffing.

Serves 4
2 zucchini (12 oz each)
For the polenta stuffing:
1 oz dried porcini mushrooms
4 scallions, cut into thin rings, white and green parts separated
2 tablespoons olive oil
½ cup finely diced celery
1 cup finely diced carrot
1 garlic clove, finely chopped
¾ cup corn meal
1¾ cups vegetable stock
1 teaspoon chopped thyme leaves
½ teaspoon chopped rosemary
1 teaspoon salt, freshly ground white pepper

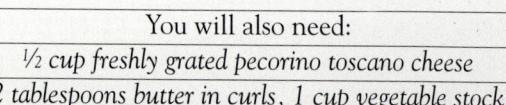

Tasty zucchini stuffed with vegetables and polenta and baked till golden brown are a welcome addition to any menu.

The distinctive taste of this dish comes from the dried porcini mushrooms, so be generous with them.

You will also need:
½ cup freshly grated pecorino toscano cheese
2 tablespoons butter in curls, 1 cup vegetable stock

Cut the stalks off the zucchini, and halve the zucchini lengthwise. Hollow out the halves as shown above on the left, leaving only a thin shell. Cut the scooped-out flesh into small dice.

Soften the porcini mushrooms in ½ cup lukewarm water for at least 15 minutes. Pour off and reserve the soaking water, and chop the mushrooms finely.

Heat the olive oil in a large saucepan and sweat

the white parts of the scallions, the garlic, diced zucchini, celery, and carrots until lightly colored. Stir in the corn meal and toast lightly. Add the porcini, the reserved soaking water, and the vegetable stock. Bring briefly to a boil, then cook over a low heat, covered, for a further 15 minutes, stirring occasionally. Stir the thyme, rosemary, and green parts of the scallions into the polenta, and season with salt and pepper.

Preheat the oven to 400°F. Lightly salt the zucchini shells on the inside. Spoon the polenta and vegetable mixture into them. Pour the vegetable stock into a baking dish and place the stuffed zucchini in the dish. Sprinkle with pecorino and dot with the butter. Bake for 20–25 minutes, until the top of the stuffing has turned an appetizing golden-brown. Arrange on plates and serve.

Peperoni ripieni
Sweet red peppers with a surprisingly light stuffing

These block-shaped peppers are known as *quadrati* in Italian. Their large capacity makes them especially suitable for stuffing.

Stuffings based on crusty white bread are a specialty of southern Italy. Stuffed bell peppers of this sort are prized there both as an antipasto and a light main course, with, for example, rice as an accompaniment, or as a snack that can be eaten either warm or cold. In the recipe given below, capers, anchovy fillets, and olives lend flavor to the stuffing. The capers must be the kind that are preserved in salt; the vinegary taste of the pickled capers makes them unsuitable for this dish. Taste the stuffing before adding any salt, as it may be salty enough from the capers and anchovies. For variety, you could add small cubes of prosciutto, and a spicy, coarsely grated cheese such as Caciocavallo — in which case you should leave out the capers, anchovies, and olives. Not only bell peppers, but also hollowed out zucchini and eggplant taste wonderful with these kinds of stuffings.

Serves 4
4 red bell peppers
For the stuffing:
2 day-old rolls, ½ cup olive oil
1 tablespoon salted capers, finely chopped
2 garlic cloves, finely chopped
6 anchovy fillets, finely chopped
2 tablespoons finely chopped parsley
1 tablespoon finely chopped thyme leaves
15 pitted black olives
salt, freshly ground white pepper
You will also need:
1 cup freshly grated Parmesan cheese
½ cup vegetable stock

Prepare the red peppers as described in the first step of the picture sequence. To make the stuffing, proceed as described in the next three steps of the picture sequence. Preheat the oven to 350°F and follow the instructions in the remaining steps of the picture sequence.

Cut off the tops of the peppers and reserve. Remove the seeds and ribs, and wash the hollowed out peppers.

Grate the crust from the rolls. Finely dice the crumb, and soak in a bowl with 3 tablespoons olive oil.

Add the remaining ingredients to the diced bread. Season with pepper, and add salt to taste.

Gradually stir the remaining olive oil into the stuffing. Mix well until the oil binds the stuffing.

Place the hollowed-out peppers in a baking dish and divide the stuffing evenly among them.

Sprinkle with Parmesan cheese and replace the tops. Pour in the stock and bake the peppers for about 40 minutes.

Tomatoes times two
Aromatic with garlic and herbs, or with a spinach stuffing

As different as the following two dishes may be, they have one thing in common: the tomatoes are baked. Make sure, therefore, that you buy firm tomatoes. For the first recipe, plum tomatoes are ideal; choose the Roma, or, even better, San Marzano variety, if available. For stuffing, on the other hand, firm, round varieties are more suitable; apart from the fact that they can take more stuffing, the tomatoes are not peeled in this recipe, and the plum tomatoes would tend to split open from the heat of the oven.

BAKED TOMATOES

These tomatoes taste especially good as an antipasto or as a side dish with broiled meat or fish, accompanied by crusty white bread.

Serves 4
2¼ lb plum tomatoes, peeled
1 bunch basil
1 bunch flat parsley, finely chopped
2 garlic cloves
6 tablespoons extra-virgin olive oil
½ teaspoon thyme leaves
salt, freshly ground black pepper

Halve or quarter the tomatoes, depending on size, and seed them. Strip the basil leaves from their stalks and cut all but 10 leaves into fine strips. Cut 1 of the garlic cloves in half. Heat the olive oil in a skillet and sauté the halved garlic clove until light brown, then lift out and discard.

Preheat the oven to 425°F. Brush a baking dish with 2 tablespoons of the garlic-flavored olive oil, and place half of the tomatoes in it. Season with salt and pepper, and sprinkle with the basil strips, two-thirds of the parsley, and the thyme. Squeeze the second garlic clove through a garlic press over them. Drizzle with 2 tablespoons of the oil. Place the remaining tomatoes on top. Season with salt and pepper, and drizzle with the remaining olive oil.

Bake the tomatoes for 20 minutes. Remove, and serve sprinkled with the reserved whole basil leaves and the remaining parsley.

STUFFED TOMATOES

These *pomodori ripieni* are seasoned with lemon balm and orange zest, lending the spinach stuffing a pleasantly fresh citrus tang. Peppermint leaves can provide an aromatic accent if lemon balm is unavailable.

Serves 4

1¾ lb firm, round tomatoes

For the stuffing:

1 lb spinach

3 tablespoons butter

⅓ cup pine nuts

2 shallots, finely chopped

⅔ cup finely diced boiled ham

grated zest of 1 orange

a few leaves lemon balm, cut into thin strips

salt, freshly ground black pepper

You will also need:

butter, 2 tablespoons olive oil

Cut a slice off the bottom of each tomato if necessary so that it will sit flat in the baking dish, and cut a "lid" off the top of each one. Hollow out each tomato with a small spoon and turn upside down on paper towels to drain thoroughly.

Bring some salted water to a boil in a large sauce pan and blanch the spinach. Drain, squeeze out all excess water, and chop coarsely.

Melt the butter in a skillet and fry the pine nuts until golden. Add the shallots and ham, and sauté briefly. Stir in the spinach and the orange zest. Season with lemon balm, salt, and pepper.

Preheat the oven to 375°F. Butter a baking dish. Stuff the tomatoes with the spinach mixture, place in the dish, drizzle with the olive oil, and bake for 20–25 minutes.

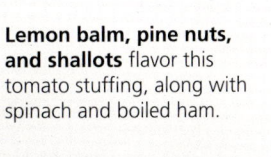

Lemon balm, pine nuts, and shallots flavor this tomato stuffing, along with spinach and boiled ham.

The Spanish Steps are a trademark of the city of Rome, just like simple but exquisite artichoke dishes are a hallmark of its traditional cuisine.

Carciofi alla romana

Artichokes, Roman style: the stuffing spicy, with lots of parsley, garlic and peppermint

Arranged stalk-up on large platters, these stuffed artichokes are served in Roman restaurants as an antipasto when in season. The stuffing may be enriched with bread crumbs, as here, or contain only herbs.

Serves 4
4 artichokes (about 1 lb each), juice of 2 lemons
For the stuffing:
9 tablespoons olive oil
3 garlic cloves, finely chopped
¾ cup finely chopped shallots
1 bunch parsley, finely chopped
2 tablespoons chopped peppermint, 3 cups bread crumbs
½ cup pitted black olives, coarsely chopped
salt, freshly ground pepper
You will also need:
kitchen string, 3 tablespoons olive oil
about ⅔ cup vegetable stock

Remove the outside leaves of the artichokes. Cut off the prickly tips of the other leaves if wished, as shown in the first step of the picture sequence. Cut the stalks back to 2 inches in length, then pare thinly.

Immediately tie each artichoke together crosswise with kitchen string and place in a bowl of water acidulated with the lemon juice. Cook the artichokes and prepare them for stuffing, as described in the final four steps opposite.

Meanwhile, make the stuffing. Heat the olive oil in a skillet and sweat the garlic and shallots until lightly colored. Stir in the parsley, mint, bread crumbs, and olives, then season with salt and pepper.

Preheat the oven to 350°F. Carefully fill the artichokes with the stuffing, pressing the leaves together again slightly. Heat the olive oil in a large pot and place the artichokes close together inside, stalks upward. Pour in enough stock to come a third of the way up the artichokes and bake for about 30 minutes. If the stalks begin to brown too much, cover the pot with aluminum foil. To serve, halve the artichokes lengthwise and arrange on plates.

Trim off the tips of the leaves with kitchen scissors, and cut off the tip of the artichoke with a sharp knife.

Cook the tied-up artichokes in briskly boiling water acidulated with lemon juice for 10 minutes.

Weigh down with a lid that will hold them under the surface of the water. Drain the cooked artichokes upside down.

Remove the string. Twist out the petals from the center of the artichoke.

Using a melon baller or a small spoon, scoop out the inedible choke from the base.

Freshness is not a worry if you grow your own fennel, like restaurateur Alfonso Iaccarino on his farm near Sorrento. If you rely on store-bought supplies, though, check for the unmistakable signs of quality: feathery, shiny green leaves, and a plump rather than dried-up appearance around cut parts.

Fennel with black olives
Baked with a crisp crust of bread crumbs and Parmesan cheese

Finocchi gratinati, or fennel *au gratin*, is prepared in a wide variety of ways in Italy. In Emilia-Romagna, for example, it is often coated with a rich sauce made of cream and delicately melting cheese before being baked. Here, however, it is prepared *al pomodoro*. The bulbs are first parboiled and then topped with stewed tomatoes. The whole is sprinkled with bread crumbs and Parmesan cheese, and baked in the oven until bubbling and golden. Bulb fennel is in season in Italy during the cooler part of the year, and is harvested from the fall to the spring.

Serves 4
2¼ lb fennel bulbs
2 thyme sprigs
1 rosemary sprig
1 bay leaf
1 teaspoon salt
freshly ground pepper
½ cup dry white wine
For the tomatoes:
2 tablespoons olive oil
⅓ cup chopped shallots
2 garlic cloves
10 oz tomatoes, peeled, seeded, and diced
You will also need:
butter
½ cup pitted black olives
¾ cup white bread crumbs
⅔ cup grated aged pecorino or Parmesan cheese
2 tablespoons chopped fennel leaves

This fennel au gratin makes a good vegetarian main course if served with rice or fresh crusty white bread. To drink, we suggest a strong white wine, preferably the one used in the recipe.

Place the herbs and bay leaf in the buttered dish, arrange the quartered fennel over the base, season with salt and pepper, and pour over the white wine.

Cut off the base of root of the fennel bulbs and the green stalks. Quarter the bulbs lengthwise and cook in briskly boiling salted water for 5 minutes, then drain well.

Preheat the oven to 400°F. Butter an au gratin dish and proceed as shown in the picture sequence on page 270. Bake for about 20 minutes.

In the meantime, heat the oil in a skillet and sweat the shallots and garlic cloves. Add the tomatoes and stew for 1 minute, then remove from the heat. Spread this mixture evenly over the fennel and scatter the olives on top.

Combine the bread crumbs, cheese, and the fennel leaves, and sprinkle over the top. Bake for a further 15–20 minutes, adding a little wine during this period if the dish is looking too dry.

Corn is a cereal grass that originated in South America. It arrived in Italy, via Spain and Portugal, in the sixteenth century.

Polenta slices with a porcini stuffing

A stylish, upmarket version of the traditional poor-man's meal

For centuries, cooked polenta was one of the cheapest foods available in northern Italy. Nowadays, it is often served only as a side dish. In this recipe it plays a starring role, accompanied by a fruity tomato sauce. When not in season, the fresh porcini mushrooms used in the stuffing can be replaced by dried ones. In this case, you will need only one-third the quantity given below, and you will need to soak the dried mushrooms before use.

Serves 4
For the polenta:
3¼ cups milk, ½ teaspoon salt, freshly grated nutmeg
6 tablespoons butter, 1¼ cups corn meal
1 teaspoon olive oil
For the mushroom stuffing:
2 tablespoons butter, ½ cup chopped shallots
1 garlic clove, crushed
8 oz porcini mushrooms, coarsely chopped
1 tablespoon chopped parsley, 1 teaspoon thyme leaves
2 tablespoons cream, 3 oz fontina cheese
salt, freshly ground pepper
For the breading:
flour, 2 eggs, beaten; fine white bread crumbs
For the tomato sauce:
3 tablespoons olive oil
½ cup diced onion
1 garlic clove, finely chopped
1¼ lb tomatoes, peeled, seeded, and diced
1 tablespoon chopped herbs
salt, freshly ground pepper
You will also need:
½ cup sunflower oil

Bring the milk to a boil in a large saucepan with the salt, nutmeg, and butter. Remove from the heat and stir in the corn meal with a whisk. Cook over a low heat for 10 minutes, stirring constantly. Turn the polenta out onto an oiled baking sheet, spread to a thickness of ½ inch, and leave to cool.

Melt the butter in saucepan and sweat the shallots and garlic until lightly colored. Add the mushrooms and sauté, stirring frequently, until the mixture is relatively dry. Add the herbs and season with salt and pepper. Pour in the cream, bring briefly to a boil, and remove from the heat. Cut the cheese into small cubes and stir into the slightly cooled mushroom mixture.

Cut the cooled polenta into rectangles about 2¾ x 4 inches, spread half of them with the mushroom stuffing, top each with a second piece of polenta, and press down lightly. Bread the stuffed polenta slices by turning first in flour, then in eggs, then in bread crumbs.

To make the sauce, heat the oil in a saucepan and sweat the onion and garlic until translucent. Stir in the tomatoes and herbs, season with salt and pepper, bring briefly to a boil, remove from the heat and keep warm.

Heat the sunflower oil in a heavy-based skillet and slowly fry the polenta slices on all sides until golden brown. Arrange on plates, and pass around the tomato sauce separately. A salad of fresh wild herbs harmonizes superbly with this dish.

Funghi freschi

Italians adore fresh mushrooms, whether gathered on a walk in the woods or bought at the market, and have a real flair for preparing them

MEDLEY OF WILD MUSHROOMS

There are many varieties of wild mushroom, and it does not matter which ones you use for this ragout, as long as you are sure they are safe to eat and absolutely fresh. The orange-colored Caesar's mushrooms may be enveloped by a thin membrane, known as the universal veil. As the mushrooms mature, the remains of this veil may form a ring, called the velum or velar remains, around the base of the stem.

Serves 4
1¾ lb mixed wild mushrooms
5–6 tablespoons extra-virgin olive oil or butter
1 small red chile pepper, thinly sliced into rings and seeded
2 garlic cloves, thinly sliced
½ bunch flat-leaf parsley, finely chopped
salt, coarsely ground black pepper

Clean and trim the mushrooms. If you are fortunate enough to find any Caesar's mushrooms, remove the velar remains and wipe clean. Peel the caps. Cut the velar remains into pieces, and cut the mushrooms lengthwise into ¼-inch-thick slices. Very carefully wipe clean and trim the remaining varieties of mushroom and leave whole, halve, or quarter them according to size.

Heat the olive oil or melt the butter in a skillet,

and briefly sweat the chile pepper and the garlic. Add the mushrooms and sauté for 4–5 minutes over a low heat, turning carefully. Season with salt and pepper, and serve sprinkled with parsley. Italian white bread, such as a Tuscan country loaf or ciabatta, goes very well with this dish.

FRESH MUSHROOMS WITH TOMATOES

Depending on the time of year and your personal preferences, this very simple but tasty mushroom dish can be prepared with just one of the varieties of mushroom rather than with both. (Not illustrated.)

Serves 4–6
8 oz each small porcini and small white mushrooms
7 oz plum tomatoes, peeled
2 garlic cloves, finely chopped
1 teaspoon rosemary leaves, finely chopped
6 tablespoon extra-virgin olive oil
salt, freshly ground black pepper

Carefully clean the white mushrooms and the porcini, preferably by wiping off any dirt or grime clinging to them with a damp cloth. Wash the mushrooms only if absolutely necessary, and then carefully pat dry. Halve the mushrooms lengthwise.

Seed the tomatoes, straining the seeds and reserving the juices. Finely dice the tomato flesh.

Heat the olive oil in a skillet. Add the garlic, and allow to color slightly. Add the mushrooms, sauté briefly, and season with salt and pepper. Stir in the rosemary. Stew the mushrooms until the liquid they give off evaporates.

Stir the tomatoes and their reserved juice into the mushroom mixture. Simmer the mushrooms over a low heat, covered, for about 10 minutes. If the mixture should become too dry, add 1–2 tablespoons water to prevent the mushrooms from sticking to the pan.

Spoon the mushrooms and tomatoes onto a warmed platter and serve. Italian white bread and a glass of red wine go superbly with this mushroom dish, which can be served as an hors d'oeuvre, or as a side dish with meat or game.

As delicious a medley of mushrooms as one could wish for: aromatic wild mushrooms — including the rare Caesar's mushroom — and young firm-fleshed porcini, with the red chile pepper providing a touch of heat.

Baked mushrooms

Two recipes: one for garlicky mushrooms, and one for Caesar's mushroom caps with a fine vegetable stuffing

GARLIC MUSHROOMS

Serves 4

¼ cup olive oil
⅓ cup finely chopped shallots
4 garlic cloves, finely chopped
1½ celery stalks, thinly sliced
1¾ lb cultivated mushrooms, trimmed, and halved
2 tablespoons lemon juice
2 tablespoons dry Marsala wine
1 bunch parsley, chopped
1 teaspoon salt, freshly ground pepper
3 tablespoons vegetable stock
½ cup white bread crumbs, 1 tablespoon butter, in curls

Heat the oil in an flameproof baking dish, and sweat the shallots, garlic and celery until lightly colored. Add the mushrooms, lemon juice, Marsala, parsley, salt, and pepper, and stir well to combine. Pour in the vegetable stock. Preheat the oven to 400°F. Sprinkle the mushrooms with the bread crumbs and dot with the butter. Bake for about 20 minutes, then serve.

STUFFED CAESAR'S MUSHROOMS

Serves 4

1¾ cups vegetable stock
1¾ lb Caesar's mushrooms, ¼ cup vegetable oil
1 garlic clove, 1 cup finely diced celery
2 slices white bread, crust removed, finely cubed
½ cup finely diced shallots, ¾ cup finely diced carrots

VEGETABLES 277

1 tablespoon chopped celery leaves
salt, freshly ground pepper; 2 tablespoons butter, in curls
You will also need:
butter, 1 tablespoon finely snipped chives

Boil the stock down to reduce by half. Wipe the mushrooms clean, remove and wipe clean the velar remains. Peel the caps and remove the stems. Hollow out any thick-walled caps slightly. Finely dice the stems, velar remains, and any fruiting bodies. Heat half of the oil in a skillet and squeeze the garlic through a garlic press into the pan. Add the bread cubes and fry until golden. Heat the remaining oil in another skillet and sweat the vegetables for 3 minutes. Add the mushrooms and sauté for 1 minute. Mix in the celery leaves and croutons, and season. Mound the mixture into the mushroom caps.

Preheat the oven to 400°F. Butter an ovenproof dish, arrange the mushroom caps in it, and dot them with the butter. Pour in the reduced stock, and tuck any leftover stuffing in between the mushroom caps. Bake for 15 minutes.

These mushrooms *au gratin* are superb served with a *frittata* as antipasti.

Before serving, arrange the stuffed Caesar's mushrooms on warmed plates with a little vegetable stock, and sprinkle with snipped chives. Sautéed potatoes go well with this dish.

Pesci FISH

Night after night, small boats sail out of the harbors along the Italian coast to supply the regional markets with fresh fish and seafood of all kinds the next morning. The Italians know how to use the abundant catch to best effect: The regional cuisines of Liguria, the Veneto, Campania, and Sicily, for example, are all famous for their imaginative ways with the the treasures of the sea.

Fine foods from the sea

A wonderful variety of fish, shellfish, and crustaceans: The Italians are spoiled for choice as far as delicacies from the sea are concerned.

Eels — at home in freshwater and saltwater

By the time it reaches Italy, the eel has traveled halfway around the world. All eels hatch in the Sargasso Sea, and then drift to Europe with the Gulf Stream. The little eels accumulate for a while in the brackish water at the mouths of rivers before traveling upstream. In this intermediate stage they are known as elvers, and are a popular delicacy in Italy, served dressed in oil and lemon juice. Fully grown river eels are smoked and served as an antipasto. This fatty fish is also braised, grilled, and pan-fried, and is part of the traditional Italian Christmas menu.

Skate and rays Commercially, no distinction is drawn between these closely related fish, so painted rays (above, far left) and spotted rays (above, left) are sold together. The thornback ray (above, right) is also eaten.

Glass eels or elvers, *cieche* in Italian, are young eels. They are caught in the mouths of rivers.

Eel Italy is one of the countries in which the fully grown fish — known there as *anguilla* — is most frequently caught and prepared.

Skate and shark

As different as they may look, Skate, *razza* in Italian, and shark, *pesce-cane* or *palombo*, are actually closely related zoologically. The species of culinary importance have firm,

light flesh, which is closer in taste to veal than fish. Although portions of the skate tail are used in cooking, it is mainly the comparatively huge pectoral fins of large skate that are eaten, after the skin and skeletal bones are removed. Filleted skate wings are served grilled baked, and poached. In Sicily, they are served seasoned with salt and pepper, dusted with flour, and pan-fried, accompanied by a cold sauce of capers, chopped anchovy fillets, and olive oil.

Shark steaks can be prepared in exactly the same way as swordfish or tuna, but taste especially delicious pan-fried or grilled.

Moray eel

The moray eel has been a popular food fish in many areas of the Mediterranean since Roman times. Its flesh is quite fatty, white, and tender, but does not travel at all well, which is why the moray eel is only of local importance. In Italy, this fish is pan-fried, grilled or used in soups.

Monkfish

The delicate monkfish is known in Italy by different names, depending on the region: thus,

The larger spotted dogfish, also known in Italian as *gattopardo* (leopard) because of its spots, occurs throughout the Mediterranean area. Although firm and tasty, its flesh is not highly regarded in Italy, and is usually cut into small pieces and braised or added to fish soups.

Opinions diverge greatly as to the culinary value of the **moray eel**. On the west coast of Italy, however, the spotted, eel-like *murena* is a popular food fish.

Sardine fishing in the Adriatic. The little silvery sardine is one of the most important European food fishes. In the Mediterranean, sardines are often caught at night by luring them with a light, surrounding whole schools with a net, and heaving them on board the boat.

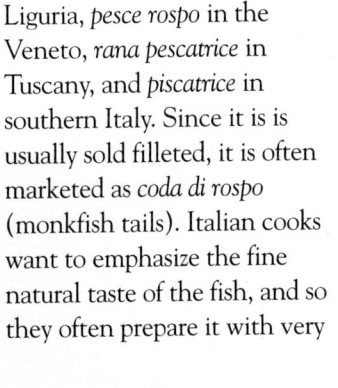

for instance, it is called *boldrò* in Liguria, *pesce rospo* in the Veneto, *rana pescatrice* in Tuscany, and *piscatrice* in southern Italy. Since it is is usually sold filleted, it is often marketed as *coda di rospo* (monkfish tails). Italian cooks want to emphasize the fine natural taste of the fish, and so they often prepare it with very few other ingredients. Usually, a few drops of good olive oil, a bit of onion, garlic, and parsley suffice if the fillets are braised or grilled, or they are cooked briefly in tomato sauce.

"Small fry," big taste

Italian cooking would be unthinkable without sardines, anchovies, and the truly tiny silversides. As if to compensate for their small size, these fish go by a number of names: the sardine, for instance, is known variously as *sarda*, *sardina*, and *sardella*, while the anchovy is referred to as *acciuga* or *alice*. The Sicilian dish *sarde a beccaficu*, or stuffed sardines, is known throughout Italy.

Anchovies, on the other hand, are most often preserved raw in oil or in salt. Also popular are freshly hatched anchovies, which depending on the region are known as *neonati*, *bianchetti*, *nudini*, or *gianchetti*. These are cooked whole and ungutted, and served, for example, as a salad. The tiny, almost transparent silversides, called *latterini* in Italian, are prepared in the same way as young anchovies, or are dusted with flour and deep-fried in hot oil until crisp.

Flying fish primarily inhabit tropical waters, and are not found as frequently in the Mediterranean. The few that turn up in fishermen's nets are usually black-finned flying fish.

Sardines (top) are often used fresh in Italy for grilling. It is usually only the fillets of **anchovies** (middle), preserved in different ways, that are used in Italy. **Silversides** (above) are small, almost transparent schooling fishes, frequently found in the Mediterranean close to the coast. As with whitebait, individual species are not distinguished when sold.

With its huge jaws, sharp teeth, and barbed dorsal fin, the **monkfish** is rather repulsive at first glance. Despite its ugly appearance, its firm, white flesh — totally free from bones except for the spinal column — is prized by gourmets.

Smooth or spiny

Although differing widely in terms of texture and quality, the fish on these two pages still have something to offer lovers of whole, fish and fans of fish soups.

The highly coveted species

Sea bass and John Dory, grouper and dentex are among the most delicious food fishes that the Mediterranean has to offer. What they have in common is firm, tasty flesh, which is well suited to a variety of preparations, but which usually tastes best when prepared with just a few seasonings that will not swamp their own fine flavor. For example, the dog's tooth bream or dentex, known as *dentice* in Italian, is either brushed repeatedly with oil and grilled, or baked with vegetables such as onions and potatoes. Dentex fillets are also available *sott'olio*, preserved in oil, and in cans. Equally popular are the black and brown grouper, *cernia*, which are also sometimes served raw, drizzled with best-quality olive oil and lemon juice.

The quality of goldlines can vary greatly according to season, and depends on which species of seaweed the fish have been feeding on most heavily before being caught.

The sea bass is sometimes also known by its French name, *loup de mer*. The Italian terms for this fish are positively legion; most common are *branzino* and *baicolo* in northern Italy, *ragno* and *spigola* in central Italy, and *spinula*, *pesce lupo*, and *lupo* (wolf) in southern Italy. In Palermo and Trapani a favorite way of cooking sea bass is to season the scaled and gutted fish with salt and pepper, drizzle it with olive oil, wrap it in parchment paper with diced tomatoes, capers, and a sprig of oregano, and then baked it in the oven for about 30 minutes.

The large-scaled scorpion fish is as well armed as it looks. It must be handled carefully, as it has poison glands at the base of its dorsal fin.

The John Dory is found in the eastern Atlantic and the Pacific oceans, as well as in the Mediterranean. In many European languages the name of this fish bears a reference to St. Peter. In Italian, for example, it is called *pesce San Pietro*. According to legend, the gold-rimmed black spots on the fish's body are the thumbprints of the Apostle. These spots can be used as an index of quality: If their edges are clearly defined, the fish is indisputably fresh. Top-quality John Dory is a guarantee of excellent eating. In Italy, the fillets are grilled or prepared in the same manner as Dover sole.

Humpback dentex are found in the southern Mediterranean. They owe their name to their sharp teeth and relatively high-arching backs.

Horse mackerel, or scad, are are often caught in tuna nets. In Italy they are prepared fresh, but are also enjoyed marinated.

The red, or cuckoo, gurnard, *capone imperiale* in Italian, is the most highly regarded food fish of the gurnard family.

Not quite so well known, but delicious nonetheless

The scorpion fishes and members of the gurnard family are often not the most economical fish, as the head alone constitutes a large proportion of the body. Despite their somewhat grotesque appearance, both species are quite tasty, and — especially in the case of smaller specimens — are superb in fish soups. Larger scorpion fish, known as *scorfano* or *scorpena rossa* in Italian, are also good steamed or fried, and can stand up to strong seasonings such as onions, garlic, and plenty of chile pepper. For gurnard, on the other hand, braising is the cooking method of choice. The horse mackerel or scad, *suro* in Italian, and the bogue or goldline, *salpa* or *sarpa*, are best grilled whole, with punchy seasonings. If you come across horse mackerel, choose smaller specimens of 2½–3 inches long; larger ones may suffer from slightly tough flesh. Ray's breams, on the other hand, known as *brama occhiuta* or *pesce castagna* in Italian, are especially fine baked in white wine with capers and onions.

The sea bass (top) is numbered among the very best food fishes, and commands a correspondingly high price. The **black grouper** (above) is also highly sought-after and expensive throughout the Mediterranean.

Despite its name, the **Ray's bream** or **Atlantic pomfret** also occurs in the western and central Mediterranean. During the fall and winter months, this fish, known in the local dialect as *pisci luna* or "moon fish," is caught primarily all around Sicily.

An excellent food fish, the **John Dory** is an international celebrity in culinary terms.

A splendid specimen of bluefin tuna, like the one on sale here at the market in Palermo, may have been 6–10 feet long. The French and German names, which translate as "red tuna," are self explanatory if you glance at the deep color of the fish's flesh.

Chub mackerel are popular food fish, as are the conspicuously striped Atlantic mackerel, or *sgombri*, also found in the Mediterranean.

The Atlantic bonito is a smaller relative of the tuna, reaching a maximum length of 35 inches. This fish is easily recognized by its dark-blue diagonal stripes.

Tuna & relatives

Tuna are caught in the Mediterranean during the summer, when they migrate to shallower waters to spawn. The fishermen drive the fish into fixed nets known as *tonnare*, which are put up near the coast. Two species of tuna are found throughout the Mediterranean: the bluefin and the albacore or long-fin tuna, known in Italy as *tonno* and *alalunga* or *albacora*, respectively. They differ in size — the bluefin can be up to 10 feet long, but the albacore will not exceed 4 feet — and in color, the meat of the albacore being distinctly lighter than that of the bluefin.

It is not just the fine, boneless flesh of the tuna that is used in Italy. In Sicily, even the light-pink milt — the sperm of the male fish, known as *latume*, and seen lying on the table in the photo above — has its enthusiastic buyers. The roe of the female is also popular; heavily salted, pressed into rectangular shapes, and dried or smoked, it is made into *bottarga di tonno*. Another tuna specialty is *ventresca*, the dark, fatty, soft underbelly of the tuna, preserved in oil, which has a particularly fine taste.

Albacore is superior in taste to bluefin; in addition, it contains more fat, making it well suited to grilling, as well as being excellent wrapped in parchment paper and baked gently. In general, however, the Italians also like their tuna steaks braised in a well-seasoned tomato sauce. Tuna is also eaten raw as a carpaccio, as well as air-dried. The latter is a specialty known as *mosciame* or *musciame*, and was traditionally made from dolphin meat, until the ban on catching them.

In the spring, schools of Atlantic bonito, or *palamita*, migrate to the Mediterranean to spawn, and are caught along the Italian coasts. The Atlantic bonito, however, is much less sought-after as a food fish than the large species of tuna.

A direct comparison between the size of fish and buyer clearly illustrates how large a swordfish can grow. Major specimens reach a length of up to 15 feet, and tip the scales at 1,430 pounds. As overfishing of stocks has made an impact, however, fishermen now seldom succeed in taking swordfish more than 11½ feet in length.

Striped red mullets, while still small and absolutely fresh, are sometimes prepared whole and ungutted in Italy. This is possible because the fish have no gall bladder.

The swordfish, or *pesce spada*, always occur singly or in pairs. When they do not get entangled in *tonnare*, they are usually harpoon- or line-fished, a method not entirely lacking in danger, since these fish are liable to defend themselves vigorously. This fish is very popular, especially in southern Italy. It is served grilled, smoked, and raw, carved into thin slices.

The light, muscular flesh of the swordfish has quite a different texture from that of most other fish, being similar only to tuna.

The mackerel's importance as a food fish owes less to its size than to the quantity caught. Mackerel is quite fatty, and is therefore superbly suited to smoking, pan-frying, and grilling. Italians group mackerel with tuna, swordfish, herring, anchovies, and others as *pesci azzurri*, or "blue fish," because of their blue tinge. Equally popular are two red fish: the red mullet, *triglia di fango* in Italian, and the striped red mullet or surmullet, *triglia di scoglio*. Since the red mullet searches for food on the sea bed in the mud, it is liable to have a slightly sludgy aftertaste, and is therefore not quite so highly prized as the striped red mullet. Both are ideal for grilling. In Livorno, mullet are dusted in flour, pan-fried in olive oil until crisp, then simmered briefly in a light tomato sauce.

Scabbardfish, *pesce bandiera* or *pesce fiamma*, are a deep-sea fish, which come to the surface near the coast in the spring, and have firm, white, pleasantly aromatic flesh.

Scabbardfish have an elongated, eel-like body. These fish are caught regularly in the vicinity of Messina.

Flatfish

As their shape implies, all flatfish are inhabitants of the sea bed — but not for their entire lives. Recently hatched young float about freely in the water, and look like other fish too. When they have grown to a few inches in length, one of their eyes "migrates" to the other side of the body, which thus becomes the top side. This side acquires a more or less dark coloring, while the underside usually remains light, ensuring that the fish is ideally adapted to its environment. Flatfish can be caught with seine nets, which are dragged over the sea bed, harvesting everything in their wake, or — a method that yields better-quality flesh, but is more labor-intensive, and thus less economical — with long lines, which can be over 65 feet long and are often baited with sardines. The fisherman needs a fair amount of strength and skill to pull a larger specimen to the surface.

Species of culinary importance...
Flatfish have been considered a particular delicacy in the Mediterranean since ancient times, with turbot, *rombo chiodato* in Italian, and Dover sole, *sogliola* (but also known in southern Italy as *palaia* and in central Italy as *sfoglia*) leading the popularity stakes. the, as now. Like all major pleasures, however, this one does not come cheap. The cost can be kept down somewhat by opting for related species, including the brill, or *rombo liscio*; the scaldfish or *sogliola variegata*, which connoisseurs compare to Dover sole; or the thickback sole, which is found in Italian markets as *suacia* or *chiancetta*.

And how to prepare them
In Italy. turbot and brill are often served cut into slices and braised — for instance, in a Marsala and cream sauce; or poached, and then served, for example, with a shrimp-and-butter sauce. Smaller specimens may be prepared whole, studded with garlic and rosemary and baked in a hot oven. The various soles can also be poached, gently pan-fried, or grilled a popular way of preparing Dover sole in the Marches. Dover sole is also popular *alla mugnaia*, or *meunière* style, sautéed over a low heat in butter and served with lemon and parsley. For a slightly more unusual variation, try *sogliole all'arancia*, in which the fillets are topped with a few orange slices.

The turbot is the only flatfish to sport numerous nodules on the dark-skinned upper surface of its body. This fish reaches a maximum length of about 3 feet.

Scaldfish resemble Dover sole in shape, but their skin is translucent. They are considerably smaller than the sole, reaching a maximum length of only 8 inches. Their delicate, tender flesh, however, may be mentioned in the same breath as that of the Dover sole.

Brill are very similar in appearance to turbot, but do not grow quite as big. In Italy they are available less often than turbot.

Dover soles are among the most sought-after of all sea fish. They are usually available 12–16 inches long.

Thickback sole are very easily recognized by their frayed-looking fin line and speckled upper surface.

FISH 287

The velvet swimming crab (top right), or *granchio*, is recognized by the velvety "fur" covering its body. In the Veneto, different names are given to the male and female **Mediterranean green crab** (below right), as well as to crabs before, after, or in the middle of moulting. Especially prized are crabs that still have their white shell.

In crabs, the sought-after meat is found in the claws, legs, and the muscular carapace.

All crustaceans are prepared in the same manner initially. If you have bought fresh, live crustaceans, add them headfirst to a large pot of boiling liquid. If you are cooking more than one, make sure that the liquid has definitely returned to a rolling boil before you add the next crustacean.

Crustaceans

This category includes the most sought-after delicacies that the Mediterranean sea has to offer: the elongate lobsters, spiny lobsters, Dublin Bay prawns, and the more compact crabs. Lobsters, *astici* or *elefanti di mare* in Italian, as well as spiny lobsters, *aragoste* (in the large photo above) are caught in special traps called lobster pots. The flesh of these two species is of equally superb quality, but the lobster yields more meat, specifically in its powerful claws; the spiny lobster, by contrast, has long antennae that are of no culinary use. Dublin Bay prawns are rather similar in appearance to lobsters, and also have claws, which are not, however, worth cracking; in principle, it is only their tender tail meat that is eaten. Dublin Bay prawns are highly perishable, so live specimens should be checked thoroughly before purchasing.

The common, or edible, crab, *granciporro* The legs, shell, and, above all, claws of this creature harbor a relatively high proportion of luscious meat.

In Venice, the meat of the large **spider crab**, *grancevola*, is often made into a salad, which is then served in the shell.

Dublin Bay prawns are also known as scampi and langoustines. In Italy, they are caught chiefly in the Adriatic and along the Ligurian coast. "Glassy" meat with no fishy smell is a sign of freshness.

The common European shrimp, *gambero sega* in Italian, is a costly catch for fishermen, since they are not trawled, but caught in hand nets and in traps. Even when they are only about 4 inches long, they are still quite expensive, but their exquisite flesh is worth the high price.

Squilla *(Squilla mantis)* are easily recognized by their long, almost uniformly wide body, and the two black spots on their tail fins.

Mantis squillid

Zoologically not a shrimp, but comparable in terms of size and suitable cooking methods, are the mantis squillids, which may be known in Italian as *canocchie* or *pannocchie*, as well as *cicala di mare* (sea cicadas) in Tuscany and Sicily. The most famous recipe for them originated in Venice: *canocchie con olio e limone* — unpeeled, boiled or steamed mantis squillids, dressed with olive oil, lemon juice, salt, and pepper.

Shrimp & Co.

In Italy, the term *gamberi* covers all crustaceans up to just over 8 inches in body length. Smaller specimens are referred to as *gamberetti*, at least in a culinary context. No distinction is made between fresh- and saltwater varieties; even a crayfish is a *gambero*. Otherwise, Italians often classify shrimp by color.

Gamberi bianchi

The top shrimp in terms of size and flavor, the *gambero imperiale* (also called *spanocchio*, and, in Latium, *mazzancolle*) belongs to the "white shrimp" category. Since they can be caught comparatively easily at a depth of "only" 130 feet, and their flesh is of superb quality, it is hardly any wonder that stocks have decreased. For this reason, Italians are now trying their hand at shrimp farming — quite successfully in the northern Adriatic. Also considered a *bianco* is the Aesop shrimp, whose flesh is not considered as fine. Both species, which grow to 6–8½ inches, are delicious seasoned with salt and pepper, and brushed now and again on with a marinade of olive oil and lemon juice as they are grilled.

Red and gray

Although all shrimp turn a reddish hue when cooked, the shells of the *gamberi rossi* are this color even when raw. The two species in this group are to be found only from depths of about 720 feet, and are caught with special trawling nets. In terms of quality and size, they come a close second to the *gamberi imperiali*. "Red" prawns, are best grilled, or pan-fried whole. Smaller specimens are often coated in batter and deep-fried, sometimes in their shell. They can also be boiled, peeled, and served as a salad, dressed with olive oil and lemon juice, or mayonnaise. The little *gamberetti grigi*, or common gray shrimp, are very good this way.

Shrimp tails, raw and in the shell, are ready to be cooked and are ideally suited to many recipes.

Shellfish

Anyone lucky enough to be offered the chance of trying one of the many delicious shellfish dishes prepared in Italy should seize the opportunity. We particularly recommend that you try the delicate fanshells, such as the scallop, or the smaller *pettine* and *canestrelle*. Offering a relatively large proportion of delicate flesh, they are usually shucked before cooking, unlike most other shellfish. Also good for a culinary surprise or two are the rod-shaped razor clams. They must be cleaned thoroughly before cooking, as their shells can be full of sand. Both species are popular grilled until their shells open, then served as an antipasto. Razor clams are also enjoyed raw in Italy, or in soups.

The scallop, or fanshell, is called *conchiglia di San Jacopo, capa santa,* or *pellegrina* in Italian. For a distinctive presentation, serve the meat in the deeper half-shell.

The striped venus clam, *cappa gallina, poverazza,* or simply *vongola,* is often eaten with pasta in Italy, particularly spaghetti and linguine.

Vongole

In Italy *vongole* refers to many shellfish, but particularly clams. The small, 1-inch long *vongole gialle* or *vongole lupini,* known in English as carpetshells, are eaten mainly with pasta, while large species are added to soups and

The grooved carpetshell (top), or *vongola verace,* is also eaten raw in Italy.

The hard clam (above), *cappa chione,* also called *fasulara* in Campania and Apulia, is one of the larger species of venus clams, up to 4 inches long.

Wedge clams, known in Italian as *telline, arselle,* or *calcinelli,* are a rather small delicacy, with their 1⅓-inch-long shell. They are eaten raw or added to soups.

sauces too. They are also savored straight from the shell. In any case, they are best combined with only a few other ingredients, so that nothing masks their delicate flavor.

Mussels

Mussels, too, are a widely distributed species of shellfish,

Mediterranean mussels are usually known to their devotees in Italy by their southern Italian name of *cozze*. In Latium, Liguria, and Tuscany, they are also called *muscoli* or *datteri neri*; in the Veneto, *peoci*

and are also farmed along the Italian coast, in the lagoon in Venice, in Liguria, and in the Gulf of Taranto. They are almost always eaten cooked — in salads and soups, deep-fried, or breaded and cooked on skewers.

Related to mussels, but even more highly prized are date shells (pictured above), *datteri di mare* in italian. Since these shellfish bore into rocks from which they must be chipped out, "harvesting" them is a labor-intensive business, a fact that is reflected in their high price.

Razorshell, or razor, clams — *cannolicchio, capalonga,* or *manico di coltello* in Italian— are fished chiefly in the Adriatic and in the waters around Sicily.

Marine-snail parade (top left to bottom right): whelks in their elegant houses, black periwinkles, and spiny purple-dye murex.

From minute to massive

Marine snails, sea urchins, and cuttlefish are a bit unusual in appearance, but prepared in the Italian style they are sure to find favor.

Snails from the sea

Land snails are a well-known delicacy, and their aquatic relatives are their equals in every way. Larger specimens must be cooked for long enough, or cut into slices and tenderized with a meat mallet before being prepared, so that their flesh is not tough. The most popular species in Italy are the purple dye murex, *cornetto di mare*, and the flat limpets, *or patelle*, which resemble shellfish with only a half shell, and the larger, similar-looking abalones or ormers, *orecchie di mare*.

Round and spiny

Sea urchins (*ricci di mare*) are covered in sharp spikes. To reach the edible part, known in the trade as the "tongues," the chalky skeleton of the urchin is cut open on the underside right around the mouth opening, and the black intestines are pulled out. Drizzled with a little lemon juice, the tongues can then be slurped directly from the shell, or scooped out with a spoon.

Cuttlefish

Cuttlefish have plump, sac-like bodies, which may have a narrow fin suture along the sides. Of their ten tentacles, eight are quite small and fleshy, and two are extended like antennae. Cuttlefish are sought after for their tender meat; they also provide the ink, or *nero di seppia*, often used to lend a dramatic black color to some rice and pasta dishes. If you buy your cuttlefish fresh, you can extract the ink yourself, as shown below on the right. Otherwise, it is available in small sachets, or dried. In Italy, the species of culinary importance are the common cuttlefish, known as *seppia*, which grows to about 10 inches, and the little or lesser cuttlefish, which is only 1–2 inches long.

Stony sea-urchins (left) are the most important edible sea-urchins in the Mediterranean. Using scissors, Sicilian fishermen skillfully prepare them for eating (above).

Octopus that are very small (*polipo* or *polpo* in Italian) are very tender; larger ones require a special tenderizing treatment.

FISH 291

Squid

The more slimline, almost torpedo-shaped squids, called *calamari*, are prepared just like cuttlefish. First, remove the brownish membrane from the body. Pull the tentacles out of the body sac; they should come away with the intestines. Now remove the transparent, supporting cuttlebone and wash the body thoroughly. Cut away the tentacles just above the eyes so that they remain joined by a thin ring. In the middle of the ring is the beak or mouth, which you pop out with your index finger and then cut out. The ink from squid can be used like *nero di seppia*. there is no culinary distinction between the common or European squid and the short-finned squid, *totano*, which has a distinctly low-slung, triangular tailfin.

Octopus

The octopus differs from the cuttlefish and the squid in that it has only eight tentacles, and no cuttlebone or fins. These creatures can grow up to 10 feet, and tip the scales at 55 pounds. It is the smaller specimens, however, that are usually eaten. Even these, however, require thorough tenderizing before they are cooked to ensure that, when boiled or grilled, the flesh will be appetizingly tender.

Very small *polpi* can be cooked whole; large octopuses, on the other hand, are prepared like cuttlefish or squid. A Neapolitan specialty is *polpo affogato* or "drowned octopus," made by slowly braising a relatively large octopus with olive oil, garlic, tomatoes, chile peppers, white wine, and herbs in a tightly sealed clay pot over a low heat until it is meltingly tender.

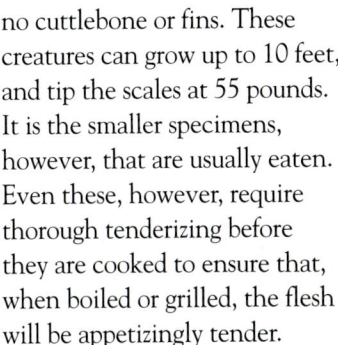

The common squid can reach a length of up 20 inches and a weight of 4½ pounds. The popular deep-fried squid rings *calamari fritti,* are prepared from the body sac, cut into rings. Squid can also be stuffed and braised. Small specimens, which can be prepared whole, are called *calamaretti*.

Little or lesser cuttlefish, *seppiole* in Italian, are so tender that they can be prepared whole. Marinated in oil with chile peppers, they make a fine antipasto.

White octopuses, called *moscardini* in Italy, grow up to 16 inches long. They are related to the octopus, but not so highly regarded as a food.

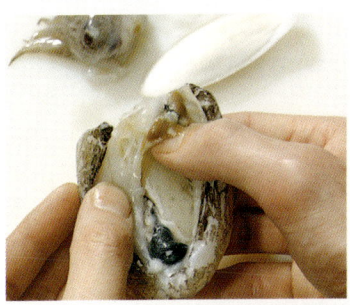

Extracting cuttlefish ink: Cut off the head with the tentacles. Carefully cut open the body sac lengthwise and pull out the cuttlebone; you should then see the shiny ink sac. Carefully remove the innards with your thumb. Squeeze the ink from the ink sac with your thumb and index finger.

From brooks and lakes

Despite the fact that *pesci e frutti di mare* inevitably play a more important role in Italy, freshwater fish and shellfish are extremely important in culinary terms. They are particularly appreciated in Trentino-Alto Adige, in Lombardy, and in Umbria, regions which have no direct access to the sea. Anyone who has had the good fortune to feast in Italy on crayfish (*gamberi di fiume*), grilled eel, or trout with truffles will certainly rank these freshwater delicacies on a par with the finest treasures of the sea.

Freshwater fish

Italy's large northern lakes and clear brooks supply even more delicacies, such as pike, *luccio* in Italian. The firm, white flesh of this fish is very tasty, and in Italy is sliced and fried, or braised in a strong-flavored tomato sauce. Pike is also good for stuffing and for making into *quenelles* and pâtés. The European perch, *pesce persico*, is one of the finest freshwater fishes, which occurs only in northern Italy, however. Around Lake Como, fillets of this fish are often prepared *alla mugnaia*, dusted in flour and sautéed in butter.

Likewise found only in northern Italy, particularly in Lombardy, is the carp (*carpa*). The variety used as a food fish there is the *carpa a specchi*, or mirror carp. It is braised with other strongly flavored ingredients such as onions, wine, and various herbs.

The most popular freshwater fish is the trout, two species of which are caught or farmed in Italy: the brook trout, or *trota fario*, and the rainbow trout, *trota iridea*. Trouts can be cooked *al blu* (boiled, when absolutely fresh, in a mixture of water and vinegar), baked in a parchment-paper parcel, or grilled or broiled; smaller fish up to a weight of 7 ounces, known as *trotelle*, are simply pan-fried in butter.

Marinating and drying

Smaller freshwater fish are also popular prepared *in carpione* in Lombardy. Originally, *carpione* was a term used to describe Lake Garda trout, which were typically prepared by first frying them in olive oil, then marinating them in white wine, vinegar, garlic, onions, and herbs, including, usually, an abundance of sage: an absolutely wonderful, summery antipasto.

A further fish specialty of the north, this time from Lake Como, is *misoltitt*. This term is derived from the name *misoltino*, given in Lombardy to the twaite shad, which is called *agone* or *cheppia* elsewhere in Italy. The little fish are gutted and air-dried. Skinned, and dressed with oil and vinegar or lemon, they are served as an antipasto, but they can also be fried or grilled without additional fat.

Fish in the kitchen

Buying freshly caught fish is naturally not a problem. When this highly perishable food has to be transported over any distance, however, it is helpful to know how to judge freshness. If you are at all dubious about the quality of fresh fish, do not to buy it; use frozen fish instead

Signs of freshness
Bright red gills and clear eyes are the surest signs of freshness in fish. In addition, skin and fins must not be damaged. A fresh fish smells of the sea, and not "fishy," sour, or of fish oil. If the fish is already filleted, the flesh should spring back when pressed with a finger.

Preparing fish
If you buy fish that have not been dressed, all you need do is first gut and scale them, then clean them thoroughly inside and out under cold running water. The slime must first be removed from eels' skin which is best done by vigorous rubbing with coarse sea salt. Afterwards, wash the fish carefully.

Filleting fish
Of course, you can buy fish that has already been filleted. If you must do this job yourself, however, it is not too difficult. First, cut off the head. With a sharp knife, make a lengthwise incision into the fish along the backbone. Next, slide the knife under one of the fillets at the head end, and, running the blade flat along the backbone, cut off the fillet toward the tail. Lift off the fillet, remove the backbone with the tail fin, and skin the fillets. Flatfish yield 4 fillets, two on the back and two on the belly side. They should be separated by making an incision in the fish along the backbone an around the fin line, and then sliding the knife underneath the fillets flat along the bones. Cut off the fin sutures. A delicate fish stock can be made from the trimmings of lean white fish.

Preparing fish stock:

Coarsely cut up 2¼ lb fish trimmings (remove gills) and rinse in a bowl under running water for 20 minutes, until the water is free from cloudy substances. Drain.

Melt ¼ cup butter in a large saucepan or kettle, and sauté the trimmings over a low heat, stirring, for 3–4 minutes, until lightly colored.

Add 1 cup diced shallot, ¾ cup chopped leek, ½ fennel bulb, ½ cup diced parsley root, and ¾ cup chopped celery.

Briefly sweat the vegetables with the fish trimmings. Carrots are left out on purpose, to keep the stock light in color. As soon as the mixture comes to a simmer, add 2¼ cups cold, dry white wine.

Pour in 9 cups cold water. It is important for the wine and water to be cold when added, since slow heating develops the flavor better.

Add 1 bay leaf, 2–3 thyme sprigs, and ½ teaspoon whole white peppercorns to the pot. More seasonings are not necessary

Bring the stock to a boil. Skim the stock repeatedly to remove the grayish-white foam that rises to the surface

After 20–30 minutes' gentle simmering, line a conical strainer with a piece of cheesecloth and ladle in the stock. Let the liquid run through completely, without pressing down on the contents.

Marinated eel in tomato sauce

A recipe from around the lagoon of Comacchio on the Adriatic, where the eel recipes are the best

Skinning the gutted eel: Loosen a piece of skin behind the head and to the side. Slide your right thumb under the skin and loosen it all the way to the opposite side. Using this "handle," pull the skin forward over the head. Grip the loose end of the skin firmly in a cloth, and then pull off backwards over the tail. Using scissors, cut off the fins in the direction of the head.

Eels are quite fatty, so are well suited to braising, and can stand plenty of seasoning. In this recipe the chunks of eel are marinated in a strong red wine with vegetables, herbs, and seasonings. An eel weighing about 2¼ lb is just right for this recipe, which provides 3 pieces per serving. Ask your fish seller to skin the eel for you, if you do not relish this arduous task.

Serves 4
1 eel (about 2¼ lb)
7 tablespoons olive oil, 1 tablespoon flour
½ cup fish stock, 2 tablespoons tomato paste
8 oz tomatoes, peeled, seeded, and diced
1 tablespoon chopped parsley
1 teaspoon chopped thyme
salt, freshly ground pepper
For the marinade:
1 onion, 1 carrot
2 garlic cloves, finely sliced
¼ cup coarsely chopped parsley root
2 teaspoons fresh thyme leaves
1 small rosemary sprig, 2 bay leaves
½ teaspoon salt, 1 teaspoon white peppercorns
2 chile peppers, halved lengthwise and seeds removed
1 cup red wine (e.g. Merlot or Cabernet)

A Merlot or Cabernet from the Veneto is highly recommend for marinating the eel. It would be a mistake to cut corners here, since the quality of the red wine used substantially affects the outcome of the dish.

Homemade ribbon noodles or polenta go particularly well with the spicy braised eel and the hearty tomato sauce.

If necessary, skin the eel, as shown in the picture sequence above left, then cut the fish into 12 pieces 1–1½ inches long.

To make the marinade, cut the onions into thin rings, and the carrot into fairly large chunks. Mix with the garlic and parsley root, and layer in a container with the eel chunks, herbs, seasonings, and chile peppers. Pour over the wine, cover with plastic wrap, and marinate in the refrigerator for 3–4 hours, turning the fish chunks at intervals so that the flavors of the marinade permeate it evenly.

Remove the eel and drain on paper towels. Strain the marinade and reserve vegetables and liquid separately. Heat 3 tablespoons olive oil and sear the drained vegetables over a high heat with the seasonings and herbs. Add the marinade and reduce by half. Strain and set aside.

Pat dry the eel chunks and dust lightly with flour. Heat the remaining olive oil, and sear the fish on all sides over a high heat. Deglaze with the fish stock, stir in the tomato paste, and pour in the strained marinade. Simmer over a low heat for 15 minutes. Add the tomatoes, sprinkle with parsley and thyme, and braise for another 10 minutes, until the eel is tender. Season with salt and pepper, arrange 3 pieces of eel on each warmed plate along with a little sauce, and serve.

Fish in a paper envelope
In Italy, people like to prepare whole fish *al cartoccio*, for an especially flavorful result

The Italian word *cartoccio* originally described a parchment-paper bag, but now the word is also generally taken to mean "cooked in foil." One advantage of the traditional parchment paper is that the food can brown a little. This method of preparation is especially good for relatively lean, single-portion fish, which might otherwise easily dry out if fried or grilled. Superbly suited to this treatment, for example, are porgy and snapper.

The parchment envelope provides the sensitive flesh of the fish with perfect protection from the strong radiant heat of the grill or oven.

Lemons are the classical accompaniment for seafood. They should, of course, be used with discretion, so that their strong flavor and acidity do not overpower the natural taste of the seafood.

Serves 4
4 white-fleshed single-portion fish, dressed (14 oz each)
¼ cup olive oil
4 sprigs each parsley and thyme
12 fennel seeds
⅓ cup finely chopped caperfruits
2 ripe lemons
salt, freshly ground white pepper
4 teaspoons salted capers
You will also need:
parchment paper

Prepare and light a charcoal grill or preheat the oven to 375°F.

Thoroughly wash the fish inside and out under cold running water, and pat dry with paper towels. Generously rub the fish inside and out with olive oil, and season with salt and pepper. Place 1 sprig each of parsley and thyme in the cavity of each fish. Evenly distribute the fennel seeds and the chopped caperfruits among the cavities. Peel both lemons, removing the white pith as carefully as possible. Slice the lemons into rounds ⅛ inch thick, and place 2 lemon slices in the cavity of each fish.

Soak the salted capers for about 10 minutes and drain well. Cut the parchment paper into 4 suitable-sized pieces, and soak in water. Lift out, place the fish on the paper, and top with the remaining lemon slices and the capers. Wrap the fish in the paper, and seal tightly at both ends.

Place the fish in their envelopes on the grill, taking care to leave sufficient space between the rack and the coals so that the paper does not catch fire, and cook the fish for about 10 minutes on both sides. If using an oven instead, bake the fish for 15–20 minutes without turning.

Prepare the zucchini chips as soon as possible before serving, so that they stay nice and crisp. They are also delectable as an antipasto, or as a nibble with a glass of wine.

Pan-fried monkfish with zucchini sauce
Crisp-fried zucchini chips are an interesting foil for the juicy flesh of this fish

This delicate vegetable sauce may also be served with pan-fried steaks of the equally choice sea bass, known in Italian as *branzino* or *pesce lupo*. The firm, virtually boneless flesh of the monkfish, called *pesce rospo* or *rana pescatrice* in Italian, has its own special appeal, however: its flavor and texture are a bit reminiscent of lobster or rock lobster.

Serves 4
4 medallions of monkfish (about 6 oz each)
2 tablespoons olive oil, 2 tablespoons butter
salt, freshly ground pepper
For the zucchini sauce:
1 tablespoon olive oil
¾ cup finely diced onion
½ cup diced celery
2½ cups diced zucchini
1 red chile pepper, seeded and finely chopped
1 tablespoon white wine vinegar
1 tablespoon butter, 1 teaspoon flour
½ teaspoon paprika
⅔ cup milk
salt, freshly ground pepper
For the zucchini chips:
10 oz zucchini, ⅓ cup flour
salt, freshly ground pepper
oil for deep-frying
You will also need:
parsley leaves

To make the zucchini sauce, heat the olive oil in a pan and sweat the diced onion and celery until lightly colored. Add the diced zucchini and the chile, and sauté for about 5 minutes. Pour in ½ cup water and the vinegar, cover the pan, and simmer over a low heat for about 5 minutes. Finely purée the vegetables with a hand blender. Using a fork, combine the butter with the flour and stir into the zucchini purée. Season with paprika, salt, and pepper. Stir the milk into the sauce, and simmer over a moderate heat for about 8 minutes, stirring constantly. Keep the sauce warm.

To make the zucchini chips, cut the ends off the zucchini, and slice it into paper-thin rounds. Combine the flour, salt, and pepper in a plastic bag, and shake the zucchini slices in the bag. Tip into a strainer and tap off the excess flour.

Heat the oil in a large skillet and deep-fry the zucchini slices in batches until golden. Lift out with a slotted spoon and drain on paper towels.

Remove as much of the skin as possible from the monkfish, as it can become tough when pan-fried and spoil the dish. Salt and pepper the monkfish. Heat the olive oil and butter in a skillet and fry the medallions for 3–4 minutes on each side. Arrange the fish on plates with the sauce and the zucchini chips. Garnish with parsley leaves and serve.

Like Pantelleria, **the Liparian Islands** — here, the most northerly one, Isola Salina — are famous for their spicy capers. The aromatic buds are painstakingly harvested by hand.

Costolette di tonno
Juicy tuna steaks, marinated and grilled, seasoned with capers and lemon

For this delicious recipe you need tuna steaks: slices cut crosswise from the tail of the fish. The skin and central bone hold the *costolette* in shape as they grill, and can easily be removed from the fish when it is cooked. Marinating food in wine, garlic, and herbs is a Palermitan specialty, and the fish, known in the local dialect as *tunnu*, is often served just with the remaining marinade, a little parsley, and lemon. In this recipe, capers lend an additional spiciness, and the toasted bread crumbs provide an interesting contrast to the juicy tuna steaks.

Serves 4
2¼ lb tuna, cut into steaks
1 teaspoon salt, coarsely ground pepper
olive oil for brushing the steaks
For the marinade:
5 garlic cloves, finely chopped
1 cup white wine
1 sprig each rosemary and thyme, chopped
For the caper and lemon mixture:
1 tablespoon salted capers
½ lemon
1 tablespoon olive oil
salt, freshly ground pepper
You will also need:
1 slice day-old white bread, crusts removed
1 tablespoon olive oil

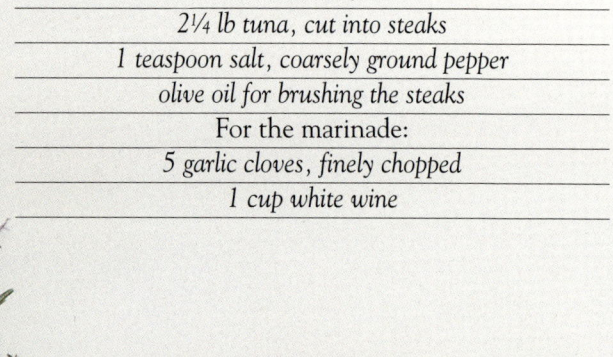

Tonno nostrano — "own-catch tuna" — is the proud claim on the sign at this fish seller's stall in Palermo: a guarantee of freshness, and, therefore, quality.

To make the marinade, combine the garlic, wine, rosemary, and thyme in a shallow baking dish. Season the tuna steaks with salt and pepper, turn them in the marinade, cover with plastic wrap, and leave to marinate in a cool place for about 1 hour.

Preheat the grill. Lift the tuna from the marinade and pat dry. Brush the steaks with oil and place on the grill. Grill the tuna on both sides for a total of 10–15 minutes, brushing frequently with the marinade.

To make the caper and lemon mixture, soak the capers in water for about 10 minutes to get rid of excess saltiness, then drain them well and chop finely. Squeeze the juice from the lemon. In a small bowl, mix the olive oil with the lemon juice, chopped capers, salt, and pepper.

Crumble the bread into fine crumbs. Heat the oil in a skillet, and toast the bread crumbs until golden, stirring constantly.

Arrange the grilled tuna steaks on plates. Spread with the caper and lemon mixture, sprinkle with the browned bread crumbs, and serve with a fresh, seasonal salad.

Sea bass with radicchio sauce
The slightly bitter notes in the sauce and vegetable garnish deliciously round out the taste of this choice fish

It is not just the unusual sauce that makes this recipe interesting, but the garnish of deep-fried radicchio strips as well. *Radicchio di Treviso*, whose elongated leaves do not form firm heads, is especially suitable here, owing to its relatively thick leafribs.

Serves 4
2 sea bass, dressed (1⅔ lb each)
4 springs each dill, parsley, and thyme
4 celery leaves
2 tablespoons olive oil, salt, freshly ground pepper
For the radicchio sauce:
5 oz radicchio di Treviso
1 leek (white part only)
2 tablespoons butter, 4 teaspoons Cognac, 1 cup fish stock
¼ cup white wine, 10 green peppercorns, salt
For the deep-fried radicchio strips:
2 oz radicchio di Treviso, 1 teaspoon flour
You will also need:
vegetable oil for deep-frying

The fine white flesh of the sea bass is a delicacy, and so is its skin when fried until crisp. The fish must be scaled especially carefully beforehand, however.

Wash thoroughly inside and out under cold running water, and carefully pat dry. Place 2 sprigs each of dill, parsley, and thyme, and two celery leaves in the cavity of each fish. Season with salt and pepper, and leave the fish in a cool place.

To make the radicchio sauce, clean and trim the leek and the radicchio. Cut the leek into rings and the radicchio into strips.

Melt the butter in a pan and stew the leek rings for about 5 minutes. Add the radicchio, and sweat for a further 3 minutes. Pour the Cognac over the vegetables and set alight, tossing the pan until the flames die down. Pour in the fish stock and wine, add the peppercorns, and season with salt. Bring to a boil, reduce the heat, and simmer the vegetables, covered, for about 15 minutes, until soft. Purée the mixture in a blender, thinning the sauce with a little fish stock if necessary. Season to taste with salt and pepper, and keep warm.

To make the deep-fried radicchio strips, trim the radicchio and slice into ¼-inch-wide strips. Transfer to a bag with the flour, and shake until the radicchio is dusted with flour. Tip into a strainer and tap off the excess flour. Heat the vegetable oil in a deep saucepan and deep-fry the radicchio strips in batches until they start to turn brown, being careful, as the oil may spatter. Lift out with a perforated spoon and drain on paper towels.

Heat the olive oil in a skillet, and pan-fry the fish on both sides for about 5 minutes until brown and crisp. Fillet the fish or halve them lengthwise, and serve with the radicchio strips and sauce.

Mullet times two

These beautiful small fish are accompanied in the first instance by mushrooms, in the second by olives, and in both cases by tomatoes

In Italy, both striped red mullet and red mullet are especially popular pan-fried or grilled. The striped red mullet or *triglia di scoglio*, however, is generally preferred to the smaller red mullet, *triglia di fango* or *triglia d'alga*, whose Italian names reveal the reason for its lesser popularity: it can occasionally taste a little muddy.

STRIPED RED MULLET WITH MUSHROOMS

Pioppini or *piopparelli* are the names given in Italy to these aromatic little mushrooms with slender, light-colored stems and brown caps, which lend a special zest to this dish. They have been cultivated in Italy only recently, but with such success that they are now even exported.

Serves 4
8 striped red mullets, dressed 5 oz each)
salt, freshly ground pepper
a little flour for dusting; ¼ cup vegetable oil
For the mushroom and tomato mixture:
1 lb pioppini mushrooms, 2 tablespoons butter
½ cup very finely diced onion
1 garlic clove, very finely diced
10 oz tomatoes, peeled, seeded, and diced
1 dash lemon juice, salt, freshly ground pepper
You will also need:
1 tablespoon chopped parsley

Wash the fish under cold running water inside and out, and carefully dry with paper towels. Season with salt and pepper and dust with flour.

To make the mushroom and tomato mixture, clean and trim the mushrooms, shortening the stems slightly. Melt the butter in a skillet and sweat the onion and garlic until golden. Add the mushrooms and sauté for 2 minutes. Stir in the tomatoes, season with salt and pepper, add lemon juice to taste, and stew for a further 2 minutes.

Heat the oil in a skillet, and fry the mullets on each side for about 2 minutes. Arrange on plates with the mushroom and tomato mixture, and serve sprinkled with parsley.

RED MULLET WITH OLIVES

Serves 4
8 red mullets, dressed (4 oz each)
¼ cup extra-virgin olive oil
1 garlic clove, finely chopped
3 tablespoons finely chopped parsley
½ cup black olives
4 anchovy fillets
3 tablespoons tomato paste
10 oz tomatoes, peeled, seeded, and diced
salt, freshly ground pepper

Prepare the red mullet as described in the preceding recipe. Heat the olive oil in a skillet and fry the fish on both sides for 2 minutes, then lift out and set aside.

Sauté the garlic, parsley, and olives in the olive oil over a low heat for 2–3 minutes. Add the anchovy fillets, and fry until they have disintegrated. Stir in the tomato paste and add the tomatoes. Return the mullets to the pan, and braise on both sides for 5 minutes. Season with salt and pepper and serve.

Skate wing in minestrone with pesto

The classic Italian vegetable soup, garnished with a crisp pan-fried fish fillet

Serves 4
1¾ lb skate wing
salt, freshly ground pepper
flour for dusting, 3 tablespoons vegetable oil
For the minestrone:
4 small artichokes, salt, juice of ½ lemon
⅓ cup finely diced lean pancetta
1 carrot, 2 oz celery root
2 leek, 4 oz Savoy cabbage, 4 oz zucchini
⅔ cup diced potatoes

Using a stable, pointed knife, make an incision in the skin along the tall side of the wing. Run the knife flat along the cartilage, loosening the top fillet.

Remove the fillet around the outer edge of the cartilaginous skeleton. Turn the skate wing around, and detach the thinner lower fillet in the same way

Lay the filets flat. Loosen the skin slightly in one spot on each wing and grip firmly with a cloth. Using a long knife, cut the fillets free from the skin.

Fillets of skate, *razza* in Italian, become crisp on the outside when pan-fried, but stay beautifully juicy inside. You could, however, use fillets of other firm, white-fleshed fish for this minestrone instead.

5 oz tomatoes, peeled, seeded, and diced
1 tablespoon olive oil, ½ cup chopped onion
1 teaspoon tomato paste, 4½ cups meat stock
1 cup cooked borlotti beans
For the pesto:
3 oz basil leaves, ½ cup pine nuts
3 garlic cloves, salt
⅔ cup freshly grated Parmesan, ½ cup olive oil

Fillet the skate wing as shown in the picture sequence on the left. Remove the tendons on the thick sides of the fillets.

To make the minestrone, break off the stalks

of the artichokes directly under the globes. Strip off the small, tough leaves around the base of the stalk. Boil the artichokes in salted water acidulated with the lemon juice for 10 minutes. Leave in the cooking water.

Cut the carrot and celery into sticks, the leek into rings, the cabbage into ¾-inch squares, and the zucchini into rounds,.

Heat the oil, and sweat the bacon and onion. Add the carrot and celery root, and continue to sweat. After 1 minute, add the leek and cabbage, and continue to cook. Stir in the tomato paste. Pour in the stock, and stir in the potatoes. Simmer for 10 minutes, then add the zucchini. After 5 minutes, stir in the tomatoes and beans, season, and simmer for another 2 minutes.

To make the pesto, blend or process all the ingredients to a paste. Lift the artichokes from their cooking liquid, drain, quarter, and add to the minestrone. Season the skate fillets with salt and pepper, and dust both sides very thinly with flour, tapping off any excess. Heat the oil, and pan-fry the fillets on both sides for 2–3 minutes. Ladle the minestrone into bowls, arrange the skate wings on top, and serve, handing the pesto around separately.

Baked gray mullet

This fish dish brings the fragrant scent of herbs and fennel to your dinner table

Several species of gray mullet — *muggini* or *cefali* in Italian — are fished in Italian waters, although no distinction is usually made between them in commercial or culinary terms. The fish are liked not only for their flesh, which is chiefly served grilled or baked, but also for their fine roe. Grey-mullet roe is made into *bottarga di muggine*, which is even more sought-after, and a good deal more expensive than, tuna *bottarga*.

Serves 4
2¼ lb gray mullet, dressed
1 tablespoon lemon juice
8 oz fennel bulbs
1 garlic clove, finely chopped
12 oz medium-sized tomatoes, peeled, quartered, and seeded
¼ cup olive oil
1 cup dry white wine
salt, freshly ground white pepper

For this dish it is best to buy a whole fresh mullet, which you can then cut crosswise into steaks or cutlets yourself.

Fish lovers can enhance the flavor of this dish further by cooking the heads of the mullet — gills removed — with the other ingredients, then removing them before serving.

You will also need:
oil for greasing the baking dish
2 tablespoons chopped herbs (parsley, rosemary, lemon balm, thyme)
2 tablespoons butter, in curls

Wash the fish thoroughly inside and out under cold running water and pat dry. Cut crosswise into steaks 1–2 inches wide. Drizzle the steaks with lemon juice, season with salt, cover, and set aside in a cool place.

Wash and dry the fennel bulbs. Cut off the base of the root as well as the green stalks, and quarter the bulbs lengthwise. Add to briskly boiling salted water and cook for 10 minutes, then remove and drain well.

Heat the oil in a skillet and quickly sear the garlic, tomato quarters, and fennel pieces over a high heat, stirring. Season with salt and pepper. Deglaze with the wine, and simmer for 4–5 minutes.

Preheat the oven to 400°F. Oil a baking dish. Spoon the fish cutlets and vegetables into the dish, sprinkle with the herbs, dot with the butter, and bake for 15–20 minutes.

Calabrian fish stew

Recipes for seafood stews like this one are in principle flexible, since the ingredients are always determined by what is freshest and best at the market

The most famous Italian fish stew is probably the Ligurian *cacciucco*, but similar dishes are prepared everywhere along the coast where fish are caught. The varieties of fish used depend on what has been netted; as a matter of principle, however, the "soup fish" are chosen. These are cheap, owing to their quite small proportion of flesh, but nonetheless provide a good, strong flavor. Chief among these are the fearsome scorpion fish or rascasse, and the gurnard, but small specimens of other species are also used. The necessary fish stock can be made in advance from the bones and trimmings.

Serves 4

2¼ lb fish (bonito, mackerel, rascasse, conger eel)
1 celery stalk, 1 carrots, 2 small leeks, 1 zucchini
10 oz cockles, 10 oz carpetshells, 3 tablespoons olive oil
¾ cup very finely chopped onions
1 garlic clove, very finely chopped
¼ cup diced parsley root
10oz tomatoes, peeled, seeded, and diced
1 red chile pepper, cut into rings and seeded
5½ cups fish stock, 1 tablespoon chopped parsley
1 teaspoon thyme leaves

Wash the fish under cold running water;, remove the fillets, and cut into chunks.

Thinly slice the celery. Cut the carrot into rounds and the leek into thin rings. Cut off both ends of the zucchini, and cut it into rounds.

Wash the cockles and carpetshells under cold running water and drain. Discard any that are open.

Heat the olive oil in a saucepan and sauté the chopped onion and garlic until lightly colored. Add the parsley root, celery, carrot, and leek, and sweat briefly. Pour in the stock and simmer for 15 minutes. Stir in the zucchini, tomatoes, and chile, and simmer for a further 5 minutes. Add the shellfish. As soon as they have opened, carefully add the fish chunks and cook 2–3 minutes, until done.

Discard any unopened shellfish. Sprinkle in the parsley and thyme leaves. Season the fish stew to taste and serve.

Fish, Dublin Bay prawns, shellfish — all seafood highly prized by gourmets — are landed fresh daily by Italian fishermen, and sold at the market immediately.

If you are lucky enough to come across such splendid, sweet, ripe tomatoes in high summer at farmers' markets or at the greengrocer's, follow the example of Italian housewives and preserve the fruit in jars — preferably in large enough quantities to last until the following summer.

Fillet of John Dory with tomato sauce

Pan-fried Dublin Bay prawns and zucchini ribbons round out the flavor of the fish perfectly

This light, summery, relatively uncomplicated dish can be prepared quickly. Essential for best results are absolutely fresh Dublin Bay prawns and aromatic tomatoes, so shop carefully.

Serves 4
4 John Dory fillets (5 oz each)
4 Dublin Bay prawns
2 tablespoons olive oil
2 tablespoons butter
For the tomato sauce:
½ cup finely chopped onion
¼ cup finely chopped celery
small bunch parsley, finely chopped
2 tablespoons olive oil
salt, freshly ground pepper
2 whole cloves
1 cup passata (sieved tomatoes)
salt, freshly ground pepper
For the vegetable accompaniment:
7 oz zucchini
1 tablespoon olive oil
salt, freshly ground pepper
You will also need:
1 teaspoon thyme leaves
4 teaspoons salted capers, soaked in water and finely chopped

The *pesce San Pietro* (John Dory) is one of the finest catches that the Italian fishing grounds have to offer. Its firm, white flesh tastes best stewed or, as here, pan-fried.

Season the fish fillets with salt and pepper. Twist the tails off the Dublin Bay prawns. With a sharp knife, halve the tails lengthwise and devein them.

To make the sauce, hat the olive oil in a skillet and sweat the onion until translucent. Add the celery and parsley, and continue to sweat for about 5 minutes. Season. Stir in the sieved tomatoes, and simmer for 10 minutes.

To make the vegetable accompaniment, cut off both ends of the zucchini, and cut lengthwise into thin slices; halve these slices lengthwise. Heat the olive oil in a skillet and sauté the zucchini strips briefly on both sides. Season with salt and pepper.

Heat the olive oil and butter together in a skillet, and pan-fry the seasoned John Dory fillets on each side for about 1 minute. Place the Dublin Bay prawn tails cut surface down in the skillet with the fish fillets, and sauté for about 1 minute.

Arrange the fish fillets on plates with the Dublin Bay prawns, some sauce, and the sautéed zucchini. Sprinkle the zucchini strips with the thyme leaves, garnish the fish with the capers, and serve.

Garlic is an essential ingredient in any seafood stew, particularly in the south of Italy. Sometimes more is used, sometimes less — but never so much as to overpower the flavor of the shellfish.

Shellfish stew
A delicious mixture of fresh shellfish, *calamaretti*, and vegetables

The shellfish used in this recipe can be varied according to taste; the varieties given below are merely suggestions, and any sorts will do, as long as they come to a total of 4 pounds. You can even replace part of the shellfish with sea snails. Whatever combination you use, *calamaretti*, complement the mollusks superbly. These little squid are left whole, and need only be carefully washed before they are pan-fried, then stewed.

Serves 4
1 lb small venus clams
1 lb razorshells, 1 lb carpetshell clams
1 lb cockles, 14 oz calamaretti
¼ cup olive oil
1 lb tomatoes, peeled, seeded, and diced
1 large onion
2 garlic cloves, finely chopped
1–2 carrots, 1½ celery stalks
½ green bell pepper, cored, seeded, and cut into strips
1 chile pepper, seeded
2 tablespoons olive oil
½ cup dry white wine (e.g. Vernaccia)
1 cup fish stock
1 parsley stalk
salt, freshly ground pepper
You will also need:
1 tablespoon chopped parsley

Carefully scrub all the shellfish under cold running water, and discard any that are open specimens,. Thoroughly rinse the *calamaretti* and drain on paper towels.

Cut the onion into rings and the carrots into rounds. Trim and slice the celery. Halve the green- and chile peppers and remove their stalks, seeds, and membranes. Cut the bell pepper into fine strips, and leave the chile whole.

Heat 2 tablespoons olive oil in a large saucepan, and sweat the onion rings and garlic until translucent. Add the carrots and celery, and sweat briefly, followed by the green-pepper strips and the whole chile. Pour in the wine and the fish stock. Add the parsley stalk and season with salt and pepper. Simmer for 5 minutes.

Heat the remaining olive oil in a skillet and briefly sauté the *calamaretti*. Lift out and keep warm. Add the shellfish to the vegetable stock and cook, covered, for about 5 minutes. One minute before the end of cooking time, add the *calamaretti*. Adjust the seasoning, sprinkle with chopped parsley, and serve.

All kinds of shellfish feature in this delicious stew. Discard any shellfish that remain closed after cooking.

Stuffed calamari
Served with a spicy pesto, and tomato sauce with clams

As a glance at their body shape will tell you, squid were just made for stuffing. Here, they are stuffed and cooked only briefly, so that their flesh stays tender.

Serves 4
1 lb fairly small squid, 3 tablespoons butter, 2 tablespoons olive oil
For the stuffing:
½ heaping cup long-grain brown rice
3 tablespoons olive oil
1 cup fish stock, 10 oz mussels
¼ cup chopped onion
1 garlic clove, crushed
2 thyme sprigs, ⅓ cup white wine, 1 cup diced zucchini
½ cup chopped sweet red pepper, ⅔ cup chopped leek
10 oz tomatoes, peeled, seeded, and diced
salt, freshly ground black pepper

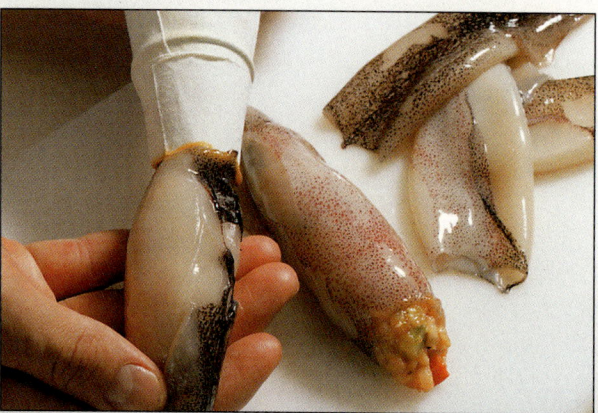

Using a pastry bag with a large round tip, pipe the stuffing into the squid, taking care to leave a bit of room for expansion as they cook. Replace the tentacles in the opening. Heat the butter together with the olive oil, and pan-fry the squid on all sides.

For the sauce:
10 oz clams, 2 garlic cloves, ¼ cup chopped onion
2 tablespoons olive oil, ⅓ cup white wine
⅓ cup finely chopped shallot, ½ teaspoon tomato paste
1 cup sieved tomatoes (passata)
salt, freshly ground pepper
1 sprig each thyme and rosemary
For the pesto:
1 garlic clove, chopped
1 teaspoon pine nuts
1 cup basil leaves, cut into strips
¼ cup freshly grated Parmesan cheese
½ cup olive oil, salt, freshly ground pepper
You will also need:
basil leaves for garnishing

Wash the rice, leave to soak overnight in cold water, then drain well. Wash the squid, and pull the tentacles out of the body sac; they will come away with the intestines. Cut off the tentacles just above the eyes so that they remain joined together by a narrow ring. Remove the beak and quill, and rinse

The calamari are stuffed with a delicious mixture of rice, vegetables, and mussels, then sealed again quite "naturally" with their tentacles.

the body sacs well inside and out.

To make the stuffing, heat 1 tablespoon olive oil in a saucepan and sweat the rice. Pour in the fish stock, season lightly with salt, and bring to a boil. Reduce the heat and simmer for about 20 minutes.

In the meantime, clean the mussels thoroughly, removing all traces of sand and chalk clinging to them, and pulling off the beards. Discard any mussels already open. Heat 1 tablespoon of oil and sweat the onion and garlic clove. Add the mussels and thyme, deglaze the pan with the white wine, and steam the mussels until they open. Discard any which remain closed. Shuck the mussels and set aside.

Heat 1 tablespoon oil in a skillet, and sweat the zucchini, sweet pepper, and leek for 2 minutes. Stir in the tomatoes and the rice. Season with salt and pepper, and simmer until the liquid has completely evaporated. Let cool, and mix in the shucked mussels.

Wash and scrub the clams for the sauce under cold running water, discarding any that are open. Crush 1 of the garlic cloves. Heat 1 tablespoon oil in a skillet, and sweat the onion and crushed garlic. Add the clams, deglaze with wine, and simmer until they have have opened. Drain, reserving the stock. Shuck two-thirds of the clams.

Finely chop the remaining garlic clove. Heat 1 tablespoon oil in a skillet, and sweat the shallots and garlic until translucent. Stir in the tomato paste, pour in the clam stock, and boil down until reduced by half. Stir in the sieved tomatoes, season with salt and pepper, add the herbs, and simmer over a low heat for 15–20 minutes.

Preheat the oven to 350°F. Stuff the squid and pan-fry them as shown in the picture sequence on the left. Place in the oven for 10–12 minutes to finish cooking.

To make the pesto, pound the garlic, pine nuts, and salt in a mortar and pestle. Add the basil and cheese, and work to a paste. Pour in the oil in a thin trickle, season with pepper, and mix together well.

Add the shucked clams to the tomato sauce to warm through, and season to taste. Arrange the squid on serving plates, drizzle with the pesto, and garnish with the clams in their shells and the basil leaves.

People who live near the lagoon of Venice are blessed with fish and seafood, as the wide range at the market proves.

Seafood, pure and simple

This dish does not need much to round it out: a few tomatoes, garlic, olive oil, and possibly some good pasta

Moscardini are a type of small octopus.

FRUTTI DI MARE CON LINGUINE

Serves 4

2 rock lobsters (about 1½ lb each), 2¼ lb cockles
7 tablespoons extra-virgin olive oil
3 garlic cloves, halved lengthwise, green shoots removed
1 sweet red pepper, thinly sliced into rings, and seeded
8 oz prepared moscardini
1¼ lb small tomatoes, peeled, halved, and seeded
8 oz linguine, salt, freshly ground pepper
You will also need:
parsley leaves

Plunge the rock lobsters one at a time into briskly boiling salted water and cook for 4 minutes. Lift out and refresh briefly in ice water. Twist off the tails, halve lengthwise, and devein. Thoroughly clean the cockles, discarding any that are open. .

Heat 5 tablespoons olive oil in a skillet and sweat the garlic and bell pepper. Add the *moscardini* and sautÈ for 5 minutes, keeping them on the move, followed by the tomatoes and cockles. Simmer, covered, for 5–6 minutes, until the cockles have opened. Discard any cockles that remain closed. Shuck half of the cockles, and mix their meat back into the dish.

Cook the noodles in lightly salted boiling water until *al dente*, then drain well and fold into the seafood mixture.

Heat the remaining olive oil. Season the lobster halves with salt and pepper, and pan-fry for 2–3 minutes on each side, starting with the cut surface face

down. Serve the lobster halves with the seafood noodles, garnished with parsley.

BAKED PRAWNS

Serves 4
1¼ lb raw shrimp tails, shell on
2 tablespoons butter, 3 tablespoons olive oil
2 garlic cloves, finely chopped
½ red and ½ green pepper (halved crosswise), seeded and cut into strips
8 cherry tomatoes, halved
2 tablespoons finely cut herbs (parsley, sage, marjoram)
salt, freshly ground white pepper
2 rosemary sprigs

Peel the shrimp tails down to the last joint with the tailfin, then devein them.

Heat the butter and olive oil in a skillet, and briefly sauté the shrimp tails on both sides.

Preheat the oven to 400°F. Mix the garlic, peppers, and herbs, and stir into the shrimp. Drain the shrimp slightly, reserving the frying fat, and transfer to an ovenproof dish. Add the tomatoes, season with salt, pepper, and the rosemary sprigs, and bake for 8–10 minutes, until done, drizzling repeatedly with the reserved frying fat. Lift out and serve.

Prawns, garlic, and herbs: Simplicity itself to prepare, but incomparably delicious, which is why just a little fresh Italian bread makes a more-than-ample accompaniment.

Baked rock lobster
Cooked on a bed of shellfish and tomatoes, and gratinéed with an aromatic sauce

Rock-lobster coral — which is shiny black when raw, but red when cooked — and the greenish liver, both of which can be removed most easily from the shell with a spoon, are particular delicacies. In this recipe, they lend a special touch to the *salsa olandese*.

In Italy rock lobsters, *aragoste* in Italian, are often served grilled or pan-fried, a treatment that really highlights the delicate, slightly sweet flavor of their firm white meat. ("Normal" lobster makes a superb substitute if rock lobster are not available.) In this recipe, shellfish, tomatoes, and a homemade *salsa olandese* (hollandaise) increase the pleasure, as does the fact that the rock lobster is baked in its shell, which enhances the flavor of the meat.

Serves 4
1 rock lobster (about 1½ lb)
2¼ lb mussels, 2¼ lb cockles
1¼ lb cherry tomatoes, peeled and halved
6 tablespoons olive oil
¾ cup finely chopped onion
2 garlic cloves, finely chopped
2 tablespoons chopped parsley
1 tablespoon snipped basil
3 thyme sprigs, salt, freshly ground pepper
For the *salsa olandese*:
¼ cup finely chopped shallot, 1 tarragon sprig
1 parsley sprig, ¼ bay leaf, 3 white peppercorns
1 tablespoon white wine vinegar, 4 tablespoons white wine
2 egg yolks, 6 tablespoons butter
pinch salt, pinch cayenne pepper, dash lemon juice
1 tablespoon heavy cream, whipped to soft peaks
You will also need:
parsley sprigs

Plunge the rock lobster headfirst into briskly boiling salted water. Boil for 4 minutes, then lift out. Cool slightly and halve lengthwise. Scoop out the coral and liver as shown above on the left, and pass both through a strainer. Keep cool until further use. Remove the stomach sac and devein the lobster.

Thoroughly scrub the shellfish under cold running water, removing any sandy or chalky residue. Pull the beards off the mussels. Discard any shellfish that remain open.

To make the hollandaise sauce, bring the shallots, herbs, seasonings, vinegar, wine, and 1 tablespoon water to a boil in a saucepan, and reduce by three-fourths. Strain into a bowl, and place on top of a double-boiler. Add the egg yolks, and beat until the whisk leaves an obvious trail in the sauce.

Heat the butter in a saucepan until almost all of the whey has settled on the bottom. As soon as light-brown flecks form, take the butter off the heat and leave to cool. Stir the butter into the sauce, first drop by drop, then in a thin stream; season with salt, cayenne pepper, and lemon juice. Stir in the strained liver and coral, and the whipped cream. Proceed as shown in the picture sequence below.

Heat ¼ cup olive oil in a roasting pan, and sweat the onions and garlic until lightly colored. Stir in the cockles and tomatoes.

Add the mussels. Simmer the cockles and mussels until they have opened. Discard any that remain closed.

Stir the herbs into the shellfish and tomato mixture, and season with salt and pepper. Salt and pepper the rock-lobster halves, too.

Heat 2 tablespoons olive oil in a skillet, and pan-fry the lobster halves cut surface down for about 2–3 minutes.

Preheat the oven to 400°F. Place the lobster halves cut surface up on top of the shellfish. Ladle the sauce into the shell. Gratinée in the oven for 10 minutes.

Gratinéed until golden brown, the lobster halves — sprinkled with parsley if desired — are arranged on top of the shellfish and tomato mixture, with which they were baked. In Italy, *gnocchetti* or thin homemade ribbon noodles are a popular accompaniment to this dish.

carni MEAT

Good meat should be well hung, nicely marbled, and appetizing. The success, for instance, of one of Italy's most famous meat dishes, *bistecca alla fiorentina,* is dependent on quality. In fact, whether the dish is braised or pan-fired beef, veal, or pork, as is usually the case in the north; or whether lamb and kid are prepared *alla griglia,* over a fire of aromatic wood, as is often the case in the south, the quality of the meat is always crucial.

Pork, veal, and beef

The Italians are as fond of meat — braised or grilled, pan-fried or boiled — as they are of fish. They relish variety meats too; indeed, many a poor-man's meal of bygone days, such as lamb kidneys or tripe, is now considered to be a delicacy, and comes with a price tag to match. Every kind of meat is served: beef, veal, pork, lamb, goat, and in the south, for instance in Apulia, sometimes even horse and donkey meat. With few exceptions, such as the famous *bistecca alla fiorentina* and the northern Italian *brasato*, large pieces of meat are rather unusual. For the most part, Italians eat little meat, but of the very best quality: tender, juicy, and full of flavor.

Pork

Pork, *carne di maiale*, is popular throughout the country, from the alpine valleys in the north, down to Calabria and Sicily in the south; probably not least of all because every part of the pig can be used. In the past, many Italians kept one or two pigs, which they would slaughter in the winter to yield a good supply of meat, sausages, and ham. The more perishable cuts, such as the variety meats, were consumed immediately, often in sociable gatherings. Today, this custom has faded out, as most people buy their sausages and hams. The predilection for pork has remained, however, undoubtedly owing to the good flavor of the Italian meat. This is a result of the animals' feed, as well as the conditions under which they are reared. The meat of pigs that are fed on corn and other grains is excellent, but the best and most aromatic meat comes, it is said, from animals that are allowed to roam freely and to snuffle after acorns. Grilled or broiled pork cuts, such as a chop on the bone (*braciola con l'osso*) or ribs (*costine*), are as prized as a pork roast (*arrosto di maiale*). While lard used to play an important role in cooking, today, with growing nutritional awareness, it is of subordinate importance. Still very popular throughout Italy, and particularly in Umbria, is suckling pig (*maialino* or *porcellino*). Slaughtered at 8–12 weeks, the young animal's flesh is still extremely tender. Traditionally stuffed and seasoned with herbs, and known as *porchetta*, it is roasted on a spit, or in a wood oven at very high heat. On Sardinia, the island where more meat than fish is consumed, it goes by the name of *porceddu*, and is roasted for at least 2 hours over the embers of a fire kindled with aromatic herbs and wood. In addition, the meat trimmings from ham production are made into boiling sausages, such as *zampone*, the heartily stuffed pig's foot from Emilia-Romagna; *cotechino*, a sausage made from pork and pork rind, which is a must for stews like *bollito misto*; and *cappello da prete*, a triangular sausage resembling a priest's hat, which must simmer for 2 hours. These hearty northern Italian specialties are served as winter warmers; they would be far too heavy as summer fare.

Veal and beef

The Italians raise special breeds of cattle, including the famous white cattle from the Val di Chiana south of Arezzo, or those from the Maremma in southern Tuscany, to produce the best quality veal (*vitello*) and beef (*manzo*) Breeds such as Marchigiana and Romagnola are also reared exclusively for classifications may serve as a guide: *Vitello* describes a young calf, *vitellone* refers to a 1-to-2-year-old animal, and *manzo* is the name given to male and female animals up to 3 years old. Later, a distinction is drawn between the *bue*, a castrated bullock or steer; *toro*, a bull; and *vacca*, a fully grown cow. Beef, and veal in particular, is very

This *macelleria* in Venice displays its wares in an appetizing fashion. In many cases, the *macellaio*, or proprietor of a butcher's shop, no longer does his own slaughtering, but specializes in selling sausages, meat, and variety meats.
From calf's foot, to variety meats such as melt (*milze*) and kidneys (*reni*), to oxtail (*coda di bue*), virtually everything is available here.
Including, of course, veal shank, cleanly sawed-off, as is essential for osso buco.
For saltimbocca, a dish in which the meat is pan-fried with prosciutto and sage, the veal cutlets should be cut thinly and across the grain, and preferably from the round.

their superb meat. A little confusingly, every area has its own names for the different cuts of meat. Neither is there universal agreement as to what to call the animals themselves, although the following popular in central and northern Italy, and is made into the widest variety of dishes such as roulades, cutlets, chops, and roasts.

This standing rib roast of beef is nicely marbled and has a sufficient proportion of fat for roasting, grilling, or broiling.

Lamb and kid

The further south you travel in Italy, the drier and more barren the soil, and the less suited it is to grazing cattle. Only in the marshy areas of Latium, Campania, and Molise are buffalo are still raised, while the mountainous regions support the less demanding sheep and goats. It is hardly surprising, therefore, that the superb recipes for lamb and kid come from the south.

Freshly slaughtered sheep and lambs hang from the ceiling of this butcher's shop, promising delicious roasts. Everything on the carcass is made use of, as can be seen to the right in the foreground.

Sheep crop the sparse grassy cover of the mountains of southern Italy. These undemanding creatures can be grazed even on rough ground, and provide the milk for pecorino cheese, as well as meat.

Lamb and mutton

For many Italians, lamb, or *agnello*, is the harbinger of spring. Roman cuisine is famous for its preparation of *abbacchio*, or milk lamb. This requires a very young animal, slaughtered at 4–8 weeks, which is extraordinarily tender but seldom available. Lamb up to the age of 6 months can also be very tender. As they get older, however, their meat becomes tougher and distinctly stronger-flavored. Lamb is the term used to describe animals up to 1 year old; older animals are sheep, or *montone*. Mutton, the meat from sheep, is very popular in Italy, particularly in the south. Castrated males up to 2 years old are wethers (*castrato*). Their deep red flesh is ideal for braising, and the meat of younger animals can also be pan-fried. Lamb, but especially the somewhat fattier mutton, should always be served hot, as it tastes best this way, especially if the fat was not removed before cooking. Older, fully grown sheep, known as *pecore*, are also sometimes used in cooking, but their meat is a bit tougher and must be cooked for a correspondingly longer period. In addition to garlic, herbs such as rosemary, oregano, thyme, and mint go well with lamb. Sometimes, though, it is eaten plain; for instance, lamb chops may be simply brushed with olive oil and char-grilled on a barbecue. Cooking over an open fire is one of the preferred methods of preparing meat, especially in the south, and it is not unusual to spit-roast a lamb at large family celebrations or other festivals. Also popular, however, are roast lamb, *arrosto d'agnello*; saddle of lamb, *sella d'agnello*; and ragùs in which cubed lamb is sautéed in hot oil or lard. Often, the lamb is accompanied by vegetables such as fennel, beans, and artichokes.

Goat and kid

Prized on a par with young lamb in central and southern Italy, if not actually more sought-after, is the meat of kid goats, known as *capretto*. This comes from young male or female animals 4–6 weeks old. The exceedingly tasty kid meat is served in Italy primarily in the spring, usually from Easter onwards. It is prepared in quite a similar fashion to lamb: roasted whole, or braised in cuts such as the leg or shoulder; spit-roasted, as in *spiedini di capretto*; baked, *alla paesana*, with potatoes, onions, and tomatoes; and hunter-style, *cacciatora di capretto*, with ham or bacon, red wine, and tomatoes. Unlike sheep, fully grown goats are rarely eaten, but used instead chiefly for milk and cheese production.

MEAT 327

For about 2 quarts of stock, you will need a mixture of 4½ pounds of meat, and 1 pound of beef or veal bones. First, blanch the bones. As soon as the water wells up in a brisk boil, pour it off and rinse the bones. Transfer the bones and meat to a large saucepan and add cold water to cover completely. Bring to a boil, repeatedly skimming off any foam that rises to the surface, and simmer over low heat for about 1 hour. Then add a bouquet garni consisting of 1 carrot, 1 leek, a small piece of parsley root, and 1 celery stalk, as well as ½ garlic clove, all peeled and trimmed. Add 1 onion, if wished, then 1 ripe tomato, a few stalks of parsley, 1 bay leaf, and 10 peppercorns. Simmer gently for 2 hours. Pour the broth through a cloth-lined strainer, as shown on the right. Defat the broth before use.

Homemade meat stock It is worth the time and effort it takes to make stocks, as they taste best and can easily be stored in the refrigerator for up to 3 days and in the freezer for much longer.

Lamb chops The light-red meat promises to be quite tender when grilled. If you want them with long bones, as shown here, be sure and order them in advance.

Light broths and stocks

For many Italian dishes such as risottos, and of course soups, a good stock is a must. As a rule, it is light and not greatly reduced. The stock can be prepared in different ways, according to the desired flavor: with and without bones, with more or less vegetables, and from different kinds of meat, either from beef alone, or a mixture of beef and veal; from veal and poultry, or from poultry alone. We highly recommend that you make different stocks in advance, as they freeze superbly and can be thawed out in batches when needed. The basic recipe that follows can be used to make different stocks.

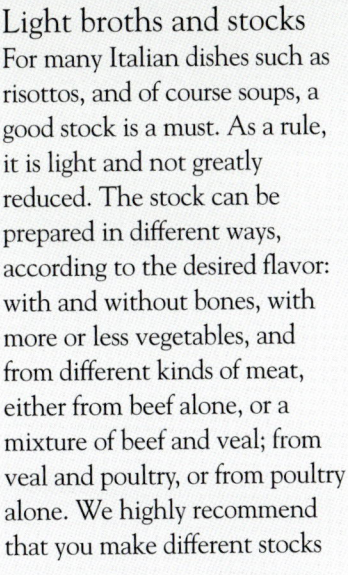

At Bertino's in Bologna, or in another good restaurant, you can treat yourself to this famous dish of boiled meats. If you would like to try this specialty from Emilia-Romagna at home, however, be sure to invite plenty of dinner guests, since the recipe works only with large quantities.

Bollito misto

In northern Italy this dish is served *con salsa verde* — with a piquant herb sauce

The main requirement of an authentic *bollito misto* (literally, a "mixed boil") is different sorts of meat. Typical ingredients are beef, tongue, chicken, and, occasionally, a calf's head, plus, of course, *zampone*, the rather sumptuous, heartily stuffed pig's foot so popular in northern Italy. The *salsa verde* can also be prepared with 4 anchovy fillets instead of the salted capers.

Serves 6-8
For the *bollito misto*:
8 oz marrowbones, 1¾ lb beef chuck
2¼ lb pickled ox tongue
1 chicken (about 3 lb)
1 onion, quartered
1–2 carrots, cut into 2-inch long pieces
2 celery stalks, cut into 2-inch long pieces
1 zampone (stuffed pig's foot weighing about 3 lb)
salt
For the *salsa verde*:
3¾ cups finely chopped flat-leaf parsley
1 garlic clove, finely chopped
½ cup coarsely chopped shallot

There is no "basic" recipe for *salsa verde*. Popular throughout Italy, widely varying versions of this sauce are prepared in each region, some with anchovies and some without; some hot with chile peppers, some mild with egg yolk. The result always tastes different, but invariably good, especially with boiled meats.

In the kitchen of Bertino's, renowned for its *bollito misto*, the whole family still lends a hand. Here, the various boiled meats wait to make their entrance.

4 teaspoons salted capers, rinsed and coarsely chopped
½ cup coarsely chopped dill pickles
2 tablespoons fresh white bread crumbs
salt, freshly ground white pepper
2 tablespoons balsamic vinegar
1 cup olive oil

Carefully wash the marrowbones under cold running water. Bring about 5 quarts water to a boil in a large pot, and lower in the chuck, tongue, and marrowbones. Reduce the heat, season with salt, and simmer gently for about 2½–3 hours, keeping the water just at boiling point.

In the meantime, make the *salsa verde*. Combine all the chopped ingredients in a bowl with the bread crumbs, and season with salt and pepper. Stir in the balsamic vinegar, mixing well. Add the olive oil in a thin stream and stir to blend.

Forty minutes before the end of cooking time, add the chicken to the pot. Add the onion, carrots, and celery 15 minutes after the chicken. If necessary, add a little more boiling water. Fifteen minutes before the end of cooking time, lower in the *zampone* and heat slowly in the broth.

Lift all the meat from the broth, then wrap the beef in foil and leave to rest for 10 minutes. Carve the beef, tongue, and stuffed pig's foot into slices, and the chicken into pieces.

Arrange the meat together with the vegetables on a warmed platter, sprinkle with parsley, and serve with the *salsa verde* and fresh white Italian bread. For complete authenticity, pass around *mostarda* (candied fruit in a mustard sauce) or *sottaceti* (pickled vegetables).

Intensely perfumed oregano is harvested in southern Italy in July, when the herb is in full bloom.

Costolette alla pizzaiola
Classic pizza ingredients give character to the sauce accompanying the pork chops

With their slightly higher proportion of fat, small pork chops are usually especially juicy, and thus excellent for this dish. However, steak, thinly sliced beef, or veal cutlets may also be prepared in this way. Fresh oregano, which grows in the karst areas of southern Italy and Sicily, is the herb of choice, owing to its particularly strong flavor. If you cannot get hold of any fresh, use the dried herb, which is in between marjoram and thyme in flavor, although a little spicier.

Serves 4
4 pork chops (weighing 6–7 oz each)
3–4 tablespoons olive oil
4 garlic cloves, thinly sliced
1¼ lb ripe tomatoes, peeled, seeded, and finely diced
⅔ cup red wine
1 tablespoon fresh or 1 teaspoon dried oregano
salt, freshly ground black pepper

Fine olive oil and dry red wine combine with tomatoes, garlic, and oregano to produce a wonderfully aromatic sauce, which tastes best with homemade ribbon noodles.

Oregano is a sought-after export of southern Italy. Although the aromatic herb is also sold fresh in local markets after the harvest, the overwhelming proportion of the crop is dried, hermetically packed, and exported around the world.

For the ribbon noodles:
2½ cups all-purpose flour
1 egg, 7 egg yolks
1 tablespoon oil
½ teaspoon salt
2 tablespoons butter, melted

First make the pasta dough. Sift the flour onto a work surface and make a well in the center. Place the egg, egg yolks, oil, and salt in the well, and mix with a fork. Gradually stir in the flour from the inside edge. With circular movements, incorporate more and more flour until you have a sticky dough. Using both hands, work in the remaining flour and knead vigorously until the dough is smooth and firm. Roll the dough into a ball,

wrap in plastic wrap, and rest in the refrigerator for about 1 hour.

Season the pork chops with salt and pepper. Heat the oil in a skillet and brown the chops on both sides for about 3 minutes. Lift out the chops, cover them, and set aside.

Sauté the garlic in the oil remaining in the skillet without letting it color. Add the tomatoes and sweat briefly. Deglaze the skillet with the wine, sprinkle in the oregano, season with pepper and salt, and simmer for a further 10 minutes.

Using a pasta machine, roll out the dough to the desired thickness and cut into ½-inch-wide ribbon noodles. Return the chops to the skillet and braise them in the sauce for about 5 minutes on each side.

Cook the noodles in rapidly boiling salted water until *al dente*, then drain and toss in melted butter. Arrange the chops on plates with the pizzaiola sauce and noodles, and serve.

The *gondolieri* are strictly optional, even though the food does taste superb in a restaurant on the spot! Stay-at-homes can console themselves with a white wine from the Veneto.

Fegato di vitello
Calf's liver, Venetian style: traditionally served with fried polenta patties

This dish is easy to prepare and tastes great. As with all simple recipes, its excellence depends upon the impeccable quality of the ingredients. If possible, the liver should come from a milk calf — a very young animal that has not yet been fed with hay — as it will be that much more tender. Aromatic sage leaves are included in almost all Italian recipes for liver — a touch too harsh, perhaps, for many non-Italian palates. There is no need to be dogmatic on this point; use or omit the sage as you like. The same is true for the deglazing of the skillet after sautéeing the onions: If you find the flavor of the white wine overpowering, use half wine, half veal stock. Similarly, you can decide to cut the liver into strips, as is the original Venetian custom, or into thin slices, as suggested in this recipe.

Serves 4
For the calf's liver:
1¾ lb calf's liver in one piece
flour (optional)
9 tablespoons butter
1 lb onions, thinly sliced into rings
1 cup white wine
2 tablespoons olive oil
salt, freshly ground pepper
For the polenta patties:
1 teaspoon salt
1 cup polenta (corn meal)
2 tablespoons butter
You will also need:
1 tablespoon chopped flat-leaf parsley

First prepare the polenta. Bring 2¼ cups water to a boil in a pot with the salt. Trickle in the polenta, stirring constantly, and taking care that the water remains at a constant boil so that no lumps form. Continue to stir constantly for about 20 minutes. The polenta is done when it comes away cleanly from the sides of the pot.

Tip the polenta out onto a wet board. Using a palette knife, spread to a thickness of ½ inch, and leave to cool.

Meanwhile, prepare the calf's liver. Carefully remove any membrane and sinew from the liver. Halve the liver lengthwise and cut crosswise into thin slices. Lightly dust with flour if wished, and set aside.

Using a 3-inch round cookie cutter, cut circles from the cooled polenta. Melt the butter in a skillet and fry the polenta patties on both sides until golden. Remove from the heat and keep warm.

Melt 6 tablespoons of the butter in a skillet and sauté the onions until golden brown. Deglaze with the white wine, reduce the heat, and simmer for another 5 minutes. Season with salt and pepper, and remove from the heat.

In another skillet, heat together the remaining butter and the olive oil, and fry the liver only briefly. Season with salt and pepper, and mix the fried onions in with the liver. Arrange the liver with the polenta patties on warmed plates, sprinkle with a little chopped parsley, and serve at once.

It is best to fry the onions and calf liver for this Venetian specialty at the same time in separate skillets, to ensure that they are done simultaneously.

Sage was highly prized in ancient Rome for its medicinal powers, hence its botanical name, *salvia*, derived from the Latin *salvare*, "to cure."

Braciole di vitello
Veal chops served with an aromatic sage butter

The vegetable accompaniment is typical of the south of Italy: spinach, with a slightly sweet note from the Vin Santo and raisins on the one hand, and a distinctly spicy flavor from the garlic and anchovy fillets on the other. Crisp-fried almond croquettes complement the flavors and textures.

Serves 4
4 veal chops (about 7 oz each)
¼ cup olive oil, 16 sage leaves, ¼ cup butter
salt, freshly ground pepper
For the almond croquettes:
2¼ lb mealy potatoes, 4 egg yolks
5 teaspoons butter, freshly grated nutmeg
¾ cup flaked almonds, 1½ cups fine white bread crumbs
¼ cup all-purpose flour
2 eggs, beaten
salt
For the spinach:
½ cup Vin Santo, ¼ cup raisins
2¼ lb spinach, 1 tablespoon olive oil
1 pinch freshly grated nutmeg, ¼ cup butter
½ cup scallion rings
1 small garlic clove, finely chopped
3 anchovy fillets, finely chopped
⅓ cup pine nuts, 1 tablespoon chopped flat-leaf parsley
1 pinch salt, freshly ground white pepper
You will also need:
fat for deep-frying

The browned sage butter should be prepared immediately before serving and poured over the meat. Only then does the herb stay beautifully crisp and flavorful.

First, prepare the dough for the almond croquettes. Boil the potatoes in lightly salted water for 20–25 minutes, then drain them and cover with a clean cloth for a few minutes to absorb some of the steam. Peel the potatoes and put through a ricer into a bowl. Mix with the egg yolks, butter, salt, and nutmeg. Shape the lukewarm mixture into ropes the thickness of your finger and leave to cool. Combine the almonds and bread crumbs. Cut potato ropes into 2-inch lengths

and turn the croquettes in flour, then beaten egg, then the combined bread crumbs and almonds. Set the breaded croquettes aside until it is time to fry them.

To make the spinach, gently heat the wine in a saucepan and plump the raisins in it. Heat the oil in a pot and sauté the spinach. Season with salt, pepper, and nutmeg, and cook until wilted. Transfer the spinach to a flat strainer and drain thoroughly.

In a separate pot, melt the butter and sweat the scallion rings and garlic until translucent. Add the anchovies and the raisins and Vin Santo. Reduce the liquid until it is almost completely evaporated. Lightly squeeze the excess liquid from the spinach, add the spinach to the pot, and cook with the other ingredients for 5 minutes. Sprinkle in the pine nuts and parsley, season to taste, and keep warm.

Preheat the oven to 100°F. Salt and pepper the veal chops. Heat the olive oil in a skillet and brown the chops for 5 minutes on each side. Remove the meat from the pan, transfer to an ovenproof dish, and keep warm in the oven. Pour off all but 1 tablespoon of fat from the skillet.

Heat the fat for deep-frying to 350°F in a pot or deep-fat fryer, and fry the prepared croquettes until golden brown. Lift out and drain on paper towels.

Briefly fry the sage leaves in the fat remaining in the skillet. Add the butter, heat until it foams, and scrape the bottom of the pan to incorporate the flavorful sediment. Remove the chops from the oven, pour the sage butter over them, and arrange on plates with the spinach and the croquettes.

Before being rolled, the boneless pork loin is topped with chopped garlic, grated lemon zest, sage, and rosemary, and seasoned with salt and pepper.

Impressions of Tuscany on a clear summer evening: the unusual perspective makes the rosemary in the foreground look as if it is growing sky high.

Arista alla fiorentina
Rolled pork roast, Florentine style, with herbs, garlic, and lemon

In Tuscany, pork loin is usually prepared with rosemary, sometimes as a boneless rolled roast, as here; sometimes on the bone as a rack of pork. The major advantage of the rolled roast is that the meat, protected by the fat, remains especially succulent when roasted.

Serves 4
5½ lb boneless pork loin with belly
12 sage leaves, 5 rosemary sprigs
grated zest of 1 lemon
4 garlic cloves, chopped
2 sage sprigs
1 cup coarsely chopped onion, 1 cup coarsely chopped leek
5 black peppercorns, crushed
2 cloves, 2 bay leaves
salt, freshly ground black pepper
For the polenta:
1 teaspoon salt, ¼ cup butter
1½ cups polenta (corn meal)
¼ cup freshly grated Parmesan cheese
You will also need:
strong kitchen string
¼ cup olive oil

Polenta, served here with freshly grated Parmesan cheese, is the classic accompaniment for this succulent, spicy pork roast.

First prepare the meat. Detach one-third of the fat from the pork. Salt and pepper the meat, and place the sage leaves, 3 rosemary sprigs, lemon zest, and garlic on the meat side and under the detached fat. Roll up the meat from the pork loin toward the belly, pressing the detached fat firmly back in place. Truss the rolled roast with kitchen string, tying in the remaining rosemary and sage sprigs.

Place the pork in a large pot with lightly salted boiling water to cover, add the onion, leek, and seasonings, and simmer over a low heat for 30 minutes. Lift out the meat and pat dry, then reserve 5½ cups of the cooking liquid. Preheat the oven to 350°F. Place the meat in a roasting pan lightly greased

with olive oil, brush all over with the oil, and roast for about 1½ hours until done, adding the reserved cooking liquid a little at a time, and basting frequently with the roasting juices.

Meanwhile, prepare the polenta. Bring 4½ cups water to a boil in a pot with the salt and butter. Slowly trickle in the corn meal, stirring vigorously with a wooden spoon so that no lumps form. Continue stirring the polenta for about 20 minutes, until it comes away from the base of the pan, the remove from the heat and keep warm.

When the roast is done (it should register 158–162°F on a meat thermometer), remove it from the oven. Wrap it in foil and rest for 10 minutes.

Meanwhile, strain the roasting juices, reduce to 2¼ cups, and adjust the seasoning.

Remove the roast from the foil and slice. Pour the juices that ooze from the meat into the gravy. Sprinkle the polenta with the grated Parmesan, and arrange on warmed plates next to the pork slices and gravy.

Brunello di Montalcino, a star among Tuscan red wines, delights with its full flavor, which it owes in part to its long aging period: a *riserva* must mature for a total of 5 years in barrel and bottle.

Brasato al Brunello
This classic pot roast from Tuscany demands a bottle of good red wine

A Brunello di Montalcino, one of the most famous, and one of the most expensive, Tuscan red wines, would be the ideal choice for this dish; but other top-quality, full-bodied dry red wines, such as those from the south of Italy, can also produce delicious results. Another alternative would be a Rosso di Montalcino (Rosso dei Vigneti di Montalcino). This wine is produced from the same variety of grape as Brunello, the *Sangiovese grosso*, but is bottled after a shorter maturation period in the barrel, which accounts for its slightly lower price.

Serves 6–8
4½ lb beef pot roast (top round, rump, or sirloin tip)
¼ cup olive oil
For the marinade:
1–2 onions, sliced into rings
2 carrots, cut into rounds
2 celery stalks, sliced
1 bay leaf, 12–15 black peppercorns
½ garlic clove, 1 bottle Brunello di Montalcino
For the porcini noodles:
2 cups all-purpose flour
2 eggs, 1 egg yolk

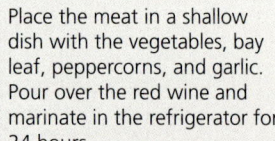

Place the meat in a shallow dish with the vegetables, bay leaf, peppercorns, and garlic. Pour over the red wine and marinate in the refrigerator for 24 hours.

Heat the olive oil in a large pot and sear the meat on both sides. Season with salt and pepper.

Add the vegetables and seasonings from the marinade and sauté briefly, stirring occasionally. Pour in the marinade liquid and bring to a boil.

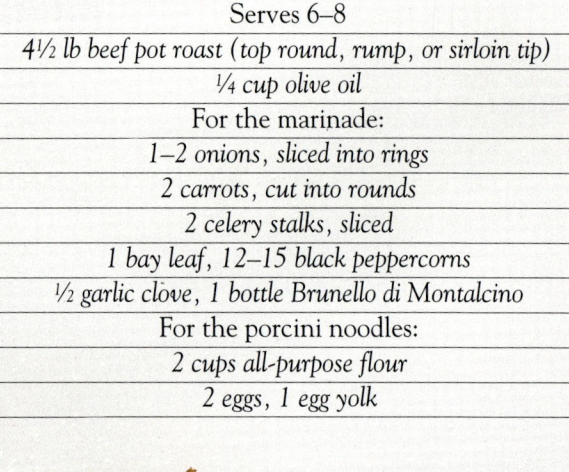

This pot roast will succeed only with the right meat. The cut of meat should be fine-fibered and not too small. Suitable cuts include top round, rump, and sirloin tip. The roast is properly cooked when it can be cut with a spoon. Polenta and porcini tagliatelle are popular accompaniments to this dish.

⅓ oz dried porcini mushrooms, finely chopped or crushed
2 tablespoons oil
½ teaspoon salt
1 tablespoon finely chopped parsley
2 tablespoons butter, melted
freshly ground pepper
You will also need:
1 tablespoon chopped parsley

Trim the meat of any sinew and membrane. Marinate the beef, as shown in the first step of the picture sequence on the left.

Preheat the oven to 350°F. Lift the meat from the marinade and pat dry. Strain the marinade, reserving the liquid and draining the vegetables. Proceed as shown in the last two steps of the picture sequence. Braise the beef, covered, in the oven for 2–2½ hours.

In the meantime, prepare the porcini noodles. Sift the flour onto a work surface and make a well in the center. Tip in all the chopped mushrooms and the remaining ingredients except the butter. Stir together with a fork, then, with circular movements, mix in more and more flour from the inside edge, until you have a sticky dough. Work in the remaining flour, and knead the dough vigorously with both hands until smooth and firm. Roll the dough into a ball, wrap in plastic wrap, and rest in the refrigerator for 1 hour.

Using a pasta machine, roll out the dough to the desired thickness, and cut into tagliatelle.

Remove the pot roast from the oven, transfer to a warmed platter, and keep warm. Strain the roasting juices, pressing the vegetables through the strainer, then bring to a boil once more and adjust the seasoning.

Cook the tagliatelle in boiling salted water until *al dente*. Drain, and toss in the melted butter. Slice the pot roast, sprinkle with parsley, and serve with the tagliatelle and gravy.

340 MEAT

Gnocchetti sautéed in butter go brilliantly with these stylishly filled roulades in their hearty, spicy sauce.

Beef roulades with mortadella sausage and vegetables

This is how the Romans like their *involtini*: spicily stuffed, and braised in a hearty tomato sauce

The mortadella sausage lends a very special touch to the roulade stuffing, which includes pancetta, garlic, capers, onions, and mustard. Fine carrot and celery strips round out the flavor of the *involtini*.

For the beef roulades:
8 beef roulades (about 3 oz each)
4 thin slices of mortadella sausage
2 garlic cloves, finely chopped
2 small onions, thinly sliced into 16 rounds
⅓ cup salted capers, 1 carrot
2 celery stalks
2 tablespoons hot mustard
8 thin slices pancetta
salt, freshly ground pepper,
For the tomato sauce:
1 cup finely chopped onion
1 garlic clove, finely chopped
1 cup finely chopped mixed root vegetables (celeriac, celery, leek, carrot)
1 small green chile pepper, halved lengthwise and seeded
10 oz ripe tomatoes, chopped
¼ cup olive oil
1 cup red wine, 2¼ cups beef stock
salt, freshly ground pepper
You will also need:
kitchen string, parsley leaves

Place the roulades next to each other on a work surface. Halve the mortadella slices. Shake some of the salt off the capers, then chop them coarsely and mix with the garlic. Cut the carrot and the celery lengthwise into ¼-inch-thick slices, then crosswise into matchsticks 2 inches long. Prepare the roulades and tie them together as shown in the picture sequence opposite.

Heat the olive oil in a skillet and brown the roulades all over. Add the chopped onion, garlic, and root vegetables, and fry briefly. Tip in the tomatoes. Pour in the wine and allow to reduce slightly. In a separate pot, bring the beef stock to a boil and reduce by half. Gradually add the stock to the roulades, then season with salt and pepper. Braise, covered, over medium heat for about 1 hour.

Lift out the beef roulades and remove the string. Strain the sauce and season to taste. Arrange the roulades on plates with the sauce, and serve, garnished with parsley.

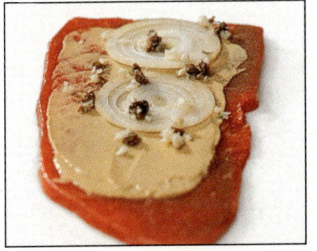

Lightly salt, then pepper the roulades, spread with mustard, top with two slices of onion, and sprinkle with the caper and garlic mixture.

Top with ½ slice mortadella sausage and 1 slice pancetta. Pile up ⅛ of the vegetable matchsticks in the lower third of the roulade.

Fold the roulades in slightly at the long sides, and roll up from the narrow side with the vegetable matchsticks.

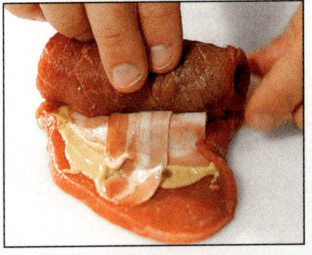

Tie the roulades with kitchen string so that the filling cannot escape, and dust with a little flour.

Involtini di vitello
Veal roulades stuffed with prosciutto, anchovies, capers, and garlic

There are countless variations of this recipe in Italy. The thin slices of veal are also occasionally stuffed with combinations of ground pork and Parmesan cheese, pancetta and Parmesan cheese, anchovies and mozzarella cheese, or even raw ham and Gorgonzola cheese.

Serves 4
8 veal cutlets from the top round (4 oz each)
salt, freshly ground white pepper
For the stuffing:
4 teaspoons salted capers
1 garlic clove, finely chopped
6 anchovy fillets in oil, drained and chopped
4 oz prosciutto, finely diced
3 tablespoons chopped parsley
2 tablespoons passata (strained tomatoes)
½ cup fine fresh white bread crumbs
salt, freshly ground pepper
2 tablespoons butter, softened
For the sauce:
1⅓ cups veal stock, 3 tablespoons cream
salt, freshly ground black pepper
You will also need:
8–16 toothpicks, flour
¼ cup vegetable oil and 2 tablespoons butter for frying

Place each veal cutlet between two pieces of plastic wrap and tenderize by pounding with a meat mallet until they are uniformly thin. Season each cutlet with salt and pepper.

To make the stuffing, tip the capers into a strainer and rinse for about 10 minutes,

A classic risotto is the ideal accompaniment for the pan-fried, stuffed veal roulades. It can be a pumpkin risotto, as shown here, or a saffron-flavored Risotto alla Milanese.

Aromatic cured prosciutto, salted capers, and anchovy fillets are some of the main ingredients of the roulade stuffing.

then chop finely. In a bowl, combine the capers, garlic, anchovies, prosciutto, parsley, and passata with the bread crumbs. Season to taste with salt and pepper and stir in the softened butter.

Divide the stuffing evenly among the veal cutlets, and spread smooth with a palette knife. Fold the long sides of the cutlets in slightly, then roll up and secure with 1–2 toothpicks so that the stuffing cannot come out. Dust the roulades with flour.

Heat the oil and butter together in a large skillet and briefly brown the *involtini* all over. Reduce the heat, and fry for a further 10 minutes, turning constantly. Lift out and keep warm.

To make the sauce, pour the veal stock into the skillet and reduce by half. Strain and reheat the sauce. Stir in the cream and reduce again slightly. Season with salt and pepper.

Remove the toothpicks and arrange the *involtini* on warmed plates with a little sauce. A risotto makes a good accompaniment.

Lamb shanks braised in red wine
The braised lamb is especially tender and succulent, and ideally partnered by homemade herb gnocchi

This is an ideal recipe when you are expecting guests. Once seared, the lamb cooks all by itself in the oven, and the gnocchi can easily be prepared a day in advance.

Serves 4
For the lamb shanks:
5 tablespoons vegetable oil
1 cup finely chopped onion
3 garlic cloves, finely chopped
1 rosemary sprig
⅓ cup finely diced celery
⅓ cup finely diced carrot
1 lb tomatoes, peeled, seeded, and diced
4 lamb shanks (about 12 oz each)
1⅔ cups red wine
1¾ cups lamb stock
salt, freshly ground pepper
For the gnocchi:
1½ lb mealy potatoes
¼ cup ricotta cheese, 1 egg yolk
¾ cup freshly grated Parmesan cheese
2 tablespoons flour
salt, freshly ground pepper
freshly grated nutmeg
For the herb butter:
½ cup butter
1 clove garlic, crushed
2 tablespoons chopped herbs (parsley, oregano, rosemary)
You will also need:
butter, ⅓ cup freshly grated Parmesan cheese

Preheat the oven to 400°F. Wash the potatoes for the gnocchi, wrap them in aluminum foil, and bake them for about 1 hour.

Meanwhile, prepare the lamb shanks, heat 2 tablespoons of the oil in a skillet and sweat the onion and garlic until lightly colored. Add the rosemary, celery, and carrot, and continue to sweat briefly.

Season the lamb shanks with salt and pepper. Heat the remaining oil in a large flameproof baking dish and sear the lamb shanks all over. Deglaze with the red wine and boil until reduced by half. Add the sweated vegetables, stir in the tomatoes, and pour in the lamb stock. Braise, covered, in the oven for 50-60 minutes.

Peel the baked potatoes and put them through a ricer into a bowl while still hot. Leave to cool slightly, then add the ricotta, egg yolk, Parmesan, flour, salt, pepper, and nutmeg, and work into a smooth dough. Roll into ropes about ½ inch in diameter, cut into ¾-inch-long sections, and roll each piece over a grater to give it a lattice pattern.

Lower the gnocchi into boiling salted water, reduce the heat, and cook for 3 minutes, until done. Lift out the gnocchi and drain.

To make the herb butter, melt the butter in a skillet and briefly sweat the garlic, then stir in the herbs. Layer the gnocchi in a shallow, buttered ovenproof dish, sprinkle with Parmesan, and pour the herb butter evenly over the top.

Bake the gnocchi with the lamb for the final 15–20 minutes of cooking time. Remove the lamb and gnocchi from the oven and season the meat to taste. Serve the lamb on a platter, passing around the gnocchi separately.

Brown the veal on both sides in plenty of butter and lift out of the pan. Sweat the vegetables, then season them. Return the meat to the pan, pour in the wine and stock, and add the tomatoes and thyme.

Osso buco

Veal shank, seasoned with a mixture of finely chopped garlic, parsley, and lemon zest

Although the vegetables used in this classic Lombardian dish vary according to the recipe followed, ripe tomatoes are usually included. The sliced veal shank also tastes very good — and this is one of the simplest methods of preparation — just seared in butter with a clove of garlic, which is removed from the pan when it starts to brown. The pan is then deglazed with white wine and meat stock, and the slices of veal are braised for about 1½–2 hours. Shortly before the end of the cooking time, they are spread with a spicy mixture of chopped parsley, ½ garlic clove, sage, rosemary, and the grated zest of ½ lemon. Traditionally, however, this *gremolata* consists only of finely chopped garlic, parsley, and grated lemon zest. If you like it very piquant, you can replace the garlic with 4 anchovy fillets. In all cases it is important to braise the veal for long enough so that it is tender. Risotto is a popular accompaniment to osso buco, either the classic Risotto alla Milanese, or the radicchio risotto illustrated below.

With osso buco, a white wine is usually used to deglaze the pan. A suitable choice would be a dry Pinot grigio or a Pinot bianco, of which northern Italy can offer a large selection. In Tuscany, by contrast, a red Cabernet is sometimes used.

Serves 4–6
3½ lb veal shank, cut into 6 pieces
flour
¼ cup butter
½ cup chopped onion
1 carrot and 1 celery stalk, trimmed and cut into julienne
1 garlic clove, crushed with a little salt
1 bay leaf
½ cup dry white win
1 cup veal stock
1 lb ripe tomatoes, peeled, quartered, and seeded
1 teaspoon thyme leaves
salt, freshly ground pepper

For the gremolata:
½ small garlic clove, finely chopped
2 tablespoons chopped parsley
grated zest of 1 lemon

Carefully wash the meat under cold running water and pat dry with paper towels. Season with salt and pepper, then dredge in the flour, tapping off any excess. Heat the butter in a large flameproof casserole dish and brown the veal slices on both sides over a gentle heat, then remove them. Briefly sauté the onion in the casserole dish, then add the carrot and celery, and sweat them. Add the garlic and bay leaf.

Preheat the oven to 350°F. Return the meat to the skillet. Pour in the wine and stock, and add the tomatoes and thyme. Braise in the oven for 1–1½ hours, basting the pieces of veal with the sauce and turning them occasionally.

Meanwhile, to make the *gremolata*, thoroughly combine the garlic, parsley, and lemon zest.

Two minutes before the end of cooking time, spread the veal with the *gremolata*, braise for the final two minutes, and serve the osso buco in its sauce with the risotto of your choice.

Trippa
Often scorned in this country, tripe is considered a delicacy in Italy

Nearly every Italian province proudly boasts its own tripe recipe. Three of the many exceedingly tasty versions have achieved fame throughout Italy: the Tuscan tripe stew *trippa alla fiorentina*, prepared with plenty of fresh vegetables; the Roman *trippa alla romana*, with pecorino cheese and fresh mint; and *trippa con i fagioli*, cooked with white beans and sprinkled with grated Parmesan cheese, the way they like it in Milan.

Serves 4
1¼ cups dried white beans
3 lb boiled tripe
¼ cup olive oil
1 cup finely chopped onion
3 garlic cloves, finely chopped
1 small red chile pepper, seeded and cut into strips
¾ cup finely diced carrot
½ cup finely diced celery
⅓ cup finely diced leek
2 bay leaves
1 rosemary sprig
1 cup white wine
1¾ cups veal stock
1 teaspoon lemon juice
2 tablespoons chopped parsley
2 tablespoons tomato paste
¼ cup freshly grated Parmesan cheese
salt, freshly ground black pepper

Place the beans in a bowl with cold water to cover and soak overnight. The next morning, drain the beans and rinse well under cold running water. Bring sufficient salted water to a boil in a pot, add the beans, and cook for 40–45 minutes, until tender.

Prepare and sweat the tripe as shown in the picture sequence below. Pour in the stock and season with salt, pepper, and lemon juice. Sprinkle in the parsley and simmer the tripe for a further 20 minutes. Dissolve the tomato paste in a little stock, and stir into the tripe. Stir in the white beans, and season generously with salt and pepper. Sprinkle the tripe with grated Parmesan and serve with fresh Italian bread.

Cut the tripe into thin strips with a sharp knife. Heat the olive oil in a large pot.

Sweat the onions and garlic until lightly colored, then tip in the vegetables and sweat briefly. Add the tripe, and sweat it briefly too.

Add the bay leaves and rosemary sprig. Pour in the white wine and reduce by half.

Lamb chops
Baked with a risotto topping and flavored with *scorzone*

A rather finicky dish, admittedly, but one whose well balanced flavors make it worth the effort. Rosemary and thyme develop their spicy taste beautifully when pan-fried, and a *soupçon* of garlic complements the tender lamb chops. Summer truffles — *scorzone* in Italian — accent the whole. The long rib bones are usually cut off, so ask the butcher specially for chops with the long bones intact.

Serves 4

8 lamb chops with long rib bones (about 4 oz each)
¼ cup butter, 1 cup finely chopped white onion
½ cup Arborio rice
¼ cup white wine, 1½ cups chicken stock
1 pinch freshly grated nutmeg
¾ cup freshly grated Parmesan cheese, 1 egg yolk
3 tablespoons olive oil
2 garlic cloves, lightly crushed
3 thyme sprigs, 1 rosemary sprig
1 teaspoon medium-hot mustard
salt, freshly ground pepper
For the truffle dressing:
2 oz summer truffle, 9 tablespoons extra-virgin olive oil
4½ tablespoons balsamic vinegar
3 tablespoons beef stock
1 pinch salt, ½ teaspoon sugar, 1 pinch grated nutmeg
For the vegetables:
1¾ lb small artichokes, juice of 2 lemons
14 oz cherry tomatoes, ¼ cup olive oil
2 garlic cloves, lightly crushed; 2 thyme sprigs
salt, freshly ground pepper
You will also need:
1 oz summer truffle, 4 small thyme sprigs

Scrape clean the bottom third of the long rib bones of the lamb chops, and refrigerate the meat until later.

Melt half of the butter in a saucepan and sweat the onion until lightly colored. Tip in the rice and sweat,

Heat the oil and the remaining butter in a skillet and brown the lamb chops for 1 minute, together with the garlic and the herbs.

Turn the lamb chops and brown for 1 minute on the other side. Lift out and place on a board.

Spoon the risotto evenly over the lamb chops and spread smooth. Return the chops to the skillet.

Spread some mustard on the meat on the rib bones, and sprinkle the rice mixture with the remaining Parmesan.

stirring, until the grains are translucent. Pour in the wine, and allow to reduce almost completely. Gradually add the stock, and cook the rice for 15 minutes, stirring several times during this period. Remove from the heat and allow to cool slightly. Season with salt, pepper, and nutmeg, stir in ⅓ cup of the Parmesan cheese and the egg yolk, and leave to cool completely.

To make the truffle dressing, carefully brush off all dirt and grit from the summer truffle. Where this is not possible because of deep cracks, peel the truffle. Rinse briefly under running water only if absolutely necessary. Cut the truffle into very small dice.

Heat ¼ cup of the olive oil in a pan, and sweat the truffle over medium heat for 10 minutes. Deglaze the pan with the vinegar. Remove from the heat and stir in the stock and the remaining oil. Season with salt, sugar, and nutmeg, and leave to cool.

To make the vegetable accompaniment, remove the tough outer leaves from the artichokes, slice off the tip of each artichoke flat with a sharp knife, and halve the artichokes lengthwise. Scoop out the hairy choke with a small spoon and place the artichokes in plenty of water acidulated with lemon juice to prevent discoloration. Drain well before using.

Heat the oil in a skillet and sauté the garlic, thyme, and artichokes over a medium heat. Add the tomatoes and sauté for a further 3–4 minutes, then season with salt and pepper and set aside.

Preheat the oven to 400°F. Salt and pepper the lamb chops. Brown the meat as shown in the first three steps of the picture sequence. Bake the chops with their rice topping for 10 minutes, then remove from the oven. Proceed as described in the final step of the picture sequence, then gratin the chops briefly under a preheated broiler. Place the cooked lamb chops on warmed plates.

Deglaze the meat juices in the skillet with ⅓ cup water, bring to a boil, and strain. Reduce a little, and season with salt and pepper to taste. Spoon the gravy and the truffle dressing onto the plates with the lamb chops, followed by a portion of artichokes. Shave some truffle thinly over the top, and garnish each plate with a sprig of thyme before serving.

POULTRY &
Cacciagione & pollame

The Italians enjoy a wide range of poultry: chicken, particularly the free-range hens of Tuscany with their firm-textured meat, ducks, geese, and pigeons. Poultry is extremely versatile and tastes excellent whether roasted, braised, or grilled.

The regions of Italy where game is in plentiful supply, like Umbria, Tuscany, Piemonte, Venice and Alto Adige, offer a wide variety of delicious game recipes, especially for *cinghiale*, the wild boar, which is particularly popular in Sardinia.

GAME

Game

Game is very popular everywhere in Italy, but there are clear differences in regional resources. At the tip of "the boot," you will rarely find anything but pigeon, hare, and perhaps the odd wild boar, whereas in Umbria and Tuscany there are plenty of wild boar, deer, hare, and pheasant. Pheasants are also bred in captivity and then released shortly before the hunting season. The north is rather spoiled as far as game is concerned; there are still chamois deer, ibex, and red deer in the Alpine regions. Venison does not often appear in the markets there, but it is sold in specialist shops.

Roe deer

The roe deer, *capriolo*, is the smallest and most common type of deer in Europe. It is found throughout Italy, especially in the wooded foothills of the Alps and the Apennines. Its reddish-brown meat is tender and tasty, and it is often cooked as a *ragù*, flavored with rosemary, juniper, and wine. In Venice it is served *con salsa d'uvetta*, with a sweet-and-sour sauce made from chicken liver, raisins, pine nuts, apples, red wine, and various herbs. It can also be sliced and pan-fried, or braised. Fawns and one-year-old animals provide particularly tender meat, which is especially highly prized.

Fallow deer

The fallow deer, *daino*, is a medium-sized member of the deer family, occurring in the wild in Sardinia, and in game parks. The meat of enclosed animals tends to be a little fattier. In other respects, the meat of the fallow deer resembles that of other types of deer and is used in similar ways. The meat of calves and one-

There are limited numbers of fallow deer in the wild, but they have been living in game parks for centuries. The short-fibered, reddish-brown meat is tender, juicy, slightly spicy and very tasty.

Useful pieces of venison: (from top to bottom) **whole leg of venison,** seen from the underside. It is usually separated into upper and lower leg pieces, and can be roasted or grilled. **Shoulder of venison,** underside, bone in. All bones are removed when the meat is prepared for roasting. **Saddle of venison,** skinned and cut, can be roasted whole or as two fillets.

year-old animals is, again, especially sought after.

Deer

Although the most prevalent member of the deer family in the world, the red deer, *cervo*, is actually very scarce in Italy, except in the national parks of the Alpine regions, in Piemonte, and Friuli. Since the meat is still very popular, it is usually imported from Eastern Europe. The meat is firm, reddish-brown and lean, and it is often marinated in wine and olive oil before braising or roasting, which helps to keep it succulent. Red deer meat is frequently made into a *ragù* or roasted and served with a white wine sauce. In *cervo con salsa di cilegie* the meat is braised with mushrooms, bacon, herbs, and spices. Red deer is equally popular pot-roasted or braised with wine, garlic and lemon.

Chamois and ibex

the meat of chamois, ibex, and wild sheep — particularly that of young animals — is a rare delicacy for the Italians. The goat-like chamois, *camoscio*, is found in the Apennines and especially in the Italian Alps. It can still be found in the Valle d'Aosta and in the Dolomites, probably because chamois hunting in Italy is subject to restrictions. Chamois meat is dark, highly aromatic, and, in the case of older animals, very fatty, which is why young animals are in great demand for cooking. A chamois stew *salmi di camoscio*, for example, tastes excellent with polenta. Salted and air-dried chamois meat — *mucetta, mocetta* or *motzetta* — is a particular delicacy in the Valle d'Aosta, cut into thin slices and served as an antipasto. In earlier times, stronger-tasting ibex meat was the preferred specialty of the region, but not today.

Wild boar

The Italians are very fond of wild boar meat because it is juicy, very firm texture, and leaner than that of the domestic pig. Animals up to one year old and those weighing up to 45 pounds are especially popular. They are made into ragouts or braised; some are roasted whole, like suckling pigs, on a spit or in the oven. Calabria, Abruzzo, Umbria, and especially Tuscany are famous for their excellent wild boar recipes and their delicious wild boar sausages and ham.

Hare and wild rabbit

Both the field, or wild, hare (*congilio selvatico*) and the wild rabbit (*lepre*), the smallest member of the hare family, play a prominent role in Italian cooking. There are numerous recipes for this tender, aromatic meat, from the subtle *lepre all vignarola*, found in Piemonte, to the Sicilian *coniglio alla cacciatora*, in which the meat is braised with capers and olives. Wild rabbit has a more delicate flavor than domestic rabbit.

Wild boar, *cinghiale*, is one of the most popular types of game in Italy. Its meat is not only eaten fresh but also made into a variety of delicious products, particularly in Tuscany.

The wild sheep, *muflone*, with its large curly horns, has become rare in Italy, as elsewhere. A few may still be found in remote mountain regions and in Sardinia.

Ibex, *stambecchi*, love the rocky mountain regions of the Alps and Abruzzo. They are very rare.

Wild rabbit and hare look very similar but can be differentiated by their size, the length of their ears, and the color of their coat. Hares are larger and have longer ears. Wild rabbits have a pale-gray to blue-gray coat.

Guaranteed fresh! Shoppers in Italy can be sure they are buying really fresh meat when live hens are for sale, as in this market in Rome.

Domestic poultry

Duck, goose, turkey, and especially chicken are the most popular types of meat in Italy.

The reasons for their popularity are simple. Firstly, the birds themselves are relatively easy to keep; if you have the space, you can always keep a couple of hens or ducks. Secondly, eggs are a welcome by-product and, thirdly, poultry —especially lean chicken or turkey meat — is very healthy.

In Italy the domestic rabbit, *coniglio*, is generally classified as poultry, and it, too, is very popular. Its light-colored meat is high in protein, low in fat, and easily digestible.

Chicken

As long as the quality of the bird is good, chicken, or *pollo*, is delicious whether boiled, braised, roasted, or grilled. Scarcely any other meat is so readily available or offers such culinary versatility. It is also relatively cheap, and if you have to dig a little deeper in your pocket for a free-range chicken, it is well worth it. It comes as no surprise that there is a huge variety of recipes for chicken, and nearly every region has its own particular specialties. The Italians use *pollo* to describe both male and female birds, but they distinguish them in other ways: *gallina* are laying hens, which finally end up as boiling chicken, weighing around 4½ pounds and guaranteeing a good broth. *Galletto* describes a very young chicken, or Rock Cornish hen, weighing about 1 pound. *Gallo* is the fully grown rooster; its comb is called *creste di gallo*. Some Italian recipes require a fattened chicken, *pollastro*, which can weigh 3–4½ pounds, or the smaller version, *pollastrello* or *pollastrino*, which normally weighs 1¾–2½ pounds. The Italians have numerous recipes using just the breast of the chicken, *petti di*

Chicken that have been kept and fed well, preferably on wheat and corn, are particularly highly prized in Italy because of their firm meat and superior taste. White leghorn hens from Tuscany are especially popular.

In shops, chicken are usually sold ready to cook, but sometimes they are still sold with the head on, probably because some people consider the comb a delicacy.

A flock of geese In Italy, the goose, *oca*, is very popular. It is kept mainly in Piemonte and in Emilia-Romagna, and eaten predominantly in the winter months because of its fatty meat.

pollo. The fleshy capon, *cappone*, weighing 4½–5½ pounds, has a distinctive flavor and very tender meat.

Turkey

The turkey has several names in Italian: *tacchino*, *dindo*, and *pito*. Its meat is very popular, especially the tender, fleshy breast. Scallops or rolled roasts, *rotolo di tacchino*, are taken from the breast. This type of bird is rarely cooked whole — it can weigh 9–15 pounds. A whole bird will be served, usually stuffed, only at large family occasions and, of course, at Christmas. In Lombardy, for example, roast turkey is served with chestnut stuffing, *tacchino arrosto ripieno con castagne*. It is also prepared *in carpione*: the meat is cooked and then left in a marinade of wine, oil, vinegar, and herbs.

Duck

Like their wild relatives, domestic ducks are descended from the mallard duck. The Italians frequently use the domestic duck, *anatra* or *anitra*, in cooking. The meat is not exactly lean, but it has a full, robust flavor that is irresistible when roasted or grilled. Grilling or roasting duck (and goose) on a rack has the advantage that much of the fat can drain off. In Italy, duck is sometimes combined with prosciutto, or is served with fruity sauces, particularly those with a sharp flavor, such as those made with oranges or morello cherries.

Goose

Wild and domestic geese, both descend from the common wild goose or gray goose. In Italy, small white or gray geese are kept for their meat. Depending on the type of food provided and the duration of fattening, they can reach a final weight of 10–12 pounds. In some parts of northern Italy, in Lomellina, for example, a special, larger breed of goose is kept, the Toulouse goose, which is popular for its liver. The Romans loved *fegato grasso*, the Italian counterpart to the French *foie gras*. Although, in the past, goose liver was destined mostly for export, today it plays a greater role in modern Italian cooking.

Goose meat, the fattiest of all types of poultry, has a very distinctive flavor and is especially good when roasted. A traditional meal served in Florence on All Saints Day, the day after Halloween, is *Oca arrosta*, roast goose stuffed with sage, rosemary, and thyme. All visible fat should be removed before cooking the goose, and rendered for use with the goose and in other recipes.

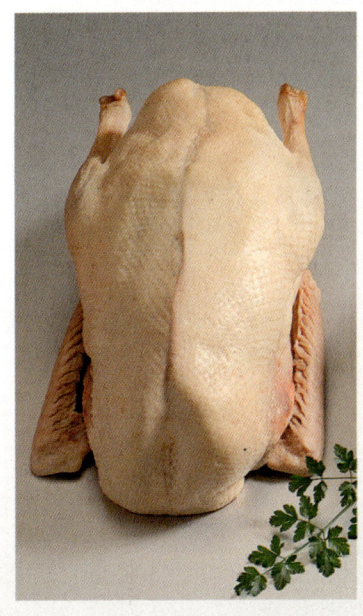

A whole turkey hen (top) weighs a good 13 pounds. The lighter breast meat is more tender than the darker thigh meat, shown diced (above).

A whole duck, *anitra*, (above right) is grilled or roasted. The breast fillets (right) are also popular pan-fried.

A fattened goose, *oca da ingrasso* After intensive rearing lasting about fifteen weeks, a goose weighs 10–12 pounds. Pasture-reared birds are fattened for up to thirty weeks. In spite of this, the birds are then only 2–4½ pounds heavier.

Guinea-fowl, *faraona* in Italian, is a member of the pheasant family. It has been bred for thousands of years, and has dark, tender, and succulent meat.

Guinea-fowl, quail, and wild poultry

Although the mountain (or gray) hen, the woodcock, and the partridge were often found in the wild, they are now largely a protected species. However, they are hunted sparingly in those areas where the fowl population is relatively stable and where there is a increase in numbers. In Italy, some types of wild poultry, such as the pheasant, are bred in captivity and then released shortly before the hunting season. Domesticated birds like guinea-fowl, pigeons, and quail are very popular because of their tender and firm meat.

Guinea-fowl

The guinea-fowl originated in Africa and was well-known to the Romans. With its blue-gray plumage, tipped with silver-white, it is one of the most attractive types of fowl. In Italy different sized guinea-fowl are available: single-portion birds, aged around six weeks and weighing 1–1¼ pounds. After being fattened for twelve weeks, they weigh 2¾ pounds and, when fully grown, they reach a weight of 3¾–4½ pounds. Guinea-fowl have a relatively high proportion of meat or their size and the lowest fat content of any poultry. Young hens are usually roasted, but they need to be covered with bacon to prevent them from becoming dry when cooked. Older birds are better suited to braising. *Faraona alla valcuviana* is a dish from Lombardy in which the guinea-fowl are seasoned with salt, pepper, and herbs, then dotted with butter, wrapped in parchment paper, placed in an earthenware pot, and baked.

Quail

The European quail is the smallest of the common partridges and occurs in the more temperate regions of Europe, particularly in the Mediterranean, and flies to North Africa in the fall. The timid, yellow-gray bird can run as well as it can fly. If it senses danger, it will take off vertically from the fields, like a helicopter. Quails have a good meat yield for their size; 40 percent of the meat is found on the breast, which is far more than in any other type of poultry. The Italians are very fond of quail, wild or domesticated, especially because of its tender meat, but also because of the eggs. Quail is usually cooked whole, and tastes delicious roasted, braised, or grilled. It must be covered with bacon or basted to prevent it from drying out.

Small quails, *quaglie,* are usually sold oven-ready. A portion is generally regarded as two birds, weighing about 4 ounces each. Quails are considered a particular delicacy because their meat is tender and full of flavor.

Pigeon

There are over 300 species of pigeon, but for culinary purposes we need only differentiate between the wild pigeon, *palombaccio* or *colombaccio*, and the domestic pigeon, *colombo* or *piccione*. Fattening pigeons are bred for their meat, of which 26 percent is found on the breast. Squabs ready for roasting weigh 9–14 ounces; their meat is tender and light, one reason why they are considered a delicacy. Older birds are better steamed or stewed, and they also

produce an excellent soup. Umbria is famous for its delicious wild pigeon recipes, including *alla ghiotta*, pigeon rolled in ham and roasted on a spit, and *alla todina*, simply roasted on a spit. The juices are full of flavor, so they are saved and made into a delicious sauce.

The meat of the domestic pigeon is delicate and not gamey. It is very popular and is bred almost everywhere in Italy.

Pheasant

The Romans brought the pheasant to Europe from Asia. Today it continues to be extremely popular in Italy. Most

weigh about 3 pounds, and older males only about 8 ounces more. The lighter female, weighing 1½–2¼ pounds when young and up to 3 pounds when older, tastes more aromatic. With their delicate dark meat

Ringed dove is the most common species of wild pigeon. Its dark, game-like meat is more highly prized in Italy than that of the domestic pigeon.

with truffles, or as *fagiano rincartato*: flavored with juniper and baked in parchment paper.

Wild duck

The mallard is the most common wild duck. The birds, which are either wild or come from breeding stations, weigh 2¼–3 pounds and are hunted in from September to January. The wild duck, *anitra selva* in Italian, is less fleshy than the fattened domestic duck, and its skin and meat are darker, more aromatic, and less fatty. The skin of these wild birds is removed with the feathers, to protect the meat from contamination with river pollutants that cannot be washed off. Wild ducks can be served whole, in pieces, or breasted, either roasted or braised. In Italy, wild ducks are also cooked in the same way as domestic birds, but the less fatty flesh is frequently covered with bacon or basted during roasting so that it does not dry out during cooking.

Wild goose

The gray goose, from which the domestic goose is descended, is the most common and the largest European wild goose. It is the only goose in Europe that incubates its eggs, and it is a migratory bird. The age of a wild goose, or *oca selvatica* in Italian, can be distinguished in the same way as that of the mallard (see right). Wild geese and those from breeding stations are hunted in late fall. Their meat is more muscular, less fatty, and less succulent than the that of the domestic goose, but has a good flavor. They are roasted whole, sometimes stuffed, or cut up and braised.

Colorful pheasant, *fagiano*, is one of the most popular species of wild poultry. Only the male sports colored plumage; the female is brown-gray. Pheasants are found in the wild in Italy, but are also bred in large numbers.

male pheasants come from the wild and their meat is pleasantly firm. Young males, which can be recognized by their short, tapered and truncated spurs,

and exquisite wild flavor, pheasants are very popular in the northern and central regions. In Tuscany and Piemonte pheasant is eaten

Amongst wild ducks, mallards are the most widespread. The drake can be distinguished from the brown-feathered duck by its bottle-green, iridescent head and the white ring around its neck. Young ducks, not yet one year old, are especially highly sought-after for cooking, and these can be recognized by their reddish-honey-colored beaks and the dark, gray-green webs. They later change color to orange-red, in their second year.

Ham and sausages made from game and poultry

Game ham and sausages are culinary delicacies in Italy and elsewhere because of both their low calorie content and their excellent and subtly spiced flavor. In some places they are difficult to come by, but in regions such as Tuscany and Umbria, they are one of the staple meats on offer in the *salumerie*, *macellerie*, and *pizzicherie*, as the Italians call their delicatessens. In Capalbio, in the southernmost part of Tuscany, a summer "celebration of the wild boar" is held in the open air. A variety of wild boar dishes simmer for hours in large vats on open fires, and a delicious aroma envelops the little town on the hill. There are also numerous stalls offering ham and sausages made from the delicate meat of the wild boar.

Leg meat from roe and red deer, and saddle fillets of hoofed game are also processed into the most delicious ham-like meats.

The Tuscans have made a name for themselves by preserving game in salt and brine. Smoked meat is also found in this region; one famous example is *prosciutto di cinghiale*, cured and dried wild boar ham, which develops its unique, delicately spiced flavor over a maturing period of an entire year. Wild boar ham can also come from the saddle of the animal, and it is then sold as *filetto di cinghiale*. Other meat products, for example, salami, are made from wild boars, which are prevalent in Maremma. In many places, you will find the small, aromatic *salame di cinghiale*, occasionally also seasoned with fennel seeds, when it is known as *cinghiale e finocchio*. There is also a larger, thicker *finocchiona di cinghiale*, the popular fennel salami. Butchers also sell *salsiccia cinghiale*, a wild boar sausage. Some butchers specialize exclusively in this highly sought-after range of delicatessen products. Sometimes they cannot keep up with the great demand for these game products, which require a

Prosciutti di cinghiale (left), a Tuscan specialty, is particularly noticeable because of its unusual appearance. To make a ham of this kind, the wild boar is cut in half lengthwise. The rear half and the leg remain in the skin. The exposed meat is rubbed with garlic and curing salt, and left to cure in the air for 6 months. It is then left for another 6 months in wood ashes, where it develops its fine flavor. A smoked ham of wild boar (inset).

long maturing period to perfect their flavor.

Meat remaining from legs, shoulder, neck, and ribs is generally used for game salami. As a rule, a certain amount of bacon and pork must be added to bind the sausage — it would be too dry and brittle if it were made just from game. Although game should normally be cooked thoroughly and never eaten raw, this does not apply to sausage and ham, as the curing process makes them safe to eat. This process can be seen as the meat slowly changes color from gray to dark red during the drying phase. Although some types of salami-like sausage, such as *finocchiona*, should be used relatively quickly after being cut, the combination of curing and smoking enables ham and sausage to keep well for months.

Goose salami from Lomellina This *salame d'oca*, or *ecumenico* salami, made by Gioachino Palestro is one of the best sausage specialties in Italy. Served with a glass of chilled, dry Pinot Brut and crisp, fresh bread, it is a rare delicacy.

This same is true of the poultry specialties found mainly in the north of Italy, such as smoked breast of duck and goose. Smoking is usually the best method of preserving the fatty meat of waterfowl, but it is also used for leaner turkey meat. Other individual pieces of meat, such as legs, can be preserved in this way, as can a whole small rooster. Smoked poultry is a useful cooking ingredient: It adds an interesting flavor to some dishes and is less rich than bacon. Goose salami from Lomellina - the narrow stretch of land between Piemonte and Lombardy that is also famous for its rice, is produced in a different way. The stuffed neck of goose is just dried, not smoked. Gioachino Palestro aims for absolute quality: he leaves his excellent goose salami to hang for three months in the refrigerating room before he finally sells it as a great delicacy.

Daniele Patestro from Mortara making his fine goose salami. He stuffs the long neck of the goose just as it was done 500 years ago.

Only the breast, the best part of the goose, is used by Palestro in his special salami. Other manufacturers also use other parts of the goose.

Dried venison salami, made from a combination of lean venison and pork fat with fine grains.

Smoked breast of duck with a thin coating of fat. The firm meat can be sliced very thinly. Goose breast is also suitable for smoking.

Ham of roe deer, highly smoked and spiced, from the hills of northern Italy. This very tender ham can be cut a little thicker when served as an antipasto.

Gnocchi with ragout of roe deer
Potato gnocchi make an excellent accompaniment for this spicy game ragout

In northern Italy, for example in the region around Verona, the Italians really know how to make gnocchi. It is important to leave the dough to stand for only a short while and then work quickly with it.

Dark-red, short-fibered roe deer leg meat is particularly well suited to this ragout, but meat from wild boar, red deer, or chamois, or even poultry such as pheasant or duck may be used instead.

Serves 4
For the ragout:
1¼ lb boneless venison leg
5–6 tablespoons oil, 2–3 tablespoons tomato paste
1⅔ cups red wine, 1 garlic clove
12 oz tomatoes, peeled, seeded, and diced
4 oz pearl onions
⅔ cup chopped leek, ⅓ cup chopped carrot
½ cup chopped celery
1 strip orange zest
1–2 sprigs thyme, 3–4 sage leaves
1¾ cups game stock, salt, freshly ground pepper

The attractive pattern on the home-made gnocchi is made by pressing the dough over a grater. The pattern enables the gnocchi to hold the sauce, and so they make a good accompaniment to the ragout.

Tomatoes and typically Italian herbs, such as thyme and sage, bring a southern flavor to this dish. The herb sprigs and leaves are removed before serving. It is well worth trying this recipe with other types of wild game.

For the gnocchi:
1¼ lb floury potatoes, ¾ cup all-purpose flour
1 egg yolk, salt
You will also need:
1 tablespoon chopped parsley

Preheat the oven to 400°F. Trim the meat and cut into ½–¾-inch dice. Heat the oil in a large saucepan and sear the meat over a high heat. Stir in the tomato paste and cook briefly, then add the wine. Cover and simmer for 25–30 minutes. In the meantime, wrap the potatoes in aluminum foil and bake for about 1 hour.

Add the garlic, vegetables, orange zest, and herbs to the pot, then pour in the stock. Season with salt and pepper, and simmer for 30 minutes, stirring occasionally.

Remove the potatoes from the oven, unwrap, and let cool before peeling. Sift the flour onto a work surface and make a well in the center. Add the egg yolk and salt, then press the warm potatoes through a strainer, making a ring of potato around the top of the flour. Quickly knead to a smooth dough, then set aside for 10–15 minutes.

Roll the dough into 2 lengths about ¾ inch in diameter and dust with flour. Cut into ½-inch pieces and press each of these over a grater to make a lattice pattern. Place a portion of gnocchi in gently boiling water and reduce the heat. As soon as the gnocchi rise to the surface, remove them from the water, drain well, and keep hot. Serve the gnocchi with the ragout, garnished with parsley.

Wild boar ragout

Served with delicate red wine figs, a good red wine being the recommended drink with this dish.

A 24-hour marinade made from vegetables, spices and a good red wine complements the flavor of the wild boar superbly and tenderizes the meat. The wine is not wasted, as the marinade liquid forms the basis of the sauce.

The concern that wild-boar meat may have an unpleasantly powerful smell or taste applies only to older animals during the mating season. For this reason and because it is more tender, the Italians, among others, prefer the meat of younger animals, those under one or, at most, two years old. In this case, the thin layer of fat can also be left on the meat.

Serves 4
2¼ lb boneless shoulder of wild boar, cut into 1¼-inch dice
3 tablespoons vegetable oil, 1½ tablespoons flour
1 cup game stock, generous pinch dried ginger
5 allspice berries, pounded in a mortar and pestle
salt, freshly ground white pepper
For the marinade:
¾ cup diced carrot, 1½ cups diced onion
⅔ cup diced celery root
1 teaspoon white peppercorns, 4 crushed juniper berries
4 teaspoons gin
4½ cups good red wine, e.g. a Barolo
For the figs in red wine:
2¼ cups red wine, e.g. a Recioto Valpolicella Classico
¼ cup sugar, 2-inch cinnamon stick, juice of ½ lemon
pinch salt, 1 small rosemary sprig
8 ripe figs

Place the diced meat and vegetables in a dish, add the peppercorns and juniper berries, pour the gin and the red wine over them, cover with plastic wrap, and leave to marinate for 24 hours.

Lift the meat from the marinade with a fork and pat dry. Strain the marinade, reserving the liquid. Drain the vegetables well.

Heat the oil in a large saucepan, and brown the meat evenly all over, stirring constantly. Add the drained vegetables, and sauté over a high heat till an even light brown. Sprinkle the flour over the meat and vegetables. Pour in 1 cup of the marinading liquid, followed by the game stock, and simmer the ragout over a moderate heat.

After 40–50 minutes, tip the contents of the pot into a strainer, reserving the braising liquid and the meat separately. Strain the sauce back into the pot, season with salt, pepper, dried ginger, and allspice, and keep warm.

To make the figs in red wine, bring the wine to a boil in a saucepan with the sugar, cinnamon stick, lemon juice, and salt. Add the rosemary sprig, and cook until the liquid is reduced by half. Meanwhile, preheat the oven to 350°F. Wash the figs, pat dry, and cut a cross in the bottom of each. Place the figs in the reduced syrup, and bake, covered, for 10 minutes.

Add the meat to the sauce and heat through. Arrange the meat with some sauce on warmed plates, spoon figs to the side, and serve.

Wild boar ragout is a popular dish wherever wild boars are found, for example, in Umbria, Abruzzo, Sardinia, and Sicily. Tuscany is especially well-known for its wild boar specialties, and there, wild boar ragout and products such as wild boar ham and salami are firm favorites.

Fresh, tasty figs harvested in southern Italy and they are the key ingredient in one of the best accompaniments to game and wildfowl: figs in red wine.

366 GAME & POULTRY

The ripening time for the elder coincides with the beginning of the game season. Elderberries are often served with venison, chamois and wild boar — usually in a compote — because their strong flavor. goes particularly well with this robust type of game.

Paillard of venison
Paper-thin slices of loin, served with ceps and vegetables

A paillard is usually made from veal or beef fillet, but the special cutting technique can also be used for delicate game meat, such as venison. A piece of loin is cut deeply at regular intervals of ¼–½ inch, but the meat is severed only at every second cut. Flattened and briefly pan-fried in a mixture of oil and butter, the meat tastes delicious. Extremely high-quality meat and very careful handling are of prime importance.

Basting during cooking with a mixture of butter and oil prevents the venison from drying out and adds flavor.

Serves 4
1¾ cups game stock, 1 lb loin of venison
1½ celery stalks
1 small carrots
14 oz cep mushrooms
⅔ cup finely chopped onion
1 garlic clove, finely chopped
¼ chopped parsley root
3 tablespoons vegetable oil,
2 tablespoons butter
2 tablespoons chopped parsley
salt, freshly ground pepper
You will also need:
plastic wrap
parsley leaves

Pour the game stock into a large heavy-based casserole dish, boil, and reduce to ⅔ cup.

Carefully trim the loin of venison, removing all skin and sinews. Cut the meat deeply at ¼-inch intervals, but sever the meat only at every second cut. There should be 12 portions of meat, each with two thin slices joined together along one edge.

Place a piece of plastic wrap on a work surface, spread out the joined slices of meat on it, and cover with another piece of plastic wrap. Flatten the slices to an equal thickness, using a meat hammer, and keep cool until required.

Cut the carrot and celery into strips about 2 inches long. Clean the ceps carefully, not washing them if possible, and slice them.

Heat 1 tablespoon oil in a large skillet and sweat the onion and garlic. Then add the carrot, celery, and parsley root, and sweat over a reduced heat for 2–3 minutes. Add 2 teaspoons butter and the ceps, and cook for a further 2 minutes. Sprinkle the salt, pepper, and half of the parsley over the contents of the pan.

Heat the remaining oil in another skillet, add the rest of the butter, and heat until frothy. Gently fry the 12 portions of meat in batches, adding salt and pepper, and basting constantly with the oil and butter mixture. Turn the venison slices and cook the second side gently, again basting constantly and adding salt and pepper.

Place one portion of venison on each warmed plate and spoon over some of the vegetable and mushroom mixture. Lay a second portion of venison diagonally across the top, again covering with a little of the vegetables and mushrooms. Finally cover diagonally with a third portion of venison.

Reheat the reduced stock, season with salt and pepper to taste, and pour over the meat. Sprinkle on the remaining chopped parsley, garnish with the parsley leaves, and serve.

Rosemary, garlic and bacon complement the delicate flavor of the rabbit legs really well. The meat is first browned on the stove and then finished off in the oven, which enables the flavors to develop fully.

Rabbit, rabbit

Rabbit legs roasted with rosemary and bacon, and a whole rabbit braised with olives, herbs, and white wine

In Italy rabbits are one of the most popular types of meat. If the Italians have space at home, they will often keep the friendly animals themselves, otherwise they will buy good-quality meat. Rabbits are sold whole or in individual pieces. The legs of young fattened rabbits are the most tasty and are also the best value.

ROAST RABBIT WITH ROSEMARY

Serves 2

2 rabbit legs
salt, freshly ground white pepper
2 small cloves garlic, 4 sprigs rosemary
4 thin slices pancetta
3 tablespoons vegetable oil
1 shallot, halved
knobs of butter

Preheat the oven to 420°F. Wash the rabbit legs under cold running water and carefully pat dry with paper towels. Season with salt and pepper.

Depending on the intensity of flavor required, either cut the garlic into pointed shapes and insert into the rabbit, or thinly slice and place under the bacon. Tie the rosemary, possibly the garlic slices, and the bacon around the rabbit legs as shown in the picture above. Heat the oil in a heavy-based casserole and brown the legs and the halved shallot on all sides. Remove from the heat, dot with butter and roast for about 20 minutes. Serve hot from the oven.

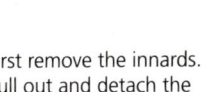

Preparing a rabbit

BRAISED WILD RABBIT

Serves 4

1 wild rabbit, ½ teaspoon salt, white pepper
1 tablespoon flour, ¼ cup olive oil,
¾ cup finely chopped shallot
2 garlic cloves, finely chopped
⅓ cup finely diced carrot, ½ cup finely chopped celery
½ cup chopped scallion, ½ cup white wine
½ teaspoon ground allspice
pinch each ground ginger and nutmeg
½ teaspoon crushed coriander
1⅔ cups game stock; 10 black olives, halved and pitted
1 tablespoon chopped parsley
½ teaspoon chopped rosemary
1 tablespoon chopped thyme, 1 teaspoon chopped oregano

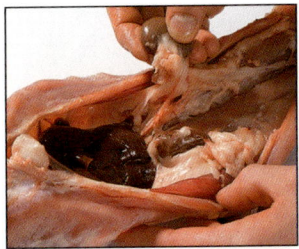

First remove the innards. Pull out and detach the heart, liver, and kidneys. Carefully pull off the thin fatty skins surrounding the kidneys. Cut off the head.

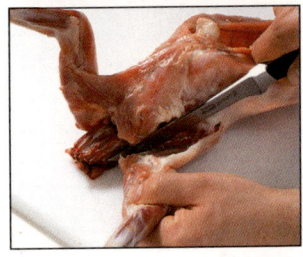

Cut into the foreleg sockets, twist the legs, and cut through the joint. Cut up the ribcage and separate the saddle.

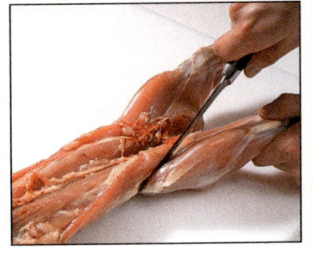

Separate the hind legs above the pelvic bones. Detach the hind legs where they begin to join the saddle.

Preheat the oven to 400°F. Prepare the rabbit, as shown on the right. Wash the pieces and pat them dry. Remove all skin, season with salt and pepper, and dust with flour.

Heat the oil in a heavy-based casserole, brown the meat all over, and remove. With the exception of the garlic, sweat all the vegetables in the remaining oil, return the rabbit pieces to the casserole, and add the garlic and wine. Sprinkle the allspice, ginger, nutmeg, and coriander on top and braise in the oven for 20 minutes. Pour over some of the stock, and add the olives and herbs. Braise for another 15–20 minutes, basting often and adding more game stock, if necessary. Remove from the oven and serve.

Squab kebabs
In Italy, all types of poultry are cooked as kebabs, *allo spiedo*

Squabs are a popular main dish in Italy because of the aromatic sauce, which takes its flavor from the fine meat. This dish from the Veneto is also very impressive because of its bread, herb, and cheese stuffing.

Serves 4
4 small, fleshy squabs
For the spiced oil:
10 juniper berries, 2 bay leaves, ¼ cup olive oil
salt, freshly ground white pepper
For the stuffing:
1 day-old roll, crust removed
2 tablespoons butter, ¼ cup diced onion
½ garlic clove, crushed
¼ cup diced pancetta
½ cup milk, 1 egg
1 tablespoon chopped sage
thyme and rosemary
salt, freshly ground white pepper
½ cup diced Gruviera or Gruyère cheese

Pour the lukewarm milk over the slices of roll and leave to soak.

Add the egg, half the herbs, and the onion and pancetta mixture. Season with salt and pepper.

Add the fried croutons and the cheese. Mix all the ingredients together well.

You will also need:
12 slices pancetta
chopped thyme, rosemary and sage

Wash the squabs inside and out, pat dry, set aside. Chop the juniper berries and bay leaves, and stir into the olive oil.

To make the stuffing, cut half of the roll into slices and dice the other into ¼-inch cubes. Melt half of the butter in a skillet and fry the cubes until golden.

Heat the rest of the butter in another skillet and sweat the onion, garlic, and diced pancetta. Prepare the stuffing as shown in the illustrations above. Stuff the body cavity and sew the opening closed, or secure with toothpicks.

Wrap 4 slices of pancetta around each squab and tie with kitchen string. Place on skewers, brush with the spiced oil, and grill over glowing wood ashes. Brush with the oil during cooking and sprinkle with chopped herbs.

Aromatic rosemary, appears in many dishes from southern Italy. Its pungent flavor goes very well with grilled squab, but you must be careful not to use too much.

Braised pheasant
Wild duck or wild goose can also be cooked in this way

SALMI OF PHEASANT

Serves 4

2 pheasants (1¾–2¼ lb each)
3 tablespoons vegetable oil, 3 tablespoons butter
3 shallots, sliced in rings, 2 teaspoons Cognac
4 teaspoons truffle stock, ½ cup white wine
3¼ cups wildfowl stock; 1 oz black truffles, sliced
12 button mushroom heads, crimped
salt, freshly ground white pepper,

Preheat the oven to 375°F. Wash the pheasants, pat dry, and season with salt and pepper. Heat the oil in a flameproof casserole and brown the pheasants on all sides. Transfer to the oven and roast for about 30 minutes. Remove the pheasants from the oven and cut the meat into pieces, removing all skin and sinews. Reduce the heat and keep the meat hot.

Chop up the carcasses. Melt half the butter and sweat the shallot until translucent. Briefly fry the bones. Pour in the Cognac, truffle stock, and wine, and reduce a little. Add the wildfowl stock and simmer for 10 minutes. Strain the contents of the pan, reheat the sauce, and reduce by half. Melt the remaining butter

Pheasant legs and breast served with a little delicate red wine sauce .Figs in red wine (see page 364) are an excellent accompaniment to this dish.

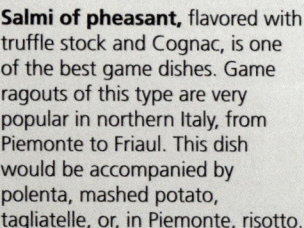

Salmi of pheasant, flavored with truffle stock and Cognac, is one of the best game dishes. Game ragouts of this type are very popular in northern Italy, from Piemonte to Friaul. This dish would be accompanied by polenta, mashed potato, tagliatelle, or, in Piemonte, risotto.

in a skillet, season, and sauté the truffles with the meat and button mushroom heads. Pour the sauce over, bring quickly to a boil, and serve.

BRAISED PHEASANT IN A FINE SAUCE

Serves 4
1 pheasant (about 3 lb), 2 tablespoons vegetable oil
¾ cup diced carrot, 1 cup diced onion
½ cup chopped celery, 10 oz tomatoes, roughly chopped
1 tablespoon flour
2¼ cups red wine, 5 allspice corns, 4 white peppercorns
2 cloves, 1 bay leaf
grated zest of 1 lemon, salt, white pepper

Wash the pheasant and pat dry. Remove the legs and breast, trim, and season with salt and pepper. Cut the carcass into small pieces. Heat the oil in a saucepan, brown the legs and breast all over, then remove. Brown the carcass in the same pan. Add the vegetables and cook until they are an even golden color. Add the tomatoes and braise until nearly all the liquid has evaporated. Dust with flour, let it burn slightly. add a third of the wine and heat, stirring constantly. Repeat this process twice more.

Add cold water to barely cover the contents of the pot and bring to a boil. Place the pheasant legs in the liquid, simmer for 5 minutes over a low heat, then add the breast. Using a pestle and mortar, coarsely grind the allspice, peppercorns, and clove, and add to the pot with the bay leaf and lemon zest. Cover and braise for 10–12 minutes over a low heat. Remove the meat and keep hot. Strain and reduce the stock, season and, if necessary, thicken slightly. Heat the pheasant breast and legs in the sauce and serve.

Braised duck

One recipe with duck braised in red wine, flavored with thyme, and one with duck braised in its own juices, flavored with orange

Braising is a particularly good method of cooking poultry, especially duck, as the meat remains tender and succulent. In some recipes, such as those below, the duck is marinated first, in others it is not. In either case, the meat is briefly seared before braising.

DUCK BRAISED IN RED WINE WITH THYME

Serves 4

1 duck (3½–4 lb)
1 teaspoon salt
2 teaspoons roughly chopped thyme leaves
2 tablespoons vegetable oil

A good accompaniment to this dish would be homemade noodles and zucchini or eggplant.

¼ cup butter
4 shallots, finely chopped
1 garlic clove, finely chopped
¼ cup finely diced celery root
1 cup finely chopped leek
1 cup dry red wine
1 cup dark duck or other wildfowl stock
¼ cup heavy cream
freshly ground white pepper

Preheat the oven to 375°F. Wash the duck inside and out and pat dry. Cut into 4–8 pieces of about equal size. Place the pieces in a dish, sprinkle with salt, pepper, and the thyme, then cover and leave to marinate for about 1 hour.

Heat the oil and 2 tablespoons of the butter in a large flameproof casserole and brown the duck on all sides. Add the shallots, garlic, celery root, and leek, and sauté for about 10 minutes. Add the red wine and braise, uncovered, for about 10 minutes.

Add the stock, cover the casserole dish, transfer to the oven, and braise for about 1 hour. Take out the duck pieces and keep hot.

Strain the sauce, pressing through as much of the vegetables as possible. Skim the fat from the sauce and reduce to about a quarter.

Beat in the cream with a wire whisk, adding further seasoning if necessary. Cut the remaining butter into pieces and whisk into the sauce. Serve the duck in the sauce, or hand around the sauce separately.

DUCK LEGS IN A DARK SAUCE

This dish tastes best made with wild ducks, which are leaner and firmer than domestic ducks. Try to select the youngest birds possible when purchasing. You will need the legs and carcasses of 2 ducks. If you cannot buy the pieces individually, buy 2 small ducks, cut them up yourself, and use the breast meat in another recipe. Fruity flavors, such as black currant and, as suggested here, orange, harmonize particularly well with the dark, rich duck meat.

Serves 4

4 duck legs (4½ oz each
2 tablespoons vegetable oil
carcasses of 2 ducks
1 onion, roughly chopped
1 carrot, roughly chopped
1½ celery stalks, roughly chopped
1 teaspoon tomato paste
1 tablespoon flour
1 orange
1 bay leaf
4 juniper berries, 2 cloves
salt, freshly ground black pepper

Thoroughly wash the legs and carcasses under cold running water, and pat dry. Season the legs with salt and pepper. Heat the oil in a large heavy-based saucepan, brown the legs on all sides, then remove.

Chop the carcasses into small pieces. Brown them in the hot oil, and proceed as shown in the first two pictures on the right.

In the meantime, peel the orange, separating the zest from the pith. Cut the zest into fine strips, blanch in boiling water, remove, and drain. Cut the orange into segments, reserving any juice, and set aside.

As soon as the water has been added, return the duck legs to the pot, add the bay leaf, juniper berries, and cloves, and simmer, covered, over a low heat. Then proceed as shown in the last three pictures on the right.

Add the onion, carrot, and celery to the duck carcasses and sauté gently until golden.

Stir in the tomato paste, dust with the flour, cook briefly, then add cold water until all the ingredients are just covered.

After 1–1½ hours, remove the duck legs and strain the cooking liquid into a deep skillet

Return the duck legs to the sauce, pour over any orange juice, and season with salt and pepper.

Arrange the duck legs on warmed plates with the orange segments, add the sauce, and serve with a spoonful of vegetable rice, if you wish.

Lemon pigeons

Northern Italian cuisine at its best: pigeons with gremolata and polenta cakes

Gremolata, also known as *cremolata* or *cremolada*, is a classic spicy herb mixture from Lombardy. It normally includes finely chopped garlic, grated lemon zest, and chopped parsley.

Serves 4
4 pigeons (about 11 oz each)
2 tablespoons olive oil, 3 tablespoons butter
salt, freshly ground white pepper
For the gremolata:
2 garlic cloves, very finely chopped
zest of ½ a lemon, finely chopped
2 tablespoons finely chopped parsley
For the polenta cakes (makes about 20):
1 teaspoon salt, 1⅓ cups cornmeal
¼ cup butter, ¼ cup white bread crumbs
¼ cup freshly grated Parmesan cheese
1 tablespoon chopped herbs (parsley, oregano, thyme)
For the sauce:
½ cup poultry stock, 1 teaspoon lemon juice
¼ cup butter, salt, freshly ground pepper
You will also need:
butter for greasing

Preheat the oven to 420°F. Thoroughly wash the pigeons, inside and out, carefully pat dry, then season with salt and pepper. Truss the pigeons tightly to retain their original shape, tucking the wings underneath and running the trussing string around the thighs and crossing it over the parson's nose.

To make the gremolata, mix the garlic and lemon zest in a bowl with the parsley, and set aside.

To make the polenta, bring 2¼ cups salted water to a boil in a large saucepan. Carefully trickle the cornmeal into the water, stirring constantly and keeping the water bubbling all the time so that no lumps can form. Continue stirring, always in the same direction if possible. When the mixture begins to thicken, the hard work really begins; the polenta will take 20 minutes to cook, and it will stick to the bottom and the sides of the pot unless it is stirred continuously.

Turn the polenta out onto a wet board and, using a palette knife, spread it out to a thickness of about ½ inch. Leave to cool slightly. Grease a baking sheet with butter. Using a plain, round pastry cutter about 2 inches in diameter, cut out the polenta cakes and place them on the baking sheet. Melt some of the butter in a skillet, stir in the bread crumbs, Parmesan, and herbs, and then evenly distribute the mixture over the polenta cakes, using a spoon. Bake in the oven for about 15 minutes.

Reduce the oven temperature to 400°F. Heat the oil and the remaining butter in a flameproof casserole. Place the pigeons in the casserole, with the breast up, and carefully brush them with the oil and butter mixture. Roast, uncovered, for 20 minutes. Take the pigeons out of the casserole and keep hot.

To make the sauce, strain off the oil and put the casserole on the stove. Pour in the stock and lemon juice, season with salt and pepper, bring to a boil, and stir to loosen the roasting sediment. Whisk in the butter in small pieces. Arrange the pigeons on warmed plates, sprinkle with the gremolata, and serve with the sauce and polenta cakes.

The gremolata gives the pigeons a special fresh spicy flavor. Homemade polenta cakes with a tasty topping of white bread crumbs, Parmesan cheese, and herbs make a good accompaniment.

In the market In Italy the hens are sometimes sold by live weight.

Pollo alla sienese
A delicious braised chicken dish from Siena, with black olives, garlic and sage

The Piazzo del Campo in Siena is one of the most famous piazzas in Italy. Here every year this medieval town celebrates its past with the spectacular *palio*, a centuries-old horse race, in which the whole town participates, one part competing against another. As well as its past and its beautiful buildings — including the magnificent cathedral dome that dominates the landscape, and the high tower of the Town Hall, the Torre del Mangia — Siena boasts a fine cuisine.

The town lies in the middle of the great fruit-farming area of Tuscany, and the black olives grown there are reputed to be the best in the world. The olives, combined with the braised chicken and sage, give this dish its typical Tuscan flavor. Ideally, serve it with a mild white wine, such as a Galestro, a Vernaccia di San Gimignano, or a Montecarlo from the Lucca region.

Serves 4
1 chicken (3 lb)
1 tablespoon flour
¼ cup olive oil
2 tablespoons butter
3 garlic cloves, finely chopped
6 small sage leaves
½ cup white wine
½ cup chicken stock
¾ cup black olives, pitted
salt, freshly ground white pepper

Thoroughly wash the chicken, inside and out, and carefully pat dry. Using a kitchen knife or poultry scissors, cut the bird into 8 pieces: First, free the leg by carefully cutting the skin between the body and the leg with a large, sharp knife. Cut through the skin as far as the joint, bending the leg outward with the hand. Twist the leg until the ball of the joint springs out. Cut through the joint, pressing lightly. Separate the wing at the shoulder joint, cutting off a small part of the breast with it. Press quite firmly to split the

A light, dry Tuscan wine is perfect both for cooking and for serving with the meal.

collarbone, then divide the back parallel to the backbone. To separate the breasts, carefully cut left and right along the length of the breastbone.

Season all the chicken pieces with salt and pepper, and lightly coat them with flour.

Heat the oil and the butter in a large flameproof casserole and brown the chicken pieces on all sides. Add the garlic and the sage leaves, and fry with the meat. Pour over the wine and the chicken stock, then add salt and pepper to taste. Cover, and simmer for about 20 minutes.

Cut the olives into strips, add them to the chicken pieces in the casserole, and cook for a further 20 minutes. Season to taste, then serve with fresh bread and a glass of chilled white wine.

Stuffed Rock Cornish hens
These young chickens taste wonderful, stuffed with delicate mixture of walnuts, pine nuts, and goose liver

Small birds can be boned before stuffing, but this does take a little time and skill. Pull the skin back at the neck end and work all the bones free, one by one. The meat and skin can then be pulled back into shape. Alternatively, the chicken skin can be slit along the backbone and all the bones worked free, then the bird can be stuffed and sewn up into its original shape.

Serves 4

4 Rock Cornish hens (14 oz each), salt, pepper
For the stuffing:
4 slices crustless white bread, ½ cup lukewarm milk
⅔ cup diced unsmoked bacon, ⅓ cup finely diced shallot
1½ cups chopped walnuts,
¾ cup pine nuts, ¼ cup freshly grated Parmesan cheese
¼ teaspoon freshly ground nutmeg
1 tablespoon chopped herbs (lemon thyme, parsley)
2 eggs, 5½ oz fresh goose liver, salt, pepper
For the stock:
¼ cup chopped onion, ⅓ cup chopped carrot
¼ cup chopped parsley root
½ cup chopped leek, ⅓ cup chopped tomatoes
1 bay leaf, 5 white peppercorns, salt
You will also need:
2 tablespoons oil, 1 teaspoon chopped herbs

Mix together in a bowl the bread, walnuts, pine nuts, bacon, shallots, Parmesan, nutmeg, herbs, and eggs. Remove skin and sinews from the goose liver, cut into ½-inch cubes, mix with the other ingredients and season. to taste.

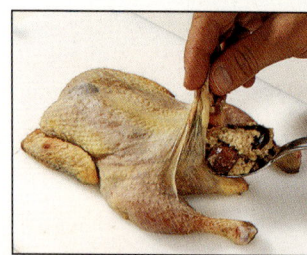

Using a spoon, stuff the hens, taking care not to fill them so full that the stuffing squeezes out during cooking.

To make the stock, put the vegetables, bay leaf, and peppercorns into a saucepan of salted water and bring to a boil. Add the hens, reduce the heat, and simmer for 10 minutes.

Bone the Rock Cornish hens, leaving the leg and wing bones in. Pull the skin at the neck end back over the carcass, carefully strip and twist out the collar bone. Make a slit in the skin on the underside (backbone side) and loosen each thigh bone using a sharp knife. Break the thigh bone away from the shoulder and pull it out. Working from the underside, loosen the meat from the shoulder along the backbone, and cut it away from the hip joint. Turn the bird over and work the breast meat free from the carcass. Free the backbone, cutting it at the parson's nose, and carefully pull out and discard the breastbone.

To make the stuffing, dice the bread, soak it in the milk, then drain it. Fry the bacon in a non-stick pan until slightly brown, then add the shallots and fry until golden. Proceed as shown in the first three pictures on the left.

Preheat the oven to 400°F. Secure the skin around the opening of the stuffed birds with toothpicks. Wind kitchen string around the toothpicks, knotting it on the last one. Season the hens with salt and pepper, then follow the instructions to the last small picture. Remove the birds from the pot, and strain and reserve the stock. Transfer the birds to a roasting pan, brush with oil, and roast for 20 minutes, basting occasionally. Remove the birds from the oven, arrange on warmed plates, and sprinkle with chopped herbs.

To make the sauce, place the roasting pan on the stove over a medium heat. Add 1¼ cups of the reserved stock, stirring to loosen the roasting sediment. Reduce by half, season to taste, and serve separately.

dolci DESSERTS

From delicately melting and cool, to crisp-fried and hot, the range of Italian desserts, or *dolci*, offers something for every taste. Just how much time you devote to creating the sweet highpoint of a meal is up to you; for dessert, Italians are as likely to place a bowl of sweet, juicy fruit on the table as they are a refreshing ice cream or sorbet, or a carefully layered *zuppa inglese*. Often, though, Italian desserts mean baking, so you will also find recipes for simple cookies and sophisticated cakes in this chapter.

Citrus fruits — fragrant and juicy

The ancestors of modern citrus fruits — lemons, oranges, and mandarins — originated in Southeast Asia, where the first varieties were being cultivated some 4,000 years ago. The citron was the first citrus fruit to become known in Europe, in the fourth century BC, not because of its juice or flesh, but because of the volatile oil contained in its peel, which was sought after for the manufacture of perfume. Even in ancient Rome, lemons were the only citrus fruit known. Enchanting murals in the towns of Campania buried by the eruption of Vesuvius in AD 79 show that lemon trees were grown then in ornamental gardens for their fragrant blossom, even though the attractive fruits were not yet being put to culinary use. It is believed that the Arabs brought the first, although still sour, varieties of oranges to the western half of the Mediterranean, with mandarin oranges following on as latecomers in the nineteenth century.

Yellow and sour

Lemons (*limoni*) are an integral part of Italian cooking. They are grown on a large scale in the country, although not everywhere. Only in the south of Italy, for instance in Campania and Calabria, and in Sardinia and Sicily, are conditions exactly right for their growth. In fact, lemons are cultivated in such large quantities in Sicily that they can be exported. Usually, lemons are harvested for export before they are fully ripe, but continue to ripen without a hitch if they are stored in a cool, dry place; under optimum conditions, they will keep for up to 6 months. Both the sour juice and the thinly pared or grated aromatic zest of unsprayed fruits are used often and lavishly in Italy: the juice instead of vinegar in salad dressings, for marinating fish and meat, or for drizzling over cooked seafood; the zest, chiefly in desserts and baking. The thick, white inner peel of the large citron, known as *cedro* in Italian, whose fruits can be up to 8 inches long and weigh as much as 4½ pounds, is primarily candied, and is an essential ingredient in many famous Sicilian desserts. The intense flavor of the volatile oils in lemon peel is also used in drinks, for example, *limoncino*, a sweet lemon liqueur that is served ice-cold.

Lemons are harvested by hand The fruits must be picked with great care, since the peel must be undamaged and blemish-free if the fruits are to be stored for any length of time or exported.

Oranges, bitter oranges, and bergamot

There are so many varieties of oranges (*arancie*) on the market that it is hard to believe that, botanically, they are all the same fruit. Oranges grown in Italy can at least be roughly divided into light-fleshed fruits and red-fleshed "blood" oranges, or *sanguigne*. They are grown in the same areas that are suitable for cultivating lemons, with the main emphasis again on Sicily. This island is also home to some of the most interesting recipes using oranges, influenced by Arab culinary traditions. It is not just the fruits that are of culinary importance, however; the small, white flowers, with their bewitching fragrance, are the basis of orange-flower water is made, which is used to flavor jams, cakes, and pastries.

DESSERTS 385

peel. Bergamot is used to flavor liqueurs, mineral waters, tobacco, and tea; the well-known Earl Grey tea, for instance, owes its characteristic scent and taste to bergamot oil.

Mandarin oranges and grapefruits

Mandarins are quite small, plump citrus fruits, which are grown mainly in Calabria and Sicily. There are many varieties, but the two main ones are the standard or "normal" mandarin orange (*mandarino*) and the clementine (*mandarancio* or *clementina*). Common to both are the thin, easy-to-peel skins, and the ease with which the segments inside — whose number ranges from 8 to 10, depending on variety — can be separated into individual

Mandarins (top) come in many varieties, one of which is the **clementine** (above).

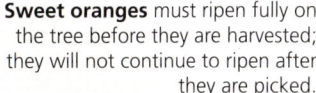

Lemon trees bloom again even before the fruit of the previous blossom has been picked. In Italy lemons are harvested up to three times a year.

Sweet oranges must ripen fully on the tree before they are harvested; they will not continue to ripen after they are picked.

The citron is easily recognized by its thick white inner rind, and its relatively small amount of flesh. In Italy, its juice is used mainly in the manufacture of beverages.

Whereas sweet oranges are grown for eating fresh or juicing, the flesh of bitter oranges (*arancie amare*) are used mainly in the manufacture of liquors and marmalade, and their thick rind is cut into pieces and made into candied orange peel. The bergamot orange (*bergamotto*) resembles the lemon in appearance and is cultivated for the volatile oil contained in its

sections. The flesh of these fruits is sweet and juicy. Italians use mandarins and clementines in exactly the same ways; eating them fresh, candied, or glacéd. These citrus fruits are also important in the beverages industry, as they yield both a robust-flavored fruit juice and a sweet liqueur known as *mandarinetto*, used chiefly in baking and in cocktails.

The grapefruit (*pompelmo*), the largest of these citrus fruits, is cultivated in Sicily, Calabria ,and Lucania. Its bittersweet flesh can be yellow, pink, or red, the reddish varieties being somewhat sweeter. They are eaten fresh on their own, in antipasti, and in fruit salads, and used juiced in cocktails and other drinks.

The bergamot has a bitter flesh and is not suitable for eating fresh, but the oil extracted from the peel is used to flavor numerous foods, as well as being used in the manufacture of perfumes.

386 DESSERTS

Prickly pears are called *fichi d'India*, "Indian figs," in Italy, although the plants originated in Latin America. They flourish well in their adopted southern Italian habitat. The fruits of the 10–13-foot high cacti are juicy and refreshing. Be careful when peeling them, though, as they have fine spines on the skin.

and prickly pears grown in the south, in Sicily.

Seasonal availability

When selecting fruit, Italians are still guided by what is in season, so that they can be certain that the fruit actually ripened on the tree or vine, and was thus able to develop its full flavor.

Pomes and drupes

Pomes (seed fruits) and drupes (stone fruits) are members of the rose family. The first group

Frutta

Such a vast variety of fruit flourishes in a country that Italians do not need to accept produce that has been harvested unripe or damaged in transit. The selection ranges from crunchy Tyrolean apples in the north to exotic pomegranates

Dessert in Italy often consists of nothing but a selection of fresh fruit.

Figs The color of the flesh and peel of *fichi* vary according to variety. As a rule, light-colored fruits are tarter than dark ones. Figs should be eaten when fully ripe, but are then very sensitive to pressure.

Medlars, *nespole comuni* (top), are often made into confectionery in Italy. **Loquats**, or **Japanese medlars**, *nespole del Giappone* (above), are eaten raw or candied, or are made into a liqueur.

comprises apples, pears, and quinces: fruits harboring several small seeds in their interior. The second group comprises those fruits with only one seed, which is usually surrounded by a hard shell, as cherries (*ciliegia*), plums (*prugna*), apricots (*albicocca*), and peaches (*pesca*). The apple (*mela*) is one of the most commonly consumed fruits in

Italy. Like the pear (*pera*), it is chiefly eaten fresh or in a fruit salad, or *macedonia*, as well as stewed and baked, often with a splash of wine. Fine brandies are skillfully distilled from both fruits, mainly in the north. The quince (*mela cotogna*), on the other hand, is not suitable for eating raw. The cooked pulp, sweetened with sugar, is made into a dessert called *cotognata*, a solid quince jelly, as well as compote and jam. Chunks of quince also find their way into many a *mostarda*.

We have the Romans to thank for the spread of the juicy stone fruits throughout the Mediterranean; the introduction of the cherry is personally ascribed to the Roman gourmet and general Lucullus. Stone fruits are often enjoyed raw in Italy, but they are also made into ice cream, compote, jam, juices, and more potent beverages, such as the aromatic, sweet maraschino liqueur, prepared from the sour marasca cherry.

Berries

Although botanically the ponderous watermelon is a berry, the term is generally used to refer exclusively to small soft fruits such as strawberries (*fragole*), raspberries (*lamponi*), blueberries (*mirtilli*), blackberries (*more di rovo*), and red- or black currants (*ribes*). Such berries flourish wild in Italy's woods, and even though they are smaller than the cultivated varieties, they are still prized for their much more intense flavor. To avoid parasites, low-hanging wild berries should be heated to 158°F before being eaten. Whether wild or cultivated, berries are very sensitive to pressure, and so should be transported carefully and washed very gently before they are eaten. They taste superb, sweetened only slightly and served with cream, in fruit salads, on pastry bases or in tartlets. They are also popular in Italy as ingredients for jams, jellies, and syrups. Somewhat exotic are medlars, which must be either touched by frost or stored for a relatively ong period before being eaten, to ensure that they are soft and sweet.

The dessert grape (*uva*) is grown in Italy in huge quantities for export as well as domestic consumption: some are eaten fresh, and some are dried into raisins (*uve passe* or *uvette*).

Pomegranates, *melagrana*, are eaten fresh, and their juicy flesh is also used for juices and sorbets. The bright red syrup known as grenadine is manufactured commercially from the juice in Sicily.

A sun-ripened melon and a typically round watermelon are proudly displayed by a Sicilian farmer (top, far left). *Angurie*, watermelons, are piled up at a market stall in Palermo (bottom, far left) and ogen melons ripen on the vine (left).

Nuts and seeds

The edible seeds and kernels of various plants are grouped together conceptually in Italy with dried fruits such as raisins

A ripe walnut still on the tree. Its hard kernel has cracked through the green, somewhat leathery husk, all remnants of which must be carefully removed at harvest.

and prunes under the heading *frutta secca*. It pays to buy nuts in the shell and crack them open yourself rather than buy shelled nuts, since almost all nuts contain a good many highly nutritious fats and oils that can very quickly turn rancid on contact with oxygen. Ideally, therefore, they should be cracked open just before they

Pistachios> are recognizable by their typically beige shells, which split open from the tip as they dry, exposing the reddish-to-purple skin and the green kernel.

are eaten or added to a dish. Unshelled supplies are best stored in a cool, dry, well ventilated place, separated according to type.

Walnuts, hazelnuts, and pistachios

Walnuts (*noci*) are among the most prized nuts. The four-part kernels nestling in the hard shell are surrounded by a bitter-tasting yellowish or brown seed

Sweet, or Spanish, chestnuts are doubly protected by the prickly husk and a brown, leathery seed coat, which splits during roasting.

coat, which is easily stripped off in the case of freshly harvested nuts. In Italy, walnuts are eaten as a snack, and used in baking and in piquant sauces. The aromatic oil extracted from walnuts is highly valued, and used, for instance, in salad dressings. Walnut oil should be used up as quickly as possible, however, as it soon turns rancid.

The unripe green nuts, together with their skins, are also sought after in northern Italy, where they are made into a *digestif* known as *nocino*. Similarly versatile are the hazelnut (*nocciola*) and the pistachio (*pistacchio*). Both are added to desserts and cakes. Pistachios, whose kernels are relatively soft, are also used in ice cream and for decorating dishes, and even as an ingredient in sausages. The variety cultivated on Sicily, *minnulara*, is easily recognized by its purple skin.

Cream-colored pine nuts are also "double-wrapped", in groups of three or more in the pine cone, and then individually in a hard, dark-brown seed coat.

Chestnuts and pine nuts

Edible chestnuts are divided into two groups: the large, rather plump *castagne* and the heart-shaped, somewhat stronger-tasting *marroni*, both known in English as sweet chestnuts. Chestnuts are the only nuts that are low in fats and oils. This means that, like potatoes, they will fall apart

when cooked, making them easy to mash or purée. Boiling and roasting are the preferred cooking methods for chestnuts. To prepare them, make a cross in the shiny brown shell with a sharp knife, especially if you plan to roast them in the oven, on the burner, or over coals, as t otherwise they can really leap. Roasted chestnuts are called *caldarroste* in Italy, where they are enjoyed as a hot snack in winter. Boiled, they are eaten plain or added to soups, but these sweetish nuts can also be candied or puréed and combined with sugar and cream to make sweet dishes. Dried chestnuts are finely ground and used in baking or pasta stuffings.

Sweet-tasting like chestnuts, but rich in oils, are the beige, shiny pine nuts. These are obtained from the cones of the

Just right for harvesting As soon as the apricot-sized, velvety, but inedible fruits of the almond tree are ripe, they burst open, and the hard stone falls out. It must be cracked open to get the kernel.

Almond trees in flower on Sicily, the largest almond-growing area in Italy. In spring, the blossom covers many hills in a lovely, delicate white veil, as here in the area around Agrigento. Almonds play an important role in Italian cooking, especially in the famous Sicilian *dolci*.

Almonds

Sweet almonds (*mandorla dolce*) are used in *torrone*, a nougat of honey, candied fruits, and almonds; in marzipan or almond paste (*pasta reale*); and in almond milk (*latte di mandorla*). Bitter almonds (*mandorla amara*) are used in small quantities, mainly to intensify the taste of sweet almonds, for example, in *amaretti*, the crisp almond cookies. They were used to make the almond liqueur, *amaretto*, but now apricot kernels are often used instead.

umbrella pine, which grows throughout the Mediterranean. The cones release the seeds either when ripe or when dried. *Pinoli* are popular desserts and in sauces, for instance *pesto alla genovese*, and *salsa di pinoli*, which is served in Genoa with cooked fish. In Sicily, pine nuts are used primarily for spicy stuffings containing rice and raisins.

Every brush stroke is made with care, even when *frutta di martorana*, or almond-paste fruit — which looks deceptively like the real thing — is manufactured in fairly large quantities. In Italy the almond paste, or *pasta reale*, is made from coarsely ground almonds.

Eggplants, pears, figs, and even onions are modeled from *pasta reale*. The sweet paste, consisting mainly of almonds, sugar, and eggs, is also made to look like little loaves of bread, flowers, and chocolates.

A long tradition Almond-paste candies used to be made in convents and are now also made at home.

Tucked away in a courtyard in Erice, this staircase leads to the delights of a little domestic confectionery, or *pasticceria*.

Gelato

The big freeze: how to turn cream into ice cream and make refreshing *sorbetti* from fruit

Ice cream and flavored ice are ideal refreshments on hot summer days, and welcome desserts at any time of year. Italy is the birthplace of ice cream, or *gelato*, and there it is made as *gelato crema* and *gelato all'uovo*. Both are custard-based, but the former also contains cream. Both are flavored according to taste, with, for instance, chocolate, nuts, or liqueurs; and they turn out best when made in an ice-cream maker. A fruit ice, or *gelato alla frutta*, on the other hand, contains neither cream nor eggs, but in the simplest case consists of puréed fruit, water, and sugar. When liqueur, tea, or coffee is used for flavoring instead of fruit, and when the frozen mixture is served as a slush in a glass, it is called a *sorbetto*, or sorbet

Transfer the custard to a saucepan. Heat carefully to just under boiling point, stirring constantly, until the custard is thick enough to "blow roses."

In other words, heat the custard until it thinly coats the back of a wooden spoon. When you blow on the surface, it should make wrinkles reminiscent of a rose.

Preparing *gelato all'uovo*:

Bring ¼ vanilla pod to a boil in 2¼ cups milk. In a mixing bowl, whisk 6 egg yolks together with ½ cup sugar.

Strain the custard to remove any lumps that may have formed.

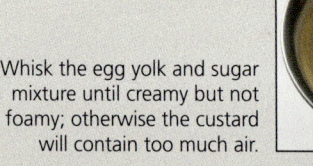

Whisk the egg yolk and sugar mixture until creamy but not foamy; otherwise the custard will contain too much air.

To make vanilla ice cream, transfer the custard to an ice-cream maker and freeze until creamy. You can, of course, flavor the mixture as you wish before freezing it.

Gradually pour the hot milk into the egg yolk and sugar mixture, stirring constantly.

To make chocolate ice cream, melt 4 oz of bittersweet chocolate and stir into the custard when the latter has reached the proper coating consistency, then freeze the mixture.

Sorbetti turn out especially creamy when made in a *sorbetière*, a small ice-cream maker. If you do not have one, whisk the mixture thoroughly at intervals as it freezes; the first time, after about 30 minutes. The more frequently you stir or whisk it, the finer and more delicate the sorbet will be.

SORBETTO DI VISCIOLE

Serves 8–10

1 cup sugar, 1 piece cinnamon bark
1 lb sour cherries, pitted
juice of ½ lemon
You will also need:
1 cup heavy cream, 1 tablespoon sugar
scraped contents of ¼ vanilla bean
16–20 sour cherries

Bring 1¼ cups water to a boil with the sugar and cinnamon bark, then leave to cool. Purée the cherries in a blender or food processor. Remove the cinnamon and stir the sugar solution into the puréed fruit. Freeze until creamy. Whip the cream to soft peaks with the sugar and vanilla. Using a pastry bag with a star tip, pipe the sorbet into glasses. Decorate each portion with a little whipped cream and 2 cherries.

SORBETTO DI POMPELMO

Serves 8–10

1 cup sugar, 1 cup pink grapefruit juice, juice of 1 lemon
1 cup white wine, ⅓ cup Campari, 2 egg whites
You will also need:
mint leaves

Bring 1 cup water to a boil with the sugar, then leave to cool. Combine the grapefruit and lemon juices, and strain. Mix the wine, Campari, and sugar syrup, and stir into the fruit juices. Whip the egg whites to soft peaks, and fold into the liquid. Freeze until creamy, stirring frequently to give it a nice foamy texture. Spoon into glasses and serve decorated with mint.

After the first baking, slice the dough logs diagonally into ½-inch-thick pieces. Space them out flat on the cookie sheet and bake a second time.

Biscotti di Prato

In Tuscany, these almond cookies are also called *cantucci* or *giottini*, depending on the area, and are traditionally served with Vin Santo

To those unfamiliar with them, these biscuits seem hard and brittle at first, since they are baked, then sliced and baked a second time to dry them out. But biscotti are not intended simply to be nibbled on their own; in Tuscany, they are served to round out a fine meal, accompanied by a strong espresso or, even better, a glass of Vin Santo, the amber-colored dessert wine. Diners dunk their biscotti in the wine to their heart's content, quite content to let the cookies crumble, for this allows their almond flavor to mingle sublimely with the wine's bouquet. Vin Santo is one of a number of dessert wines, or *vini passiti*, produced in many places in Italy by similar methods. In Tuscany it is made mainly from white Trebbiano and Malvasia grapes. To make Vin Santo, producers take the unusual step of leaving the harvested grapes to dry in a closed space for two months, either spread out on straw mats or hung up so air can circulate around them. This causes the grapes to shrivel like raisins and their sugar content to become concentrated. Then they are pressed and the wine is aged, traditionally in small oak casks in attics, where temperature fluctuations from summer to winter "regulate" the fermentation process in an entirely natural fashion. The wine remains in the cask for a minimum of three years, developing a relatively high alcohol content of 15–17 percent, and an intense color resulting from the oxidation processes. Like sherry, Vin Santo can be made dry as well as medium-dry and sweet, which is the best type for serving with biscotti.

Makes about 70
2½ cups all-purpose flour
1 teaspoon baking powder
⅞ cup sugar
2 eggs, 1 egg yolk
1 pinch salt
⅔ cup unblanched, very coarsely chopped almonds
½ cup unblanched, ground almonds
You will also need:
1 egg yolk for glazing
2 tablespoons milk
butter and flour for the cookie sheet

Sift the flour and baking powder together into a bowl. Add the sugar, eggs, egg yolk, salt, and the chopped and ground almonds. Knead into a firm dough.

Preheat the oven to 350°F. Divide the dough into 4 equal pieces. On a floured work surface shape each piece into a log about 12 inches long and 1 inch in diameter. Beat the egg yolk with the milk and use to glaze the dough logs. Grease a cookie sheet with butter and dust lightly with flour. Place the dough logs on the sheet and bake for about 20 minutes, until golden brown.

Remove from the oven and allow to cool slightly. Slice the still-soft logs as shown above left. Return to the oven and bake the cookies for another 5 minutes. Remove the biscotti from the oven, and leave to cool on a wire rack before serving.

There is no shortage of good-quality almonds in Italy. The best come from the south of the country, from Apulia, Calabria, and, above all, Sicily. The almonds in this picture are not yet shelled, and some of them are still surrounded by their outer covering of velvety, inedible fruit.

Grape cake

Schiacciata con le uve is baked in Tuscany at the time of the grape harvest

Schiacciata means "squashed," and is the name given in Tuscany to flatbreads and cakes made from a simple yeast dough. In this recipe the dough sets off the flavor of the fruity grapes to best advantage. Use fruit that is fully ripened and aromatic to produce an exceedingly delicious cake, which, freshly baked, is great served as a dessert or with coffee.

Place one of the disks of dough on a greased baking sheet and spoon half of the grapes over the top, leaving a 1¼-inch edge free.

Carefully lay the second sheet of dough over the grapes, positioning the edges to fit perfectly over those of the disk below.

Press the edges of the two sheets of dough firmly together to prevent the "pocket" opening up as it bakes.

Scatter the remaining grapes over the surface of the dough, and pierce the dough at intervals with a toothpick.

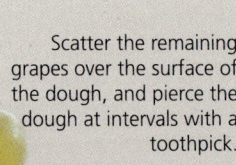

Serves 8

For the dough:
2¾ cups all-purpose flour
1 tablespoon dry active yeast
1 cup lukewarm water, 3 tablespoons olive oil, 1 pinch salt

You will also need:
1 lb each seedless red and green grapes
¾ cup superfine granulated sugar
3 tablespoons butter, melted

Sift the flour into a bowl and make a well in the center. Add the yeast, dissolve in half of the water, and mix with a little flour. Sprinkle this starter with flour, cover with a cloth, and let rise in a warm, draft-free spot, until the surface shows cracks.

In the meantime, remove the grapes from the stalks, mix them with the sugar and melted butter, and set aside.

Continue making the dough. Add the oil, salt, and remaining water to the starter. Using a mixing spoon, work in all the flour, and beat until the dough bubbles and comes away from the sides of the bowl. Knead into a smooth dough. Divide the dough in half and roll out into 2 disks. Proceed as shown in the picture sequence on the left. Cover the cake and let rest for about 1 hour.

Preheat the oven to 400°F and bake the grape cake for 35–40 minutes, until golden brown.

Serving this cake from the baking sheet or a wooden board enhances its rustic quality.

Frittelle di riso, a specialty from northern Italy, are dusted with confectioner's sugar while still warm and served at once.

Freshly fried delicacies

Frittelle di riso, fritole venessiane, and *fiori di zucca fritti* are extremely popular throughout Italy

In Italy, small and large sweet fritters are often made with yeast. For the pumpkin flowers, though, a thin batter of flour, milk, and egg is sufficient.

FRITTELLE DI RISO

Makes about 20
⅓ cup raisins
⅛ cup glacé cherries, chopped
4 teaspoons pine nuts, chopped
¼ cup chopped walnuts
4 teaspoons Vin Santo, 2¼ cups milk
¼ teaspoon salt, 3 tablespoons sugar, 1 cup Arborio rice
¼ cup butter
2 eggs, separated
grated zest of ½ lemon, grated zest of 1 orange
2 teaspoons dry active yeast
5 tablespoons all-purpose flour

You will also need:
oil for deep-frying, confectioner's sugar

Mix the raisins, cherries, pine nuts, walnuts, and Vin Santo in a small bowl, and leave to steep for 1 hour. Bring the milk to a boil in a saucepan, and add the salt and 2 teaspoons of the sugar. Tip in the rice and cook for 4–5 minutes, stirring. Stir in the butter and simmer until you have a nearly dry rice pudding. Let cool to lukewarm. Beat the egg whites to firm peaks, trickling in the remaining sugar. Gently mix the citrus zests, egg yolks, and the yeast into the rice pudding. Fold in the sifted flour and the soaked fruit and nuts. Fold in the egg whites. Heat the oil to 350°F in a deep pan or deep-fat fryer. Using two tablespoons dipped in water, form dumplings from the rice mixture, and fry them in the hot oil for 2–3 minutes, turning. Lift out, drain on paper towels, and dust with confectioner's sugar.

FRITOLE VENESSIANE

Makes about 30
For the dough:
2½ cups all-purpose flour, 1 tablespoon dry active yeast
⅔ cup lukewarm milk
2 tablespoons butter, melted
1 egg, 3 tablespoons sugar, 4 teaspoons Grappa
grated zest of ½ lemon, ¼ teaspoon salt
3 tablespoons each chopped candied lemon and orange peel
2 tablespoons pine nuts, 2 heaping tablespoons raisins
For the red-wine zabaione:
3 egg yolks, ½ cup sugar, ½ cup red wine
You will also need:
oil for deep-frying, confectioner's sugar

Sift the flour into a bowl and make a well in the center. Add the yeast, pour in the milk to dissolve it, mixing in a little flour from the sides, and dust with flour. Cover the bowl with a cloth and let the starter rise in a warm spot for 15 minutes.

Mix the butter with the egg, sugar, grappa, lemon zest, and salt, and stir into the starter with a wooden spatula. Beat the dough by hand until it is smooth, shiny, and bubbly, and clearly coming away from the sides of the bowl. Cover the dough with a cloth and let rise in a warm spot until doubled in size.

Quickly need the candied citrus peels, into the dough with the pine nuts and raisins. Cover, and leave to rise again for 10–15 minutes. Heat the oil to 275°F in a deep saucepan or deep-fat fryer. Use a tablespoon to form little balls, and deep-fry them for 6–8 minutes, until light brown. Lift out with a slotted spoon and drain on paper towels.

To make the *zabaione*, cream the egg yolks and sugar. Place the bowl in the top of a double boiler over water kept at just under boiling point. Pour in the wine and whisk until the mixture is foamy and has doubled in volume. Place the bowl inside a second bowl filled with ice water, and whisk the *zabaione* until cold. Sift the confectioner's sugar over the *fritole*, and serve them with the *zabaione*.

FRIED PUMPKIN FLOWERS

Makes 8–12
½ cup all-purpose flour, ¾ cup milk
1 egg yolk, 1 egg white, 1 pinch salt
8–12 pumpkin flowers
You will also need:
oil for deep frying, confectioner's sugar

Sift the flour into a bowl. Add the milk and egg yolk, and stir to a smooth batter. Beat the egg white and salt to stiff peaks, then fold into the batter. Chill. Strip the sepals from the flowers, then cut out the stamens or pistils. Press the flowers together slightly. Heat the oil to 350°F in a deep saucepan or deep-fat fryer. Holding the flowers by the stalk, dip them in the batter, letting the excess drain. Fry one at a time for 1–2 minutes, turning often. Lift out and drain on paper towels. Trim the stalks slightly, and dust the flowers with confectioner's sugar before serving.

A tempting selection of deep-fried doughnuts at a market in Palermo. Fried foods, both sweet and savory, are held in high regard everywhere in Italy.

Deep-fried pumpkin flowers with fresh raspberries and a classic zabaione made with Marsala can form the crowning finale to a summery meal.

398 DESSERTS

At the Ferron brothers' *riseria* near Verona, best-quality short-grain rice is processed in the mill, and afterwards in the kitchen — with superb results, as the recipe on this page shows.

Rice torte
This cake, based on a rice pudding, is beautifully moist

In some areas of Italy, people like their rice cakes fairly substantial: made from rice pudding and a mixture of nuts and glacé fruits. This Venetian version is lighter, combining an airy dough with the golden-yellow rice. At the Riseria Ferron the chefs prefer to use Vialone nano rice a variety more often used for creamy risottos.

Serves 16
For the rice pudding :
4½ cups milk, 1 pinch salt
1 strip lemon zest
1 cup Vialone nano rice
1 cup sugar
2 tablespoons butter
5 egg yolks
scraped contents of ½ vanilla bean

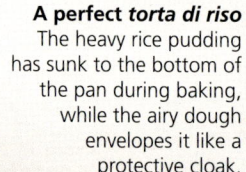

A perfect *torta di riso*
The heavy rice pudding has sunk to the bottom of the pan during baking, while the airy dough envelopes it like a protective cloak.

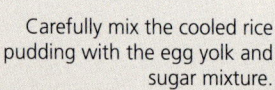

Carefully mix the cooled rice pudding with the egg yolk and sugar mixture.

Spread the dough from the center outward, coating the sides thoroughly.

Thoroughly grease a springform pan, and dust its base and sides with flour.

Ladle the rice pudding into the center of the pan.

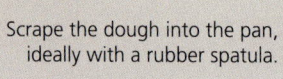

Scrape the dough into the pan, ideally with a rubber spatula.

Fold the dough down from the sides of the pan onto the rice pudding.

For the dough:
¾ cup + 2 tablespoons softened butter
1½ cups sugar
2½ cups all-purpose flour
1 tablespoon baking powder
½ teaspoon grated lemon zest
5 egg whites
You will also need:
a 10-inch springform pan
confectioner's sugar

First prepare the rice pudding. In a large saucepan, bring the milk to a boil with the salt and the strip of lemon zest. Stir in the rice and teaspoons of the sugar, and simmer for 40 minutes, stirring at intervals. Take the rice pudding off the heat, remove the lemon zest, stir in the butter, and let cool.

In the meantime, prepare the dough: Stir the butter with one-third of the sugar until foamy. Mix together the flour and baking powder, and stir into the butter and sugar mixture with the grated lemon zest. In a clean, dry bowl, whip the egg whites to peaks. Trickle in the remaining sugar, and continue beating until the sugar has dissolved and the egg white is firm. Gently fold the egg white into the butter and flour mixture.

Next, finish preparing the rice pudding. Stir the egg yolks, remaining sugar, and the scraped contents of the vanilla bean together until creamy. Proceed as shown in the picture sequence.

Preheat the oven to 300°F and bake the rice cake for 60–70 minutes. Leave to cool in the pan, and dust with confectioner's sugar before serving.

Crema fritta
Fried vanilla custard slices, served in a fruity sour-cherry sauce

The custard for these delightful little bars has to chill in the refrigerator for at least 1¼ hours before it can be sliced. Then the individual pieces are coated in bread crumbs and deep-fried.

Serves 4
For the custard:
2¼ cups milk, scraped contents of ½ vanilla bean
1 cup all-purpose flour, ½ cup sugar, 1 pinch salt
2 eggs, 6 egg yolks, 2 tablespoons butter, melted
For the sour-cherry sauce:
¼ cup red wine
¼ cup orange juice, strained
⅜ cup sugar

Using a large palette knife, slice the chilled custard crosswise into bars ¾ inch wide.

Turn the board through 90°, and cut through the bars lengthwise at 1½-inch intervals.

Turn the custard chunks first in the beaten egg, then in the bread crumbs.

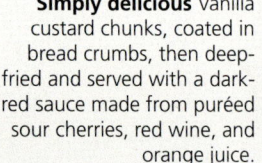

Simply delicious Vanilla custard chunks, coated in bread crumbs, then deep-fried and served with a dark-red sauce made from puréed sour cherries, red wine, and orange juice.

5 oz sour cherries, pitted
generous pinch ground cinnamon
generous pinch ground cloves
¼ teaspoon cornstarch
You will also need:
a 6 x 6-inch mold or baking sheet
1 tablespoon butter, melted
2 eggs, 1 cup fine dried white bread crumbs
oil for deep frying, confectioner's sugar
peppermint leaves

Scald the milk with the vanilla and remove from the heat. Sift the flour into a bowl. Add the sugar, salt,

eggs, and egg yolks, and whisk vigorously till well blended. Pour in the hot milk a little a time through a strainer and carefully mix in. Transfer the mixture to a saucepan. Bring to a boil, stirring constantly, then reduce the heat and simmer for 5 minutes. Remove from the heat and stir in the butter. Brush the mold with a little of the melted butter. Pour in the custard and smooth with a palette knife. Brush the top with the remaining melted butter. Refrigerate the custard until completely cold and set.

To make the sauce, bring the wine to a boil in a saucepan with the orange juice and the sugar. Add the cherries and spices, and simmer for 5 minutes. Purée with a hand blender and pour through a fine strainer. Bring the purée back to a boil. Dissolve the cornstarch in a little water and use to thicken the purée. Leave to cool.

Prepare the bread-crumb coating. Crack the eggs into a soup plate and beat with a fork. Shake the bread crumbs onto a plate. Unmold the custard onto a platter and proceed as shown in the picture sequence opposite.

Heat the oil to 350°F in a deep saucepan or deep-fat fryer and deep-fry the breaded custard slices in batches until golden. Drain on paper towels. Dust the *crema fritta* with confectioner's sugar, decorate with mint leaves, and serve with the sour-cherry sauce.

Dairy products, especially milk, cream, and butter, play a major role in northern Italian cuisine. In the Valle d'Aosta and Piedmont, for instance, they lend a touch of class to many dishes, and form the basis of numerous delicious *dolci*.

Panna cotta

A delicate, creamy dessert, which is especially popular in Liguria and Piedmont

Whether eating out or at home, Italians have a soft spot for their *dolci*, and northern Italians are particularly fond of creamy desserts like this one. The best foil for luscious, mild, and creamy panna cotta is a fruity sauce. In Liguria and Piedmont, it is often served with a strawberry sauce. In the recipe below, it is teamed instead with an apricot sauce, whose delicate tartness is the ideal complement for the rich dessert. It is important to begin preparations well in advance, as the panna cotta needs to set in the refrigerator for several hours. You can make the decorative chocolate leaves yourself; all you need is chocolate, fresh leaves (orange-tree or bay leaves, for instance, are suitable), and a little patience. Melt milk chocolate, semisweet, or bitter chocolate in a bowl, and allow it to cool a little, to precisely 82°F. Then slowly reheated it to 90°F, a process professionals call "tempering." The rest is quite easy. Simply draw clean, dry leaves over the surface of the chocolate, and let it cool on them. Let the chocolate harden completely, then strip it from the green leaves, starting at the stalk end.

This panna cotta with apricot sauce is a creamy, fruity delight. The very natural-looking, decorative leaf is made entirely of chocolate.

Serves 4
For the panna cotta:
3⅓ cups heavy cream
1 vanilla bean, slit open
⅜ cup sugar
1 strip lemon zest
2½ teaspoons gelatin
For the apricot sauce:
9 oz fully ripe apricots
¼ cup sugar syrup (see caption p.405)
1 tablespoon lime juice
4 teaspoons apricot brandy, 2 teaspoons cognac

You will also need:
four 1 cup molds
2 apricots
4 chocolate leaves

Bring the cream to a boil in a saucepan with the vanilla bean, sugar, and lemon zest. Simmer for about 15 minutes, stirring frequently. Remove the pan from the heat, fish out the vanilla bean, and scrape its contents back into the cream. Remove the lemon zest.

Dissolve the gelatin according to package direction and stir into the still-hot cream.

Rinse out the molds with cold water, pour in the cream mixture, and leave to set in the refrigerator for at least 5, but preferably 6, hours.

To make the sauce, blanch, refresh, and skin the apricots, then halve and pit them. Purée the flesh in a blender, then strain. Bring the purée to a boil with the sugar syrup, lime juice, apricot brandy, and cognac, and simmer for 5 minutes. Remove from the heat and leave to cool.

Blanch, skin, halve, and pit the apricots for the decoration. Take the molds out of the refrigerator. Run a knife along the inside of the molds between the panna cotta and the edge, dip the molds briefly in hot water, and unmold the panna cotta onto serving plates.

Place an apricot half next to each panna cotta, and pour some apricot sauce over the fruit, but not over the panna cotta itself. Decorate each portion with a chocolate leaf and serve.

A view from the hills of the Veneto. Like many small towns and villages in Italy, Bassano del Grappa is enclosed by protective walls and stands on a hill.

Zuppa inglese

A favorite dessert of the Italians: liqueur-steeped ladyfingers between layers of custard and chocolate cream

This dessert owes its name far less to any "English soup" than to the vanilla custard it contains, known in food circles as *crème anglaise* — English cream. Another theory claims that it is named after the ladyfingers, which some older Italians call *inglesi*. Wherever the name comes from, however, this *zuppa inglese* is i one of the best Italian desserts.

Serves 4
For the ladyfingers:
6 egg yolks, ⅔ cup sugar
scraped contents of ½ vanilla bean
4 egg whites, scant ½ cup cornstarch
½ cup all-purpose flour
For the vanilla custard:
2¼ cups milk
½ vanilla bean, slit open
5 egg yolks
½ cup sugar, 2 egg whites
For the chocolate cream:
1 heaping cup ricotta cheese, ¼ cup sugar
3 oz semisweet chocolate, finely chopped
You will also need:
parchment-paper strips 2 inches wide
⅓ cup sugar syrup
⅓ cup amaretto
1 oz bittersweet chocolate, shaved
½ cup amarena cherries (sour black cherries in syrup)
confectioner's sugar

To make the ladyfingers, whisk the egg yolks, a quarter of the sugar, and the scraped contents of the vanilla bean in a mixing bowl until creamy. Whip the egg whites to stiff peaks, trickling in the remaining sugar. Using a wooden spoon, carefully fold the sifted cornstarch into the egg whites, followed by the egg-yolk mixture, and then the sifted flour. Line a baking sheet with the parchment-paper strips and preheat the oven to 400°F. Spoon the batter into a pastry bag with a round tip and pipe out the fingers, with the ends

Moisten the ladyfingers with the sugar syrup and amaretto mixture, and spread the chocolate cream over them. Top with a layer of ladyfingers, moistening them well. Spread half of the vanilla custard on top, cover with ladyfingers, and moisten these well, as before. Ladle the remaining vanilla custard evenly over the top, and arrange ladyfingers over it to resemble the spokes of a wheel.

slightly thicker than the middle. Sift confectioner's sugar on top, and bake for 8–10 minutes. Remove from the oven, and strip off the parchment paper.

To make the vanilla custard, scald the milk with the vanilla bean. Remove the vanilla bean, and scrape its contents back into the milk. Whisk the egg yolks with a third of the sugar in a bowl until creamy. Slowly stir the hot milk into the egg-yolk mixture. Transfer to a saucepan and heat the custard until it thickens, stirring evenly with a wooden spatula so that it does not stick to the pan. Do not let it boil.

Remove the custard from the heat, and reserve a third of it in a bowl. Beat the egg whites to stiff peaks, trickling in the remaining sugar. Stir this meringue the still-hot vanilla custard in the saucepan.

Stir the ricotta and sugar together until creamy, then blend in the reserved custard, followed by the chocolate. Mix the sugar syrup with the amaretto.

Line the bottom of a serving bowl with ladyfingers, and proceed as shown in the picture sequence on the left.

Place the bowl in the refrigerator and chill for 3–4 hours. Take out, and decorate with the shaved chocolate and amarena cherries. Dust with confectioner's sugar just before serving.

All but the top layer of ladyfingers are moistened with amaretto and sugar syrup. You can make the latter yourself quite easily by bringing 1 lb sugar and 2⅛ cups water to a rolling boil for 1 minute. The sugar syrup can be stored in the refrigerator for up to 6 months.

Meringues with chocolate cream
In the Piedmont and Lombardy regions, people have a predilection for these sweet *meringhe*

In Italy, meringues are usually eaten with whipped cream. Sometimes, though, they are sandwiched together with a chocolate cream, as in the recipe below. Here, the bitter chocolate takes the edge off the sweetness of the *meringhe*, and offers a contrast in taste and texture. The recipe below makes 30–40 piped meringues, depending on size, which are then assembled into 15–20 "sandwiches." The meringues must be made a day in advance, and can be stored in an airtight jar for 2–3 weeks, provided that they are completely dry. The basic chocolate cream, without the rum, can also be kept, well sealed, for at least 1 week in the refrigerator.

For the meringues:
8 egg whites, 1¼ cups sugar
2 cups confectioner's sugar
¼ cup cornstarch
For the chocolate cream:
1 lb bitter chocolate
1¾ cups heavy cream
1 vanilla bean, slit lengthwise
3 tablespoons brown rum
You will also need:
2 baking sheets
parchment or wax paper
raspberry jam
cupcake cases, cocoa powder

To make the meringue, beat the egg whites in a clean, dry bowl until they stand in peaks. Slowly trickle in the sugar and continue beating until completely firm. Mix the confectioner's sugar and cornstarch, sift over the meringue, and gently fold in with a wooden spatula.

Preheat the oven to 120°F. Line the baking sheets with parchment paper. Spoon the meringue into a pastry bag with a round tip, and pipe out

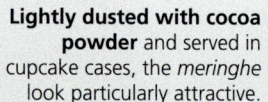

Lightly dusted with cocoa powder and served in cupcake cases, the *meringhe* look particularly attractive.

meringues 2 inches in diameter on the paper.

Place the baking sheets in the oven, leaving sufficient vertical space between them, and keep the oven door slightly open to let the moisture escape. Leave the meringues in the oven overnight to dry out completely.

To make the chocolate cream, cut the chocolate into small pieces. Pour the cream into a saucepan, add the vanilla bean, and bring to a boil. Remove the vanilla bean, scraping its contents back into the pan. Tip all the chocolate into the boiling cream, stirring vigorously with a wooden spatula, so that the chocolate dissolves completely without burning. Remove from the heat and let cool.

When the chocolate cream is completely cold, beat it with an electric hand mixer until foamy, slowly blending in the rum. Spoon , into a pastry bag with a star tip. Pipe a large rosette onto half of the meringue shells and place ½ teaspoon raspberry jam in the center of each. Top with a second meringue shell. Place the sandwiched meringues in cupcake cases, dust with cocoa powder, and serve.

Apricot and wine custard cake

A delicate, fruity filling and crisp pastry base are hidden under a pretty meringue topping

Serves 6–8
8 oz frozen puff pastry, defrosted
For the apricot compote:
1 lb fresh apricots
heaping ½ cup sugar
juice of ½ lemon, 2 teaspoons amaretto
For the wine custard:
2 teaspoons gelatin, ½ cup Vin Santo
⅜ cup sugar, juice of 1 orange
3 egg yolks
1 ⅔ cup heavy cream, whipped to stiff peaks
For the meringue topping:
4 egg whites, 1 cup sugar
You will also need:
parchment or wax paper, a 9½-inch cake ring
1 cup flaked, toasted almonds

Preheat the oven to 400°F. Roll out the pastry on a floured work surface to a circle 11 inches in diameter. Place on a baking sheet lined with parchment paper, prick at intervals, and refrigerate for 30 minutes. Bake for 15–20 minutes, until light brown; the pastry base will have shrunk a little. If necessary, cut it into shape using the cake ring as a guide.

To make the apricot compote, blanch, refresh, skin, halve, and pit the apricots. Simmer the sugar with 1 cup water and the lemon juice in a saucepan for 2–3 minutes. Add the fruit, and cook for 8–10 minutes, until soft. Remove from the heat, and pour in the amaretto. Cool the apricots and drain well.

To make the wine custard, dissolve the gelatin according to package instructions. In a saucepan, thoroughly combine the Vin Santo, sugar, orange juice, and egg yolks. Heat the mixture, stirring constantly and making sure it does not boil, until the custard thinly coats the back of a wooden spoon. Strain to remove any lumps that might have formed. Dissolve the gelatin in the still-warm custard, and leave the custard to cool until it begins to set. Fold in the whipped cream.

Place the pastry base on a cake platter and enclose it with the cake ring. Spread about a third of the custard evenly over the base. Top with the apricots, cut sides down. Spread the remaining custard on top, smoothing with a palette knife. Chill the cake in the refrigerator for about 3 hours, then lift off the ring.

To make the meringue topping, whip the egg whites in a clean, dry bowl with ¼ cup sugar. Trickle in the remaining sugar, and continue to whip until the meringue is firm. Spoon about two-thirds of the mixture into a pastry bag with a round tip, and pipe ¾-inch domes close together on top of the cake. Use the remaining meringue to ice the sides of the cake. Place in a preheated oven with an overhead element, or under the broiler, until the meringue is light brown. Stud the sides of the torte with toasted flaked almonds, scattering a few over the top.

A sweet surprise Fruit and delicate Vin Santo-flavored custard are hidden under little meringue domes. A glass of the sweet dessert wine makes a fine accompaniment to this delicious cake.

The almond harvest is still carried out by hand in the rural areas of Sicily, by shaking the trees until the almonds fall to the ground.

Focaccia di mandorla

This cross between a pie and a cake boasts a delicate almond pastry base and top, and a light custard filling

Throughout Italy, but especially in the south, almonds are used a great deal in cooking and baking. In this recipe, they are not, for once, an ingredient in a custard filling, but are used in the pastry, which tastes best when really fresh, .

Makes 2
For the pastry:
1 ⅔ cups unblanched almonds
1 cup + 2 tablespoons butter
1¼ cups sugar, 2 cups all-purpose flour
For the filling:
¾ cup sugar, ¼ cup cornstarch
4 egg yolks, 2¼ cups milk
scraped contents of ½ vanilla bean, 3 egg whites
You will also need:
a 8½-inch springform pan
parchment or wax paper
flaked almonds, confectioner's sugar

To make the pastry, pour boiling water over the almonds and let sit for a couple of minutes; refresh under cold water, then slip off the skins. Grind the almonds in a food processor. Add the remaining ingredients for the pastry gradually and process until you have a soft, kneadable dough. Wrap the dough in plastic wrap and refrigerate for 2 hours.

Preheat the oven to 375–400°F. Roll the pastry out to about ¼-inch thick. Using the springform pan, press 4 circles in the pastry. Cut them out, and bake one at a time in the parchment paper-lined springform pan for 15–17 minutes. Cut two of the bases into 12 wedges while still hot, and leave all the bases to cool.

To make the filling, place ¼ cup of the sugar and the cornstarch in a bowl. Add the egg yolks, and a few tablespoons of milk. Whisk well, making sure that no lumps form. Bring the remaining milk to a boil with ¼ cup sugar and the contents of the vanilla bean. Pour the cornstarch mixture slowly and steadily into the boiling milk mixture, stirring constantly. Allow to well up repeatedly, until the milk thickens.

Beat the egg whites to stiff peaks, trickling in the remaining sugar, until you have a firm meringue. Fold the meringue into the vanilla custard, and heat, stirring constantly, until the custard wells up again.

Spread the hot custard onto both pastry bases, working quickly, as it will not spread once cool. Top each cake with 12 wedges of pastry, sprinkle with flaked almonds, and dust with confectioner's sugar.

The heavy sacks of almonds are then loaded on donkeys. The roads from the hills to the Sicilian towns and villages are usually long, and the sure-footed donkey is often the only possible means of transport in this beautiful but inaccessible area.

Luscious vanilla custard is sandwiched between two crisp-baked almond-pastry disks. To stop the custard from squelching out when the cake is sliced, the top pastry disk is cut into 12 pieces while still warm.

BREAD

Pane e pizze AND PIZZA

Man does not live by bread alone, but there are few places he could do so quite so happily as in Italy. There, bread is not something that is simply sliced and buttered or made into sandwiches; it also takes the form of delicious flatbreads that often come with their own topping — the best example being the most famous Italian dish of all, pizza. But there are other specialties waiting to be discovered, from tomato-flavored breads, to generously stuffed calzoni, to artistically layered piquant pies with cheese and vegetables.

Their daily bread

The phrase "daily bread" applies to Italian cuisine as it does to few others, since hardly a meal is served in Italy without bread in one form or another. Bread is not just as an accompaniment, but an essential component of many antipasti — *crostini* or *bruschette*, for example — or of soups such as *pancotto*, whose literal translation is "boiled bread." There is also the Tuscan bread salad, *panzanella*, which is prepared with day-old bread soaked in olive oil.

Flatbreads

Flatbreads are the earliest form of bread. Basically, not much more is needed for their preparation than flour and water, and perhaps some salt. The ingredients are kneaded together, rolled out thinly, and cooked on both sides on a hot surface — stone, terracotta, or cast iron. These flatbreads are usually meant to be eaten immediately, since they quickly become hard and brittle. To extend their shelf life, they are first cooked in the traditional way, then dried out individually in the oven. *Pane carasau*, *crescentine* and *piadina* are all examples of peasant breads. *Piadine* are baked on special cast-iron or clay griddles. Thicker flatbreads prepared with yeast are baked entirely in an oven, like *focaccia*. In the simplest version of this bread, a yeast dough is rolled out on a baking sheet, baked, and cut into rectangular pieces that are eaten plain or topped with various ingredients. In a better-known version, however, focaccia is baked with a topping. This may consist of only olive oil and coarse salt, or may also contain sardines, onions, olives, or cheese. It is only a small leap from focaccia to the more elaborately topped pizza.

Pizza

Even though it is not considered a bread in Italy, pizza is included here because it is traditionally prepared from the same dough. Like many of the most popular Italian dishes, pizza can trace its roots to the *cucina povera*, and was once a spicy but not lavishly topped snack.

Bread and rolls

Much more varied in shape than the flatbreads are the Italian loaves and rolls. These range from the more or less round, country bread, to the *pane a cassetta* or *pancarré* ("sandwich loaf") used for melts, *tramezzini* (Italian sandwiches), and *tartine* (delicate canapés), to braided loaves, croissant shapes, large rings, and imaginatively shaped rolls like those shown at the top of the page, which were all baked from the same dough. In Rome the *bastone* or "stick," a long, thin white loaf, is especially popular. Many Roman rolls, or *panini*, look like a smaller version of it.

In Italy, bread and pizza were traditionally baked in a wood-fired stone oven, as they are on some farms even to this day. While the oven temperature is really high, it is used to bake larger loaves of bread; flatbreads such as pizza are slipped in afterwards. These bakers must rely entirely on their own experience to determine how long bread should be baked, and at what temperature.

Piadina is the typical bread of Emilia-Romagna. It can be eaten plain or stuffed with various delicious fillings.

Ciabatta and ciabattini can be prepared from the same dough; the rolls, of course, have a shorter baking time than the loaf.

Pane carasau or **carta di musica**, "manuscript paper," is the name of this wafer-thin flatbread, a Sardinian specialty.

Known well beyond the borders of Italy is the *ciabatta*, an elongate country bread whose name means "slipper." This description refers to the bread's texture, for ciabatta is made from a very soft yeast dough with olive oil. To make ciabatta yourself, you will need 6 cups all-purpose flour, 2 tablespoons active dry yeast, 2¼ cups lukewarm water, 2 teaspoons sugar, ⅔ cup olive oil, and 3 teaspoons salt. Make a starter from the flour, water, yeast, and half of the sugar, and let rise for 1 hour. Mix in the remaining ingredients, and let rise for 3 hours. Knead the dough and let rise for another 3 hours, then shape into three 12-inch long loaves rounded at the ends, sprinkle with a little flour, and let rise for a final 30 minutes. Preheat the oven to 475°F and bake for 25–30 minutes. This recipe is certainly time-consuming, but it is the long rising periods that help give the ciabatta its characteristic soft crumb and thin, soft crust. Sometimes ciabatta dough is enriched with chopped black olives or sun-dried tomatoes. Freshly baked, it is delicious even without a topping.

Almost as famous as ciabatta is the Tuscan white loaf. A peculiarity of this bread is that is is baked without salt. Why this is so has never been explained, but one thing is certain: The various Tuscan *crostini*, *fettunta* (slices of bread rubbed with garlic, drizzled with olive oil, and toasted), and the above-mentioned *panzanella* taste so incomparably good only when made with this unsalted bread.

Small baked goods

Grissini are made from a white-bread dough. When they are commercially made, each stick is the same length and thickness. Handmade grissini are irregular, and often much longer. Sometimes they are sprinkled with poppy seeds or sesame seeds before being baked. They are served mainly with antipasti, as are *taralli*, which come in the form of rings, pretzels, or knots, and may be spiced with fennel seeds and pepper or *peperoncini* (chiles).

Grissini, the crunchy breadsticks that grace the tables of Italian restaurants the world over, originated in Turin.

Breads from Sicily in every imaginable shape, are arranged on a boldly painted market cart. This large island has a long tradition of baking, which is hardly surprising, as its fertile soil earned it the reputation of a granary back in ancient times. This made it the declared target of all manner of conquerors, who also left behind their culinary mark.

Different varieties of flour and seasonings determine the final taste

The grain varieties

By far the most popular flour in Italy, and the one most frequently used in baking, is that made from the soft, floury kernels of the variety of wheat known as soft wheat. Fine semolina from durum, or hard, wheat, which cannot be ground into fine flour, is also used for baking. The preference for these flours follows a north–south divide in Italy: Whereas in the north, the flour cannot be white and fine enough, in the south — in Apulia, for example — durum wheat is also frequently used. Durum wheat gives special "bite" to bread, and loaves made with it do not grow stale as quickly as those made from soft wheat flour. Rye flour is also made into bread, especially in the Alpine regions of Italy, and there are also a number of other specialty breads prepared with cornmeal.

What's so special about wheat flour?

In principle, a dough can be prepared from the flour of almost any type of grain, with the addition of water, and possibly salt. However, such a dough will produce only thin flatbreads. If you wish to bake loaves or cakes with an attractive porosity and a light crumb, you also need a leavening agent such as yeast. And it is precisely here that the special characteristics of wheat flour come into play. Wheat contains gluten, a protein that gives the dough elasticity and creates a sort of framework that can be stabilized by the addition of salt. The gas bubbles generated by the yeast can attach themselves to this structure, making the bread porous. The gluten needs time to work properly, which is why the yeast dough must be kneaded long and thoroughly before it is left to rise. Other grains contain a different type of gluten, so almost all other types of flour must be mixed with wheat flour for baking. The only exception is rye. Loaves of bread can be baked from pure rye flour, but a special leavening agent, a sourdough starter, is then required.

The different types of wheat flour

Not all wheat flours are the same: There are differences in terms of how finely the grains have been ground, and which constituents of the grain are present in the flour. The more of the outer layers surrounding the kernel that are ground, the darker and more nutritious the flour. When only the starchy inner portion of the wheat grain is ground, a fine, white flour is produced, which is not very rich in minerals and fiber. In Italy wheat flour is sold according to standard classifications, from 00 (*doppio zero*) via 0, 1, and 2, up to *farina integrale* or whole-wheat flour. (If you can find Italian flour in specialty stores, use type 00 or 0 instead of all-purpose flour in the recipes in this chapter.) The Italians classify different types of bread according to the variety of flour from which they were baked.

Further ingredients for breadmaking

However, bread in Italy is not categorized only according to the flour, but also according to the other ingredients in the dough. *Pane di tipo speciale*, "specialty bread," is the name given to breads with an enriched dough. Even if only milk, butter, olive oil, or lard is added, the Italians speak of *pane di tipo speciale*, although the term also applies to the addition of sugar or raisins in the case of sweet yeasted breads. Bread made from specially spiced dough falls into this category too, although it is also called *pane condito*, "spiced bread."

Seeds and seasonings

In general, Italian cooking is inconceivable without fresh herbs, garlic, and onions. The first two "seasonings" cited here are a bit different, being the seeds of (**1**) sunflowers (*girasole*) and (**2**) pumpkins (*zucche*).

Wheat flour, from finely ground to whole wheat flour.

Apart from the fact that their nutty flavor is superb in baking, which is why they are often sprinkled on bread and rolls, they are also enjoyed as a tasty, and healthy, snack. **(3)** Green and red chiles (*peperoncini*) are prized in Italy as a way of spicing up many dishes, particularly in the southern part of the country. Calabrians, who usually put dried chiles on restaurant tables beside the salt and pepper shakers, are infamous for their lavish use of the sometimes diabolically hot peppers. And it's for good reason that an extremely hot variety of chile is known as *diavulillo* or *diavoletto* — "little devil" — in the Abruzze, while the slightly elongate, somewhat tamer one pictured here is called a *sigaretta*. *Peperoncini* lend a special zing even to simple dishes, such as a plate of pasta with garlic and olive oil. Piquancy is also lent by *olio santo*, the curiously named "holy oil," made by pouring best-quality olive oil over finely chopped *peperoncini*, and leaving the mixture to marinate for several days, sometimes even weeks; only a few drops are needed to lend an agreeable heat to meat, vegetables, or salad. Sesame seeds, whether **(4)** black and unhulled, **(5)** light-colored and unhulled, or **(6)** hulled, are sprinkled over a wide variety of baked goods: mainly bread, but also breadsticks and cookies. A distinctive seasoning made from the dried young leaf tips of a sweet clover is **(7)** melilotus, an Alpine specialty that is also used in Switzerland and Austria to flavor breads and cheese. In Italy, the oil extracted from **(8)** cardamom pods (*cardamomo*) nowadays is used primarily to flavor liqueurs and confectionery. In the Middle Ages, by contrast, the pods, pounded to a powder, were also commonly used, chiefly in Venice, but also in Pisa and Genoa. Perhaps it is from an old tradition rooted in that era that cardamom is still used in Siena to flavor the famous *panforte*, a disk-shaped cake containing sugar, almonds, nuts, and candied fruits. **(9)** Fenugreek seeds (*fieno greco*) are unpleasantly bitter when raw, and so are usually toasted for use as a seasoning for bread, as well as for stews and soups. **(10)** Allspice (*pimento*), also known as "pimento" or "Jamaica spice," tastes somewhat like cloves, cinnamon, and nutmeg combined, and is used in spiced breads and pastries.

(11) Poppyseeds (*papavero*) are used in bread and breadsticks in Venice, perhaps as a result of the influence of the neighboring Austro-Hungarian cuisines, in which poppyseed pastries and desserts are popular.
(12) Aniseed (*anice*) is a popular spice in Italian baking — *anicini*, small, spicy cookies, are even named after their main seasoning — and is also found in confectionery, dried figs, and even marinated olives. Very similar in taste are **(13)** fennel seeds (*finocchio*), which are used in the south and in Tuscany, where *finocchiana*, a fennel-flavored sausage, originated. *Taralli*, a piquant yeast pastry often served instead of bread with antipasti in Campania, Apulia, and Calabria, is also typically flavored with fennel.
(14) Coriander seeds (*coriandolo*), with their characteristic taste reminiscent of oranges, are found in baked goods, and are also used to flavor sausage, for example mortadella. **(15)** Linseed (*semi di lino*) appears in Italy in a type of bread made from a mixture of rye and wheat flour. The linseed is specially treated before use, giving it a nutty taste.
(16) Caraway seeds (*comino tedesco*) are used only in the northeast of Italy, in the southern Tyrol, Friaul, and the Veneto, mainly in bread, potato, and cabbage dishes, as well as in meat stews and sausages. Aromatic, slightly hot **(17)** black cumin (*nigella*) is used in the Mediterranean for sprinkling on flatbreads made from wheat flour. **(18)** Cumin (*comino*) comes from the Mediterranean and has a bitter-hot taste.

Basic doughs for breads

Except for the simplest flatbreads, almost all types of breads require a leavening agent to produce a soft crumb. The two traditional rising agents are yeast and sourdough.

Sourdough
Sourdough (*lievito di pane* or *crescente*) aerates bread without the use of other ingredients: The bacteria and yeast present in the flour begin to ferment when water is added and the starter is placed in a warm spot. The dough should be kept as close as possible to a constant 77°F, and therefore the water added to the flour should be warm (105–115°F). Even when all the rules are followed to the letter, however, a sourdough starter can sometimes go wrong, in which case it will produce a strong vinegary odor. This risk is avoided with the sourdough shown in the picture sequence below, which is started with added yeast. Most sourdough starters are made from rye flour, and in Italy they are usually used for pure rye breads.

Yeast dough
In Italy, baked goods, from loaves of bread to grissini to

Preparing a simple yeast dough without a starter:

Mix 2½ cups all-purpose flour with ½ teaspoon salt. In another bowl crumble 1 cake compressed fresh yeast, or 2 teaspoons active dry yeast, and dissolve in ⅔ cup lukewarm water.

Mix 2 tablespoons vegetable oil into the yeast solution (for pizza dough, olive oil is recommended, as it also imparts flavor to the dough), and pour the liquid into the flour-salt mixture.

Using a mixing spoon, stir the yeast-oil mixture, gradually incorporating more and more flour until the dough begins to get firmer.

Ease the dough from the bowl with a dough scraper, turning it out onto a floured surface. Continue working the dough with your hands.

Knead the dough by hand for at least 5 minutes, repeatedly slamming it down hard on the counter, until it is smooth and elastic.

Roll the dough into a ball and place in a bowl. Dust with a little flour and cover with a clean cloth.

Let rise in a warm spot for 30 minutes, until the dough has doubled in size. Before proceeding with the recipe, knead the dough again vigorously.

Preparing a rye sourdough starter with yeast:

Stir 1 cake compressed fresh yeast, or 2 teaspoons active dry yeast, in 1 cup water until dissolved. The water must be at a temperature of 105–115°F.

Using a mixing spoon, gradually stir the dissolved yeast into 1 cup rye flour.

Stir the starter until smooth, cover the bowl with plastic wrap and a cloth, and place in a warm spot for 24 hours.

Stir in 1 cup rye flour and ½ cup water. Cover and place in a warm spot for 3 days, until the dough bubbles.

BREAD AND PIZZA

In Emilia, **crescentine** are always freshly prepared, as at the Ristorante Gallida in Castel Franco, pictured below. To make them yourself, sift 4 cups all-purpose flour onto a surface and make a well in the center. Sprinkle a little salt at the edges of the flour. Dissolve 1 tablespoon active dry yeast in 2¼ cups milk, and pour into the well. Stir, incorporating more and more flour from the edges, until the dough becomes firmer. Work in 2 tablespoons softened butter in small pieces, and knead the dough until smooth and elastic. Transfer to a bowl, cover, and place in a warm spot until the dough has doubled in size. Roll out into a rectangle ⅛-inch thick, then cut into 1½-inch diamonds. Heat some vegetable oil in a skillet or deep-fat fryer to 350°F, and deep-fry the diamonds of dough, turning, until golden, 3-4 minutes. Lift out, drain on paper towels, and serve while still warm.

pizza, are made mainly from light wheat-flour doughs, and the most common leavening agent used is *lievito (di birra)*, baker's yeast obtained from brewer's yeast. Yeasted doughs are not especially difficult to prepare, but make sure that all ingredients are at room temperature, and that warm water (105–115°F) is used. Baker's yeast is available fresh, compressed into cakes weighing about ⅗ ounce, or dried in envelopes weighing ¼ ounce; 1 envelope of active dry yeast is equivalent to 1 cake of fresh compressed yeast. Both types must be dissolved in warm liquid, but it is not strictly necessary to make a starter dough when using fresh yeast; the picture sequence on the left of p. 418 gives an alternative.

Breads from yeast dough

A yeast dough like the one described here is suitable primarily for flatbreads and pizzas, as it does not need to rise very much. The preparation of most other Italian breads from a yeast dough requires a little more time, however. The ciabatta dough, for example, must prove for almost half a day, and the unsalted *pane sciocco* from Tuscany requires several hours. The fact that baking at home is so time-consuming is certainly one of the reasons that, even in Italy — a country in which people place the highest demands on the quality of food — a majority of the bread is now produced industrially. The old artisanal baking methods, in wood-burning or stone ovens, have by no means been forgotten, however, and the simple, often rustic recipes still enjoy great popularity. A good example of this are the *crescentine*, "crescents" or "half moons." This is the name given in Emilia-Romagna to the small breads that are often served warm with antipasti. The most captivating thing about *crescentine* is the way they are cooked, which is unusual for a bread: The dough is deep-fried in small batches, and so they are also called *gnocchi fritti*. The simplest version of the dough calls for only flour, water, yeast, and salt, and oil for deep-frying. The recipe above on the right, which uses milk, is a bit more substantial. In addition, the yeast can be replaced by baking soda, and finely chopped herbs may be mixed into the dough. For another, more luxurious variation, known as *gnocco ingrassato*, knead finely diced bacon into the dough. These rounds of dough — which, unlike *crescentine*, are baked — are still freshly prepared daily and eaten in Emilia-Romagna as a hearty breakfast after the first work of the day is done.

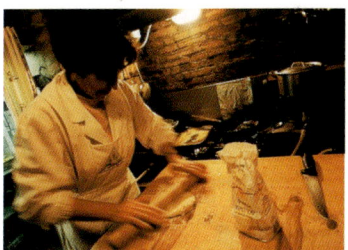

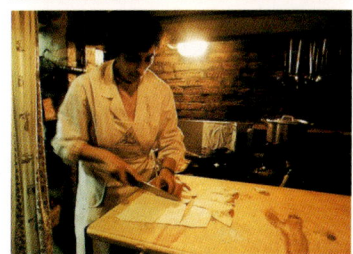

With its aniseed-like flavor, fennel seed goes well with dark, heavy breads made from rye flour, such as the Vinschgauer flatbreads.

Flatbreads from the southern Tyrol
Strongly spiced with aniseed or coriander, fennel, and caraway

This traditional flatbread is still made from scratch on many a southern Tyrolean farm and in many an Alpine hut. Once prepared chiefly with sourdough, it is now often made with yeast instead.

ANISEED FLATBREADS

Makes two 12-inch round breads
4 cups all-purpose flour
2 teaspoons active dry yeast
about 1½ cups lukewarm water, 1 teaspoon salt
You will also need:
1 egg yolk; crushed aniseed
fat and flour for the baking sheet

Sift the flour in a bowl and make a well in the center. Dissolve the yeast in 1 cup of the water, pour into the well, and mix with a little flour from the edges into a sticky paste. Dust with flour, cover, and

In order for the yeast dough for aniseed flatbreads to turn out as light and coarse-pored as intended, it must rise for several hours, in principle, just like baguette or ciabatta dough.

leave to rise overnight in a not-too-warm place.
 The next day, add the salt and almost all the remaining lukewarm water to the starter and knead to a smooth dough. Dust with flour, cover, and leave to rise again for 2 hours.
 Briefly knead the dough and divide in half. Shape each half into a ball, and roll each ball out on a floured surface into a disk about 12 inches in diameter. Leave to rise once again for 20–30 minutes.

Vinschgauer loaves, which are often baked in joined pairs, taste superb with the spicy south Tyrolean bacon called *speck*.

Preheat the oven to 400°F. Brush the dough with egg yolk and sprinkle with the crushed aniseed. Place on a greased, lightly floured baking sheet and bake for about 20 minutes.

VINSCHGAUER

Makes four 7–8-inch round loaves

4 cups rye flour
1 recipe sourdough (p.418)
1½ teaspoons salt
about 1½ cups lukewarm water
½ teaspoon crushed coriander seeds
½ teaspoon crushed fennel seeds
½ teaspoon crushed caraway seeds

You will also need:
fat and flour for the baking sheet

Sift the flour into a bowl and make a well in the center. Stir in the sourdough, add the salt, and gradually work in the water and spices to make a medium-firm dough. Dust with flour, cover, and leave to rise in a warm, draft-free spot for about 2 hours.

Briefly knead the dough and shape into 4 balls on a floured surface. Roll these into disks 7–8 inches in diameter. Dust with flour and leave to rise again for 1 hour. Preheat the oven to 400°F. Place the disks on a greased, lightly floured baking sheet and bake for 15–20 minutes.

Spicy tomato bread
Onions and thyme lend additional flavor

If you are lucky enough to get hold of really ripe, aromatic tomatoes, you may wish to try preparing your own *pomodori secchi*. If you cannot dry the tomatoes in the sun according to the Italian example, you will be pleased to learn that oven drying also works well. Lightly brush a baking sheet with olive oil. Peel, quarter, and seed the tomatoes. Preheat the oven to 160°F. Place the quartered tomatoes on the baking sheet cut surface downwards, and dry in the oven for at least 5 hours. Thus prepared the tomatoes will keep in the refrigerator for 3–4 weeks. For the bread recipe, you will need to start with about 10 ounces of fresh tomatoes, although you can, of course, dry and preserve a larger quantity.

Makes 2 loaves
For the preserved tomatoes:
½ cup dried tomatoes
2 chile peppers, halved and seeded
2 garlic cloves, halved
2 thyme sprigs
6–8 basil leaves, about 1 cup olive oil
For the dough:
5⅔ cups all-purpose flour
4 teaspoons active dry yeast, 1 cup lukewarm milk
⅓ cup extra-virgin olive oil, 1 egg, pinch of salt, 2 tablespoons sugar
1 cup finely chopped onions, 1 tablespoon olive oil
1 teaspoon chopped thyme leaves

You will also need:
flour for dusting
coarsely cracked white pepper, coarse salt

First, preserve the tomatoes. Layer the dried tomatoes in a large jar. Place the chiles, garlic, thyme, and basil on top of the tomatoes. Pour in enough olive oil to completely cover all the ingredients. Screw on the jar lid and put the jar in the refrigerator for 3 days.

The flavor of thyme also develops well at high temperatures, making it an ideal ingredient in baked goods.

Sift the flour for the bread into a bowl and make a well in the center. Add the yeast, pour in the lukewarm milk to dissolve it, and mix in a little flour from the edges. Dust the starter with flour and cover the bowl with a cloth. Place the bowl in a warm, draft-free spot, and let the starter dough rise for about 20 minutes, until the surface shows cracks.

Remove the tomatoes from the seasoned oil and drain. Measure ¼ cup of the seasoned oil, and mix with the extra-virgin olive oil and the egg. Mix into the starter with the salt and sugar. Knead together well, until the dough is smooth and shiny. Roll the dough into a ball, place in a bowl, cover with a cloth, and leave to rise for about 40 minutes, until the dough has doubled in size.

Cut the tomatoes into very small dice. Sweat the tomatoes and onion in 1 tablespoon olive oil until the onion is translucent, then leave to cool. Knead the tomatoes, onion, and thyme into the dough, then cover the dough and leave to rise again for 30 minutes.

Divide the dough in half and shape into two loaves. Place the loaves on a baking sheet dusted with flour, cover, and leave to rise for about 40 minutes. Preheat the oven to 400°F. Brush the loaves with a little water and sprinkle with the pepper and salt. Bake for 35–40 minutes. After 20–25 minutes, cover them with parchment paper to prevent overbrowning. Remove the loaves from the oven when done and place on a cake rack to cool.

It's not absolutely necessary to preserve the tomatoes for this bread yourself, of course, but if you do, you can be sure of achieving just the right spicy touch for this recipe.

Bread with ricotta and Swiss chard
An artistically layered piquant bread, with a succulent vegetarian filling and Mediterranean seasoning

The Italians call this culinary masterpiece *Torta cappuccina*, "Capuchin cake." Such layered vegetable breads and pies are popular in Italy; for example, the *torta pasqualina*, with spinach, and perhaps artichokes too, is baked at Easter, and in Liguria they make an exquisite pie with Swiss chard and pine nuts.

Makes two 10-inch round breads
6 cups all-purpose flour
¼ cup olive oil
½ teaspoon salt, freshly ground pepper
For the filling:
2¼ lb Swiss chard
2 tablespoons butter, ¾ cup finely chopped onion
1 tablespoon chopped oregano
1¾ cups ricotta cheese, 1 egg,
freshly ground pepper, salt
You will also need:
6 tablespoons butter, melted
1 cup freshly grated Parmesan
½ egg yolk, beaten with a little water

Using the rolling pin, lift one of the other small rounds and place it to fit exactly over the prepared first round.

Cut off 4 of the marked portions from the roll of dough, and shape each of them into a ball. Roll out these balls into rounds 9½ inches in diameter. Shape the remaining two portions into a single ball and roll it out into a 14-inch round. Brush one small round with melted butter and sprinkle with Parmesan cheese.

Using a palette knife, spread half of the filling evenly over the second round.

Place the third round on top, brush with butter, and sprinkle with Parmesan. Cover with the fourth round.

Brush the large round with butter, leaving a 1¼-inch edge free. Sprinkle with Parmesan, and place the pile of 4 rounds on top.

Brush the exposed rim with egg wash and fold in loosely toward the center, so that the filling is completely enclosed.

To make the dough, sift the flour into a bowl. Add the oil, about 1 cup water, salt, and pepper, and knead into a smooth dough. Cover, and leave to rest for about 20 minutes.

To make the filling, remove the stalks from the Swiss chard and save for another recipe. Wash the leaves under running cold water and cut into ½-inch-wide strips. Blanch in boiling salted water for 2–3 minutes. Lift out with a slotted spoon, drain, and leave to cool, then squeeze out all excess moisture.

Melt the butter in a skillet and sweat the onion until lightly colored. Add the chard and sweat for 3–4 minutes. Season with salt, pepper, and oregano. Remove the skillet from the heat and leave the chard to cool. Stir the ricotta and egg together in a bowl until smooth, mix in the chard, and season to taste with salt and pepper.

Briefly knead the dough once more, then divide in half, shaping both halves into cylindrical rolls on a floured surface. Mark each roll into 6 equal-sized pieces. Proceed as shown in the picture sequence on the left. Preheat the oven to 400°F. Brush a baking sheet with a little oil. Place the stuffed bread on the sheet with the folded-in edges on the bottom. Brush the top with melted butter and pierce at intervals with a fork. Prepare the second loaf in the same manner. Bake the bread for 20–25 minutes.

Renzo Depellegrin rolls his *piadina* dough out really, really thinly. At his restaurant, Al Palazzo Tesorieri, in Bagnocavallo, the flatbread is constantly baked fresh.

Piadina
Flatbread from Emilia-Romagna that is baked on a hot griddle

Piadina romagnola, or *piada* for short, is seen as the favorite food of the inhabitants of the Adriatic coast between Ravenna and Cattolica, since this thin flatbread is *de rigueur* at almost every meal. It is sold in special shops known as *piadinerie*, but many a beach stand or kiosk offers baked *piadine* hot off a clay or cast-iron griddle. Almost every village seems to have its own secret recipe for them — literally secret, since *piadina* bakers tend to keep their own recipes strictly to themselves. The cult of the *piadina* has grown to such an extent that a dedicated school, the *Scuola internazionale di piadina romagnola*, has been founded in Rimini. Whatever the secret variations, the basic recipe is not in doubt: the dough consists of nothing more than flour, lard, water, and salt. It is known, too, that in Ravenna *piadina* is occasionally enriched with milk, honey, or lemon rind, and olive oil is substituted for the lard. In the villages around Rimini, the dough is made with hot water, whereas in the environs of Cattolica cold mineral water is used; in Coriano, the liquid of choice is dry white wine, while in Cesena the flatbreads are aerated with yeast, as in the recipe given here. *Piadina* is eaten plain, freshly baked and still warm, or else stuffed — sometimes quite lavishly. To stuff a *piadina*, halve it while still warm, top with the filling of your choice, and clap the other half on top. Common fillings consist of ham, salami, tomatoes, and mozzarella, blanched spinach, cheese, arugula, anchovies, *salsiccia*, and sweet peppers; the only limit is your imagination.

A freshly baked *piadina* tastes superb with ham, olives or fresh cheese — here, the Italian squaquerone.

Carefully place the dough on the hot griddle, taking care that no air bubbles form.

Pierce repeatedly at close intervals with a fork to let air escape.

Bake the *piadine* for 8–10 minutes, turning repeatedly, until they are nicely browned.

Makes 5
4 cups all-purpose flour
1 tablespoon active dry yeast
1 cup lukewarm milk
¼ cup soft lard
1 egg
½ teaspoon salt
a pinch sugar

Sift the flour into a bowl and make a well in the center. Add the yeast and pour in the milk to dissolve it, mixing in a little flour from the sides. Sprinkle some flour over the starter. Cover the bowl with a clean cloth and place in a warm, draft-free spot. Leave the starter to rise until the surface shows cracks. Add the lard, egg, salt, and sugar to the starter and stir with a wooden spoon. Knead by hand to a smooth dough. Roll the dough into a ball, place it in the bowl, cover, and leave to rise again. Knead the dough once more and shape into a cylindrical roll 2¼ inches thick. Divide the roll into 5 equal pieces. On a lightly floured surface, roll out each piece into a 10-inch round. Heat an ungreased clay or cast-iron griddle (special *piadina* griddles, which may be difficult to find here, can be used on both gas ranges and electric hotplates) or heavy cast-iron skillet. Cook the flatbreads one at a time, as illustrated in the picture sequence on the left. Let them cool before topping or filling according to taste.

Focaccia: two different ways

Two versions of the famous Ligurian flatbread, one sophisticated, one simpler

The olive oil poured into the dimples of the flatbread is not completely absorbed by the dough, but it is what keeps the focaccias so beautifully moist.

FOCACCIA WITH SARDINES

Makes two 10 x 15-inch focaccias
For the dough:
5¼ cups all-purpose flour
2 tablespoons active dry yeast, 1 tablespoon sugar
1¾ cups lukewarm water
4 tablespoons olive oil, 1 tablespoon salt
For the topping:
1¼ lb fresh sardines
5 oz onions
3 garlic cloves, finely chopped
1 tablespoon chopped parsley, 2 tablespoons olive oil
coarse sea salt, freshly ground pepper
You will also need:
olive oil for the baking sheets

Sift the flour into a bowl and make a well in the centre. Add the yeast and sugar, and pour in a little water to dissolve the yeast, mixing in a little flour from the sides. Dust the starter with flour, cover, and leave to rise in a warm, draft-free spot for about 15 minutes, until the surface shows cracks.

Add the remaining water, the oil, and the salt to the starter, and knead to a supple dough, working in a little more flour if it remains sticky. Roll the dough into a ball, dust with a little flour, and leave to rise, covered, for another 30 minutes, until it has doubled in size.

To make the topping, fillet the sardines. Cut off the heads and the fins. Using a small, sharp knife, carefully cut open the belly of each sardine. Release the center bone by moving it gently to the right and left with your thumb, without damaging the fillets, and carefully pull out the bone. Thoroughly wash the two joined fillets under running cold water and carefully pat dry. Separate the fillets and cut each one into 3–4 pieces. Peel and halve the onions, and cut into thin half-moons.

Knead the dough, divide in half, then roll out each half on a floured surface into a 10 x 15-inch rectangle. Place each rectangle of dough on an oiled baking sheet and prick with a fork at regular intervals. Scatter the sardines and onions on top. Sprinkle with garlic, salt, pepper, and parsley, and drizzle over the olive oil. Preheat the oven to 400°F. Leave the focaccias to rise for a further 30 minutes, then bake for 20–25 minutes.

FOCACCIA WITH OLIVE OIL

Makes two 12 x 15-inch focaccias
9⅔ cups all-purpose flour
2 tablespoons active dry yeast
2¼ cups lukewarm water, ¼ cup olive oil
2 teaspoons salt
You will also need:
oil and flour for the baking sheets
½ cup extra-virgin olive oil
about 50 small, pitted black olives, coarse sea salt

Sift the flour into a bowl and make a well in the center. Add the yeast and the water to dissolve it, mixing in a little flour from the sides. Dust the starter with flour and cover the bowl with a cloth. Leave to rise in a warm, draft-free spot until the surface shows cracks. Knead the oil and salt into the starter. Roll into a ball, cover, and leave to rise again, until the dough has doubled in size.

Knead the dough and divide in half. Roll out each half on a floured surface into a rectangle measuring about 12 x 15 inches. Place on oiled, lightly floured baking sheets, cover, and leave to rise in a warm place for about 15 minutes.

Dimple the surface of each rectangle by pressing down with your index and middle fingers at regular intervals. Drizzle ¼ cup olive oil per focaccia into the dimples, as shown in the picture above on the right. Sprinkle some coarse salt over one of the flatbreads, and place an olive in each dimple of the other.

Preheat the oven to 400°F. Place the focaccias on an oiled baking sheet and bake for about 20 minutes. Remove from the oven and cool on a wire rack.

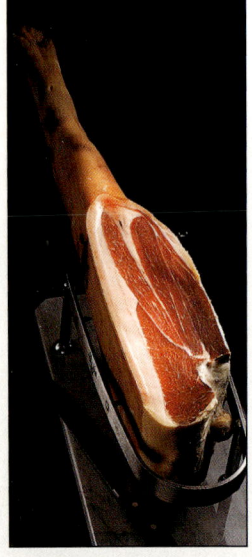

Prosciutto, or air-dried ham — here a splendid San Daniele — is a luxury that can transform even a simple focaccia into an exquisite delicacy.

Focaccia with pecorino cheese and prosciutto

Seemingly simple, with the right ingredients this is truly a connoisseur's bread

Just which type of prosciutto and pecorino cheese you choose for this recipe is a matter best left entirely to your own taste and pocketbook. As far as the ham is concerned, the choice ranges from *prosciutto di Parma*, to the milder San Daniele, to the new hot tip *culatello*, a specialty from the district of Zibello in the province of Parma, which is still relatively unknown outside Italy. For *culatello*, only the succulent centerpiece of the pork haunch, carefully seasoned and air-cured for about nine months, is good enough, a fact that is, of course, reflected in its high price. Even wider is the choice of pecorinos, the hard sheep's-milk cheese made throughout central and southern Italy, with recipes differing from region to region. We recommend a medium-aged pecorino — known in Italy as a *semifresco* — which will not be as crumbly as a cheese that has matured for longer, and can therefore melt gently as it bakes.

If wished, the focaccia can be sprinkled with cubes of cheese and prosciutto while it bakes. This produces an attractive surface, as can be seen from the focaccia in the background; on the other hand, when hidden in the dough, as in the bread in the foreground, the cheese and prosciutto are less exposed to the heat of the oven and stay juicier.

Pecorino cheese is still often made in the traditional manner by Sicilian farmers. Here, sheep's milk is heated with rennet in copper kettles over a wood fire until it curdles.

Makes two 8 x 12-inch focaccias
4½ cups all-purpose flour
1 tablespoon active dry yeast
⅞ cup lukewarm milk
½ cup butter, softened
2 small eggs
½ teaspoon salt
You will also need:
5 oz medium-aged pecorino cheese
7 oz prosciutto
olive oil and flour for the baking sheets

Sift the flour into a bowl and make a well in the center. Add the yeast and some of the milk to dissolve it, mixing in a little flour from the sides. Dust the starter with flour. Cover the bowl with a cloth and

leave the dough to rise in a warm, draft-free place for about 15 minutes, until the surface shows cracks.

Add the remaining milk plus the butter, eggs, and salt to the starter, and knead to a smooth dough. Roll the dough into a ball, dust with flour, place in a bowl, cover, and leave to rise in a not-too-warm place for about 2 hours.

Cut the cheese and prosciutto into ¼-inch dice. Knead the dough again, working in the cubed cheese and prosciutto as you do so; you might want to reserve a little of each to sprinkle over the top of the foccacias before baking.

Divide the dough in half and roll each half into an 8 x 12-inch rectangle, ¾ inch thick. Place each rectangle of dough on an oiled, lightly floured baking sheet, cover, and leave to rise for about 30 minutes, until considerably increased in size.

Preheat the oven to 400°F. Brush the foccacias with olive oil and bake for 30–35 minutes. If wished, sprinkle the remaining cheese and prosciutto cubes over the dough halfway through the baking time. Remove the *focaccias* from the oven and leave to cool on a wire rack.

In Sicily, this round of dough with its hearty topping is a staple of *la cucina povera,* as it is made without any expensive ingredients and still constitutes a complete, filling, and, above all, delicious, meal.

Sfincione
The Sicilian "sister" of the Neapolitan pizza

Whether pizza and sfincione both go back to common roots or whether one of these two hearty pies gave rise to the other will probably never be determined for certain. In any case, Sicilians strenuously deny that sfincione and pizza are identical. Certainly the crust for the piquant Sicilian *sfinciuni*, as it is called in the local dialect, is different from a Neapolitan pizza crust: thick and tender, yet crisp underneath and at the edges, but we might recognize it as a deep-pan pizza crust. The toppings may be similar to those for pizza and, as for pizza, improvisation is allowed; many a sfincione is topped with salami slices, or a ground meat and tomato sauce (*ragù*), or has anchovy fillets added to the basic recipe. A must, however, is the Sicilian Caciocavallo, a hard cheese that resembles the better known Provolone in terms of production method and texture. Sfincione can be baked as rounds sufficient for a single portion, or as a single large rectangle to be shared. If you choose the large rectangular pie, note that some of the ingredients increase slightly in quantity.

Sfincionari — **sfincione** bakers and sellers — traditionally offer their hearty wares fresh from the pan, simply cutting off individual portions for their customers.

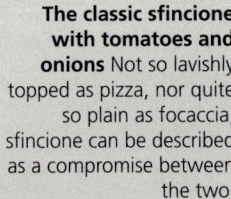

The classic sfincione with tomatoes and onions Not so lavishly topped as pizza, nor quite so plain as focaccia, sfincione can be described as a compromise between the two.

Makes 4 rounds, or 1 large rectangle
For the dough:
4 cups all-purpose flour
1 tablespoon active dry yeast
1 cup lukewarm milk
1 egg, ½ teaspoon salt
Topping for 4 rounds:
2¼ lb tomatoes, peeled, seeded, and diced
3 garlic cloves, finely chopped
1¼ cups finely chopped onions
1 teaspoon salt, ¼ cup olive oil
7 oz Caciocavallo cheese
20 black olives, halved and pitted
1 teaspoon finely chopped oregano leaves
Topping for 1 large rectangle:
2¼ lb tomatoes, peeled, seeded, and diced

3 garlic cloves, finely chopped
1¼ cups finely chopped onions
1 teaspoon salt, ¼ cup olive oil
9 oz Caciocavallo cheese
40 black olives, halved and pitted
coarsely torn mint and basil leaves
You will also need:
olive oil for the baking sheets

Sift the flour into a bowl and make a well in the center. Dissolve the yeast in the milk and pour into the well. Add the egg and salt, and work to a light dough. Shape into a ball, cover, and leave to rise for about 40 minutes.

To make the topping, mix the tomatoes, garlic, onions, and salt with half the olive oil.

To make the 4 individual rounds, knead the dough and divide into 4 pieces. Shape into thick rounds with ¾–1-inch-thick edges, and place these on two oiled baking sheets. Preheat the oven to 400°F. Spread the tomato mixture over the dough. Cut the cheese into ¼-inch dice. Sprinkle the olives, cheese, and oregano over the tomatoes. Drizzle over the remaining olive oil, and bake for 20–25 minutes.

To make the large rectangular sfincione, preheat the oven to 425°F and oil a baking sheet. Roll out the dough to the size of the baking sheet and place on it. Prick in several places with a fork to stop the crust from producing bubbles as it bakes. Prepare the tomatoes, onions, garlic, cheese, and olives as for the round sfincioni, and top the dough with them. Scatter the mint and basil on top, and bake for 20–25 minutes.

A Pizza Capricciosa, is made of the same dough as the Margherita, but in addition to the tomatoes, the crust is topped with ham, mushrooms, anchovy fillets, and artichoke hearts, with mozzarella and herbs being added last.

Pizza Margherita
The basic pizza with ingredients in the colors of the Italian flag

According to tradition, this pizza was created in honor of Margaret of Savoy, the first queen of Italy. The monarch was staying at the Capodimonte palace in Naples when she expressed a wish to try a pizza, a local specialty. One of the most famous *pizzaiol* was quickly summoned, and, seized with patriotism, he baked this piquantly topped pizza in the nation's colors.

Makes 2
For the crust:
2½ cups all-purpose flour
2 teaspoons active dry yeast, ½ cup lukewarm water
½ teaspoon salt, 2 tablespoons olive oil
For the topping:
2 x 14-oz cans peeled tomatoes
2 balls of mozzarella cheese
20 basil leaves, ½ cup olive oil
salt, freshly ground pepper
You will also need:
oil for the baking sheets

To make the crust, sift the flour into a bowl and make a well in the center. Add the yeast and pour in the water to dissolve it, mixing in a little flour from the sides. Dust the starter with flour. Cover the bowl with a clean cloth and leave the dough to rise in a warm, draft-free place, until the surface shows cracks.

Add the salt and oil to the starter, and knead to a smooth dough. Roll into a ball and leave the dough to rise again until it has doubled in size. Brush two baking sheets with oil.

Knead the dough again, divide evenly in half, turn out onto a floured surface, and shape each portion into a ball. Roll each ball out into a thin, round disk and place on a baking sheet. Preheat the oven to 425°F. Pierce the pizza bases in several places with a fork, and top them as shown in the first three steps of the picture sequence. Drizzle over the oil, as shown in the fourth photo. Bake each pizza for 18–22 minutes.

Topping a Pizza Margherita:

Drain the tomatoes, then chop them coarsely. Top the pizza bases with the tomatoes, stopping short of the edge of the crust.

Slice the mozzarella into rounds and distribute these evenly over the tomatoes. Season with salt and pepper.

Place the basil leaves on top. Chopped, they flavor the whole pizza better, but they look more decorative left whole.

After 10–15 minutes, drizzle over the olive oil with a spoon, or with a traditional Italian oil can.

Bake the pizzas one at a time. The Pizza Margherita should emerge from the oven with a crisp crust and a juicy, tender topping.

Instead of prosciutto and onions, salami, black olives, and mozzarella can be used to top this pizza.

Pizza with artichokes

With its thick, juicy topping, this southern Italian pizza is sumptuous in every respect

Makes two 9½-inch pizzas
For the crust:
2½ cups all-purpose flour, 2 teaspoons active dry yeast
⅔ cup lukewarm water
2 tablespoons olive oil, ½ teaspoon salt
For the tomato sauce:
2 tablespoons olive oil, ½ cup finely chopped onion
1 garlic clove, finely chopped
12 oz tomatoes, peeled, seeded, and diced
1 tablespoon tomato paste
½ teaspoon salt, freshly ground pepper
For the topping:
3 young artichokes with their stalks, about 4½ oz each
about 6 tablespoons lemon juice
9 oz tomatoes, 4 oz prosciutto
1 onion, sliced into rings
2 tablespoons olive oil
1 tablespoon chopped herbs (parsley, thyme, basil), salt

First prepare the artichokes. Cut off the stalks directly under the flower heads and brush the bases immediately with lemon juice. Strip off the small, tough leaves around the base of the stem. Use kitchen scissors to cut off the prickly tips of the outer leaves, and use a sharp knife to cut off the tip of the artichoke evenly. Place the trimmed artichokes immediately in a bowl of water acidulated with 2 tablespoons lemon juice, to prevent them discoloring.

Artichokes and prosciutto teamed with ripe tomatoes and spicy herbs — who could resist such a pizza?

Bring sufficient salted water to a boil in a pot with 2 tablespoons lemon juice and boil the artichokes for 15 minutes. Lift out, and turn upside down to drain. Cut each artichoke lengthwise into 6 and scrape out the inedible choke.

To make the crust, sift the flour into a bowl and make a well in the center. Add the yeast and pour in the water to dissolve it, mixing in a little flour from the sides. Dust the starter with flour, cover, and leave to rise in a warm place until the surface shows cracks. Add the oil and salt, and work to a smooth dough. Cover, and leave to rise until doubled in size.

To make the sauce, heat the oil in a saucepan and sweat the onion and garlic. Add the tomatoes and stew briefly, then stir in the tomato paste and season with salt and pepper. Reduce the heat and simmer for about 10 minutes, then leave to cool.

To make the topping, core the tomatoes and cut into eighths. Slice the prosciutto, then cut across into ¾-inch-wide strips.

Preheat the oven to 425°F. Briefly knead the dough, then divide it in half and roll each half into a disk 9½ inches in diameter. With floured hands, build up a rim by working the dough outward from the center. Place the pizza bases on a baking sheet, prick with a fork, and dust the edges with flour. Spread with tomato sauce, then top with the artichoke and tomato pieces, the onion rings, and the strips of ham. Drizzle the pizzas with olive oil and bake for about 20 minutes. Remove from the oven and sprinkle with the herbs. Serve hot.

Brightly painted donkey carts such as this one still add their picturesque touch to street scenes in Sicily. Farmers use them to bring their wares to the market, like the freshly harvested artichokes shown here. The sides of the carts are illustrated mainly with scenes from the Middle Ages.

When spreading the filling over the crust, leave a ¾-inch edge free and brush it with egg white. Fold the other half of the crust over the filling and press the edges down firmly to seal. Turn over the calzone, place on a baking sheet, and crimp the now-thick edge with a knife at ⅓-inch intervals.

Calzone times two
Large turnovers from Campania with a spicy filling, baked and sliced

In this country, the calzone is known chiefly as a folded-over pizza, which is prepared with fillings ranging from the simpler to the more sumptuous. In Italy, on the other hand, the most widely varying stuffed-dough pockets are termed *calzoni* — literally, "trouser legs." A strong bread or pizza dough can form the basis of this dish, but so can a more delicate yeast dough. Even more varied are the fillings, and the variations presented here are among the most delicious. If you prefer, you can bake two small turnovers instead of one large one for either of the following recipes.

ONION AND TOMATO CALZONE

Makes 1 large or 2 small
3⅓ cups all-purpose flour, 1 teaspoon salt
1 tablespoon active dry yeast, 1 cup lukewarm water
3 tablespoons olive oil
For the filling:
5 tablespoons olive oil
10 oz onions, sliced into rings
4 oz black olives, pitted and finely chopped
6 anchovy fillets, finely chopped
1 tablespoon capers, finely chopped
10 oz small tomatoes, peeled, seeded, and diced
1 bunch parsley, finely chopped
5 oz mild pecorino cheese
oregano, salt, freshly ground pepper
You will also need:
oil for the baking sheet
1 egg, separated

Sift the flour into a bowl and mix with the salt. Dissolve the yeast in the water and pour into the flour with the oil. Knead to a supple dough. Form the dough

Three types of cheese go into the filling of this calzone, which is also lent flavor by the salami slices and fresh herbs.

into a ball, place in a bowl, and dust with flour. Cover with a clean cloth, and leave the dough to rise in a warm place for about 30 minutes, until doubled in bulk.

To make the filling, heat the oil in a pan and stew the onion rings over a low heat, covered, until they have softened. Mix in the olives, anchovies, capers, tomatoes, and parsley. Season with oregano, salt, and pepper, and leave the mixture to cool. Coarsely shred the cheese and stir into the cooled onion mixture.

Knead the dough again, and roll it out on a floured surface into an oval ¼–1-inch thick.

Spread the onion mixture over one half of the dough, as shown above on p.438, leaving free an edge the width of your finger. Brush this edge with egg white. Fold the other half of the crust over the filling and press the edges together firmly to seal. Paint the outside edge with egg white too, and fold inwards.

Turn over the calzone, place on an oiled baking sheet, and crimp the newly formed thicker edge with the back of a knife, as shown in the second photo above on p.438. Cover and leave to rise again for about 20 minutes. Preheat the oven to 400°F.

Beat the egg yolk and brush it over the top of the calzone. Bake for 25–30 minutes, until golden.

CHEESE, SALAMI, AND HERB CALZONE

Makes 1
dough as in the preceding recipe
For the filling:
4 oz mozzarella or mild Provolone cheese
1 cup ricotta cheese, ½ cup finely grated pecorino cheese
1 small thyme sprig, a few rosemary needles
4 oz Italian salami, thinly sliced
1 egg, ¼ cup light cream, 1 tablespoon chopped parsley
salt, freshly ground pepper
You will also need:
1 egg, separated; flour for the baking sheet

Prepare the dough. To make the filling, cut the mozzarella or Provolone into ¼-inch dice, and press the ricotta through a strainer. Strip the thyme leaves from their stalks, and chop the leaves with the rosemary. Mix the cheeses with the salami, egg, cream, and herbs. Season with salt and pepper.

Preheat the oven to 400°F. Knead the dough and roll out into a large, round disk. Spread the filling over one half of the disk, leaving an edge of about ¾ inch free. Brush this edge with egg white, fold over the other half of the crust, and press the edges together firmly to seal. Form the edge of the crust as shown above left. Beat the egg yolk and brush it over the top of the calzone. Bake for 25–30 minutes, until golden.

The filling of the onion-and-tomato calzone is pleasantly spicy, thanks to the capers, black olives, anchovies, and herbs. Be careful when seasoning, however, so that this folded pizza does not become too salty.

Indice
INDEX

A

Abalone 290
Abbacchio 326
Abruzzese 38
Acciuga 281
Aceto 60, 61
    Balsamico Tradizionale di Modena 60
Affettato 40
Aglianico del Vulture 21
Aglio 64, 69
Agnello 326
Agone 292
Air-dried chamois meat 354
Alalunga 284
Albacora 284
Albicocca 386
Alice 281
Allspice 417
Almond biscuits 389, 392
Almond croquettes 334
Almond liqueur 389
Almond milk 389
Almonds 389, 392, 410
Amaretto 389
Amaretti 389
Anatra 357
Anchovies 281
    Cavolo Nero with 252
Anguilla 280
Angurie 387
Anice 417
Aniseed 417
Aniseed Flatbreads 420
Anitra 357
Antipasto di peperoni 48
Aperol 22
Apple 386
Apricot 386
Apricot sauce 402
Apricot and Wine Custard Cake 408
Aragoste 287
Arancia amare 385
Arancie 384

Arista alla Fiorentina 336
Arneis 20
Arrosto di maiale 324
Arselle 289
Artichoke, 104, 150, 236, 237
    Bucatini with 150
    Pizza with 436
Artichoke hearts, preparing 237
Artichokes with Tomatoes 44
Artichokes, cooking whole young globe 237
    Roman style 268
    Tuscan Vegetable Soup with Beans and 104
Arugula, wild 63
    Arugula and Pecorino, Orecchiette with 187
    Soup, Cream of 96
Asiago 122, 194
Asparago selvatico 239
Asparago 239
Asparagus 228, 239
Asparagus Risotto 228
Astici 287
Atlantic bonito 284
Atlantic pomfret 283
Averna 22

B

Bacon 36, 37
Bagna caoda 12
Baicolo 282
Baked Rock Lobster 320
Baked Shrimp 319
Baked Tomatoes 266
Bambolo 123
Barba di frate 238
Barbera 20
Barista 23
Basil 68
    Risotto with 205
Basil sauce 50, 57
    Carpaccio with 57
Batavia lettuce, 63

Battuto 249
Bay 67
Bay boletus 247
Bean and Olive Salad 80
Bean Salad with Rosemary 45
Bean soup (Ribollita) 100
Bean Soup with Penne Rigate 91
Beans 88, 89, 239
Beans, Soup with Cabbage and 90
    Tuscan Vegetable Soup with Artichokes and 104
    White, with Peppers 250
    White, with Shrimp 40
Bechamel sauce 190
Beef 324, 325
Beef and veal stock 327
Beef Roulades with Mortadella and Vegetables 341
Bel Paese 123
Bergamot 385
Bergamotto 385
Bianchetti 281
Bianco sporco 22
Bigo'li with Quail 188
Biscotti di Prato 392
Bitter orange 385
Black cumin 417
Black currants 387
Black grouper 282, 283
Black Olives, Fennel with 270
Black pasta dough 144
Black Pasta with Zucchini 144
Black Ravioli Stuffed with Rock Lobster 157
Black truffles 246
Black-eyed peas 89
Blackberries 387
Blue fish 285
Blueberry 387
Boar Ragout, Gnocchi with 180
Bocconcino Modense 38
Bocconcino 121
Bogue 283
Boiling chicken 356
Boldro 281

Boleto baio 247
Boleto dal piede rosso 247
Bollito Misto 328
Bolognese sauce 131, 190
Borage Leaves, Deep-fried 70
Borlotti beans 89
Bottarga di tonno 284
Braciola con l'osso 324
Braciole di Vitello 334
Braised beef 338
Braised duck 374, 375
Braised Lamb Shanks in Red Wine 344
Braised Pheasant in a Fine Sauce 373
Braised Wild Rabbit 369
Branzino 282
Brasato al Brunello 338
Brazino (sea bass) 12
Bread 414, 415
Bread dough 418
Bread Salad, Tuscan 74
Bread with Ricotta and Swiss Chard 424
Bresaola 33
Brill 286
Broccoletto di rapa 241
Broccoletto 240
Broccoli 240
Broccoli Aspic 46
Broccoli rabe 241
    with Croutons 255
    with Prosciutto 254
Broccolo 240
Brook trout 292
Broth, Garganelli in 140
Broth, Ravioli in a Clear 154
Brunello di Montalcino 21, 338
Bruscandoli 63
Bruscette 414
Bruschette, Tomato 43
Bucatini ai carciofi 150
Bucatini with Artichokes 150
Buck's horn plantain 238
Buckwheat pasta dough 134
Buckwheat dumplings 174

C

Cabbage 240
  Soup with Beans and 90
Cabernet Sauvignon 21
Cacciatore 39
Cactus figs 386
Caesar's mushroom 247
Caesar's Mushrooms, Stuffed 276
Caffè 22
Cairina 357
Calabrian Fish Stew 310
Calamari 291
  risotto 222
  Stuffed 316
Calcinelli 289
Caldarroste 388
Calf's foot 325
Calf's Liver 332
Calzone with Cheese, Salami and Herbs 439
Calzone with Onions and Tomatoes 438
Camoscio 354
Campari 22
Campotosto 38
Canestrelle 289
Cannellini beans 88
Cannelloni, Mushroom 164
Cannolicchio 289
Cannonau 22
Canocchie 288
Cantarello 247
Cantucci 392
Capa santa 289
Capalonga 289
Capello da prete 324
Caperfruit 27
Capers 26, 76
Caper Sauce, Spaghettini with 139
Capon 356
Capone imperiale 283
Cappa chione 289
Cappa gallina 289
Cappelletti Croccante 153
Cappelletti in Duck Broth 152
Capperi 26
Capperone 27
Cappone 356
Cappuccina torta 424
Capretto 326

Capriolo 354
Capsicum, sweet 244
Caraway seeds 417
Carciofi 236
  grigliati 30
  alla romana 268
Cardamom pods 417
Cardoon 236, 258
Cardoon with Tomato Sauce 258
Carne di maiale 324
Carp 292
Carpa a specchi 292
Carpaccio with Basil Sauce 57
Carrots, dicing 248
Carta da musica 415
Castagna 388
Castrato 326
Catalogna di Galantina, Salad 79
Catalogna Salad 78
Cauliflower 240, 241
Cavolfiore 240
Cavolo 240
Cavolo cappuccio rosso 240
Cavolo cappuccio 240
Cavolo di Milano 241
Cavolo nero 240, 241
  cutting 253
Cavolo Nero with Anchovies 252
Cavolo verza 241
Cayenne pepper 244
Ceci 87
Cedro 384
Ceps *see* Porcini
Cerasuolo di Vittoria 22
Cernia 282
Cervo 354
Chamois deer 354, 355
Chamois meat, air-dried 354
Chanterelle mushroom 247
Chard, Bread with Ricotta and Swiss 424
Cheese, types of 116–125
  Asiago 122, 194
  Bambola 123
  Bel Paese 123
  blue-veined 124
  Bocconcino 121
  Caciocavallo 120
  Caciotta 106, 122, 123
  Canestrato 118, 119

  Cicillo 120
  Extra-hard 116
  Fior di latte 121
  Fontal 123
  Fontina 123
  Formaggi caprini 125
  Formaggini 124
  Fresh cheese 124, 125
  Goat's-milk cheese 125
  Gorgonzola 124
  Grana Padano 116, 117
  Grana Trentino 116, 117
  Marzolino 123
  Mascarpone 124
  Montasio 122–123
  Mozzarella 52, 120, 121
  Panerone (Pannarone) 124
  Parmesan 116
  Parmigiano-Reggiano 116
  Pecorino (sheep's-milk cheese) 95, 118, 119, 430
  Provolone 120
  Quartirolo 123
  Ragusano 120, 121
  Ricotta 125
  Robiola 124
  Semi-hard cheese 122
  sheep's-milk 95, 118, 119, 430
  Stracchino 124
  Taleggio 123
Cheese
  Calzone with Salami, Herbs and 439
  Eggplant with Mozzarella 53
  Gnocchi 177
  little yeast cakes with 71
  Pecorino, Focaccia with Prosciutto and 430
  Pecorino, Orecchiette with Arugula and 187
  sauce 148
  for slicing 122
  Tomatoes and 53
Cheppia 292
Cherries 386, 387
Cherry tomatoes, yellow, plum 234
Chervil 67
Chestnuts 388
Chiancetta 286
Chianti 21
Chick-peas, preparing 87

Chicken 356
Chicken breast 35
Chicken broth 140
Chile Peppers in Oil 49
Chiles 417
China Martini 22
Chiodino 247
Chocolate cream 404, 406, 407
Chocolate Cream, Meringues with 406
Chocolate leaves 402
Ciabatta 415
Ciabattini 415
Ciala di mare 288
Cicciolata 37
Ciccioli croccanti 37
Ciccioli 37
Cieche 280
Ciliegia 386
Cima alla Genovese 50
Cima di Rapa 241
Cinghiale e finocchio 360
Cinghiale 355
Cipollata 100
Cipolle borettane 30
Citron lemon 384, 385
Citrus fruit 384, 385
Clams 289
Clams, Salad with Scallops and 82
Clear Broth, Ravioli in a 154
Clementina 385
Clementine 385
Cloves 417
Coda di bue 325
Coda di rospo 281
Cold cuts 40
Colombaccio 358
Comino tedesco 417
Comino 417
Common wild goose 357
Conchiglia di San Jacopo 289
Coniglio selvatico 355
Coniglio 356
Cooked ham 33
Cooked, kneaded cheese 120, 121
Cooking from the Italian regions 6–19
Capocollo 37
Coppa 36–37
Coriander seeds 417
Coriandolo 417

Cornetto di mare 290
Corretto grappa 22, 23
Costine 324
Costolette alla Pizzaiola 330
Costolette di tonno 300
Cotechino 324
Cotognata 387
Cozze 289
Crabs 287
Crema fritta 400
Crescentine 414, 419
Creste di gallo 356
Crostini 414, 415
Crostini with olive paste 42
Cucurbita 220, 242, 243
Culatello di Zibello 34, 35
Cuore di bue 234, 235
Cuttlefish
 extracting ink from 291
 Risotto 222

D

Daino 354
Dandelion 62, 63, 220
Dandelion Flowers, Risotto with 220
Datteri di mare 289
Datteri nero 289
Deep-fried Borage Leaves 70
Deer 354
Denominazione di Origine Controllata (DOC) 19, 116
Dentex 282
Dentice 282
Desserts 382–410
Dessert grapes 387
Dill 66
Dindo 357
Dolcetto 20
Domestic duck 357
Domestic goose 357
Domestic pigeon 358, 359
Dried pasta *see Pasta secca*
Dried porcini 166
Dublin Bay prawns 287
Duck 357
Duck breast 361
Duck Broth, Cappelletti in 152
Duck, Braised in Red Wine 374
Duck Legs in a Dark Sauce 375

E

Eel 280
 Marinated, in Tomato Sauce 294
 skinning an 294
Eggplant 244, 245
Eggplant with Mozzarella 256
Eggs, Wild Herb Salad with Olives and 72
Elder 366
Elefante di mare 287
Ellettaria cardamomum 417
Elver 280
Espresso coffee 23
European quail 358

F

Fagiano 359
Fagioli al fiasco 250
Fagioli 88, 89
Fagiolini 238
Fallow deer 354
Faraona 358
Fasulara 289
Fava beans 88
Fazzoletti, Striped, with Quail Ragout 172
Fegato di Vitello 332
Fegato grasso 357
Fennel 66, 216, 245
 with Black Olives 270
 game salami 360
 leaves 66
 Risotto 216
 seeds 417
 Soup 102
 wild 245
Fenugreek seed 417
Fernet Branca 22
Fettuccine with White Truffles 142
Fettunta 415
Fichi d'india 386
Fichi 386
Fieno greco 417
Figs 365, 386
Filetto di cinghiale 360
Filita cheese 120, 121
Fillet of John Dory with Tomato Sauce 312
Finger biscuits 404
Finocchi gratinati 270
Finocchiella 245
Finocchio 245, 417
Finocchiona di cinghiale 360
Fiori di Zucca Fritti 397
Fish in a Paper Envelope 296
Fish stock, preparing 293
Fish, preparing 293
 see also Pesce
Flageolet beans 88
Flatbreads 415
Flatfish 286
Flying fish 281
Focaccia 414
 di Mandorla 410
 with Olive Oil 429
 with Pecorino and Prosciutto 430
 with Sardines 429
Fragole 387
Fragola di bosco 387
Fresh porcini 166
Fresh Mushrooms with Tomatoes 275
Fresh pasta *see Pasta fresca*
Fresh pasta dough, preparing 126
Fresh tomato sauce, preparing 129
Freshwater fish 292
Fried Pumpkin Flowers 397
Fried Vanilla Custard Slices 400
Fritelle di borragine 70
Fritelle di riso 396
Fritole Venissiane 397
Fruit 384-387
Fruit ice 390
Frutta di martorana 389
Frutta secca 388, 389
Frutta 384-387
Frutti di Mare con Linguine 318
Funghi freschi 274
Funghi 246, 247
Funghi di muschio sottolio 30

G

Galletto 356
Gallina 356
Gallo 356
Gamberetti grigi 288
Gamberetti 288
Gambero imperiale 288
Gamberi rossi 288
Gambero sega 288
Game 354, 355
Game salami 360, 361
Game stock 155
Garbanzos 87
Garganelli in Brodo (in broth) 140
Garlic 69, 314
Garlic Mushrooms 276
Garlic, Sweet Peppers with 45
Gattopardo 280
Gelato 390
Gewurztraminer 21
Gheriglo 388
Gianchetti 281
Giant pumpkin 220
Giottini 392
Gnocchetti di patate 184
Gnocchetti Don Alfonso 184
Gnocchi 178, 180, 182, 344, 362
Gnocchi alla romana 178
Gnocchi, Cheese 177
Gnocchi fritti 419
Gnocchi with ragout of roe deer 362
Gnocchi in Tomato Sauce 182
Gnocco ingrassato 419
Gnocchi with Boar Ragout 180
Gnocchi, Spinach, with Hare Ragout 176
Goose 357
Goose salami 361
Gorgonzola Risotto with Spinach and 210
Grancevola 287
Granchio 287
Granciporro 287
Grano saraceno 135
Grape 387
Grape cake 394
Grapefruit 385
Grapefruit Sorbet 391
Grappa 22

Green beans 238
Green olive paste 31
Green pasta, preparing 126, 127
Green zucchini, marinated 261
Gremolata 346, 347, 376
Grenache 22
Gray goose 357, 359
Grissini 415
Grooved carpetshells 289
Grouper 282
Guinea fowl 358
Guinea fowl ragout 140
Gurnard 283

H

Ham 32, 33
Hare 355
Hare Ragout, Spinach Gnocchi with 176
Hazelnut 388
Hedgehog mushroom 247
Herb Risotto 205
Herb Risotto with Rock Lobster 227
Herbs, aromatic 64-69
Herbs, Calzone with Cheese, Salami and 439
Honey mushroom 247
Hops 62
Hop shoots 63
Horse mackerel 283

I

Ibex 354, 355
Ice 390
Ice cream, preparing 390
Indicazione Geografica Tipica (IGT) 19
Insaccati 37, 38, 39
Insalata Caprese 52
Insalata 62, 63
Involtini di manzo 341
Involtini di Vitello 342

J

John Dory 282, 283
John Dory with Tomato Sauce, Fillet of 312
Jumbo Shrimp, Minestrone with Monkfish and 106
Jumbo Shrimp Risotto 226

K

Kale 240, 241
Kid 326
Kidney 325
Kirsch liqueur 387
Kohlrabi, Lasagne with Swiss chard and 192

L

Lacrimae Christi 21
Lagreiner 21
Lamb 326
Lamb Chops 326, 350
Lamb Shanks Braised in Red Wine 344
Lampascione 245
Lamponi 387
Rock Lobster 287
    Black Ravioli Stuffed with 157
    Herb Risotto with 227
    oven-baked 320
Lard 324
Lardo 37
Lasagna with Swiss Chard and Kohlrabi 192
Lasagna, Bolognese style 190
Latterini 281
Latume 284
Layered almond cake 410
Laying hens 356
Leavened dough 418
Leavened rye sourdough with yeast 418
Leg of veal 346
Leg of venison 354
Legumes 86–89
Legumi secchi 86–89

Lemon 296, 384, 385
Lemon liqueur 384
Lemon pigeon 376
Lenticchie 87
Lentils 87
Lettuce, types 62–63
Lievito (di birra) 419
Lievito di pane 418
Limoncino 384
Limone 384
Linguine, Frutti di Mare con 318
Linseed 417
Lisca 114
Little yeast cakes 71
Lobster 287
Loquat 386
Loup de mer 282
Luccio 292
Luganega 37
Lupo 282

M

Macaroni and Spinach *au gratin* 170
Macaroni bake 194
Mackerel 284, 285
Mackerel, horse 283
Maialino 324
Mallard duck 357, 359
Mallo 388
Malvasier 21
Mandarancio 385
Mandarine 384, 385
Mandarine liqueur 385
Mandarinetto 385
Mandarino 385
Mandorla amara 389
Mandorla dolce 389
Manico di coltello 289
Manzo 324, 325
Marasca 387
Maraschino liqueur 387
Marinated Eel in Tomato Sauce 294
Marinated Green Zucchini 261
Marinated Peppers 48
Marinated Yellow Zucchini 261
Marjoram 65
Marroni 388

Marsala 22
Martini 22
Marzipan 389
Mazzancolle 288
Meat Sauce, Bolognese 131, 190
Medlar 386
Mela 386
Melagrana 387
Melanzane grigliate 30
Melanzane alla parmigiana 256
Melon 387
Menta 68
Meringues 406
Meringues with Chocolate Cream 406
Merlot 20, 21
Milk lamb 326
Minestrone di verdura 92
Minestrone from Campania 93
Minestrone with Monkfish and Jumbo Shrimp 106
Minestrone with Pesto, Fillet of Ray in 306
Mint 68
Mirror carp 292
Mirtilli 387
Medley of Wild Mushrooms 274
Mocetta 354
Monica di Cagliari 22
Monica di Sardegna 22
Monkfish 106, 281
Monkfish, Minestrone with Jumbo Shrimp and 106
Monkfish, Pan-fried, with Zucchini Sauce 298
Montone 326
More di rovo 387
Moray eel 280
Morello cherries 387
Morello cherry sauce 400
Morello cherry sorbet 391
Mortadella 36, 37
    Beef Roulades with Vegetables and 341
Moscardino 30, 291
Moscato 22
Mosciame 284
Mostarda 31, 387
Motazetta 354
Mozzarella 52, 120, 121
    Eggplant with 53

Mucetta 354
Muflone 355
Mullet
  Baked Gray 308
  red 285
  Red, with Olives 304
  Striped Red, with
    Mushrooms 304
Murena 280
Muscat de Chambave 19
Musciame 284
Muscoli 289
Mushrooms 246, 247
  Cannelloni with 164
  fresh, with tomatoes 275
  Pappardelle Con Funghi 168
  Striped Red Mullet with 304
Musk octopus 291
Mussel Soup 108
Mussels 289
Mutton 326

N

Navy beans 88
Nebbiolo 20
Neonati 281
Nero di seppia 290, 291
Nero di Toscana 241
Nespola del Giappone 386
Nigella 417
Nocciola 388
Noce 388
Nocino 388
Noodles, ribbon 330
Norcian truffles 246
Nudini 281
Nut liqueur 388
Nuts 388

O

Oca di ingrasso 357
Oca selvatica 359
Oca 357
Octopus 290, 291
Ogen melon 387
Olio al tartufi 247
Olive oil 28-29

  Focaccia with 429
Olive paste 31, 133
  Crostini with 42
Olives 26
  Black, with Fennel 270
  Red Mullet with 304
  Salad, Bean and 80
  Taggiasca 28
  Wild Herb Salad with Eggs
    and 72
Onion
  Calzone with Tomato and
    438
  dicing 248
  soup 100
  wild 245
Orange 384, 385
  Salad 75
Orecchie di mare 290
Orechiette with Arugula and
  Pecorino 187
Oregano 65
Ormers 290
Orvieto 21
Osso buco 346
Ovolo 247
Oxtail 325
  Stuffing, Tortelli with 146

P

Palaia 286
Palamita 284
Palombaccio 358
Palombo 280
Pan-fried polenta slices 332
Pancarre 415
Pancetta 37
Pane a cassetta 415
Pane carasau 414, 415
Pane sciocco 419
Pan-fried Monkfish with
  Zucchini Sauce 298
Panforte di Siena 13
Panini 414
Panna cotta 402
Pannocchie 288
Pansoti with Walnut Sauce 159
Panzanella 74
Papavero 417
Paper Envelope, Fish in a 296

Pappardelle con Funghi 168
Parma ham 32
Parsley 64
Passato di pomodoro 235
Passito di Pantelleria 22
Pasta
  alla Norma 149
  Au Gratin, Vegetables and
    148
Pasta, cooking properly 128
Pasta, cutting 127
Pasta, dried *see Pasta secca*
Pasta, filled 112
Pasta, fresh *see Pasta fresca*
Pasta, green, making 126, 127
Pasta fresca (fresh) 112, 126
  black 144
  buckwheat 134
  dough 112
  fresh, making 126–127
  green, preparing 126–127
  porcini 166
  ripiena 112
Pasta secca (dried) 114–115
  Conchigliette tricolori 114
  corta 114
  Elbow macaroni, plain,
    colored with spinach
    and beet juice 114
  Gnoccetti di zite 114
  letters 114
  lunga 114
  Mezze penne rigate 114
  pastina all'uovo 114
  Pennette rigate 114
  Pipette 114
  Strozzapreti 114
Pasta reale 389
Pasta rigata 114
Pasticcio di maccheroni 194
Pâté de fois gras 357
Patelle 290
Peach 386, 387
Pear 386
Peas 87, 238
Pecora 326
Pecorino, Focaccia with
  Prosciutto and 430
Pecorino, Orecchiette with
  Arugula and 187
Pelati 235
Pellegrina 289
Penne all'Arrabiata 138

Penne Rigate, Bean Soup with
  91
Penne Rigate with Porcini in
  Cream 168
Peoci 289
Pepe di Cayenna 244
Peperonata 253
Peperoncini in oil 49
Peperoncino 417
Peperoni all'olio 48
Peperoni all'acciughe 250
Peperoni Ripieni 264
Peperoni 244
Peppermint 68
Peppers
  Marinated 48
  skinning 48
  Stuffed 264
Pera 386
Perch 292
Pesca 387
Pesce 278–321
  al Cartoccio 296
  bandiera 285
  castagna 283
  San Pietro 282, 312
  fiamma 285
  lupo 282
  persico 292
  rospo 281
  Spada 285
Pesce-cane 280
Pesci azzurri 285
Pesto 132, 306, 316, 389
Pesto, Fillet of Ray in
  Minestrone with 306
Pettine 289
Petto di pollo 356
Pheasant 359
  Braised, in a Fine Sauce 373
  Salmi of 372
  stock 155
  Tortelloni with 155
Piada 426
Piadina romagnola 426
Piadina 414, 415, 426
Piccione 358
Pig's head brawn 36
Pig's foot 324
Pigeon 358
Pike 292
Pimento 417
Pine nuts 388, 389

Pino Nero 20, 21
Pinoli 389
Pinto beans 89
Pinzimonio 44
Piopparelli 304
Pioppini 304
Piscatrice 281
Pisci luna 283
Piselli mangiatutto 238
Piselli 87, 238
Pistachio 388
Pistacia vera 388
Pistazie 388
Pito 357
Pizza 414
   with Artichokes 436
    Capricciosa 434
    Margherita 434
Pizzoccheri with Sage 134
Plum 386, 387
Plum-shaped yellow tomatoes 234
Polenta 178, 272, 336
Polenta Filling, Zucchini with 262
Polenta Slices, with Porcini Stuffing 272
Polenta cakes 376
Polenta slices, pan-fried 332
Pollastrello 356
Pollastrino 356
Pollastro 356
Pollo 356
Pollo alla Sienese 378
Polpo di pomodoro 235
Polpo 290
Pomegranate 387
Pomes 386, 387
Pomfret, Atlantic 283
Pommarola 129
Pomodori secchi 235, 422
Pomodorini 234
Pompelmo 385
Poppyseeds 417
Porcellino 324
Porcinello grigio 247
Porcini 166, 246, 247
   in Cream, Penne Rigate with 168
   noodles 338
   in Olive Oil 30
   pasta dough 166
   Stuffing, Polenta Slices with 272

Pork 324
Pork Chops with Tomato Sauce 330
Pork, Rolled Roast in the Florentine style 336
Poverazza 289
Preserved tomatoes 422
Prickly pears 386
Prosciutto 32, 33
   di cinghiale 360
   Focaccia with Pecorino and 430
   di Parma 32
   di San Daniele 33
Prosecco 20
Prugna 386
Pumpkin 220, 242
   flowers 243
   Flowers, Fried 397
    preparing 243
   purée 242
   risotto 221
   Salad 81
   seeds 416
   Stuffing, Tortelli with 145
Purple broccoli 240
Purple cauliflower 241
Purple sage 67

Q

Quaglie 358
Quail 358
   Bigo'li with 188
   European 356
   Ragout, Striped Fazzoletti with 172
Quince 386, 387
Quince bread 387

R

Rabbit, preparing 369
Rabbit, Roast, with Rosemary 368
Radicchio, Risotto with 230
Radicchio Sauce, Sea Bass with 302
Ragno 282

Ragusano pepeto 121
Rainbow trout 292
Raisins 387
Rana pescatrice 106, 281
Raspberry 387
Ravioli
   Black, Stuffed with Rock Lobster 156
   Clear Broth with 154
   di magro 158
   with Shrimp Stuffing 156
Raw ham 32, 33
Ray 280
Razza 280
Red chiles 417
Red deer 354
Red gurnard 283
Red mullet 285
Red Mullet with Olives 304
Red Wine, Duck Braised in 374
Red Wine, Lamb Shanks Braised in 344
Red wine figs 364
Red currant 387
Remoulade sauce 46
Reno 325
Ribes 387
Ribollita 100
Ribs 324
Ricci di mare 290
Rice 198–203
Rice doughnuts 396
Rice Torte 398
Rice, cooking by the absorption method 203
Rice, Spinach Soup with 96
Rice, types of 202
Ricotta, Bread with Swiss Chard and 424
Ringed dove 359
Riso greggio 200
Risotto
   Asparagus 228
   basic preparation 203
   with Basil 205
   Calamari 222
   with Dandelion Flowers 220
   Fennel 216
   Herb 205
   Herb, with Rock Lobster 227
   Jumbo Shrimp 226
   alla Milanese 204
   Porcini 214

   Pumpkin 221
   Radicchio 230
   Saffron, with Summer Truffles 218
   Savoy Cabbage 212
   Shrimp, with Savoy Cabbage 206
   with Spinach and Gorgonzola 210
   with Sweet Peppers 224
   Tomato 209
   Vegetable 213
   with White Truffles 215
   with Zucchine Fiorite 208
Ristretto 23
Rivarossa 21
River eel 280
Roast Rabbit with Rosemary 368
Roast Veal with Tuna-fish Sauce 54
Roasted chestnuts 388
Rock Cornish Hen 356
Rock Lobster, Baked 320
Roe Deer, Gnocchi with Ragout of 362
Roman mint 68
Romanesco 240, 241
Rombo chiodato 286
Rombo liscio 286
Rosemary 65
   Bean Salad with 45
   Roast Rabbit with 368
Rosso dei vigneti di Montalcino 338
Rosso di Montalcino 338
Rotolo di tacchino 357
Round zucchini 243
Rucola aromatica 63
Rucola selvatico 63
Rue 67
Ruta 67

S

Saddle of venison 354
Saffron Risotto with Summer Truffles 218
Sage 66, 334
Sage, Pizzoccheri with 134
Sagra dello stoccafiso 18

Salad
　with Beans and Olives 80
　Catalogna di Galatina 79
　Orange 75
　Pumpkin 81
　with Scallops and Clams 82
　Seafood 83
Salami, Calzone with Cheese, Herbs and 439
Salami, types of 38–39
Salame di cinghiale 360
Salice Salentino 21
Salmi of Pheasant 372
Salpa 283
Salsa al Dragoncello 43
Salsa olandese 320
Salsa di pinoli 389
Salsa verde 328
Salsicce 37
Salsiccia cinghiale 360
Salsiccia fresca 37
Saltimbocca 325
Sangiovese 21
Sanguigna 384
Sarda 281
Sardella 281
Sardelle Ripiene 56
Sardina 281
Sardine 281
Sardines, Focaccia with 429
Sardines, Stuffed 56
Sarpa 283
Sassicaia 21
Sauce Mornay 133
Sausage 36–39, 324
Sauvignon Blanc 21
Savoy cabbage 240–241
　Risotto 212
　Shrimp Risotto with 206
Scabbard fish 285
Scaldfish 286
Scallops 289
Scallops, Salad with Clams and 82
Scampi 287
Schiacciata con le uve 394
Scorfano 283
Scorpena rossa 283
Scorzone 247
Sea bass 282, 283
Sea bass with Radicchio Sauce 302
Sea snails 290

Sea-urchins 290
Seafood Salad 83
Seafood, Risotto with 206
Seafood, Tagliatelle with 162
Seafood, Truffle Fazzoletti with 160
Seeds 388, 389, 417
Seme di lino 417
Sepia ink 290, 291
Sepiolini 30
Seppiole 291
Sesame seeds 417
Sfincione 432
Sfoglia 112, 286
Sforzato 20
Sgombri 284
Sgonfiotti 71
Shanks, Lamb, Braised in Red Wine 344
Shark 280
Sheep 326
Shellfish Stew 314
Short-grain rice 198
Shoulder of venison 354
Shrimp 288
Shrimp, Baked 319
Shrimp, White Beans with 40
Shrimp Risotto with Savoy Cabbage 206
Shrimp Stuffing, Ravioli with 156
Simple yeast dough 418
Skate Wing in Minestrone with Pesto 306
Snow peas 238
Soave 20
Soffritto 248, 249
Soft fruit 387
Sogliola variegata 286
Sogliola 286
Sole 286
Soleras 22
Soppressata 36
Sorbet 390
Sorbetti 390
Sorbetto di Pompelmo 391
Sorbetto di Visciole 391
Sott'aceti 31
Sott'oli 31
Soup
　Arugula, Cream of 96
　with Cabbage and Beans 90
　Cipollata 100

　Fennel 102
　Minestrone with Monkfish and Jumbo Shrimp 106
　Mussel 108
　Ribollita 100
　with Spinach and Rice 96
　Tomato 103
　Tuscan Vegetable 104
　Zucchini-flower 98
Sourdough starter 418
Sour-cherry sauce 400
Spaghetti
　con Aglio, Olio e peperoncino 138
　alla Carbonara 137
　alla Chitarra 136
Spaghettini with Caper Sauce 139
Spanocchio 288
Sparico di spagna 239
Speck (bacon) 36, 37
Spices 417
Spicy Tomato Bread 422
Spider crab 287
Spigola 282
Spinach
　Au Gratin, Macaroni and 170
　Gnocchi with Hare Ragout 176
　and Gorgonzola, Risotto with 210
　pulp, making 126
　soup with rice 96
　Risotto with Gorgonzola and 210
Spinula 282
Spotted ray 280
Spring Salad 76
Squab kebabs 370
Squid 291
　preparing 291
　stuffed 316
Squid-ink Pasta with Zucchini 144
Stambecchi 355
Steccherino dorato 247
Stew, pheasant 372
Strawberry 387
Stringoli with Tomato Sauce 186
Striped clams 289
Striped Fazzoletti with Quail

　Ragout 172
Striped red mullet 285
Striped Red Mullet with Mushrooms 304
Stuffed
　bell peppers 264
　Breast of Veal 50
　Caesar's mushrooms 276
　Calamari 316
　Rock Cornish Hens 380
　Sardines 56
　squid 316
　Tomatoes 267
　zucchini flowers 99
Suacia 286
Suckling pig 324
Sugo 129
Summer truffles 161, 218, 247
　Saffron Risotto with 218
Sun-dried tomatoes 30
Sunflower seeds 417
Suro 283
Sus scrofa 355
Sweet almonds 389
Sweet chestnut 388
Sweet melon 387
Sweet peppers 244
　with Garlic 45
　Risotto with 224
Swiss Chard and Kohlrabi Lasagna 192
Swordfish 285

T

Tacchino 357
Taggiasca olives 28
Tagliatelle with Seafood 162
Tapenade 133
Tarragon 66
　Sauce 43
Tartine 414
Tartufi bianchi d'Alba 246
Tartufi 142, 215, 246, 247
Tartufi bianchi 215
Tartufi nero 246
Telline 289
Thornback ray 280
Tomato
　Bread, Spicy 422
　Bruscette 43

broth 154
paste 235
pulp 103, 235
Risotto 209
salad 174
Soup 103
Tomato sauce 120, 144, 150, 166, 178, 184, 256, 341, 436
    Basic 129
    Cardoon with 258
    Fillets of John Dory with 312
    Gnocchi in 182
    Marinated Eel in 294
    Pork Chops with 330
    Stringoli with 186
Tomatoes 234, 235
    Artichokes with 44
    Baked 266
    Calzone with Onions and 438
    and Cheese 53
    Fresh Mushrooms with 275
    oven-dried 422
    sun-dried 30
    with Peppers 253
    Stuffed 267
Tonno 284
Toro 325
Torrone 16, 389
Torta cappuccina 424
Torta di riso 398
Torta fritta 71
Tortelli with Oxtail Stuffing 146
Tortelli with Pumpkin Stuffing 145
Tortelloni with Pheasant 155
Totano 291
Toulouse goose 357
Tramezzini 22, 415
Triglia di fango 285
Triglia di scoglio 285
Tripe 348
Trota fario 292
Trota iridea 292
Trout, brook 292
Truffle
    dressing 350
    Fazzoletti with Seafood 160
    oil 218, 247
Truffles 246
    White, Fettucini with 142
White, Risotto with 215
Trumpet chanterelles 247
Tuna fish, 284
    Sauce, Roast Veal in 54
    Steaks 300
Turbot 286
Turkey 357
Turkey, rolled roast 357
Tuscan Bread Salad 74
Tuscan Vegetable Soup with Beans and Artichokes 104
Twaite shad 292

U

Unleavened bread 414
Uva 387
Uve passe 387
Uvette 387

V

Vacca 325
Vanilla cream 390, 404
Vanilla cream slices, frittered 400
Vanilla ice cream 390
Veal 324, 325
    and beef stock 327
    Chops 334
    Roulade 342
    scallop (saltimbocca) 325
    shanks (Osso buco) 346
    Stuffed Breast of 50
Vegetable Risotto 213
Vegetable Soup 92
    Tuscan, with Beans and Artichokes 104
    stock, preparing 249
Vegetables
    and Pasta Au Gratin 148
    Beef Roulades with Mortadella and 341
Veltliner 20
Velvet swimming crab 287
Venetian yeast doughnuts 397
Venison 354
Venison ham 361
Venison, Paillard of 366
Venison salami 361
Ventresca 284
Vergine 22
Vetellone 325
Vin Santo 392
Vinegar 60, 61
Vino Nobile di Montepulciano 21
Vintschgauer bread 421
Vitello Tonnato 54
Vitello 324, 325
Vongole (clams) 289

W

Walnut 388
Walnut Sauce, Pansoti with 159
Watermelon 387
Watercress 67
Wedge clams 289
Wheat flour, types of 416
White Beans with Peppers 250
White Beans with Shrimp 40
White cauliflower 240, 241
White truffle risotto 215
White truffles 215, 246
White Truffles, Fettucini with 142
Wild arugula 63
Wild asparagus 239
Wild boar 355
Wild boar ham 360
Wild boar ragout 364
Wild boar sausage 360
Wild duck 357, 359
Wild fennel 245
Wild goose 357, 359
Wild hare 355
Wild Herb Salad with Eggs and Olives 72
Wild Mushrooms, Medley of 274
Wild onions 245
Wild pigeon 358
Wild poultry 358, 359
Wild rabbit 355
Wild rabbit, braised 369
Wild sheep 355
Wild strawberry 387
Wines 19–22

Y

Yeast 419
    doughs 418
Yellow plum cherry tomatoes 234
Yellow zucchini, marinated 261
Young globe artichokes, cooking whole 237
Young pigeon 358

Z

Zampone 324
Ziti 151
Zitoni 151
Zucca 242
Zucchini 242, 243
Zucchini and Tomato Gratin 260
Zucchini
    chips 298
    green, marinated 261
    Soup, Cream of 99
    -flower Soup 98
    Flowers, Risotto with 208
    Flowers, stuffed 99
    Sauce, Pan-fried Monkfish with 298
    with Polenta Stuffing 262
    Squid-ink Pasta with 144
    yellow, marinated 261
Zuppa inglese 404